Malachy McCourt's History of Ireland

MALACHY McCOURT'S

history of

IRELAND

RUNNING PRESS
PHILADELPHIA · LONDON

Photography and Illustration Credits

Cover photograph top: John Dolan/Getty Images

Cover photograph bottom: Bert Hardy/Getty Images

p. 8: Map of Ireland. © 2004 Digital Wisdom Publishing Ltd., cartography by Nicholas Rowland.

Illustration insert:

Drombeg Stone Circle, County Cork, Ireland (photograph, 20th century) by Simon Marsden. The Marsden Archive, UK/Bridgeman Art Library.

After the battle of Clontarf, Brian Boru is killed by Brodar, a Dane (engraving, 19th century). Mary Evans Picture Library.

Clonmacnoise Celtic Cross (modern photo of 10th-century cross). The Art Archive/Dagli Orti.

Study portrait of Jonathan Swift (oil on canvas, 18th century), by Charles Jervas. Philip Mould, Historical Portraits Ltd., London, UK/Bridgeman Art Library.

Robert Emmet, Irish patriot (c. 1850–1910). Courtesy of the National Library of Ireland.

The Irish Famine (oil on canvas, 19th century), by George Frederick Watts. Trustees of the Watts Gallery, Compton, Surrey, UK/Bridgeman Art Library.

The Battering Ram Has Done its Work [County Clare] (photograph, c. 1887–88). Courtesy of the National Library of Ireland.

Evicted Family (photograph, c. 1900). Mary Evans Picture Library.

Charles Stewart Parnell, cartoon by Amand, Brussels. Mary Evans Picture Library.

Portrait of William Butler Yeats (lithograph, 1898), by Sir William Rothenstein. Private Collection/The Stapleton Collection/Courtesy of the Sir William Rothenstein Estate/Bridgeman Art Library.

Easter Rising Aftermath (photograph, 1916), by Keogh Brothers, Ltd. Courtesy of the National Library of Ireland.

Who Fears to Speak of Easter Week? (1916) by Francis Joseph Rigney, New York. Courtesy of the National Library of Ireland.

Proclamation of Independence. Image supplied by The National Museum of Ireland. Permission granted for this publication. All Rights Reserved.

Portrait of Eamon de Valera (photograph, c. 1914–23) by Keogh Brothers, Ltd. Courtesy of the National Library of Ireland.

Portrait of James Joyce in Paris at age 20 (photograph, c. 1902). The Art Archive/British Library.

Portrait of Brendan Francis Behan (photograph, 1959), by Ida Kar. Mary Evans Picture Library/Ida Kar Collection.

Bloody Sunday (photograph, January 30, 1972). AP/Wide World Photos.

Bernadette Devlin (photograph, February 1972). AP/Wide World Photos.

9   8   7   6   5   4   3   2
Digit on the right indicates
the number of this printing

Library of Congress Control Number: 2003114585

ISBN 0-7624-1965-2

Picture research by Susan Oyama
Cover design by Whitney Cookman
Interior design by Matthew Goodman
Edited by Jennifer Leczkowski and Michael Washburn
Typography: Garamond and Mason

This book may be ordered by mail from the publisher. Please include $2.50 for postage and handling. ***But try your bookstore first!***

Running Press Book Publishers
125 South Twenty-second Street
Philadelphia, Pennsylvania 19103-4399

Visit us on the web!
www.runningpress.com

Contents

IRELAND BEFORE PATRICK

Chapter I:
PEIG SAYERS:
A Modern Look at an Ancient World

To anyone who knows me, it's no secret that I was never much for the formal
schooling when I was a young fellow, paying scant attention when I did happen to
attend, remembering little, and leaving it off completely at the ripe old age of thirteen. The way I see it now, the masters at Leamy's National School in Limerick
and I had what might be called philosophical differences over pedagogy and curriculum. Needless to say, I came to America at the age of twenty with no
Certificates to prove I had ever been at school, far less learned anything there.

However, there was one thing I do clearly remember from my days at the
Leamy's College of Surgeons, as we called it because they cut us up so much—a
woman named Peig Sayers. To say she was the bane of every schoolboy's days is no
exaggeration. We all had to read her, and read her in the Irish, for it was her tales
that were the basis of our Irish primers. And as the world often goes, it wasn't
until much later in life that I realized what an amazing woman Peig Sayers actually
was and how important she is to my history.

Peig Sayers was one of the last of the great Irish storytellers—the seanachai—
and she was a direct line to Ireland's past, telling tales that had been passed down
not for years but for centuries. In many ways, she was of the same tradition as the
blind Greek poet Homer, who recited his grand epics *The Iliad* and *The Odyssey* to
kings and shepherds alike. But she regaled her listeners not only with stories of the
great heroes like Cúchulainn and Finn mac Cool, but with local tales as well: the
drowning of a boat, a pilgrimage to St. Kathleen's cemetery, or race day in Dingle.

It is a grand tradition, the telling of a tale, one that many an Irishman or woman has followed. Sure, myself and the brothers have done all right for ourselves telling the odd tale here and there. But Peig Sayers was in many ways different from the McCourt boys; her tales were timeless, her memory extraordinary, and her ways with the Irish language a peek into the glorious days of the original Celtic bards and storytellers. It is the noble art of tale-telling that informs this book—a book that gives the reader a history of Ireland as told through the lives of the people who created it. And because Peig Sayers—through the tradition of the seanachai—is a link to those early pre-Christian days, I begin with her story before reaching back into the golden mist of Celtic Ireland.

Peig Sayers was born in 1873 in the small town of Dunquin, out on the Dingle Peninsula. Her father was known as a great storyteller, and her mother was one of the finest singers ever. Peig was the last of fourteen children, although only the first three and Peig survived infancy—a position guaranteed to win her favor as the baby within the family.

As a very young girl, younger than most, she was allowed to go to school. Her mother, weakened by age, poverty, and countless pregnancies, spent most of her days in a bed in the corner of their hut, and Peig's going to school offered the old woman some rest from the task of looking after her child. Peig loved school, her classmates, and her schoolmasters, and in her account of her days there, one can see the joy with which she embraced this time of her life. The great Irish writer, Flann O'Brien, a grand fella who used dozens of pseudonyms for his writings, wrote an uproarious parody of the school days that Peig described in his book *The Poor Mouth.*

Peig's world, however, could not and did not include the luxury of going to school for long, and when she was twelve, her father found her a situation with a shopkeeper and his family in the town of Dingle. Many a young girl has left her home to act as a maid or laundress in the household of those who were better off. In a way, Peig was luckier than most, for Dingle was only a day's walk from her home; countless young girls have traveled the deep, gray seas to America or to England to do the same with the chances of seeing their loved ones becoming more and more remote after landing on foreign shores.

For most women at the time, there were two choices in life: service in the employ of a strange family, or marriage. After a time, Peig's family arranged for her to marry Peats Guiheen from the Great Blasket Islands. Now, the Great Blasket Islands sit out in the Atlantic, just west of the Dingle Peninsula, and they are a stark and rough place, and the crossing is often wild and dangerous. Yet the people are warm and friendly, and when Peats Guiheen brought his new wife to his rugged home, the Blasket Islanders welcomed her.

Before too long, Peig came to consider the Islanders her family, and the Great Blasket her home. In the world of fishermen, the life of a fisherman's wife was filled with worrisome waiting, and it was perhaps on these long nights as the women looked out toward the wild sea, hoping to see the first sign of their returning men, that Peig's skills as a storyteller blossomed, for before long word of her talent began to spread. Soon, folklorists and sociologists, teachers and students of Irish, and people of all sorts who just loved a good story were visiting Peig Sayers. At the end, they say she had nearly four hundred narratives at her disposal to recall, tales that contained the very marrow of the Irish world.

Peig died in 1958, and in the picture of her that looked out at us from our dusty schoolbooks, she looked liked a wizened old apple, her big hands poised in the act of storytelling. Her life had less to do with the twentieth century than it did with the nineteenth or even the eighteenth, for she lived in the same world as her father's father's father. A hard life untouched by modernity. What amazes me now is that the year that she died was the year that Malachy's opened in New York

City—the Irish saloon named after myself, where I held court on both sides of the bar and spun a yarn or two myself. There I was, living the fast, modern New York life, acting in the theater, appearing on television, serving drinks to America's celebrated and the world's powerful, having not a few jars myself, and making a name for myself doing the very thing that she was noted for—telling a good story. And she was an ocean away; she was several centuries away as well. She never learned the English, spoke only Irish, and wove tales as old as the rocks that guard her barren part of the world from cultivation.

Peig inherited the tale-telling talent from her father, Tomás Sayers, who was a great one for the story. Night after night, Peig, the youngest child, sat quietly by the fire while her father entertained the neighbors with tales tall and long, and remembrances. I remember the same in our own poverty-stricken Limerick slum at the end of the lane: the father—when he was there—entertaining a trio of friends by the fire, urged on by yet one more "tell us the one, about the . . ." and the small fire in the grate glowing and the sweet smell of the turf filling the room.

And so it is with Peig Sayers that I begin. For this history is a series of stories: the stories of the men and women who made Ireland's history. Each is individual in itself, and makes a wondrous tale alone. But together, as a whole, they tell a story of Ireland.

CHAPTER II:
Cúchulainn,
Fionn mac Cumaill, and Deirdre

The early history of Ireland is of course a mixture of fact and legend. Scholars tell us that before the arrival of the Celts, the island was peopled by stone-age men, then by a dark, small race from the Mediterranean, and then by the Picts. Legend, however, tells us that the great king, Mileadh of Spain, sent his three sons to Ireland. There they conquered the three races of the island: the Tuatha de Danann, a semi-divine race well skilled in wizardry; the Firbolgs, a short, dark, physical people; and the Formorians, the somber giants from the surrounding seas. Indeed, among Irish-speaking peoples, it is still a great honor to be able to claim descent from the Milesian invasion.

It was not until 350 B.C. that the Celts—a tall, fair-haired race whose empire once covered central Europe—came to Ireland, conquering the natives and establishing their culture. That culture—with the coming of Christianity and of writing in the fifth century—was preserved by the learned, scholar class of Celts called Filí, who were able to write down the sagas and records that they had for so long passed along by the power of the tongue.

For the most part, Irish mythology can be separated into four groups: those that speak of the Tuatha de Danann; those that relate the deeds of the Red Branch knights of whom Cúchulainn is the most famous; those that tell the story of Fionn mac Cumaill, his son Oisín, and the warriors of the Fianna; and those that deal with the high kings of Ireland. The story of Cúchulainn is perhaps the most famous.

Cúchulainn

When you take a walk up O'Connell Street in Dublin, just a bit north of the Liffey, a short block up from the statue of Daniel O'Connell and across from that modern monstrosity that they call the Spire, you'll see the General Post Office, a building rich in history for the Irish people. Go inside, you'll see in the lobby there Oliver Sheppard's ferocious, beautiful statue of Cúchulainn. It depicts a dying Cúchulainn tied to a rock, whilst perched on his shoulder a raven waits and watches for eternity for death. A hero of the ancient past, Cúchulainn became a symbol for the Ireland that emerged in the early twentieth century.

It is no exaggeration to say that Cúchulainn is Ireland's greatest mythological hero. He is similar to the Hercules of the Greeks. The tales we have of him come mainly from Ireland's first great epic, the *Tain Bo Cuailnge, The Cattle Raid of Cooley*. But as with many other mythological heroes, stories abound elsewhere and everywhere—stories of his childhood, his courtship, his training in arms, and his death.

When Cúchulainn was a boy of five, he had heard that Conor, the King of Ulster, had an elite corps of boys, the *macrad*, who spent their days training in sport, at chess, and in disciplining the mind. Against the wishes of his mother, who believed he was too young, Cúchulainn set out on his own to find this training ground—the famed plains of Emain Macha. The boy, traveling with his sliother, his hurley (hurling stick), a javelin, and a toy spear, liked to drive the sliother as far as he could, toss the hurley after the ball so that it hit and drove it further still, throw the javelin and the spear, and then race ahead picking up all three—ball, hurley, and javelin—before catching the spear as it was about to touch the ground. In this way, he quickly moved towards Emain Macha.

Upon arriving at Emain Macha, Cúchulainn saw 150 boys on the field hurling and practicing martial exercises. When Cúchulainn tried to join in the game, the boys attacked him with their hurleys and sliothers and also with their toy spears. Cúchulainn fended off their attacks and laid low fifty of the boys while the others ran off to tell Conor, who was playing chess. The king chided this new young fellow for his rough play, and Cúchulainn chided the king and the boys for their inhospitable greeting. (For hospitality was an important aspect of ancient Celtic society!) Conor had to agree that Cúchulainn had a point, and so the king arranged for the young warrior to play among his elite group of boys. Yet, even as Conor welcomed Cúchulainn and brought him onto the field of play, the five-year-old so overpowered the older boys that many of their fathers wrongly believed their sons were dead as they lay there on the pitch.

Cúchulainn grew in strength and wisdom, and his fame spread across the land. The other Ulster soldiers, aware that their wives and daughters were dazzled by Cúchulainn's prowess, suggested that it was time for him to find a wife of his own. He found and courted the beautiful Emer, who, before she would submit to his charms, sent him on a great quest of courage and extraordinary feats. On these journeys Cúchulainn learned important skills from Domnall Míldemail in Alba and greater skills yet from Scáthach, the Shadowy One. It was prophesized that after this training and discipline, no hero in Europe would be able to defeat Cúchulainn. And the boy had only just reached his seventh year.

It was his lone defense of Ulster against the armies of Queen Meadh and her husband King Ailil that is undoubtedly Cúchulainn's greatest feat. The story of Cúchulainn's brave stand is the crux of the *Tain Bo Cuailnge, The Cattle Raid of Cooley.*

Now, before Christianity came to Ireland, the Celts were loosely ruled by a system known as Brehon Law, although the country was not a single nation but an array of small, tribal kingdoms, and it would be wrong to say that the law applied to the entire island. However, it was a code of both honor and legislation that covered such matters as surety, education, heredity, hospitality, and succession. And what was remarkable about it was that there was a semblance of equality between men and women, or at the very least, a noble-born female had more rights than she would have on the European continent. It is against this background that the beginnings of the *Tain Bo Cuailnge* are set. Queen Meadh, as she boasted herself, was the daughter of the high king of Ireland, the Ard Rí. She outshone her six sisters in both grace and combat, and, as she proudly admitted, was the highest and haughtiest of them all. Indeed, in her household alone, she commanded well over five thousand soldiers and ruled over an entire province of Ireland.

The story begins one night when Meadh (pronounced *Maeve*) and her husband were comparing each other's possessions—and thus their individual prestige. In cataloguing her assets, Meadh realized that she was one bull short of what her husband had. Determined to right this wrong, she learned that Dare mac Fiachna in Cooley in the province of Ulster owned a bull of like quality, and she sent messengers to ask if she could borrow his bull. But Meadh was a ruthless and powerful ruler and truthfully had no intention of anything but simply stealing the bull. When the Dare refused Meadh's offers, she and her husband amassed "eighteen troops of three thousand men" from around the island and marched towards Ulster.

Now unfortunately, at the time, the men of Ulster were incapacitated by a sorceress's spell. This left seventeen-year-old Cúchulainn with the task of fending off the entire host of Meadh and Ailil's armies until his comrades woke. His feats during this period equal any in the great epics of the world, and his prowess thwarted and frustrated Meadh.

At first, Cúchulainn threw obstacles in front of the approaching armies, warning them not to cross any further into Ulster and dispatching those men who tried to do so, three or four at a time. He slew them in one-to-one combat, or together when groups of men attacked him. Once when the armies were camped at Druim Féne in Conaille, Cúchulainn, a great man with the sling, slew 300 men on each of the three nights they remained there! Frustrated by this single warrior who was destroying her army, Meadh bribed and deceived warriors into facing him, tempted him with her own daughter, and tried to bring him down through ruse and deceit. But all failed. Battle-weary and greatly wounded—his father reported that no area larger than the point of a reed had not been pierced by a spear—Cúchulainn was finally assisted by the men of Ulster; the spell had worn off them and they charged into battle.

As befitting a hero, Cúchulainn's death was as noble as his life. In battle, he knew that his mere presence was enough to strike fear into any opponent. So when the life was ebbing out of him, he tied himself standing upright to a rock with a spear in his hand, so that his enemies would still believe he was vigorous and in the thick of battle. His final stance worked for a while, for it was some time before his opponents dared to come close enough to make certain that he was dead, and did so only when they saw the raven pecking out his eyes. A hero in death as in life, Cúchulainn is remembered as a man of passion, a symbol of defiance and bravery, of determination and strength of purpose.

Fionn mac Cumaill

If Cúchulainn was the Hercules of Ireland, then Fionn mac Cumaill is King Arthur. In fact, the connection between the two is stronger than that, for there are many who argue that the Arthurian legend is based on the stories of Fionn and his warriors, the Fianna, and that the code of honor promulgated by Fionn mac Cumaill is the basis for the stories of Camelot and the knights of the Round Table. Indeed, the story of Fionn, his poet son, Oisín, and the Fianna may be the best known and most beloved among all the ancient Irish legends.

When Tuathal, a Gaelic prince, put down a final revolt of the pre-Celtic peoples around A.D. 100, he united the kingdoms of Meath and Connaught. A century after Tuathal, his descendant Conn Céd-cathach centralized the kingship. At the time, there were roughly 100 small kingdoms scattered throughout Ireland, and these kingdoms fell into five larger realms (Ulster, Meath, Leinster, Munster, and Connaught). Depending on the strength of his personality and his power, the High King would rule independently over these five kingdoms, or he would rule merely by the consent of the others.

Conn's grandson Cormac was the first king to attempt to consolidate Ireland to a single nation. He established Tara as the capital and held there on its sacred hill a great national assembly that not only engaged in legislating and "homaging," but also celebrated with music, games, and literary contests. The Fianna, an elite military force dating back to the High King Fiachadh around 300 B.C., had under Conn's rule split into two rival factions: the Clan Morna and the Clan Baiscne. And it is here that Fionn mac Cumaill's story begins.

Now during Cormac's reign, the Clan Morna were contesting the leadership of Cumaill, a great warrior from the Clan Baiscne. When Cumaill was wounded in battle, his satchel of magic was taken from him, leaving him open to death. A warrior of the Morna clan saw the advantage and beheaded the brave leader.

Cumaill's wife Muirne was pregnant at the time and shortly after gave birth to a handsome fair-haired son, who she called Demne. Knowing her son's life was in danger from the Morna clan, she sent the boy off to be raised by two sisters: the Druidess Bodhmal and her sister, the great warrior Liath Luacha. With the help of the Druid Finegas, who tutored the young boy, these two women raised Demne so he grew into a fierce warrior, skilled in weaponry and warfare and possessed of both the healing and magical arts.

Because Demne's name was known to the Morna, he never used it. Instead, he was referred to as "the fair" or "the fair-haired." In Irish, it is *Fionn mac Cumaill*—the fair-haired son of Cumaill.

FİONN MAC CUMAİLL
AND THE SALMON OF KNOWLEDGE

In the river by Slieve Bladhma where Fionn had been living, there lived a salmon that fed on hazelnuts that fell into the water. Now, the hazel tree was revered among the Druids, for it purportedly contained all the knowledge of the world. In this way, the salmon had ingested all that was to be known. One day, the Druid Finegas caught the salmon and was cooking it over a fire. The learned man assigned Fionn mac Cumaill to sit and tend to the fish as it roasted on the spit. At one point, when he attempted to turn the fish, he burned his thumb on it and instinctively put his thumb in his mouth and sucked on it, and swallowed a fragment of salmon which besotwed on him the gift of prophecy. From this moment on, whenever Fionn sucked on his thumb, he was able to see what the future held.

When Fionn became of age, he set about to restore the Clan Baiscne and bring them back into the Fianna. First, he had to pass a series of tests set up by the warriors. These tests included standing waist-deep in a hole and defending himself with just a shield and a hazel rod against nine warriors; escaping from nine warriors by running through the forest without breaking a twig under his feet or tearing his clothes; jumping over a branch as high as himself and running under another as low as his knee; running at top speed through the forest and picking a thorn from his foot without stopping; and memorizing twelve books of poetry by heart as well as many of the old legends and tales.

The young Fionn fared so well in these tests that he became chieftain of the clan, and soon after the clan rejoined the Fianna. It was not long after, when Fionn saved Tara from attack, that the High King Cormac bestowed on Fionn the leadership of the Fianna. It was a wise decision by Cormac, for under Fionn's stewardship the Fianna changed from an unruly band of elite warriors into an honorable assembly, whose fame spread far and wide. In other ways, also, it was a boon to Cormac, for Fionn proved to be a most loyal and powerful protector of his king.

After his wife Manissa had died, Fionn asked the hand of Cormac's daughter, Grainne, in marriage. So great had Fionn's loyalty been and so frequent his demonstrations of such that the King heartily agreed, and Finn mac Cumaill and the Fianna made their way to the feasting hall of Tara. Now, Grainne was a beautiful young woman, and clever, so she had no desire to marry an old man such as Fionn mac Cumaill, no matter how great his renown. She turned for help to the warrior who sat next to her at the feast, the high-minded and noble Diarmuid, the greatest warrior in the Fianna. Placing the noble warrior under a "gessa"—a druidical bond (spell) that not even the greatest hero could break—she drugged the wine so that all but Diarmuid would fall into a deep sleep. Then, she persuaded the knight to run away with her, and he—torn between his loyalty to Fionn and the strength of the "gessa" for Grainne—agreed. For sixteen years, Fionn and the Fianna pursued Diarmuid and Grainne, and their adventures were the basis for many dramatic tales and legends—legends later applied to King Arthur, Guinivere, and Lancelot.

Finally, Diarmuid's foster-father, who of all the De Danaan was the wisest and who possessed the greatest magic, persuaded Fionn to reach a peace with his once-beloved companion and warrior. The two were reunited, and a semblance of friendship grew. One day, however, when Diarmuid, Fionn, and the Fianna were out hunting wild boar on Ben Bulben, a boar attacked Diarmuid. As his companion writhed in pain, Fionn went twice to a mountain stream to get water, but each time the water slipped through his fingers when he remembered the betrayal of Diarmuid and Grainne. Finally, on the third try, he overcame his resentments and brought the water to Diarmuid, but it was too late. He saw Diarmuid's head droop and the life abandon the once-proud warrior.

There are many versions of Fionn's own death, but a persistent story tells that Fionn did not die at all. Some believe that Fionn is sleeping in a cave and will return once more when Ireland finds itself at its greatest need. Now this all sounds similar to the concept of "the once and future king" that surrounds the story of Arthur—a Celtic tale itself by the way—but if I had my preferences as to who I would want returning to help when my back was against the wall, my choice would be Fionn mac Cumaill every time. Warrior, magician, healer, and prophet, a good man to keep in step with on life's journey.

There is another story, one that concerns Fionn and the creation of the beautiful and wondrous Giant's Causeway in County Antrim. This extraordinary place is a geological wonder where hundreds of naturally formed hexagonal pillars of volcanic stone stretch out into the sea towards Scotland. The story goes that a giant in Scotland had been ridiculing Fionn's prowess. Fed up with the giant's insolence, Fionn threw a rock across the Irish Sea with a challenge attached. The Scottish giant threw a rock back with a message that said he could not fight Fionn because he could not swim and the sea lay between them. Now Fionn was not going to let this giant off that easy, so he began pulling great rods of volcanic rock from the coast and making a pathway from Ireland to Scotland. The giant now had an easy walk across the Irish Sea and came to fight Fionn. But when the giant reached Ireland, instead of meeting a fierce warrior, he found Fionn who was disguised as a baby—an eighteen-foot-tall baby, mind you, but a baby nevertheless. Fionn bit the giant's hand, and the giant, calculating that if the babies of this land were so formidable he didn't want to meet the adults, rushed back to Scotland. Fionn chased after him throwing huge rocks at him. One of the rocks missed the giant and landed in the sea, and this became the Isle of Man. Another created a gaping hole that filled up with water, and this became Lough Neagh, the largest lake in Ireland.

Deirdre and the Sons of Uisneach

The great Cattle Raid of Cooley, if you remember, had Irish warriors fighting Irish warriors. That is to say, they finally fought against each other only after the valiant stand by Cúchulainn, who had taken on the opposing army by himself. In truth, in these wars there were King Conor's own sons and soldiers, fighting against him and aligned with Meadh and Ailil. And, according to legend, there was a reason for all that, and that reason was a woman. (This story has long reminded me of those other mythical tales: the one of Eve eating the apple or Pandora opening the box. It seems the male storytellers love to throw the blame on the female half of the population!)

So, the story goes that Conor the King of Ulster and his Red Branch warriors were feasting at the home of Feidhlimidh, the king's storyteller. As they all were feasting, a hair-raising scream came from the unborn child within the womb of Feidhlimidh's wife. It was then that the Druid Cathbad predicted that the child was a girl who would grow into the most beautiful woman ever seen, but who would also be the cause of death and destruction in the house of Ulster.

When the child was born, she was called Deirdre, which means "rampageous," a nod to her disrupting a feast even before she was born. The Red Branch warriors, remembering Cathbad's prophesy, wished to kill the child on the spot, but

Conor restrained them.

"Leave her to me," he said. "I will raise her in seclusion, away from the sight of men, and when she is of age, I will bring her back to the royal court as my wife."

And so, the king arranged for a tutor and a nurse to take the girl to a remote spot, and no one was ever to see her until the time came for Conor to take her as his wife.

One day, however, when the girl had grown into quite a beauty, her tutor was flaying a calf on the snow-covered ground. Nearby, a raven was drinking the blood that had collected in the snow.

"Those three colors remind me of the man I would love, a man I see in my dreams," Deirdre told her nurse. "He has hair as black as the raven, cheeks as red as the calf's blood, and skin as white as the snow."

"There is such a man," said the nurse, "and he lives in the household of Conor. He is Naoise, son of Uisneach."

Now it happened that one day this very same Naoise was hunting in the vicinity of Deirdre's secluded hut, when he saw the beautiful girl—who had made a point of walking into his view. "Fair is the heifer that walks past me," Naoise said. And Deirdre returned with "Heifers are wont to grow big when there are no bulls around." Naoise understood who this beautiful creature was and knew well that she was intended for Conor, and so he told her, "You have the best bull in the province, the King himself!" But Deirdre replied that she would rather go with a young bull like Naoise. The young warrior was no fool, and despite her beauty and her willingness, he knew that this girl was the king's, so he begged off, but she put a "gessa" on him from which he could not extricate himself.

So it happened that Deirdre and the sons of Uisneach (Naoise and his two brothers) as well as 150 soldiers, fled the wrath of Conor by escaping to Scotland, knowing they could never return to their beloved Ireland, as the Red Branch knights would kill them on their return. Even in Scotland, however, their troubles continued. A messenger of the Scottish king, for whom the brothers had done great service, spied Deirdre as she lay next to her beloved Naoise and decided she would be the perfect queen for his master. And once more the lovers were forced to flee. This time they landed on a small island west of Scotland.

Soon rumors of the plight of Naoise and his brothers reached the Red Branch warriors in Ulster, and they felt sorry for their once-brave companions. They went to Conor and argued that the exile of Naoise and his brothers was not just—it was caused by a wicked woman and the caprice of destiny. Conor agreed. The king sent Fergus as his messenger to Naoise and his brothers. Now, long before, Fergus had married Conor's mother and taken over the kingship when her husband had died. The two were married only a short while when the mother asked Fergus if her son, Conor, could be king for just one year. To be truthful, it lasted far longer than a year, for Conor was a good and popular king, and Fergus enjoyed his new life with little responsibility and plenty of benefits, so the situation remained and no one seemed to mind.

So Fergus was charged with telling Naoise, his brothers, Deirdre, and their men that on his honor they should all return to Ireland, where they would be welcomed and unharmed. He sent his son to the island to deliver the message.

When the exiles reached Emain Macha, the seat of Conor's realm, they were met almost immediately by Conor's treachery in the person of Eoghan mac Durrthacht, prince of Fermfey. Eoghan went forward to welcome Naoise and thrust a spear through his body. When Fergus's son saw this, he stepped in between the two, but he too was impaled with Eoghan's second thrust. Then Eoghan and his army slew all the sons of Uisneach and all the men who had traveled with them into exile.

Deirdre was brought back to Conor, but for a full year she did not smile, nor raise her head. Nothing that Conor could do or command would bring her out of her gloom. And so he sent for Eoghan mac Durrthacht, the man who had slain her beloved. Since he, Conor, could not bring her out of her sorrows, he would give her to Eoghan for a year and see how he could please her.

Conor accompanied Eoghan in his chariot as the warrior took Deirdre away to his own lands. Bewildered and broken, the young girl looked first at Conor and then at Eoghan, the two men whose power seemed to shape her destiny. Conor noticed her looking at the two, and with a sadistic sneer, stated that she seemed like a sheep glancing between two rams. At this, Deirdre jumped from the chariot and smashed her head onto the rocks, her death the only escape from her tragic destiny.

And yet the Druid's prophecy was not completed yet. Fergus was outraged at the breach of his word of honor and the death of his son, as was Conor's son Cormac. Upon first hearing of Conchobar's treachery, they marched towards Emain Macha and slew three hundred of the king's men. They then traveled to Connaught, which was ruled by the powerful Queen Meadh. From Meadh's kingdom, they nightly raided the holdings of Conor for seven years. This was the first great split among the Red Branch warriors, a split that culminated in the story of Cúchulainn and the *Tain Bo Cuailnge* and was the cause of much bloodshed and ruin in the house of Ulster.

THE LAND OF
SAINTS AND SCHOLARS

CHAPTER iii:
Patrick: From Slave Boy to Patron Saint

St. Patrick was a gentleman, he came from decent people.
He built a church in Dublin town and on it put a steeple.
His father was a Gallagher, his mother was a Grady.
His aunt was an O'Shaughnessy and his uncle was a Brady.

Now I'm not certain if Patrick ever built a church in Dublin, with a steeple or without. He spent most of his time up around Armagh. (I've read that there was another fellow with the similar name of Patroculus, who came a little before Patrick, and who did his missionary work closer to Dublin, but it's pretty sure he's not the man we're talking about here.) Neither am I am so certain about that lineage, either. But if the song rings true, and he has Gallagher, Grady, O'Shaughnessy, and Brady blood in him, then your man Patrick would hardly qualify for sainthood. Because the fellows I've met with those names were men you would remember as blackguards not beatified.

Patrick first came to Ireland not of his own accord, but in the galley of a slave ship. At the time, the Celts were raiding the west coast of England pretty regularly and taking slaves—young men to work herding cows and sheep and young women to serve their masters. Now, around the year 405, the great warrior king Niall of the Nine Hostages raided a town with the impressive name of Bannavern Taberniae. Among the slaves that he brought back from the town was a sixteen-year-old Patrick, who was taken from England, thrown into the ship and brought to Ireland.

It is truly odd how the world works, for here you have a great pagan king and a seemingly somewhat helpless Christian boy, whose grandfather was a priest, and yet, it would be that Christian boy's role in history to be the one who would cause the decline of pagan kings in Ireland.

There is no documentary evidence of Patrick's time as a shepherd slave. It is said in Ireland he was proud of his Roman heritage—for the Roman Empire still thrived in Britain when Patrick was taken—and that in this pride, he pitied his captors, believing them to be missing the advantages that he enjoyed: Roman "civilization." We can imagine that he often thought of his home in Western Britain and that he must have suffered great loneliness beyond the mistreatment that comes with being a slave.

Like many of the stories that would come to surround Patrick over the years, the story of his escape from Ireland is a bit fanciful. Apparently, after six years in captivity, in the isolated world of shepherding and in a land where the language was alien to him, Patrick now turned to the religion with which he had been raised. Now surely he was not the first and certainly would not be the last to come upon religion when things were a dire mess, so he got God in the hills. One night, a voice told him to leave Ireland, that his ship was ready. And so Patrick set out towards the sea. Now, at the time, Ireland was a wild place, with forests and bog covering much of the land, and for a young slave to make his way from Antrim to the sea is a wondrous feat. The legend has him walking to Wexford, no less, which is a great distance from where he started. Sure enough, when he arrived he found a ship loading cargo for the continent. One story states that it was Irish hounds they were exporting, but that sounds wrong to me. At the moment, Europe was being overrun by barbarians, so I'm not so sure how great the market would have been

among the nobility for fancy, imported dogs. Regardless, Patrick needed passage
out of there, and so finagled his way onto a ship headed to the continent. (I think
here is where Patrick and myself have something in common, for it was more than
once that I had to use my imagination and the telling the right tale to get myself
booked from one place to another.) As sailors are often a rough crowd, the seamen
teased Patrick about his Christianity. The teasing stopped, so the story goes, when
Patrick's God brought the sailors food.

The ship had come to port, but as they moved inland, they found waste and
desolation. (Again, these were the days of the barbarian invasions and Europe was
in ruins.) Starving and half-dead, the sailors mockingly called on Patrick to ask his
God for help. Patrick did, and instructed them to bow their heads quietly. After a
moment or two, the silence was shattered by the sound of stampeding pigs.
Patrick's God had answered their prayers, and Patrick had gained his first converts.

From Britain, Patrick traveled to Gaul, where he spent long years in study. He
had much to make up for, as his childhood had been stolen from him. Finally, at a
relatively old age, he was ordained a priest. In his book *Confession*, he stated that
in a dream he had heard the Irish people calling him and pleading with him to
return. Whether the dream was true or not, events proved to bring it to fruition.
The Gaulish church where Patrick studied was charged with tending Roman
Britain and pagan Ireland, and it had asked the pope to send an emissary to
Ireland to convert the population. The pope sent a man named Palladius, who
never arrived. Some say he died beforehand, some say he went elsewhere.
However, the pope had no man there on the spot, so he sent Patrick. He was con-
secrated a bishop, and the rest, as they say, is history.

Patrick settled in Ulster, and before long a prince presented him with a church
in Armagh. This town was to become the center of Irish Christianity for a great
while afterwards. Once, I met a man from Armagh who told me a wonderful story

about Patrick that I had never heard elsewhere. The saint had been working hard to convert a particular chieftain and finally succeeded. On the day of the man's taking the sacraments, all his underlings came to the church and watched the ceremony with keen interest. Patrick counted their number and knew it was only a matter of time before they too would come to the church. So there you have the chieftain and his men in bare feet and robes of animal skins and Patrick with his crosier and his impressive vestments. During the ceremony, Patrick in his passion pounded the ground with his crosier and on one instance the crosier pierced the chieftain's foot. Patrick was unaware and the warrior made not a move, thinking that this pain and suffering was part of the initiation into this new religion. The rest of the ceremony went on, with the man's foot impaled by the crosier. Afterwards Patrick had trouble understanding why the chieftain's men were not as willing to follow their leader, as he had believed they would. I am sure it was the prospect of a lanced foot that was keeping them from the altar and had nothing to do with religion at all.

Patrick sent for helpers from the continent, and soon had set up bishops in northern and southern Leinster and in Meath. At first, his mission was readily accepted by the lower classes, but the High Kings, the Druids, the Filí, and the rest of Celtic aristocracy were not as willing to go along. This would change, however, much to Patrick's surprise, as the upper classes began to flock to the monasteries established by Patrick and his successors, which had become centers of learning and scholarship. But in fact it would not be until 490, after Patrick was dead, that the first High King himself would be converted, and not until 565 that the last of the High Kings of the pagan world would disappear.

What I love about Patrick's story is that in a way, he didn't do what he had set out to do, but in the opinion of many, he achieved something greater. Remember, Patrick was a Roman citizen grounded in the Roman church, and it was his intention to bring that church to the land of his captivity. Sure, he brought Christianity to Ireland, but once there it evolved into something much different from that centered in Rome. The fact that the country itself had no central authority, but was ruled by tribal kings, worked against the establishment of a central church. And the Filí—the powerful class of bards and poets—kept a strong grip on the culture and learning of the people. Patrick would bring his religion, but the Irish would shape it to their needs.

A story that illustrates this tension between Patrick and the ancient Celtic order is the story of Oisín. Oisín was a warrior, a poet, and the son of Fionn mac Cumaill. He lived 300 years before Patrick came to Ireland. And yet he had not died. During a battle, Oisín was rescued by a beautiful woman on a brilliant white horse. Niamh, as the woman was called, was a princess, and she brought Oisín to her kingdom, *Tir na Nog*, the land of eternal youth. Once there Oisín married the woman and enjoyed all the advantages of the kingdom.

Now, it seems to me that in all the stories of "eternal youth" I have ever heard, the fortunate fellow whoever he might be soon tires of his situation. And Oisín was no different, except he waited some 300 years until he began to feel homesick for his friends and family.

"Can I go back for a short visit?" he said, and Niamh told him yes, as long as his feet did not touch mortal ground. So he returned riding a horse and stayed mounted the entire time. (A difficult trick, I would think!) Now, when he returned to the modern world, Oisín was greatly disappointed, for the people he longed for and wanted to see had been dead for centuries. But he met and debated with Saint Patrick. It got the better of him. Or at least, he got more lines in the tale that tells the story. It was a witty conversation between the old Gaelic order and the new Christian world. Patrick had him describe *Tir na Nog* in detail, and Oisín did with great enthusiasm. When Oisín complained about the size of the food in the world that Patrick inhabited, Patrick simply claimed that this was how food was in his world. But Oisín would not accept this, and went about performing mythic feats to bring about food that he felt was fit for the heroes of the past.

Later, however, as he was traveling, he came on a group of puny men trying to move a boulder. He leaned down and with one hand did the job but he overbalanced and fell off his horse. Upon touching *terra firma,* the great poet turned into 300 year-old dust. I'm not sure how much Patrick had to do with this part of the tale, but it was certainly a dramatic way to end an argument.

Patrick's arrival was important in many ways. Sure, he brought the new faith and the so-called "civilizing" forces that were Roman. He founded a Christianity different from that emanating from Rome, one in which Patrick could empathize with women (imagine St. Paul doing so), could denounce slavery (perhaps the first man in recorded history to do so), could see God's glory in the natural world about him, and could concentrate on the natural God-given joy of life rather than the sin of man's soul. But perhaps most important of all, Patrick's importing Christianity to Ireland brought "writing," a skill that would not only advance Irish civilization immeasurably but, would also save the civilization of the western world.

As Tom Cahill wrote in his book, *How the Irish Saved Civilization,* the Gaelic world had a primitive writing called *ogham,* but its usage was limited to signposts signifying challenges, past events, and territorial claims. With the coming of the alphabet—and the development of the Irish monasteries—writing captured much that had heretofore been transmitted orally, with the result that there is not a country left untouched by Irish literary prowess.

Most people, Irish or not, know St. Patrick because of the bacchanalia that goes on in his name on March 17. Until very recently, "St. Paddy's Day" was an American phenomenon, and in Ireland the day was more of a holy day beginning with attendance at mass, with all the pubs closed on Sunday. But economic forces are powerful, the world is a smaller place, and tourists bring in cash, so now Ireland itself has grand parades with marching bands from America, revelers, floats, and unlike the New York parade, they welcome gay contingents. The brave, holy man from the fifth century whose color is St. Patrick blue seems somewhat lost in the green, and I have been known to look condescendingly on the whole thing. Yet, given that through most of human history, when large groups of people got together, they demonstrate wars, invade lands, or subjugate nations, who am I or anyone else to begrudge them this silly day of unattached fun? There is no record as far as I know of Patrick being made a saint and by whom. Not that it matters.

Chapter IV:
Brigid: "The Mary of the Gael"

One of Patrick's strengths in Ireland was his ability to integrate the Gaelic culture with the Christianity he was trying to bring. He did not, as other missionaries in other places would later, condemn the Celts as ignorant infidels or uncouth pagans. Instead, he took the Druidic world and tried to explain it in Christian terms. (The story of the shamrock and the Holy Trinity is a good—if unauthenticated—example.) This combination of the Druidic and Christian seems particularly strong in the story of Brigid.

Although Patrick had had great success in his mission in Ireland, there was still widespread resistance from many Gaelic chieftains and kings. One of these was Dubhtach, the chieftain of Leinster. Particularly worshipped by Dubhtach and his clan was the mother-goddess Brid or Brigid, a protector of the arts and culture, of harvest and the fields. Her feast on the first day of February was accompanied by bonfires lit in her honor (and would later become St. Brigid's feast day in the liturgical calendar).

A Christian slave woman became pregnant by Dubhtach, and the king sent her away. To his disappointment, the woman delivered a girl—he had wanted a son—and the mother was sold to a chieftain in Connaught while the girl was given to a Druid to be raised. The girl was named Brigid, in honor of the powerful goddess. Yet from the very beginning, the young girl seemed to be separate from mere humans. It was said that the house she was born in burst into flames after she left it, perhaps a subconscious connection to the pagan goddess's bonfires. (In 1814, some workers in Lismore Castle in County Waterford uncovered a damaged manuscript that became known as *The Book of Lismore*. The book contained *Lives of the Saints* written sometime in the sixteenth century, yet the section on Brigid seems to have been taken from works written in the seventh and tenth centuries. *The Life of Brigid* is not really a life at all, as a modern reader might describe it, but a catalog of the miraculous occurrences that surround her name. The presence of flame, both around her and her domiciles, is a quite common occurrence in the Lismore life.) Hot stuff you might say!

Brigid, according to her birth, was brought back to Dubhtach's home as a slave, although she enjoyed what were called "privileges of family." She remained a vestal virgin in the worship of Brid, her namesake. She must have been a dedicated follower, for she ultimately became high priestess of the Temple of the Oak, where she and Brid's devotees kept a vigil over a perpetual fire in honor of the mother-goddess. It is notable that the Irish words for Temple of the Oak are Kil Dara. Later the site where Brigid would build her nunnery would be named Kildare. When she and her followers converted to Christianity, they doused the fire of Brid and lit a new one in honor of Christ. The fire was kept burning for seven centuries, until Henry II extinguished it in the twelfth century.

The true story of Brigid's conversion to Christianity is lost in legend. One story states that it was Patrick himself who converted and baptized the woman; another has the influence of her Christian mother weighing heavy on the girl. Regardless, Brigid and her fellow virgins all converted and became the first community of Christian women in Ireland. They were the first order of nuns in the country, the first group in a long line of Irish women who dedicated themselves to Christ.

Yet, Brigid was more than a nun as we know one today. It is said that when she took her vows, a flame appeared above her head. It was also said that when the Bishop pronounced the words upon Brigid that attend the conferring of the veil, he instead used the words that ordained her as a bishop. When challenged, the man stated that he was powerless and the words had emerged from a spirit more powerful than he. The notion of Brigid as bishop of Kildare, although controversial for many, was perhaps not as extraordinary in fifth-century Ireland as we might think. Patrick's Christianity was far separated from Rome, and the ordinary misogyny of the Roman church was not as entrenched on this "pagan island." Indeed, Brigid's episcopacy in Kildare was a magnificent community of men and women where scholarship, piety, and generosity abounded. It is this concept of community and of scholarship that would define Irish Christianity for the next several centuries and would spread from Ireland itself to the rest of continental Europe.

As abbess of the community at Kildare, Brigid won renown for her generosity and her hospitality—traits that ultimately spread beyond the religious community and were embraced by the Irish people in general. Her generosity was legendary; even as a young girl, she drove her father mad with giving away the things he owned to the poor and needy. The various *Lives* that were written about her are filled with stories of her giving food to the poor, giving livestock to the needy, and, by example, getting others to do the same. These *Lives* were also replete with marvelous doings; the accounts of her miracles are numerous. It was believed that even her shadow had the power to cure the sick.

When Brigid died in around 525, she was buried by her altar at Kildare. In the ninth century her remains were removed to Downpatrick and placed alongside the supposed remains of Patrick and Columcille. The tomb was desecrated, however, with the coming of the Reformation and the relics were dispersed throughout the island.

There is one story about Brigid that I have always loved, and I'm not very sure when I first heard it for it seems that I have always known it. Brigid's fame spread quickly throughout the European continent, and what might be called a cult arose around her. There were numerous churches in England named after her, and in Europe there were devout communities in France, Portugal, and Belgium, communities that still revere her example today. Indeed, during medieval times Brigid was considered the very ideal of femininity. So great was her name, so exemplary her reputation, and so admired her character, that noblemen, gentlemen, and knights took to calling their own loved ones by her name—Bride. It is from this usage that we get the term used to describe a woman who is to be married. An honor for a woman who was never married except symbolically to Christ.

CHAPTER V:

COLUMCILLE: †HE DOVE OF †HE CHURCH

Of the three major Irish saints, Patrick, Brigid, and Columcille, the latter is probably the least known, but he's also the most fascinating. He came from a race of kings—great ones with still great powers in those early days of Christendom in

Ireland. And he had that arrogance and confidence that come with warriorblood. Now this was a two-edged sword for Columcille, for it served him greatly in his development and the operations of the numerous monasteries that he founded, but it also was the cause of his getting into trouble frequently. His name Colum means "dove," but originally he was named after the "fox" and these two opposite titles illustrate the dual personality of St. Columcille. For the fox implies sly ruthlessness while the dove—in addition to its Christian symbolism—a creature of warm gentleness. (Cille means church; thus "dove of the church" is the meaning of the saint's name. The word Cille—with a hard "C"—is found in many Irish place names, from Killarney to Kilgarvan.) If the early naming is not confusing enough, Columcille is also known as Columba, which becomes even more mired in confusion when you take in the fact that a late contemporary of Columcille is another saint, named Columbanus.

Columcille was born in 521 in Gartan, County Donegal. It is a gentle place with the Donegal hills rising from the shore of Lough Gartan, yet it bred hard, steely men. Columcille was born into a family of such men, the O'Neill clan, perhaps the most powerful family of its day and a dynasty that had given ancient Ireland many of its kings. Columcille was the great-great-grandson of Niall of the Nine Hostages, one of the most powerful of all the Irish High Kings of all time. (It was during this Niall's rule that the west coast of England was frequently raided and a young boy named Patricus was taken from there as a slave!)

Columcille was sent out as a foster-son to live with the priest Cruithneachán. To the modern sensibility, the concept of fostering out one's children might seem cruel at worst and uncaring at best, but in Irish society, it was a practice established to promote closeness and strength among the families within a clan. For always, the ancient Irish order was based on familial or tribal dynasty more than anything else. Under Cruithneachán's fosterage, Columcille demonstrated an uncanny sense of wisdom and determination, and there were not few who believed that this young man was destined to become High King himself. Yet it was not the hills of Tara on which Columcille had his eye but on the monasteries that dotted the Irish landscape.

Again, Patrick's success—remarkable even to himself—was the degree of enthusiasm that many Irish took to the new religion, particularly the upper classes. Because Ireland's political and social system at the time lacked villages (from whence parishes would blossom) and cities (from which dioceses would stem), the Irish church was anchored by monasteries which became not only religious sites of scholarship and spirituality, but economic and market centers, as well as places of refuge in time of attack. And more often than one would expect, kings and chieftains offered land and buildings for the building of monasteries in their domain.

So it was that Columcille found himself moving from monastery to monastery. He visited monasteries in Down, in Leinster, in Clonard, in Glasnevin, and in Clonfad, and at many, according to the various accounts written afterwards, he performed miracles at these sites. For instance, at Down he was said to have changed water into wine—an apparent favorite within the early Christian history and one that is certain to attract the attention of many. Even Brigid was credited several times with conjuring up ale when the need was apparent. In Leinster, he not only protected a young woman who was being pursued by some blackguard, but struck the pursuer dead by merely uttering some words. In each of these monasteries, Columcille's reputation grew, and he gathered around him a host of disciples.

By the time he returned to Donegal, Columcille had been ordained a priest, renowned for his learning and his spirituality, as well as for his miracles. When he reached the territory of the O'Neills, he set about building his first monastery. The High King, Aodh mac Ainmhireach, donated both the land and his own residence. Columcille tore the building down and started anew, building his monastery next to a rich forest of oak. It is this oak grove that gave the monastery—and the future town—its name: Derry. (You will remember Brigid's Kildare as the Irish for "the temple of the oak.") The monastery, through the actions of Columcille, became noted throughout Ireland for its generosity, particularly its care of the poor.

One story that I love about Columcille's generosity is this. Two men came to the monastery asking for alms. The one was a very poor man and the other, a dissolute gambler. When they appeared before Columcille, the saint gave the poor man a single coin and the gambler four times as much. His disciples were appalled and questioned Columcille about the wisdom of such an action. Columcille told them to follow him, and they set out to seek the two men. When they found the gambler, he was in a tavern, spreading his money around and sharing his newfound—but soon to be gone—wealth. Then they tracked down the poor beggar who had been given the single coin. They found him dead by the side of the road, the coin safely sewn into the hem of his jacket. Now Columcille pointed out that the money given to the gambler reached a greater number of people and was the source of greater joy and good. The coin given to the poor man, however, would never have provided anyone with any good at all. It's an odd angle for a holy man's wisdom, but that's Columcille. Were he president, he might reduce taxes on the middle class.

After several years, when the monastery at Derry was firmly established, Columcille set about establishing more monasteries throughout Ireland. He founded sites at Raphoe, at Durrow, at Kells, at Clonmore, two monasteries in Brega, and three at Swords, and various others are attributed to him as well.

The monasteries at Durrow and Kells became well known as centers of learning and spirituality, and the way that Columcille acquired Kells again demonstrates the dual side of his nature: the humble monastic and the regal authority. The High King at the time now was Diarmaid mac Cearrbheoil, and his residence was at Kells. Columcille went to visit the residence and was turned away at the door. In his defense, Diarmaid was away at the time and Columcille was rebuffed by the king's underlings. Now, hospitality as I have said before was a revered concept in Irish law that often transcended mere politeness and was more a matter of duty. As you can imagine, Columcille was outraged by this insult, and with much drama announced that the king's hall would soon house monks and that the soldiers would have to find new quarters. When the king returned and heard what happened, he was embarrassed at the breach of hospitality now associated with his residence. He apologized to the holy man, and as restitution gave him the residence to found his monastery. In a matter of days, Columcille's prophecy came about, and thus a monastery replaced a place of war at Kells.

The monasteries at Durrow and Kells are noted today for two of the most extraordinary books of medieval times. One of the primary tasks of the Irish monasteries was copying texts for preservation, and these copies were illustrated with beautiful and intricate works of art. And unlike their European counterparts who had often censored or refused to copy works they felt were "pagan," the Irish monks copied everything. For that reason, these monks have been credited by many with saving much of civilization after the fall of Rome, for they copied not only the scriptures and lives of the saints, but the works of antiquity which would have been lost to us otherwise. It was to be the copying of a book that would also change the course of Columcille's life.

A Book, a Copy, a Battle, an Exile

The story of copying a book is pivotal in Columcille's life, and it is the one that caused him to leave Ireland forever and to begin a mission of restoring Christianity to Europe. One time, Columcille was visiting a monastery in County Louth. He was very much taken by a beautiful book, a Psalter that the head abbot Finian possessed in his scriptorium. Secretly and without permission, Columcille "borrowed" the book and began making his own copy of the book. When Finian learned of Columcille's actions, he was incensed and brought his case to the High King, Diarmaid mac Cearrbheoil. This was the same king who had given Columcille the residence at Kells and, given Columcille's royal ancestry as well, one can imagine that Columcille felt pretty confident about the outcome of the case. Both men presented their side of the story to the king, and the king found on the side of Finian. His judgment, "to every cow its calf, to every book its copy," is considered the first copyright decision in history, and it caused great anger in Columcille.

Not a man to forget a wrong, real or perceived, Columcille returned to his monastery. A young prince of Connaught, having killed Diarmaid mac Cearrbheoil's son during a game of hurling, panicked and came to Columcille. The monk gave the boy sanctuary in his church, but Diarmaid mac Cearrbheoil disregarded this sacred right and had his soldiers take the boy and kill him. This now was an insult to both Columcille and his church, and the monk leapt into action. He amassed a huge army from among his families and clans and set out to avenge his wrongs.

The battle took place in Cooldrevny, County Sligo, and Columcille's forces destroyed their opponents. Three thousand of Diarmaid mac Cearrbheoil's men died and only one of Columcille's. Yet, Columcille allowed Diarmaid to keep the High Kingship; he got the copy of his book and that is what he wanted.

Of course, the church could not have one of its leading figures go around starting personal battles that would be the cause of numerous deaths without stepping in, and soon a council of holy men instructed Columcille to appear before them. They simply could not abide this behavior and after much agonizing and deliberating, they passed sentence on the man who had done so much single-handedly for Christianity in Ireland. They exiled him from his beloved country, with the command never to set foot again on Ireland's shores.

EXILE

There is a moving song about leaving Derry by Bobby Sands (a fine songwriter more famous for a hunger strike), and I am sure that Columcille would understand the emotion involved, even though almost fifteen centuries separate the two. In fact, Columcille himself wrote a beautiful poem about his feelings on that day. One of the verses ends with the lines "Many the tears of my soft gray eye/As I look back upon Ireland." But leave Columcille was forced to do, and with a following of loyal monks and an abundance of supplies, he sailed off towards the unknown, trusting in his God with his heart surely breaking. It is said that Columcille's boat landed at different small islands, but that he decided to stay on Iona, Scotland, because it was the first island from which his beloved Ireland could not be seen.

The various *Lives* written about Columcille imply a change of heart in the exiled man. Despite his greatness in Ireland—he had founded many, many important monasteries and had attracted hundreds of dedicated and holy men—there was always an arrogance that seemed to demean his character. After the battle of Cooldrevny, however, the man did change. He is described as gentler and more compassionate, chastened by events. This gentle and holy monk is the man who ultimately landed on the island of Iona and began the process of restoring Christianity to mainland Europe. For there were many monks inspired by his example who also left Ireland in order to bring their faith to the barbarian-ravaged Europe that had evolved since the fall of Rome and which Ireland, in its remoteness, had escaped.

Columcille's wish was to convert and minister to as many souls as had died on the battlefield of Cooldrevny. In Scotland, he concentrated his attentions on two groups of people: the Dal Riada, a group of people that had come from northern Ireland and who were probably already Christian; and the Picts, a ferocious band of warriors with little or no knowledge of Christianity, and little will to accept a strange missionary into their isolated community. Columcille's plan also included building monasteries in northern England, but this was only accomplished after his death by his followers, who established Lindisfarne and who converted the Angles who had now spread into England. Stories of Columcille's life in exile are filled with wonder and miracles, and the devotion of those who followed him was fierce.

One story includes perhaps the first written account of the Loch Ness monster. One day when Columcille and his men were traveling by the River Ness, they came upon some of the Picts burying a man who had been killed by a monster in the river. Columcille told one of his men to swim across the river to get their boat, and when he did, the man too was attacked by the huge monster. Columcille raised his hands, made the sign of the cross, and told the monster to leave the man alone and to go no further than the spot where it now was. (The River Ness connects Loch Ness with the sea.) The man survived, the monster left, and the Picts were quite impressed.

Another story revolves around Columcille's only return to Ireland. The Dal Riada had renounced their allegiance to the High King of Ireland upon settling in Scotland, and now paid service to their own king, Aedán. The Irish king was insisting that he was due both taxes and services, and thus relations were growing tense. The only man believed capable of resolving the issue was Columcille. It was said that when he arrived in Ireland to negotiate between the two kings, he wore clods of Scottish earth on his feet and walked blindfolded in obedience to his sentence of never seeing or touching the Irish soil again. Yet it was not the squabble between the kings that was Columcille's greatest moment on this mission. There was also a controversy surrounding the Irish poets, a class of people, mind you, that inspired both much reverence and much fear. In fact, the satires and barbs of the poets were more greatly feared by the Irish princes than the weapons of their enemies; they were powerless against words. The Irish royalty were bristling at these traveling poets, who went from one chieftain's residence to another taking food, lodging, and payment in return for their poetic praises and elegies, as well as for guarantees against their savage satires. But now, enough was enough, said the chieftains, who wanted to eliminate the class altogether.

Columcille saved the poets and protected the chieftains. He persuaded the High King not to ban the class of bards if the poets themselves agreed to a variety of conditions. Both parties were satisfied with the arrangements, and, of course, the poets sang highly the praises of the man who prevented their extinction.

There was no lack of drama in Columcille's life, having dotted Ireland with monasteries that became the centers of Christianity and scholarship, and when he was forced to leave, he did the same in western Scotland. His disciples, caught up in his zeal and holiness, continued his work. It is no exaggeration to say that this influx of Irish missionaries on the European continent was a turning point in European history, a wave of learning washing into barbaric Europe.

A unique individual, both humble and arrogant, a regal prince and a simple monk, Columcille is known to us through the reverent biographies of the men who followed him. It is one of the difficulties in knowing such a man, for his life story has been preserved by loving—though not always accurate—hagiographers.

Yet through the stories of miracles and wonders, the personality of the man emerges and we come to understand a little of the greatness of such a man, a man who possessed great extremes of humanity and spirituality and who inspired unwavering love, loyalty, and obedience in those he led.

THE VIKING INVASION AND THE
HIGH KINGS OF IRELAND

Chapter Vi

The Vikings and Brian Ború

As monasteries rose on the Irish landscape, as Columcille set off for Scotland, and as Irish monks began making their mark on the recivilization of Europe, Ireland itself was enjoying a period of relative peace, especially when compared to the rest of the European continent. This peace was not to last for long. Ireland had avoided the hordes of barbarians that had ravaged Europe, but now a new force was gathering to the north and preparing to invade.

The word "Viking" simply means "sailor," but it has come to mean those particular sailors from Scandinavia who raided Europe during the end of the first millennium. For the most part, the Swedes went to Russia, the Danes to England, and the Norsemen to Ireland. (Ironically, the Irish tend to call all the Viking invaders "Danes," who were in fact a very small percentage of the Scandinavian invaders who landed on Irish shores.) Vikings had come to Ireland before. Their long boats periodically raided the coastline, plundering and pillaging and heading back to sea. One defense for these "hit and run" incursions would be for the people to escape into the monasteries, which gave rise to the marvelous Roundtowers which one can still see in the monastic ruins of Ireland, towers that acted as lookouts and ultimately, sanctuary. The difference, however, with their arrival at the end of the eighth century is that when the Vikings came ashore this time, they stayed!

As would happen again with the Normans, Ireland's social and political system played a role in the invaders' success. Christianity, despite its gains, could never

centralize the system; the island was still a conglomeration of many small kingdoms. Because of clan and familial loyalties, the concept of one single Irish nation
had been difficult to attain, and thus a united defense against a common enemy
was nearly impossible to mount. And so the Vikings established themselves with
relative ease.

The Viking invasion would have a lasting effect on the history of Ireland, and
much that they brought to the island would become part of the very nature of
what we think of as Irish. Marauding sailors, the Vikings set up a system where
they would not need to return home for supplies. Instead, they established outposts where supplies could be stored, meetings arranged, fleets gathered, and ships
fitted out. Soon the Vikings brought their families on their excursions, dropping
them off into the safety of their outposts, before sailing out on their expeditions.
The presence of families brought on the emergence of shops, and before long what
had originally been various stopping-off points for the warriors now became communities and would ultimately expand into towns such as Dublin, Wexford, and
Waterford. It was an important development in Ireland, for the very concept of a
town was unknown to the Irish people.

In 795, Norsemen attacked Columcille's monastery in Iona. They continued
raiding the site until 830, when after the slaughter of scores of monks, the abbot
abandoned the site and moved the community back to Kells, taking some relics of
Columcille and the monastery's most famous book—known as *The Book of Kells*.
That same year, 795, saw the first large-scale Viking invasion of Ireland at Lambey
Island near what is Dublin today.

For the Vikings, Ireland was an ideal land to invade. The unique advantage
and strength of the Viking fleet was that the longboats were not only strong
enough to withstand the North Atlantic and the open sea, but also agile enough to
navigate shallow rivers and lakes. Ireland, with its large system of rivers and lakes,

must have seemed a modern superhighway to the Norsemen, who could travel deep into the country.

In 837, two large fleets of about sixty ships each entered the mouths of the River Boyne and the River Liffey. The Vikings were about to establish their permanent bases. Developing these bases into fortified, wall towns, the Norsemen used these sites to travel inland. Situated in locations that were geographically advantageous for defense and trading, the Norse sites were much more suitable for growth and development than the isolated sites of monasteries that were the Irish communities for the previous five centuries. By 841, Dublin was firmly established, and the town was growing exponentially with new Norse immigrants as well as the native Irish.

The Norse came in waves. The first surge came in the middle of the ninth century and saw the warrior king Thorgest sail as far north as Armagh, where he looted the rich monastery, inland to the River Shannon, where he crushed the settlements, and eastward to Clonmacnoise, where he not only plundered the famous abbey, but boldly set up his wife as a pagan priestess in charge of the altar. Ultimately, he was killed by a king of Meath.

The tenth century saw another surge of Viking activity. In 914, they landed on the southern coast and established what would become the town of Waterford. From here, they again attacked the Shannon valley, as Thorgest had a century before. Inland, they established a base at what is now Limerick (former home, by the way, of the McCourt gaggle), and then traveled to the southeastern corner and set up what would become the town of Wexford. The names Waterford and Wexford both come from Norse words, a constant reminder of the Norse legacy.

So great were the number of Vikings that one ancient Irish text spoke of the sea "vomiting the foreigners onto the land." With fortified bases along the eastern and southern coastlines and another within center of the island, and with shipload

after shipload arriving on the shores, the Norse must have seemed invincible to the
Irish who witnessed their arrival.

However, Norse domination would come to an end, and the man who is credited with bringing it about is the great Irish king, Brian Ború.

BRIAN BORÚ

Now although we are out of the world of ancient saints and mythic figures, history is still a world where legend often runs in front of the facts, where the "facts"
are always recorded by the victorious and where truth has no business getting in
the way of a good story. And so, we have Brian Ború, a great man, mind you, in
both legend and history. Didn't he compare himself to Charlemagne, and even
claim at Armagh that he was *Imperator Scottorum*? (As far as I know, this is the
only time a fellow ever claimed to be Emperor of Ireland!) Others saw him as a
sort of Irish Alfred the Great and wove tales of a young guerilla fighter fending off
the Viking invader. Of course, the truth, say the academics, is probably a bit less
romantic than the stories that have come down about him, but then again, why let
the truth get in the way of a good story?

In Irish history, Brian Ború is considered the last of the great High Kings,
the last of the Ard Rí. He very well may have been the first of the great ones as
well, although to be fair, there were some other notable names before Brian,
effective kings, perhaps, but not great. It was Brian, however, who is credited
with expelling the Vikings and unifying Ireland. Unifying this island has never
been an easy task, and Brian got as far as any man, I would say. And as for the
Vikings, no one was going to expel them; for by the time Brian Ború was being
crowned at the Rock of Cashel, many of the Vikings had already intermarried
with the Irish, settled into their walled towns, and had become as "Irish as the

Irish themselves," in the words of another man at a later time in history.

The High Kingship was not really ever a countrywide position, or at least was never accepted by the entire country at any one time. That simply was not the Celtic way. The High King was an elected position, not hereditary, which caused much havoc among those who got their way and those who didn't. For the most part of twelve centuries, the country was marked by territorial battles among the separate tribes, various families, and over 100 small kingdoms. Often these battles wrought much more damage on the countryside than any invader had done. One particular ruler, Feidhlimidh—who was both King *and* Bishop of Cashel—is said to have destroyed more monasteries and churches than any Viking.

Perhaps, before Brian Ború, the last effective High King had come a century early in the form of Máel Seaclainn, a prince of the Uí Néill clan, who was given the High Kingship in 859. Another by the same name (coincidentally, "Máel Seaclainn" translates into English as "Malachy") would play a role in the story of Brian Ború. But it was with this first Máel Seaclainn that the concept of an Irish nation began to form, a concept that would reach its ideal with Brian Ború.

The Uí Néill's possession of the High Kingship (seated in Tara) continued after Máel Seaclainn's death and left a power vacuum in the west, a void that was filled by a tribe called the Dál gCais. It was into this family that Brian Ború was born.

Born sometime around 940, Brian Ború (or Brian Bóraimé or Boruhma as you will see it sometimes written) was the second son of Cennedig who was chief of the Dál gCais. It was a time of great turmoil and displacement, and the Dál gCais had been driven deeper and deeper into what is now County Clare. As a boy, Brian had seen his mother and other members of his tribe brutally murdered, a foul deed he never forgot or forgave. There was a clan, the Eoganacht, who had begun to seize more and more power in the absence of the Uí Néill, and it was they who were forcing the Dál gCais further west. The Dál gCais resisted this power, and with the Uí Néill's help—who feared the overreaching grasp of the Eoganacht—they ultimately routed their enemy. As a result of these victories, Brian's brother Mahon became chief of the Dál gCais, and he quickly made peace with the Norse ruler Ivar of Limerick.

But Brian would brook no such reconciliation. He broke with his brother and set off with soldiers for the hills, from where, for several years, they attacked the surrounding Norse settlements. As his success grew and his fame spread, more and more men joined his ranks. Soon he had a sizeable army of Dál gCaissians, and a formidable fleet as well.

Sometime around 963, Brian and Mahon re-united. Realizing that with Brian's army at his side, he had a stronger negotiating tool than before, Mahon rescinded the agreements he had made with the Norse. With Brian's help, Mahon took Cashel and was named king of Cashel. Then the brothers marched to Tipperary, and with their victory there, Norse rule in Munster collapsed. Ivar of Limerick fled to Norway, and Mahon ruled peacefully (always a relative term among these chieftains) for eight years.

But Ivar hadn't returned to Norway to retire; he was planning his return and revenge. He landed again in Ireland around 974 and killed Mahon himself in battle. Brian, calculating that a war with Ivar would entail a huge loss of life, asked for one-to-one combat with the man who had killed his brother. Ivar accepted and Brian was victorious. Brian Ború was about to get his name as a great king in the annals of Irish history.

The Only High King of Ireland

With Mahon dead, Brian took his brother's titles. He returned to Cashel in 978, defeated the reigning King of Cashel, and crowned himself. Next he took the

Kingship of Munster. In 983, his troops overran Connaught, and five years later his ships sailed up the Shannon, from where he conquered Meath. His forays into Meath would have great impact later. (For those who have trouble envisioning this on a modern map, Brian Ború and his army were making forays throughout the entire west up to County Mayo, all of the south and across the center almost to Dublin.)

A fierce battler, Brian was an even greater tactician and politician, and within ten years, he had taken under his control pretty much all of the south of Ireland. Indeed, for the first time ever, unity was present in the south. And yet, there was another force with which he would have to contend. That force was Malachy II, the man who now formally held the title of High King.

Malachy was one of the Uí Néill clan and had parlayed his Kingship of Meath into the High Kingship to which he was elected in 980. At the battle of Tara, Malachy had destroyed the Norse army and taken control of Dublin, the most important of the Norse outposts. Now while in the history books, Malachy might stand in the shadow of Brian Ború, he was a great warrior and an effective ruler. He was also wise enough to know that the power he possessed was no match for Brian's forces in the south. So in 1002, when Brian proposed a conference between the two, Malachy readily agreed.

Brian suggested that the country be divided between the two of them. In effect, there would be two High Kings—a northern and southern one—but only one man would claim the title: Brian Ború. In addition, Brian wanted control of Dublin. As the final sign that the Uí Néills no longer had a monopoly on the High Kingship of Ireland, Brian had himself crowned not at Tara, the traditional site, but at the Rock of Cashel, his own domicile as it were. There was doubt that Brian was now in charge.

As a matter of course, while these two men divided the country, there were others who were not satisfied by the arrangement, particularly, the men of Leinster, who had no great love for Brian Ború. There would be various uprisings, with the last—during Holy Week in 1014—considered one of the greatest battles in the history of Medieval Europe.

The Battle of Clontarf and a Woman Named Gormfhlaith

There have been all kinds of claims for the Battle of Clontarf. It has been said that Brian's victory there finally drove the Vikings out of Ireland. It didn't. It's been said it was the pinnacle of Brian's reign. It wasn't—he died violently. And it has been called the most famous battle of Medieval Europe. Perhaps it was. The legend surrounding the Battle of Clontarf grew quickly, but was permanently centered in Irish history through two literary works. One, the thirteenth-century Norse epic *Brennu-Njáls Saga*, tells the story of Njal, an Icelandic voyager, and his family, who travel throughout Europe. Stopping off in Orkney, Njal is present during the planning for Clontarf. And though Njal himself does not take part in the battle, the event is recounted in great detail. Surprisingly, coming as it is from the Viking point of view, it is Brian Ború who is described most gloriously and heroically. The second source is the famous *Cogadh Gaedhel re Gallaibh* (roughly translated as *The War of the Irish with the Foreigner*.) This text gives a rich account of the Viking invasions culminating in the Battle of Clontarf. And while it does draw on contemporary accounts and historical annals, we have to keep in mind that it was commissioned by Brian Ború's descendants. In modern terms, we might say it was an early exercise in political spin, concentrating on a glorious tradition of a political dynasty.

The battle, which took place on Good Friday in the year 1014, had its beginnings several years earlier. The Viking King of Dublin, Olaf Cuaran, had married Gormfhlaith, the beautiful Irish daughter of the King of Leinster. Olaf and Gormfhlaith had a son, Sitric. When Malachy took control of Dublin in 981, Olaf fled to Scotland, leaving Sitric and Gormfhlaith behind. Malachy fell in love with and married Gormfhlaith, and in deference to his new bride, he named her son Sitric king of Dublin. All this occurred before Malachy and Brian's famous "summit meeting" in 1002, before Malachy had ceded so much power to his rival.

One of the aspects of the Irish Brehon Law that later shocked foreigners and caused great upheaval among the European church hierarchy was its cavalier approach to marriage and divorce. A man—or a woman—could simply put aside a spouse for a variety of reasons. Malachy, after seventeen years, decided to divorce Gormfhlaith. The proud and outraged princess returned to Leinster and began to conspire with her son and her brother, Máel Morda, whom Brian had once ousted from the kingship of Leinster. Mother, son, and uncle led an uprising against Brian Ború in 999, which he put down. But in doing so, he spied Gormfhlaith; the princess—who must have been an amazing woman—captured Brian's heart, and before long she was Brian Ború's wife and queen. With her new source of influence, Gormfhlaith persuaded Brian to set up Sitric once more as the chieftain of Dublin and to reinstate Máel Morda as the King of Leinster. Atypically for such a shrewd political mind, Brian agreed, not anticipating this family alliance would cause him trouble down the road.

Like Malachy before him, Brian soon tired of Gormfhlaith and set her aside. Gormfhlaith was furious and once more conspired with her brother and her son. Sitric enlisted the help of Norsemen living on the Scottish Isles, and promised one of them, Sigurd the Stout, not only all of Ireland but his mother for a wife as well, if he would help them defeat Brian once and for all. The stage was set for the greatest battle of medieval times. It was not, however, strictly a battle between

Norsemen and Irishman, but between Brian's forces and an alliance of Leinstermen and Norsemen. Brian himself was now in his late-seventies, still a magnificent strategist but incapable of fighting.

The story goes that the aged Brian spent the battle in his tent, saying his prayers and listening. For most of the day, the battle raged fiercely with either side vacillating between victory and defeat. Sigurd himself commanded two thousand Norseman; Máel Morda led the men of Leinster; and Brian's forces were composed of men from Munster and Connaught. At the last minute, Malachy refused to assist Brian. Contemporary accounts are inflated, but modern scholars do set the minimum of fighting men at 5,000. The fighting was on an epic and bloody scale. Finally, one of Brian's sons broke through the rebel forces. He killed both Sigurd and Máel Morda, throwing the rebels into panic and disarray. Some fled to the shelter of Dublin's walls, while many of the Norsemen tried to flee in their boats back to Scotland. A combination of high tides and panic caused most of the escaping Vikings to drown. One of the fleeing Norsemen happened upon Brian Ború alone and unguarded in his tent. The High King was slain, and with his death came the end of an era. In the course of the day Brian's forces had put down the uprising, and dispersed the Vikings, but had lost their leader.

Later his body was taken to Armagh for burial, attended with great pomp and ceremony—the outward recognition of the true High King of Ireland. Always the great politician, Brian no doubt saw that his burial in Armagh, coupled with his coronation in Cashel, was a rich symbol of the unity that he tried to bring to his nation.

THE LEGACY OF BRIAN BORÚ

For Brian Ború, militarism meant more than just a Celtic tradition of warfare. In Brian's hands, it was part of a political and personal plan. With military power, he was able to do much for Ireland—a country that had seen the ravages of Viking invasions for over a century. His might, and the prestige that came with it, allowed him to rebuild the Irish church, repairing many of the monasteries that had been pillaged by the Norse and building new ones as well. Making Armagh the center of the Irish church did much to empower the church, improve communication throughout the island, and consequently help to unify the country. He is said to have sent emissaries into Europe to bring back the countless books, relics, and treasures that had been sent abroad for safekeeping in anticipation of the plundering Viking hordes. He must have had a vision of an Ireland restored to its glory, and he used his military might and power to try to achieve it.

When Brian Ború took the kingship from Malachy, he set a precedent that would affect the High Kings of Ireland until their final demise. No longer was the title given to an "elected" candidate, chosen perhaps with all the backroom dealings and manipulating implicit, but was now assumed by the man who had the power to take it and keep it. This alone was an important progression from the earlier chaos that surrounded the naming of a High King.

Most important, however, when considering Brian Ború, is the concept of a united Ireland. He was the first to truly see the island as a single entity, and in no small way, he used his reign to pursue this vision. It is for this that later generations would see him as the great unifier. And in this nation—forged by Celtic Druidic tradition, Christian mysticism, and the poetry of the bardic classes—the power of the symbol is very strong. Thus whether historically accurate or rising from the mists of legend, the person of Brian Ború—the great High King who envisioned a united Ireland, the warrior king who vanquished the foreign invader—became that symbol that men would turn to when their dreams of a united Ireland hardened to reality and memories of a glorious past encouraged their hopes.

Chapter VII:

High Kings and High Villains—Turlough O'Connor, Rory O'Connor, and Dermot MacMurrough

Turlough O'Connor

After the death of Brian Ború, his heirs ruled Ireland for a while, but never with the same success. The High Kingship continued but now in the annals there is recorded a new category of High Kingship: "High King with opposition." With the death of Brian, there was a power void, one that various families tried to fill, but which was ultimately filled by the Norman invaders.

In addition to the O'Brien clan, which held sway in Munster, the most important families were the MacLoughlins in Ulster and the O'Connors in Connaught. Leinster—where Brian Ború and other High Kings had such contentious difficulties—was ruled by various families but most important were the MacMurroughs. Indeed, it is Dermot MacMurrough and his dealings with various kings and High Kings that ultimately brought about the Norman invasion. But we are getting ahead of ourselves. By the mid-twelfth century, the O'Connor clan was looming large in Ireland's affairs.

Turlough O'Connor was a strong High King, perhaps the last with any great power; in his son, Rory O'Connor, we have a much lesser man who is remembered primarily for being the last of the High Kings; Dermot MacMurrough is remembered as one of the greatest villains in Irish history.

Even by the twelfth century, O'Connor was a great and glorious name with much honor attached to it. In Irish the name was Ua Conchobair, and it implied descent from the great Conchobar and the days of Cúchulainn. Today the name still is revered. To get some idea of the popularity of the name, type in the words "Turlough O'Connor" or "Rory O'Connor" into the Internet and search for either name. You will find scores of Irishmen bearing the name: from rock stars and footballers, photographers and psychiatrists, and a slew of others who bear the names of these two Irish High Kings. It is a proud family name, in all its permutations, and most modern bearers are well aware of the connection with their past.

In 1119, more than a century after Brian Ború's death, Turlough O'Connor took the High Kingship. He was a strong and ambitious leader, a king of Connaught, and like Brian he seemed to understand the concept of nationhood. Like Brian, Turlough also became a patron of national culture, attempting to revive once again the glory of Ireland's golden age that had died in the years right after Brian's death. More importantly, perhaps, Turlough worked hard for Church reform. This was a critical moment for the Irish Church; Church reform had been implemented on the continent and Ireland lagged well behind. The century of Viking rule had devastated the Irish monasteries, and those Christian Vikings who remained in Dublin after the Battle of Clontarf increasingly looked towards the east and to Canterbury as their center of spirituality. Turlough presided over a convocation of Irish bishops that assembled at Kells with the purpose of bringing the Irish Church more into line with its European brethren, yet despite these attempts at reformation, the Irish Church was still out of line with the rest. The desire of the Europeans to bring Ireland back into the fold of the Roman Church would soon have drastic consequences for the country.

To maintain his power, Turlough ringed his native Connaught with forts. He bridged the Shannon. Dividing and conquering, he split Munster, the long-standing stronghold of the O'Briens, into two kingdoms. Yet he also made mistakes that proved catastrophic. In 1126, he ousted the king of Meath, placing his ineffectual son on the throne; he had tried earlier to do the same in Leinster. Both of these acts would have disastrous results, for they formed new alliances out of former rivalries that would stand in opposition to Turlough. In the north, Murtough MacLoughlin united Ulster and placed the minor kingdoms of Ulidia and Oriel under his rule, and in Leinster, Dermot MacMurrough ousted Turlough's son Conor, whom the High King had installed there as king. (This son was the same son Turlough later set up in Meath and who was killed within six months of taking the throne.) Both these men, MacLoughlin and MacMurrough, would play roles in the cataclysmic events to come.

When Turlough died in 1156, his son Rory was made king of Connaught, but the more powerful MacLoughlin in Ulster claimed the High Kingship. There are many who claim that Turlough was the last of the great High Kings, but in hindsight the matter seems inconsequential. For within a few years of his death, Anglo-Norman forces would land in Ireland, and the High Kingship of Ireland would be relegated to the annals of history alone. As the forty-eighth High King of Ireland, Turlough tried to control the island and its many kings by strengthening his own power base in Connaught, by dividing troublesome regions, and by enlisting the support of the Church. Whether he would have been able to defend against the Norman invaders is a moot point, one that underscores the tragedy of both his death and his lack of strong heirs.

Rory O'Connor

Rory O'Connor was never the king his father was. The youngest of Turlough's sons, he was not even his father's favorite. That honor went to Conor, who Turlough tried twice to position into a kingship. In the first instance, Conor was defeated by a more powerful king, and in the second, he was murdered, unable to fulfill the dreams of his father.

Rory became king of Connaught on his father's death in 1156, but his claim to the High Kingship was challenged by Murtough MacLoughlin. For several years, these two battled for the over-kingship, continuing a war that seemed endless to the two families. Various alliances were made and inducements were offered to the numerous minor kings. In the end, however, these lesser kings supported MacLoughlin, who by all standards was a more powerful and forceful ruler, and in 1162, MacLoughlin was named "High King without opposition" by the Ostmen of Dublin, who also accepted Dermot MacMurrough—MacLoughlin's greatest supporter—as the lord of the city. And while MacMurrough was politically shrewd enough to back MacLoughlin, Tiernan O'Rourke, the king of Breifne, stayed loyal to Rory. For reasons we'll learn later, there was no love lost between O'Rourke and MacMurrough, and the sides that were drawn there in 1062 would play out for the rest of the decade.

MacLoughlin was a fierce and harsh man, and even his own people grew tired of his cruelty. When he blinded the king of Ulidia in 1166, after the king had submitted to MacLoughlin's terms and offered various princes as guarantors, the people finally rose and fought back, killing MacLoughlin at the battle of Leitir Luin.

Once again, there was a power void and Rory O'Connor filled it quickly. He marched to Dublin, where he was proclaimed High King. As Rory completed the "Circuit of the Ard Rí," Dermot MacMurrough found himself beset by chiefs of Waterford, Leinster, Osory, and Dublin who were terrified of MacMurrough. Among them was Rory's ally Tiernan O'Rourke, who had his own grudge against MacMurrough. After O'Rourke and his armies looted and burned MacMurrough's palace to the ground, MacMurrough escaped with his daughter to England. O'Connor joined O'Rourke, and as High King supported his actions against MacMurrough. Neither could have known the impact that

MacMurrough's flight would have on their country. But for the time being, O'Connor settled the various kingships and principalities, and Ireland, it seemed, was in a relatively peaceful state.

MacMurrough was a proud man, and he had fled to England to seek help in regaining his crown. When he returned again in 1167, he was accompanied by a small force of Anglo-Norman knights and archers. In the meantime, Rory O'Connor had grown quite strong, and as the firmly ensconced High King, he met MacMurrough in Dublin. He insisted that MacMurrough recognize his High Kingship, pay an "honor price" of gold to Tiernan O'Rourke, and hand over two of his sons as hostages (a time-honored practice among the Irish kings). In return, Rory granted MacMurrough his familial lands—a far cry from his kingship of Leinster. But MacMurrough agreed, for after all, he had much bigger plans in the future.

In 1169, MacMurrough joined his army with two Anglo-French armies that had landed in Ireland, and together they marched on Wexford and took the city within a day. Rory O'Connor needed to act. He marched into Leinster and began negotiations with MacMurrough. He would give MacMurrough the kingship of Leinster, if MacMurrough continued to acknowledge him as High King. He also, O'Connor insisted, must send the foreign soldiers back and bring no more into the country. MacMurrough agreed, but had no intention of keeping his word.

Rory O'Connor's problems with the foreign soldiers were just beginning. In 1170, Richard de Clare, called Strongbow, landed with his troops as he had promised MacMurrough and took Waterford. With an eye toward the High Kingship, MacMurrough met him there, and together they marched to Dublin. O'Connor and O'Rourke, allied once again, came to the town's defense, but Strongbow and MacMurrough's forces slipped by them, and the Ostman chief Asgall surrendered the town to them. O'Connor and O'Rourke retreated and left Dublin to the

Normans and MacMurrough. Firmly situated, MacMurrough's forces drove deep into Meath.

O'Connor now had a challenger for the High Kingship. With the Anglo-Norman forces on his side, MacMurrough led the superior military force, and the defenders were stymied by the modern techniques of the European soldiers. O'Connor and O'Rourke decided to lay siege to Dublin. For two months, O'Connor and 30,000 soldiers camped out in what is now Phoenix Park and waited for the Norman enemy to starve. Rory even offered to recognize Strongbow's kingship of Leinster—MacMurrough had died and had promised such to his ally—if Strongbow would recognize him as High King of Ireland. Strongbow refused.

Now, there are tragic events, momentous events, that nevertheless are comical in a way. Strongbow picked two of his best men who led 600 men out of the castle and into Phoenix Park. The beseigers had no guard, and most of them, including Rory O'Connor, were naked and bathing in the Liffey. Strongbow's men attacked and routed the naked natives. As he gathered his clothes about him, Rory O'Connor may have realized that politically and militarily, Ireland was turning into something different. That this was the end.

When the English King Henry II arrived in Ireland in the autumn of 1171, he claimed much of the land that his English barons had won for themselves. At Cashel, he met with a convocation of Irish bishops who bemoaned the state of the Irish church. Henry assured them that he would take care of the problem. Spending the winter in Ireland, he accepted the allegiance of the Irish kings one by one. By winter's end, every king had submitted but one: Rory O'Connor. The High King of Ireland—together with the chieftains of the north—would not submit. But Rory was the High King of a dissolving kingdom; the foreign King was distributing land at a quick pace to his own people.

In 1175, Rory O'Connor finally submitted to Henry II. In the Treaty of Windsor, Rory accepted Henry II as the overlord and promised to pay annual tribute gathered from all of Ireland to him. For his part, Rory would remain King of Connaught and High King of all unconquered lands in Ireland. The breadth of that realm was shrinking rapidly, and before long the treaty was broken.

Even in Connaught among his own people, Rory's power was eroding. There was general dissatisfaction, and Rory was forced to name his son Conchobar (Conor) king in 1183. He once more attempted to regain his power, but fell far short. In his heart, he must have known that the world he inherited from his father was long gone, that an enemy much greater than he—or any Irish King—had ever known was building castles throughout the land, and that a return to power was a desperate hope.

Rory O'Connor died in 1198, and like his father Turlough, he was buried at Clonmacnoise. He was the fiftieth High King of Ireland. And the last.

Dermot MacMurrough

There probably isn't a man in all of Irish history who is reviled more than Dermot MacMurrough. (You'll find his first name written as Dermott, Diarmaid, and Diarmait.) His death notice from the *Annals of Tigernach* in 1171 is more a curse than an obituary:

> *Diarmait MacMurrough, king of Leinster and the Ostmen, the man who troubled Banba and destroyed Ireland, after mustering the foreigners and after ruining the Irish, after plundering and razing churches and territories, died at the end of the year of an insufferable disease, through the miracles of Finnian, Columcille and other saints whose churches he plundered.* *

The passage of time is no kinder to the man, and historians throughout the

---

* As quoted in Donnchadh Ó Corráin, "Diarmait MacMurrough (1110–71) and the Coming of the Anglo-French" in Brady, Ciaran, ed. *Worsted in the Game: Losers in Irish History.* Dublin: Lilliput Press, 1989.

centuries do not let the Irish forget MacMurrough's perfidy. He is blamed for "inviting" the Anglo-Normans to invade Ireland, and, in many a man's mind, he is responsible for all the troubles since.

The story of MacMurrough's treachery begins in 1151 during the reign of Turlough O'Connor as High King. Turlough had, twenty-five years earlier, invaded Meath, deposed the king, and set up three separate rulers. One, an underling of Turlough's, controlled west Meath, and MacMurrough and a man named Tiernan O'Rourke shared rule over east Meath.

In 1151, Turlough held a meeting with MacLoughlin, where the two powerful men swore loyalty and friendship to each other. Turlough also tried to restore the kingdom of Meath, which he had divided earlier, to its proper ruler. O'Rourke rebelled against these new arrangements and so the three kings, O'Connor, MacLoughlin, and MacMurrough, invaded and sacked his territory. And to add insult to injury, MacMurrough also stole O'Rourke's wife, along with all her treasures and cattle.

Now there are those who love to couch this story in the mists of romantic passion, and within a grand comparison to the Trojan War and the story of Helen and Paris. And sure enough we have seduction, betrayal, and grave consequences. But neither MacMurrough nor O'Rourke's wife was a young lover over-brimming with passion; to be kind, both were what we might call of "a sober age." Indeed, one historian stated that instead of a vibrant Paris, Ireland's "Helen" was ravished by an "athletic grey-beard." The circumstances of the battle, and the accounts of the chroniclers, as well, seem to imply that MacMurrough's actions were aimed more at insulting O'Rourke than at carrying off his true love. There are some who say that O'Rourke's wife, Dervorgilla—also reviled in Irish history for her small part in all this—saw MacMurrough as an attractive suitor and invited him to carry her off, for the man has been described as tall and handsome. But it seems to me these accounts are by those who simply like a "femme fatale" wrapped up in their history. Nevertheless, MacMurrough sent her back to her husband within a year, with not a little encouragement from Turlough O'Connor.

As you can imagine there was no great love between O'Rourke and MacMurrough, and O'Rourke, while making no secret of his hatred, waited until the right time to have his revenge. As the saying goes: "Revenge is a dish best eaten cold."

When Turlough O'Connor died in 1156, the rivalry for the High Kingship settled between Rory O'Connor and Murtough MacLoughlin. This rivalry would dominate the Irish political scene for the next thirteen years. It was here that Dermot MacMurrough perhaps made his biggest mistake—he allied himself with MacLoughlin. It seemed a wise alliance, as MacLoughlin was more powerful and claimed the High Kingship, and during his reign rewarded MacMurrough with grants and military support. But MacLoughlin was murdered by his own people and when Rory O'Connor took the High Kingship he marched against MacMurrough. The O'Connor foray against MacMurrough was assisted by a fervent ally with a score to settle—Tiernan O'Rourke. MacMurrough, a harsh ruler, found himself beset by men who had long memories and no loyalty to him. He had made many enemies, and now, as his fortunes waned, he could find no supporters.

Crushed and deposed, on August 1, 1166, MacMurrough sailed for England. Learning that Henry II was in France, he quickly followed the English king there. Desperate, MacMurrough swore allegiance and loyalty to Henry II. In return, he received permission to raise an army from any of Henry's lands. Returning to England, he found little success in recruiting men. He traveled to Wales, where there were soldiers aplenty looking for adventure, but MacMurrough's most important "recruit" was Richard de Clare, known throughout Irish history as "Strongbow."

MacMurrough promised de Clare the hand of his daughter, Aoife, as well as right of succession after his death, should the two be successful in regaining MacMurrough's kingship back. (Surely, MacMurrough, who had for so long been immersed in the wrangling over kingships and succession, must have known that his offer to Strongbow had no legal precedent in Ireland. But de Clare's armies would prove to have more power than any Irish tradition or laws.) De Clare, for his part, promised to help MacMurrough by bringing troops to Ireland to support him the following spring. MacMurrough was also aided by two of de Clare's allies, Robert FitzStephen and Maurice FitzGerald. Both men also promised to come to Ireland in the spring of the year. As compensation, MacMurrough promised them the town of Wexford and surrounding lands. For MacMurrough now, his job was to wait.

A year later, in August 1167, he landed back in Ireland, accompanied by Anglo-French knights and archers. Surprisingly, he was welcomed. Always the politician, MacMurrough acknowledged Rory O'Connor's High Kingship and made amends with Tiernan O'Rourke by giving his old enemy 100 ounces of gold as "honor payment." In a gesture that was more magnanimous than wise, O'Connor reinstated MacMurrough as king of his familial lands. As surety, the High King took two of MacMurrough's sons as hostages.

When FitzStephen and FitzGerald landed with two small armies in May 1169, MacMurrough joined them, and they attacked and took Wexford, which MacMurrough gave to the two Englishmen as promised. Immediately the victors built the first Norman edifice on Irish soil, the first of what would turn out to be a great number. Rory O'Connor quickly marched into Leinster to negotiate an agreement with MacMurrough. The agreement—negotiated by MacMurrough's brother-in-law, the Archbishop of Dublin, St. Lawrence

O'Toole—gave MacMurrough kingship of Leinster, and in turn he supported O'Connor's claim as Ard Rí. More importantly to O'Connor, MacMurrough also agreed to bring no more Anglo-French soldiers into Ireland, and to send back those he had with him then. MacMurrough agreed, but reneged on his promise. He may never have intended to, or perhaps he no longer had the power to.

In August 1170, Richard de Clare—Strongbow—arrived in Ireland with 2,200 troops. Another Anglo-French leader, Raymond de le Gros, joined him, and the two armies attacked and took Waterford. MacMurrough, FitzGerald, and FitzStephen joined them with their armies, and Strongbow was married to MacMurrough's daughter. From Waterford, they marched to Dublin, an obvious strategic and symbolic target. O'Connor's armies raced to the city to protect it, but the combined forces of Strongbow, MacMurrough, and his Norman allies outflanked them by traveling through Wicklow and easily took the city and set fire to it. The armored Norman knights with their troops of archers must have seemed invincible to the Irish warriors, who wore no protective clothing, used spears, battle-axes, and stone, and who were seeing for the very first time the efficiency of the crossbow and the power of these trained legions. They were armies from two separate periods of time—and the poorly armed Irish warrior was no match for the modern warfare of the Anglo-Norman.

With the arrival of Strongbow, it seemed that MacMurrough was no longer in control—he had ceded that to the foreigners. And as Strongbow's power grew, Rory O'Connor's disintegrated. With the High King weakened, old tribal enmities rose quickly in Ireland. O'Connor's enemies aligned themselves with the Anglo-French, and the foreigners marched deeper into Ireland to abet these uprisings. Irish history was at a defining moment.

When MacMurrough died in May 1171, Strongbow was made King of Leinster. Five months later, Henry II himself landed in Waterford with 4,000 men. MacMurrough had invited these foreigners in, had welcomed them and set them up. It was an action that would echo down through the centuries.

CHAPTER VIII:

"STRONGBOW"—RICHARD DE CLARE

As an actor and as a reader, my knowledge of the English monarchy comes primarily through Shakespeare and the movies. It is Shakespeare's *Henry IV* and *Henry V*
who come to mind when I see those names on the printed page. It is Shakespeare's
tragic *Richard II* whom I know, and for me the English War of the Roses unfolds
within the context of his plays. And what Shakespeare hasn't covered, Hollywood
has filled in. I would bet most Americans know King John from the Claude Rains'
portrayal in Errol Flynn's *The Adventures of Robin Hood*, not to mention the
appearance of a noble King Richard the Lionhearted at the end of the film. Even
younger moviegoers know much of their British history from Hollywood movies.
Who can forget the cruel Edward I and his feckless son, the future Edward II, in
Mel Gibson's *Braveheart*? Or how in the 1990s, Hollywood treated us to two por-
trayals of *Elizabeth I*, as well as a sniveling and sickly *Mary Tudor* and a mad
George III? And since most lads today spend little time studying their history in
school, this is it, no matter.

Yet while Shakespeare's *Henry IV* was worrying about his son's recklessness
and King John was colluding with the Sheriff of Nottingham and Edward was
worrying about William Wallace in the north and the Houses of Lancaster
and York were warring over succession, their actions—and as often their
inaction—were determining the course of Ireland's history for the next millennium. Indeed, from the moment that MacMurrough brought the Anglo-
French to Ireland to well into the twentieth century, the history of Ireland is

inexorably bound to the doings of the English monarchs.

Like history in general, Dermot MacMurrough's invitation to Strongbow, and Strongbow's acceptance, did not happen in a vacuum. There were many outside forces working towards the Norman invasion of Ireland. As so often in Irish history, one of the forces involved was the Church. As noted before, the Irish Church had developed differently from the Roman Church, and, despite reformation dating back to the days of Columcille, was still felt to be quite out of line with the orthodoxy. The cavalier attitude toward marriage was disturbing. A system of nepotism that could allow the diocese of Armagh to be run by the same family for years was problematic—as was its married archbishop. By the twelfth century, the Church had outgrown its monastic system with its symbiotic relationship between Irish royal families and church leaders, and a system of geographically divided dioceses was suggested and drawn up.

The pope, at the time, was receiving communications from both Irish prelates (notably a fellow named St. Malachy), and through English emissaries from Canterbury, about the state of the Irish Church. Theobald, the archbishop of Canterbury, was particularly concerned about Irish irregularities, and besides reporting to Rome, had also suggested a plan to Henry II for taking and reforming the island. Whatever he proposed, the plan was trumped by Pope Adrian IV himself in 1155 who in the infamous *Bull Laudabiliter* gave permission for Henry to "invade Ireland and reform its church and people." (The fact that no one has ever seen this "Bull" has challenged historians for a long time, but the point becomes inconsequential, for in 1172, Pope Alexander III gave Henry the "Lordship of Ireland"!) Again, nothing happens in a vacuum, and Henry at the time needed good relations with Rome, for he was trying to repair the damage done by his murder of Thomas Beckett the previous year.

So when Dermot came to Henry II and to Strongbow in 1169, Henry already had papal permission to invade Ireland. And in the year that Henry first landed in Ireland, he has already been named "Lord of Ireland." But Henry did not come primarily to rule Ireland—he came to rein in Strongbow. For Strongbow, and others like him, were gaining great power and wealth in Ireland, and from that position were a threat to Henry and to England itself.

Indeed, Strongbow's successes in Ireland tempted many other ambitious nobles from England to do the same, and many great Irish names actually come from these early invaders, who much to the chagrin of their English peers became "more Irish than the Irish."

Strongbow was described as a tall man with red hair, freckles, and a small voice. For the Irish, he has long been the embodiment of the Norman invasion. Though he may not have been the first, he was the most important of that first wave of Anglo-Normans to invade Ireland, though "invasion" is probably the wrong word, as he was actually invited. But, there was more going on than Dermot MacMurrough merely inviting some foreigners into Ireland to help him settle old scores. For Strongbow, it was the chance for adventure and advancement—an attitude that would later bring many young men to Ireland's shores.

Strongbow's grandfather had died in battle against a Welsh uprising in 1136, and in gratitude Henry I made Strongbow's father, Gilbert de Clare, the Earl of Pembroke (while at the same time further reducing the lot of the Celtic Welsh). Strongbow's mother had been a young mistress of Henry I, and, in fact, she bore an illegitimate daughter to Henry. Thus Strongbow was the stepbrother of the king's daughter, who herself was a half-sister of Empress Matilda.

When Henry I died in 1130, Richard's father and uncles supported the claims of Stephen against those of Empress Matilda in Scotland, yet when Stephen confiscated their lands and castles, he turned his Pembroke supporters against him and toward Matilda. This partisanship was such that twenty-five years later, Henry

II—Matilda's son—still refused to acknowledge the title "Earl of Pembroke," and the title was not used again until 1199 when Strongbow's son-in-law claimed it. To put it simply, neither Strongbow nor his family was in favor with Henry II.

Now, twelfth-century Wales was a land of young adventurers, young Normans with war in their blood who had helped conquer the southernmost part of the island, and who were eager for some excitement. Henry II had given these young warriors in Wales a wide swath to cut—and they were permitted to wage small wars in the Welsh wilderness, claiming whatever lands they could carve out for themselves. These young nobles had little loyalty to their king and probably less to Strongbow, who had made Pembroke into a feudal state. It was this attitude of self-serving adventure, acquisitiveness, and lack of fealty to England's monarchy that they brought to Ireland.

So when Dermot MacMurrough—doesn't it always seem to come back to that fellow?—invited Strongbow over, he also invited a few others of these Norman princes living in Wales. For MacMurrough, though, Strongbow was the most important recruit, and one who could deliver a sizable force. But the others would also make their name in Ireland—men with names such as FitzGerald, Butler, and Carew.

In 1167, when Strongbow found himself disposed of title and lands by his king and in debt to a usurer in Lincoln, the arrival of MacMurrough must have seemed a godsend. And the deal seemed too good to pass on. Not only was MacMurrough promising him the hand of his daughter Aoife, but he was also guaranteeing him the kingship of Leinster in inheritance—something that was actually not in his power to offer in the tradition of Gaelic succession. For Strongbow, it must have been an easy decision. He was undoubtedly feeling pinched in Wales, and Ireland offered him wealth and power. Raising an army among the Norman bucks in Wales would not prove difficult. The men he brought were connected through family, friendship, and geography.

When Strongbow landed near Waterford on August 23, 1170, he brought with him a thousand soldiers. Waterford fell easily to the superior Norman forces, the earl of Waterford was beheaded, and Strongbow married Aoife MacMurrough, in Waterford cathedral.

Now, some might say that the importance of this day lies in the victory of the Normans against the native Irish, and I wouldn't dispute it. But just as important, I believe, was the wedding between Aoife MacMurrough and Strongbow. For in marrying the Irish princess, Strongbow began a tradition that would continue among the English invaders. Men like de Lacy and FitzGerald and Desmond and Butler and DeBurgh would marry Irish princesses, and with their marriages would become more and more Gaelicized, more and more immersed in Irish tradition and Irish interests, binding ties with the Irish nobility and setting up a situation where the Anglo-Irish would, as the complaint sounded, become more "Irish than the Irish." This was a situation that future English monarchs would have to contend with—for there would arise a new class in Ireland, the Anglo-Irish.

Following his marriage to Aoife MacMurrough, Strongbow and his army marched up to Dublin. Now, the numbers were 3,000 Anglo-Normans under Strongbow and 1,000 Irish troops under MacMurrough. They took the city— while negotiating a deal with MacMurrough's relation St. Lawrence O'Toole—and the High King Rory O'Connor and his men withdrew, having been outflanked by the Norman invaders.

Now you might think that old Henry II would be pleased with one of his own boys having such success in this foreign island, but as Shakespeare himself said about another English king, "uneasy lies the head that wears a crown." And to be honest, Henry feared that Strongbow was getting too powerful—he now claimed the Kingship of Leinster as his inherited right. If Strongbow could attain such power independent of Henry, so could the other nobles who had set out on this adventure. Henry issued an edict saying that ships could no longer carry men or supplies to Ireland and recalling all his subjects back within six months, or they would lose their lands. For Strongbow, however, something important happened. Dermot MacMurrough died suddenly. And with his death, Strongbow became king of Leinster.

It was not Henry alone who was concerned with the successes of Strongbow and the other Norman invaders. The Irish kings were also worried about these foreigners who with modern warfare so easily defeated their armies. With Strongbow and his men in Dublin, Rory O'Connor and some lesser kings gathered an army and set siege to Strongbow and his forces in Dublin. But in an embarrassing setback for the High King, Strongbow once again outwitted the native army. One night as Rory and his forces were camped in what we now know as Phoenix Park, many of them bathing in the lake, Strongbow sent a small band of 600 men out of Dublin Castle to surprise the Irish armies. The Irish were unprepared for this sort of maneuver, and Strongbow was able to rout the unsuspecting soldiers easily. Dublin was now his.

Yet, Strongbow was a shrewd and a patient man, and he knew that his successes would not sit well with Henry. He knew there was no need to antagonize his king. At his uncle's advice, Strongbow went back to England to negotiate with Henry, just before Henry was about to set out for Ireland. The result of the visit was that Strongbow gave Dublin and all its adjacent lands to Henry. Those lands that he had won through conquest or by marriage, he also gave to Henry, and Strongbow would be permitted to maintain them as Henry's tenant.

In October 1171, Henry II arrived in Waterford, as Strongbow had several years earlier. Henry, however, had many more men. He landed with 400 ships, 4,000 men at arms, thousands of archers, and 500 knights. He also brought a good number of his most trusted men, the most famous of whom was Hugh de Lacy. (It is noteworthy that this vast force may have been gathered not so much against the Irish, but against the Norman invaders whom Henry believed were amassing too much land and power. Ironically, it is Henry's man, Hugh de Lacy, who grows controversial. He too will marry the daughter of an Irish king, have his allegiance questioned, and be removed from office because of it.)

While in Ireland, Henry—perhaps remembering the edicts the pope had charged him with—assembled a synod in the town of Cashel to deliberate on ecclesiastical reform. He accepted submission from many of the Irish kings, although Rory O'Connor refused to submit. And throughout this time, he deployed his men in such a manner as to protect royal interest and curtail Strongbow's growth. As Henry tried to chop down Strongbow's power, he at the same time allowed Hugh de Lacy to flourish. De Lacy was given custody of the city of Dublin and environs and was made Lord of Meath. Wisely, he stationed Strongbow's strongest military men in Dublin, separating them from Strongbow himself.

Yet at this time, Ireland was one of the lesser problems Henry was facing, and when he left Ireland in April 1173, it was not because of a job completed but to defend his crown from a rebellious son. Strongbow—whether politically astute or enormously loyal to his king—left Ireland also to help Henry fight in Normandy. Later, in gratitude for his loyalty, Henry named Strongbow the Royal Justiciar of Ireland—a powerful position that would be contested for centuries.

In the years that followed, he, de Lacy, and others like them ran rough over the Irish kings, despite the kings' pledges of submission to Henry, and greedily satisfied their ever-growing lust for land and wealth, which seemed so plentiful in this new frontier. Several members of Strongbow's family married into other Anglo-Norman families, two of them marrying FitzGeralds, a family that would gain great power in the coming centuries. Marriage was a means for the foreign invaders to form and strengthen alliances in their new land, and within decades of Strongbow's initial arrival in Ireland in 1169, their presence in Ireland was growing both geographically and politically.

Strongbow returned once more to England in the fall of 1175, when the Irish High King Rory O'Connor met with Henry II to hammer out the Treaty of Windsor. He returned to Ireland to quell a minor revolt at the beginning of 1176, but before the year was half-over, he was dead. He was buried with great pomp at Holy Trinity Church in Dublin.

Surprisingly, since Henry had long maintained such an intractable and guarded stance against Strongbow and his familial titles in Wales, the King was nevertheless quite generous to Strongbow's widow and heirs. Indeed, it is his son-in-law who finally was able to claim the title Earl of Pembroke, some sixty years after it had been stripped from the de Clare name.

How Richard de Clare earned the name "Strongbow" is uncertain. His father had it as well, and the area from which they came was noted for men expert in archery—so much so that the official seal of Gilbert de Clare shows a man holding an unusually long arrow. Yet, despite the uncertainty of its origin, the name fit well. For as a military man, a political tactician, and survivor, Richard de Clare stretched a powerful bow over the opening scenes of the Irish-Anglo drama. He amassed huge tracts of land, wealth, and power for himself, a feat repeated by many other Anglo-Norman invaders. At the same time, however, unknown to himself, he was the seedling for a class of Anglo-Irish with whom the English kings would face off for many centuries to come.

Chapter IX

The Earls of Kildare—Gerrold Mór, Gerrold Óg, and Silken Thomas

The death of Strongbow had little effect on the Norman colonization of Ireland. He was merely the first, and by the time he died, the Norman presence was well established in Ireland. And as years turned to decades and decades to centuries, the English kings paid varying amounts of heed to their neighbor to the west. Henry II made his son John—you remember him from Magna Carta fame—the Lordship of Ireland in 1177. John, by the way, was nine years old. Good old Hugh de Lacy fell into disrepute for marrying an Irish princess and so John de Courcey was made Justiciar in his place. De Courcey lost his position when he backed Richard against John upon the death of Henry II. John returned the Justiciar to the de Lacy family. (Are you getting all this? The madness of royalty is something I'll never understand.) Anyway, John took the throne in 1199 and merged the Lordship of Ireland into the English monarchy. He visited Ireland in 1210—nearly forty years after his father had come and 184 years before the next English monarch stepped foot on the island. For a group of kings, they weren't much for "hands-on-management," I'll tell you. And I am not sure whether that was a symptom or one of the causes for the weakness of the English conquest.

So, while the kings stayed away, what was going on? Well, in the fourteenth century, there was a relatively successful and noteworthy rebellion against the English invaders. Donal O'Neill had asked Edward the Bruce to come to Ireland—invited him in fact to be High King. It was a time when Edward's brother Robert the Bruce was causing quite a stir in Scotland and the English forces were concentrated there—a perfect opportunity for Ireland. Edward's campaign was at first greatly successful; he had arrived with more than 6,000 men as well as a great number of gallowglasses (foreign soldiers), and for a while, even his brother joined him. Yet, like so many such movements before and after, it was ill-fated. Edward's troops were brutal and cut a savage path across the land—so much so that although he was fighting for the Irish cause, there was little love for him or his troops by the native Irish. Edward was defeated in 1318, and his head sent over to the king. The warring forces had ravaged the land; the land itself suffered a famine; and then the Black Death struck the population. Forty percent of the Norman settlers died. The fourteenth century was certainly not a good time for Ireland.

The settlers who survived grew more and more like the people they were lording over. Take for instance, the deBurgh family whose ancestors had come over in the first wave of Norman settlers. By the fourteenth century, they had changed their names to their Gaelic forms, they spoke Irish, they intermarried with the Irish, and they maintained the Gaelic custom of hospitality—opening their homes to minstrels, poets, and bards. Such actions by the very men who were supposedly carrying out the conquest soon became an irritant to the English monarchy, and in 1310 Edward II made a rather bold statement (a statement which many wish that others after him had taken heed of!): Edward stated that Ireland could not be conquered. So it was concluded that lines had to be drawn between what was Irish and what was English. From this conclusion came the Statutes of Kilkenny of 1366.

The Statutes of Kilkenny

Since the English government had given up on the notion of conquering the whole of Ireland with its military, it believed it was essential to keep things English separate from things Irish. Most importantly, and arrogantly in hindsight, it wanted to make sure that its English settlers stayed pure, unadulterated by Irish ways. (When the Viking invaders came in the ninth and tenth centuries, the Irish didn't become Norse, the Norse became Irish. The assumption that the Irish would become like their English invaders was not being realized, and as with the Norse, the opposite was occurring much more often!) Among many things, the law proclaimed that there be no Irish-English intermarriage. An Englishman could not claim his own children if born to an Irish wife; no English person could stand for an Irish child in baptism; they were not allowed to speak Irish, use Irish names, hire poets, sell horses to the Irish, or even wear their hair in the Irish style (known as "coolun" or "glibs"). It was ordered that they revert to English law, rather than use the Gaelic Brehon laws to settle disputes among the Irish and the settlers. It was a full raft of rules and regulations, and like foreign impositions that had preceded them, the Statutes of Kilkenny failed to do what they set out to do. (Not only was the conquest not going as well as they had hoped, but the fellows they were sending over were assimilating into this foreign world at a rapid rate.) These laws of discrimination were promulgated time and time again, with threats of savage penalties—but futile in later attempts to stop human integration.

When legislated separation did not work, the next step was geographical. In 1394, Richard II came to Ireland (remember no king had been there since John in 1210). There he seemed to designate that the Pale—an area from Dundalk to Waterford—as the English part of Ireland, separate from the land of the native Irish, which he recognized. But the Pale, too, would shrink.

To get a better idea of how Irish the English settlers had become, one can look at the FitzGerald family, who for many years held the title of earl of Kildare, and who had become the most powerful family on the island. Of the many notable FitzGeralds, perhaps the most interesting are the eighth, ninth, and tenth earls of Kildare: Gerrold Mór, Gerrold Óg, and Silken Thomas.

GERROLD MÓR

Thomas FitzGerald, the earl of Kildare, who the Irish called Gerrold Mór, had a knack for taking control of a situation when he saw the time was right and was cleverly adept at fooling a long line of English monarchs. In the old chronicles, it was emphasized that he was an Englishman and that he fought against the Irish Burkes (but they also came over, like the FitzGeralds, with the twelfth century Norman settlers and had changed their name from the Norman de Burgh to the Irish Burke). In a way, he was quite English: he had married a cousin of the king and had been granted the Knight of the Garter—the King's highest honor—for his service to the Crown. But as the King's Deputy of Ireland, Gerrold Mór surely was his own man, and he began a family dynasty that would result in proud Anglo-Irish defiance.

The rise of the FitzGeralds of Kildare was the unintended result of Edward IV's attempt to weaken the power of the Anglo-Irish in Ireland and to crush the growing independence movement among the aristocracy. Edward—whose father was Richard, the duke of York—had become king as a result of his father's battle with Henry IV for the throne of England. Much of Ireland had placed its support behind Richard and the Yorkist cause, and, in gratitude, Richard had overseen an Irish parliament in 1468 that had given Ireland legislative and judicial independence of the crown, virtual home rule for the Anglo-Irish aristocracy. Richard died in 1470, and a year later his son Edward was crowned king. At first, it was believed Edward would continue Richard's pro-Ireland policies, but Edward was not going to have any independent Irish parliament. In 1468, Edward convened his own Irish parliament in Drogheda. The earl of Desmond, a Yorkist who had supported Richard, and was now the Lord Deputy of Ireland and arguably the most powerful man in Ireland, arrived at the assembly, as did the earl of Kildare, and Edward's forces arrested both. Desmond was convicted of violating the

Statutes of Kilkenny and was beheaded. Kildare, however, got off. It was Edward's goal to break the power of the strongest Anglo-Irish family and its grip on Ireland. Instead, it sent Desmond's son to align with the Irish chieftains and attack royal lands, which horrified the Anglo-Irish aristocracy. And by pardoning and advancing Kildare, Edward brought in the FitzGeralds who in their roles as the earls of Kildare, justiciars, and lords deputy of Ireland would for the next century wield greater power than the Desmonds could ever have attained.

On the death of Desmond, the earl of Kildare became justiciar, and by 1470 was appointed Deputy. On his death in 1477, his twenty-one-year-old son replaced him in both positions. This son was Gerrold Mór, the eighth earl of Kildare. He was described as a large man who was open and plain. He was noted for a violent temper, but he was respected by Irish, Anglo-Irish, and English alike.

During his lifetime, Gerrold Mór served as the governor of Ireland for more than thirty years, would serve under five English kings, and would, in fact, crown a sixth king, Edward VI, in Christ Church, Dublin. So great was Gerrold Mór's influence that one English king said about him, "He is meet to rule all Ireland, seeing as all Ireland cannot rule him." If Edward IV thought he had a problem with Desmond growing too big for his comfort, he could not have foretold the rise of Gerrold Mór.

First of all, Gerrold Mór's power stemmed from being well connected with English and Anglo-Irish families as well as to the British royalty. Second, he had immense wealth and a large loyal army. And lastly, he was a willful man of defiance. For example, in 1478, Edward, concerned that Gerrold had grown too powerful and too popular, sent Lord Grey to replace him as Lord Deputy. Gerrold simply refused to hand over the office and the king's emissary was sent packing. This Anglo-Irish earl had successfully—and boldly—defied the king of England.

Because of great turmoil in the English monarchy (Edward IV died and was followed by his son who became Edward V, who was killed by his uncle who crowned himself Richard III who was killed in battle by the man who would be crowned Henry VII), the respective monarchs had little inclination to meddle in Ireland so Gerrold 's power grew unchecked for some time.

During this time Gerrold behaved as if he were sovereign of Ireland—as if the declaration of Irish legislative and judicial independence of Richard's parliament was in full effect and a prelude to even greater freedoms. In 1488, he treated another royal emissary with contempt, so that Henry decided now it was time to step in and put down this upstart. In 1494, Henry VII sent an army to Ireland, arrested Gerrold Mór and replaced him with Sir Edward Poynings as deputy. But, as before in Irish-Anglo affairs, Henry was forced to turn his attention away from Ireland to deal with a more imminent threat from Scotland. He recalled Poynings from Dublin and reinstated Gerrold as Lord Deputy.

But Poynings did not leave Ireland unscathed. While in office he had rescinded the parliamentary declaration of Ireland's legislative and judicial independence, thus crushing the independence momentum. Poynings' Laws wrought destruction on Irish aspirations toward freedom for the next three centuries.

Gerrold re-establishing his rule did not come without condition; he had to leave his son, Gerrold Óg, at the English court as a pledge of his loyalty to the king and as a guarantee of his obedience. It would not be the last time this son would be held prisoner in London.

Also at this time, Gerrold Mór, once more reinstated, married the king's cousin Elizabeth St. John, further cementing his relations with the monarchy, as well as enhancing his image among the Anglo-Irish. At the same time, he was forging strong ties with the Gaelic chieftains, primarily through marriages, and except that he was very much an Anglo-Irish earl, one might very well assume that he was a Gaelic chieftain himself in the manner of his actions, dealings, and alliances.

Indeed, by the end of the fifteenth century probably no man had gathered greater sway over more of Ireland since the Norman conquest as Gerrold Mór. Gerrold Mór could be considered the uncrowned king of Ireland.

It was through these alliances and marriages that brought about Gerrold Mór's greatest military victory. Ulrick de Burgh (Ulrick Burke) was a powerful man who controlled much of Connaught—a small but irritating rival to Gerrold Mór. Now, as one who was always trying to forge relationships that would enhance his power, your man Gerrold had given his daughter to de Burgh (or Burke) in marriage. The story goes that Gerrold Mór received reports that Burke was abusing his daughter, and so he amasssed an army to confront this wayward son-in-law. (There are some who say it was Burke's seizing Galway city and its environs that sent Gerrold Mór off—which seems to be a lot more likely!)

Anyway, on April 19, 1504, Gerrold Mór's men met with Ulrich Burke's. The Battle of Knockdoe was a large battle with more than ten thousand men—and it is notable for being the first battle in Ireland in which guns are mentioned being used. And while historians often paint the battle as a clash between the Irish Burkes and the English FitzGeralds, Gerrold Mór's forces had as much a claim as the Burkes to their Irishness. They were both old Norman families from the first Norman invasions who had been greatly assimilated into the Irish culture. Indeed, so entrenched were the Irish ways, that one of the barons in Gerrold Mór's army stated that he would be the first to throw a spear at the Burkes. Deliberately or not, the baron was flouting a parliamentary law that required English troops to use only English weapons and not the spears and darts of Irish warriors. Apparently, the baron was thinking with his Irish heart at the time. The battle was fierce, and great numbers of men died before Gerrold Mór claimed victory. For his valor, Henry VII granted to Gerrold the Order of the Garter. (Henry saw Gerrold's victory as a glorious moment for the English monarchy in Ireland;

Gerrold saw it for what it was—a consolidating of his power and a blow to his greatest rival.)

If he was not the first, Gerrold Mór was then very close to being the first Irish leader who was killed by a gunshot. Involved in a minor battle with the O'Mores, Gerrold Mór was testing a new gun and using it upon his enemies. The O'Mores had guns as well, and one returned fire, hitting Gerrold Mór. He died shortly after of his wounds.

Gerrold Mór had ruled Kildare and the English Pale for nearly forty years, and for the most part had remained a popular ruler during the entirety. He had kept a range of English kings from meddling too drastically in the affairs of Ireland and had stretched his influence over much of the island. During his rule, the European Renaissance arrived in Ireland, and Gerrold himself was instrumental in establishing great schools, universities, and libraries. There was a Gaelic Renaissance as well, and under Gerrold Mór both the Irish and Anglo-Irish enjoyed its artistic and intellectual bounty. The cause of the Irish and the Anglo-Irish seemed never so united. His son Gerrold Óg, however, would not be so lucky, for the new English King—Henry VIII—would have little patience with the FitzGeralds and their hold on Irish rule. Gerrold Mór had built a dynasty large enough to worry a king . . . and soon the king would react.

Gerrold Óg

As the son of any great man can tell you, it's never easy taking over the da's business. And for Gerrold Óg, it was no exception. Now, this was not entirely due to any lack on the younger FitzGerald's part, but more so on the strength—and the foibles—of the monarch who now sat on England's throne—none other than your man Henry VIII. For like his father, Gerrold Óg was shrewdly political and had

great success in increasing the landholdings of the FitzGerald clan. He was popular
and skillful in his governance. And he also was apt in keeping both his Gaelic and
Anglo-Irish alliances strong, although he did maintain a feud with the earl of
Ormond, Piers Butler, for a long time, which probably proved fatal to the Kildare
dynasty in the long run. During his career, he was Lord Deputy of Ireland three
separate times—echoing his father's own knack for coming back to power when it
seemed all was stacked against him. Yet, history would seem to play out against
the new earl of Kildare, and ultimately Henry VIII and his advisors were too
clever and too Machiavellian for Gerrold Óg to maintain his power for long.

It is one of history's ironies that in the very year of Gerrold Mór's death—and
of Gerrold Óg's ascension to the position of Lord Deputy—that Thomas (later
Cardinal) Wolsey came to power and quickly gained Henry's ear and confidence.
Wolsey did not like Gerrold Óg and continually preached to Henry against him.
Wolsey believed—and continually tried to convince Henry—that the young
FitzGerald was a self-appointed king and a threat to Henry's sovereignty. Wolsey's
name for the young FitzGerald was the "king of Kildare"—a term certain to rattle
in Henry VIII's mind. To make matters worse, the earldom of Ormondy was
bequeathed to Sir Thomas Boleyn—whose daughter would soon figure greatly in
the history of Henry VIII's reign—and taken over by Piers Butler who was decid-
edly anti-Gerrold Óg. (Henry would later give Ormond back to Thomas Boleyn
and make Butler settle for the earl of Ossory!) The upshot of all this was that in
addition to Wolsey's frequent bad-mouthing of Gerrold Óg, there was a sizeable
pro-Tudor Anglo-Irish contingent that was sending complaining reports of life in
Ireland under Gerrold's governance back to England.

Finally, Henry VIII decided to act. In 1520, Henry sent an army of 1,100 soldiers under the command of Thomas Howard, Earl of Surrey, who had proven
himself defending the crown against Scotland. (If one is wondering about the

miniscule size of this invading army while the FitzGeralds maintained a sizeable

force and the Irish chieftains had upwards of 22,000, Henry VIII's Irish policy was

always cut with an eye on the purse. He did not like spending money on Ireland,

and, in fact, believed that Ireland should be providing revenue to the Crown.

Thomas himself complained about the size of the force and requested six times as

many men.) The reports Henry had been receiving complained more about the

Gaelicized English than about the Irish, so Henry replaced Gerrold Óg and set up

Thomas as the new Lord Deputy. Henry hoped that Thomas would be "more

impressive" to both the Irish and the Anglo-Irish as an English governor represent-

ing the English crown, rather than Gerrold Óg, who walked that fine line in

Ireland between Irish and Anglo-Irish, and who, as Cardinal Wolsey like to claim,

was as good as a self-appointed king. In short, he wanted an English alternative to

Gerrold Óg—a desire that would affect his actions for the next fourteen years.

Henry also ordered Surrey to reform Ireland "at once," a tall order for even the

most capable statesman. As for Gerrold Óg, he was arrested, brought to London,

and placed in the Tower. It would not be his last time in those infamous lodgings.

Surrey was not the impressive figure Henry had wished for. As I have often

mentioned, in the case of the Tudors' interference in Ireland, economy played

an active role in Henry's decisions. Surrey wanted additional soldiers and

increased funds, but Henry had already spent more on Ireland than planned.

Again, for Henry, Ireland was to be a source of income, not a drain on the

treasury. And with both plague and famine wracking the country, there was

even less revenue to be counted upon. At this time, Henry was deploying forces

on the Scottish borders and in the Welsh marches and had also allied England

with the Holy Roman Emperor, Charles V, in a war against France. Monies and

men were thus earmarked for those arenas rather than for Ireland. Frustrated

and stymied, Surrey, before too long, asked to be recalled. Henry, annoyed and concerned by his constant request for funds, assented.

So in 1522, Gerrold Óg was reinstated as Lord Deputy, but his power was now somewhat shakened by the Anglo-Irish forces gathering against him. By now Anne Boleyn had become Henry's favorite, and her father had aligned with the Butler clan to present a formidable foe to Gerrold Óg. However, it was Anne Boleyn's alignment with Henry—and Henry's argument with Rome about that relationship—that would soon bring Gerrold Óg once more to London's grim Tower.

However, at the moment, Gerrold Óg's return in 1522 was evidence of the FitzGeralds' hold on Irish power. In many ways, it had been the long reach of the Kildare dynasty that had frustrated Surrey's rule even from the confines of the Tower. For years, the Geraldine dynasty had always acted as a buffer between the Gaelic Irish and the English, and without Gerrold Óg's governing hand, Surrey had found it very difficult in Ireland indeed. Whether Gerrold Óg was in the Tower or not, the FitzGeralds were still *the* power to reckon with in Ireland and Wolsey was probably right in warning Henry about Gerrold Óg and his clan. This is why it was imperative for Henry to find an alternative to Gerrold Óg.

In 1528, Henry, upon hearing reports of lawlessness and disorder, again replaced Gerrold Óg. This time he appointed Piers Butler, who had long been anti-Geraldine and who continually had complained to the Tudor court of Gerrold's independence in his place. But if Surrey had been unable to succeed in 1520, Butler was even less capable, and Henry had to try a new approach with governing Ireland. This time, he named his only son (illegitimate, but his son) as Lord Lieutenant of Ireland. That this son was merely ten years old indicates the confusion and uncertainty of the Tudor court in dealing with a Geraldine-free Ireland. To help the boy, Henry appointed Sir William Skeffington as "Master of the King's Ordnance." With Skeffington in charge, Gerrold Óg was permitted to return to Ireland.

Like Surrey before him, Skeffington was undermined by Henry's unwillingness to spend money. While Henry was liberal with granting offices—Skeffington was named Lord Deputy in 1530—he continued to be tight with funds. Skeffington was issued few soldiers and less money. Rather than conquering and safeguarding Ireland for the English crown, he was forced to bargain with Kildare, Ormond, and Ossory and use his military in a defensive position in Dublin.

Now, these were eventful times for the Tudor monarchy, and concerns with Ireland often took second place to more urgent matters. Yet, as everyone knows, border wars and international politics were not the only distraction that Henry VIII had in the 1520s. His relationship with Rome was straining under his insistence on divorcing Catherine of Aragon and marrying Anne Boleyn. In Henry's court alone, the shake-up was cataclysmic. Wolsey fell from power in 1529, in one of the most dramatic smash-ups of all time. Sadly, for Gerrold Óg in particular and the Irish in general, the man who replaced him, Thomas Cromwell, believed in the unquestioned supremacy of the English crown and in the necessity of squashing any force that acted independently of the Crown. This attitude would change Henry's attitude about and actions in Ireland.

However, for the time being and with Wolsey—the architect of the Skeffington experiment in Ireland—gone, Gerrold Óg began planning his return to power. He began forming alliances in the Dublin and London courts, forming coalitions of men who would counter the anti-Geraldine forces that had grown strong during the 1520s. Men like his brother-in-law, Lord Leonard Grey and even Surrey—who had always acted as a counterpoise to Wolsey—became integral to Gerrold Óg's plans and argued convincingly for his reinstatement.

Henry's divorce was beginning to cause an unwanted commotion. He was receiving reports that Ireland under Skeffington was spinning out of his control, and Henry saw the necessity of having, in these potentially explosive times, a proven power instated there as Lord Deputy. In 1532, Skeffington was removed, and once again, Gerrold Óg was made Lord Deputy. It was a victory for Gerrold Óg and the third time he held the position. It seemed the Tudor court was aware that, despite its wishes, ruling Ireland was impossible with the Geraldines' involvement.

When Henry broke away from the Roman Church in 1533, the repercussions were far-reaching. In Ireland, the English clergy had for the most part given up preaching in the Irish hinterland long ago—preferring to remain in the Pale or better yet to return to England—and sought to preach to the Anglo-Irish alone, leaving the Gaelic Irish alone. The Irish church therefore was being served by mendicant friars: Dominicans, Franciscans, Augustinians. The great cathedrals had fallen into disuse and clergy were scarce. Now, when Henry VIII decided to separate from Rome and head his own church, his English clergy in Ireland for the most part followed their king. But the mendicant orders that had been tending to the Irish people had no loyalty to the English crown, and they criticized Henry VIII harshly and publicly.

Henry was furious. (Despite his size, your man Henry was very sensitive about his critics. It was one thing to be criticized by the countries on the continent to which England yet felt a bit inferior, but to withstand criticisms coming out of Ireland—which in a true perversion of logic had been given to England by the pope, whose power he now denounced—was too much for Henry to bear.) More than ever, he needed security in Ireland, and to Henry, Gerrold Óg was not the man to provide peace of mind for the English Crown.

So once again, in 1533, Henry VIII determined to rein in his Irish Deputy, Gerrold Óg, who to Henry represented all that was problematic and disloyal with Ireland. So Henry had been advised by Thomas Cromwell, who had now become the chief minister for Irish affairs. Cromwell had also allied himself with Butler, the earl of Ossory.

In August 1533, a year after Gerrold Óg had been reinstated for the third time, he was recalled once more to London. Henry felt it necessary to stop the FitzGeralds once and for all. This time, however, Gerrold Óg simply refused to go to London. Pleading that he was sick—he had been severely wounded by a gun-shot when aiding a son-in-law in a family dispute—and realizing his resilience in the Tudor world of Irish politics might be beginning to ebb—Gerrold Óg bought as much time as he could in order to arrange the future of the Geraldine clan. First, he removed all ordnances from Dublin castle to his own strongholds, thus in practicality disarming the pro-English enemies that had paved the way for his arrest while fortifying his own keeps. In the past, the FitzGeralds had always treat-ed disruptions into their governance with a bilateral response: first, they launched a consolidated public-relations campaign within the English court and second, they allowed or encouraged violent disruptions within the various Irish lordships. By amassing his armaments, Gerrold Óg this time was apparently prepared to lean more on the latter of the two. Nevertheless, he did send his wife, Lady Elizabeth Gray, to London in the hope that her familial connections in court might help affect a change in the recall order. Her mission, however, failed.

Gerrold Óg continued to ignore all commands and communications from London. Finally, in February 1534, he was forced to comply, but only after first demanding some concessions, the most important of which was the right to name his successor who would act in his place during his absence. Gerrold Óg then named his son, Thomas, Lord Offaly as Lord Justice. He also granted him the lordship of Rathwere in Meath. In a chess game of politics, Gerrold Óg was attempting to deploy his pieces in the most advantageous arrangement for him and his family. More importantly, he surrounded his son with his most trusted and experienced advisors.

One can imagine that the young, handsome boy, who had been raised in England and had never shown any particular interest in politics or governing in the first twenty-one years of his life, inspired no fear in Cromwell or Henry. With Gerrold Óg in the Tower of London, and this mere boy—whom the Irish would dub Silken Thomas—in Dublin, the Tudor court was confident that the rule of the FitzGeralds would finally be quashed. Yet Gerrold Óg's life was not yet over—even from prison, he would in his final year still greatly affect events in Ireland—and Silken Thomas would defy Henry like no one had ever before.

Silken Thomas

The tenth earl of Kildare was thrust into power with the arrest of his father, Gerrold Óg. Now, the two previous earls had known how to play the political game among the English monarchy, the Anglo-Irish, and the Irish themselves. They knew the conspiracies, the alliances, the men who could be trusted and those who could not. They also were patient with the monarchs they served, allowing these English kings, it seemed, enough leeway so that it appeared the Crown was in charge in Ireland, when in reality the FitzGeralds had run the country—or at the very least the Pale—for the past sixty years. Young Thomas did not have this background. And he was facing a king who was growing more and more frustrated at the whole Irish situation, wanting to play a more active role in governing Ireland, and no longer content to depend on Anglo-Irish deputies like the FitzGeralds to represent the crown for him.

When Gerrold Óg arrived in London, he was not immediately put in the Tower. One report suggested that Henry was playing coy in order to lure Lord Thomas to London as well. Another possibility was that seeing that Gerrold Óg was truly sick, the English court decided to let nature play out rather than exacerbating the Geraldines more than necessary. Nevertheless, in May 1534, Gerrold Óg was questioned by council, and the position of Lord Deputy was officially stripped from him. His old nemesis, Sir William Skeffington, was appointed in his place.

Now historians often tend to dismiss Silken Thomas as a hotheaded, rash young man, unschooled in the niceties of Tudor politics. But that was not necessarily the case. He had been raised and educated in Henry's court—a common occurrence among the Irish nobility, although in Thomas's case it also served to keep the boy as hostage in order to guarantee his father's good behavior. His mother, the daughter of Sir John Zouche of Derbyshire, had learned to read, write, and speak in Irish as soon as she had come to Ireland, and two of his sisters were married to Gaelic chieftains. Perhaps this Gaelicization rubbed off on the young FitzGerald.

Also, from the moment Henry had sent to Ireland for Gerrold Óg—which summons he refused to honor for as long as he could—Thomas had been under intense tutelage from his father and his advisors. He was wise enough to understand that Skeffington's appointment was a direct rebuff of his own title of lord justice and that the appointment of so many anti-Geraldines in the Dublin council did not bode well for him or his family.

In May of 1534, the dying Gerrold Óg sent all his servants and retainers back to Ireland and into Thomas's service. He also warned his son not to trust any of the King's council in London, for he would be brought to London and executed. Gerrold Óg's information seemed well founded, for in early June, letters from Henry to Thomas arrived in Dublin ordering him to appear in London before the court.

Thomas had two choices. He could acquiesce to Henry's orders and travel to London, where at best he would be removed from office and at worst killed, or he could revolt. He chose the latter.

The story of Thomas's revolt has been enlarged, revised, misunderstood, down-played, belittled, forgotten, and mocked throughout the years. But if nothing else, it was truly a moment of great drama, and, in truth, a turning point in relations between Ireland and the Tudor monarchy.

On June 11, 1534, Lord Thomas rode into Dublin to appear before the King's council. The Tudor faction in Dublin had been deliberately feeding him with false reports of his father's execution, and rumors abounded that he and his uncles were all to be arrested and executed as well. Thomas had thus decided that now was the time to act. In his mind, he was now the tenth earl of Kildare, and he was fighting for his family's honor. He was also fighting for something larger—an Irish stance against Henry.

Thomas rode into Dublin with 1,000 horseman and footmen. As an act of Irish identity, Thomas and his men wore leather coats embroidered lavishly with silk ribbons. (The Irish warriors were known to embellish their armor and cloth-ing gaily, and, in fact, Thomas Cromwell was warned not to let his own soldiers do the same. Lord Thomas's men flaunted their silk.) The Irish bard, de Nolan, describing the actions of the day, gave the name "Silken Thomas" to the young Thomas FitzGerald, and the name has remained for posterity.

Flanked by 140 horsemen, Thomas then rode to St. Mary's Abbey where the King's council was in session. Now, if there was anyone surprised at his arrival, it would be those who figured the young FitzGerald would stay away out of fear of extradition. No one could have anticipated Thomas's actions. In an extraordinary grand and public gesture, Thomas denounced royal policy in Ireland, surrendered his sword of state, resigned from all offices appointed by the King, and renounced his allegiance to King Henry VIII. It was indeed a bold action, but not a thought-less one as historians have been wont to portray it. Thomas had been conferring with family members for the weeks preceding his renunciation of Henry, gathering support in Ulster, Munster, and Leinster as well as pursuing the possibility of Spanish aid.

Thomas's aim was to put pressure on Henry VIII, by defiance and by the threat of a united Ireland against Henry's limited English Pale. He desired that Henry acknowledge the importance of the Geraldine dynasty to the Irish government, and perhaps most unusual of all, he demanded a pardon for these very actions. Finally, he demanded the title of Lord Deputy for life.

One could only imagine the utter shock of the council members present at Thomas's protest. They probably also were a bit fearful, for a man who would so rashly renounce his loyalty to the king was a man to be wary of. The Tudor court was shocked into inaction, giving Thomas time to formulate his next move.

First, Thomas ordered that all who were English by birth leave Ireland. This is notable in that it presented a serious distinction between the English and the Anglo-Irish. And it played well with the Irish chieftains on whose support Thomas was depending. The English on the king's council were understandably nervous about this turn of events, and began their exodus as well. (Thomas and his followers killed the fleeing Archbishop of Dublin, a deed for which Thomas received "papal absolution" and for which Henry VIII wanted Thomas excommunicated! The muse of history sometimes has a wicked sense of irony.)

In fact, this religious aspect was an important element of Thomas's revolt. If he was to gain and maintain support from both the Irish chieftains and from the French and Spanish who were showing great interest in this disruption in Henry's dominion, he had to expand the reasons for his revolt beyond personal revenge for his father's "falsely-reported" execution and later to effect Gerrold Óg's release. Religion provided the perfect cause.

By June 1534, Henry had already begun actively to suppress any criticism to his excommunication and break from the Roman church. He closed all the Observant Franciscan houses—the Franciscans being the most vociferous in their condemnation of Henry—and he ordered Skeffington to take whatever measures necessary to bring the English reformation into Ireland. Thus, coupling his personal revolt with religious outrage, Thomas gave his actions a certain legitimacy. Henry's excommunication had certainly focused European governments on the possibility of a revolt, whether from within England or from within Ireland. And while much was deliberated—and much more promised to Thomas—assistance from Spain, Rome, or France never materialized.

Henry's court was in turmoil, caught unawares, and unsure how to react to Thomas's revolt. There were arguments and finger pointing, and Henry, as usual, was concerned about spending too much money on this new Irish situation. In anger, Henry formally arrested Gerrold Óg in mid-June and placed the sick man in the Tower; this did little except induce Thomas to ratchet the revolt to a new level. As he had done just prior to Thomas's denuciation, Henry once again tried to lure the young FitzGerald to London, promising him pardon and the release of his father. Henry also considered sending Gerrold Óg himself as an emissary to his son, but Gerrold Óg was too sick, and besides, was in full support of his son's actions. Not surprisingly, Thomas rejected all of Henry's proposals—for the moment, he was acting from a position of strength.

It was not until October 1534, four months after Thomas's dramatic renunciation before the council, that England finally sent troops over to address the crisis. Two thousand men set sail—the largest force deployed in Ireland in over a century—although there still seemed to be no strategy except putting down the Geraldines. However, in the meantime Gerrold Óg had died in the Tower, and Henry perhaps saw that by stopping Thomas, he would be ridding himself of the

Kildare dynasty once and for all. Throughout the summer of 1534, Henry and his councilors had vacillated and delayed their reaction to Thomas's revolt. However, now that they were committed to action, they were determined to raze the Geraldine dynasty.

During the summer, Thomas took control of the Pale, but failed in his attempt to take Dublin Castle, which he besieged throughout August and September. One reason for his failure—and there were many—was the FitzGeralds' long-standing antagonism with the Butlers, particularly Sir Piers Butler, earl of Ossory, who had long been the fiercest anti-Geraldine among the Anglo-Irish. In August, Thomas had ravaged Butler's earldom to the west, but this was a drain on his forces to the east. The FitzGerald base was situated between Dublin and the Butlers' lands, and so while besieging Dublin, Thomas also had to use men and armaments to protect his rear from the Butlers. The cost of men and arms of this two-front battle made taking Dublin Castle all the more essential, as it was the stronghold of the crown's ordnance. Thomas's failure to take it deprived his cause of a needed supply of armaments.

Also at this time, Thomas was actively negotiating with the Spanish. (Charles V was more than just politically involved with the situation. His aunt was Catherine of Aragon, whom Henry divorced in order to marry Anne Boleyn. As early as February, well before Thomas's revolt, Spain had decided to "embarrass" Henry VIII. Assisting the Irish rebels seemed an excellent opportunity to do so.) In June, a Spanish ship had landed in Dingle and provided Thomas with gunpowder and ammunition. In September, a Spanish agent landed in Galway, and two friars escorted him to Thomas, who was promised Spanish assistance in arms and in soldiers. In fact, up until the very end, Thomas believed that Charles was sending 100,000 men to assist his cause. So widespread were Thomas's appeals for foreign aid, and so receptive were the governments he addressed, that England made a formal protest to the Spanish ambassador. Thomas's revolt was undermining Henry's monarchy.

From this optimistic beginning, Thomas's campaign faltered quickly. In October, Skeffington arrived in Dublin with the English forces. He publicly proclaimed Thomas a traitor to the Crown, yet did little militarily at first. Thomas's forces continued to ravage small outposts, hoping merely to pester the Crown until the spring and the arrival of the promised Spanish troops, but there were few decisive engagements. In November, two of Thomas's uncles turned to Skeffington, and reports were circulated that Thomas was losing the support of the Irish chieftains. On December 1, 1534, the Kildare castle at Trim was taken by the English. (Thomas regained it within two weeks.) All in all, things were starting to worsen. During a truce that took place over Christmas week, Thomas sent his chaplain to Spain to ask for immediate assistance, but it was not forthcoming.

The early months of 1535 saw many of Thomas's best men captured, as well as his foster mother, who the English believed was a prime instigator of Thomas's rebellion and who—rightly so—was considered a valuable hostage. But the worse news came in March. Maynooth Castle, which Thomas had fortified with most of his ordnance, had fallen to Skeffington.

How such a valuable garrison was taken so easily has interested historians almost from the moment it fell, with the most prevalent interpretation that Maynooth fell through the workings of a traitor. The destruction of Maynooth was also notable for introducing the "Maynooth Pardon" into military parlance: Skeffington executed everyone in the garrison!

Thomas's fortunes continued to sink so that by the end of the summer in 1535, he was no more than an exile, his earldom destroyed and his existence limited to the bogs and woods of the Irish hinterland. He sent his wife back to England, where she was immediately arrested. (The Spanish ambassador reported that Thomas had stated he would have nothing to do with the English, and thus sent the wife packing, although it is more likely that Thomas, realizing that events were growing dire, wanted to protect his wife from what was sure to come.)

On August 24, 1535, Thomas with Brian O'Connor, the one Irish chieftain who had remained with him throughout the summer, surrendered. Although his hopes for pardon and the restoration of his lands were a bit unrealistic, he was given guarantees that his life would be spared. Lord Leonard Grey—his uncle-in-law who had assisted the Geraldine cause in the past—transported Thomas to London. Henry was pleased at his capture but infuriated at the promises made to Thomas. No matter what was guaranteed, Henry VIII wanted Thomas dead, but wisely put off executing him until he had gathered the rest of the Geraldines in Ireland. He rightly believed that executing the tenth earl of Kildare after having made promises to the contrary would stir the remaining FitzGeralds to rise again. In October, Thomas was placed in the Tower, and before long was joined by five of his uncles. Even James and Richard FitzGerald who had fought with Skeffington against Thomas were brought to London. Henry was going to eradicate this FitzGerald problem once and for all.

On February 3, 1537, Silken Thomas and his five uncles were taken from the Tower and carted through London to Tyburn, where they were hanged. In Tudor times, however, hanging was only the beginning of an execution. When the FitzGeralds were half-dead, they were cut down and their bodies violated. Their genitals were cut off, their stomachs torn open, and their bowels burned. Then they were beheaded and their bodies cut into four pieces. The head and the four quarters were then displayed throughout the city. However, because Thomas, as the Earl of Kildare, was a member of the nobility, he was merely hanged and beheaded. No such pardon for the uncles.

While the rebellion of Silken Thomas ended in failure, it did have wide-rang-

ing effects in Ireland and throughout Europe. It aligned for the first time Irish
nationalism with Roman Catholicism, and in doing so, it also fostered European
interest in the course of Irish governance. Indeed, in Europe, much to Henry's
chagrin, Ireland was again considered a distinct country. The quashing of
Thomas's rebellion brought an end to the independence and ascendancy of the
Anglo-Irish in Dublin—and for the most part ended the power and stature of the
house of Kildare. The army Skeffington had quartered in Dublin would stay there;
Dublin city would be occupied by an English army for the next 400 years.

An Irish eulogist at the time called Silken Thomas "the best man of the English
in Ireland," and in an odd way, his death and the ensuing confiscation of his lands
galvanized the Gaelic chieftains, who now saw the extent of the Tudor monarchy's
power and desire. The formation among these chieftains of the "Geraldine
League" soon after Thomas's execution was more than mere sympathy with
Thomas. It was the understanding that now their own lands were in jeopardy
under Henry's new Irish policy.

A new era had begun.

THE TUDOR CONQUEST
AND THE FALL OF THE GAELIC WORLD

Henry VIII's defeat of the FitzGeralds signaled a new attitude toward Ireland within the English court. For the most part, in the years before Silken Thomas's revolt, the English monarchy looked at Ireland as something irksome which would not go away, but which could be made palatable with a minimum of governance and expense within its own limited Pale. However, now, Henry VIII decided on a new tactic: he wanted to subdue the entire island. There were two monumental pieces of legislation passed by the Irish Parliament that allowed him to begin this process of bringing Ireland into line. The first was in 1536, when the Irish Parliament confirmed Henry as Supreme Head of the Church of Ireland—analogous to his title in the Church of England. This confirmation came about—with not a little bullying help from the Butlers who had been so supportive during Henry's battles with the FitzGeralds—by Henry's seizure of Irish monastic lands, which he then granted to supportive Anglo-Irish families. The second was in 1540. Henry's deputy, Sir Anthony St. Leger, believed that the problem with governing Ireland stemmed from its status within the monarchy. To correct this, St. Leger claimed that Ireland was no longer a lordship, but a kingdom, and Henry VIII was the King of Ireland.

But simply naming Henry King of Ireland would not be effective, particularly beyond the Pale where Gaelic chieftains tolerated Henry's rule within the Pale, but actually had little truck with his authority. Henry began to bring the chieftains into English governance by a process called "Surrender and Re-Grant." By this, the Gaelic chieftains would surrender their land to Henry, and then he would re-grant it back to them, making them English nobles in the bargain through the beneficence of the King. In this way, the chieftains would be incorporated into the

English system. (The infamous Statutes of Kilkenny seemed to be abandoned, for now Irish and English were not to be separated but united under Henry's rule.) In a very short while, Henry used the policy of "Surrender and Re-Grant" to bring in over forty Irish chieftains who were given earldoms—albeit the lands they were "granted" were theirs in the first place. This tactic failed—especially when one considers that three of the most powerful earldoms that Henry created—the O'Neills, the O'Donnells, and the O'Briens—helped stir the greatest rebellion against the English Crown in a very long while.

Although Silken Thomas had tried to incorporate it into his rebellion, the subject of religion was at the moment pretty much a non-issue. The Irish had been abandoned by the Anglo-Irish clergy long ago, and were served primarily by mendicant friars. The changes of Henry's Reformation in Ireland, if any, were minimal, and religion beyond the Pale pretty much remained what it was. At least, that is, until the ascent of Edward VI. The policies of Henry's successor, who ruled for only six years, had the result of driving the Irish clergy back into Catholicism. He had printed in Dublin the English *Book of Common Prayer*—the first book ever printed in Ireland, mind you—and tried to insist on English in religious services. The Irish clergy simply refused. Even the Anglo-Irish vehemently opposed the edict. In short, Edward's insistence on the *Book of Common Prayer* fomented an opposition that undermined his own authority as Head of the Church—and tangentially as King of Ireland. In theory, the English prayer book would have been fine in the Pale—although much of the Anglo-Irish opposed it and the Archbishop of Armagh even left the country because of it—but in the hinterlands, English was still a foreign language, often among the Anglo-Irish themselves, and there was no contingency for translating any part of the new rituals into Irish. (In the 1590s when Sir Henry Sidney traveled through Ulster, he was taken aback by the number of Anglo-Irish nobles who no longer could speak English!)

As was said, Edward VI's influence was short-lived for he reigned only six years and died when he was sixteen years old. (One can only imagine the maneuvering and wrangling for power among the ministers of that adolescent boy!) He was succeeded by Mary, who was the daughter of Catherine of Aragon and Henry VIII and who was also a Catholic. Although Mary reversed the religious colonization of Ireland—and in truth probably solidified Catholic resistance to the English Reformation—for the most part, she continued her father's political policy of confiscating and re-granting Irish lands.

In all, while Henry VIII, Edward IV, and Mary Tudor each had been dubbed the official kings and queen of Ireland, nothing changed too greatly in Ireland. The Pale still had to be secured by an army, the Irish chieftains were still warring amongst themselves, and the success of Crown authority depended on a succession of deputies of varying degrees of skill. That was until the ascension of Elizabeth I.

With Elizabeth I's ascent to the throne came an increased desire to bring the Reformation to Ireland, and thus created an increased divisiveness. Division and dissent grew as Elizabeth set about to establish firmly the Reformation in Ireland, and this dissension was encouraged by the many European powers that were antagonistic to the new queen. Because of this overt dissent—and the overt support of the European countries—Elizabeth saw Ireland as a real source of insecurity, as a source of disaffection and thus the logical springboard for any military campaign against her. Her fears were well founded, for within ten years of her reign, England would face the strongest—and most viable—challenge from Ireland that had risen in more than 250 years: Hugh O'Neill.

Chapter X

Hugh O'Neill, the Battle of Kinsale, and the Escape of the Earls

---

"In Hugh O'Neill, the Irish cause was to find at last a man of real greatness,
a statesman as well as a soldier, a born leader who combined thought with action and
caution with energy . . . a man of intellect who understood his times."
—Edmund Curtis, *A History of Ireland*

Hugh O'Neill is one of those figures in Irish history whose life has been clouded in mystery and romanticism, and not a little wistful second-guessing. At the very least, he was that rare combination of skillful soldier and masterful politician. To many others, he was much more than that; he was the embodiment of Ireland's greatest—and last—hope against Elizabethan colonization and plantation. His success against the English Crown earned him legendary status on the European continent, who saw in him an attractive amalgamation of the Renaissance man and the Irish chieftain.

Although he was descended from the High Kings of Ireland, Hugh O'Neill's real story began with his grandfather, Conn O'Neill. Conn had submitted to Henry VIII during the "Surrender and Re-Grant" policy and had abandoned his title of The O'Neill to become the first Earl of Tyrone. Now while for Conn this may have seemed an advantageous decision, giving him feudal jurisdiction over lands that once were his through the tenuous Gaelic system of chieftainship, for those in the O'Neill territories it was not, and internecine wars flared up. Exacerbating the situation was Conn's decision to make his adopted son, Matthew, baron of Dungannon and heir to his title. His eldest, legitimate son, Shane, naturally contested the designation, and civil war broke out.

When Conn died, the Crown recognized Matthew as his heir, with one of Matthew's sons, Brian, the Baron of Dungannon. Shane continued his battle for legitimacy and in 1595 killed Matthew. Within a year, Shane claimed the title of The O'Neill (which Conn had disavowed years ago) and began expanding his territory. From that point on he became an intractable opponent of English law in Ulster, and in doing so, made himself a focal point of England's malignant interest. Three times (in 1560, 1561, and 1563) the Earl of Sussex mounted campaigns against him and three times Shane outfoxed him. Of more concern to Elizabeth, however, was that Shane was also in conversation with rebels in Scotland as well as with Catholic Spain and Catholic France. To allay Elizabethan fears—and no doubt to buy himself some time—Shane submitted to Elizabeth in 1562, and in gratitude for this submission, in 1563, she granted to him the title of The O'Neill. Shane also won a promise that the Tudor court would investigate the legitimacy of Matthew's claim to the earldom of Tyrone.

Yet, the titular concessions did not quell Shane's subversions in Ulster, and finally, in 1567, the Crown—assisted by the O'Donnells from Donegal—defeated him, and he had to flee to Scotland. Taking refuge with the MacDonnells, Shane was killed and his head sent back to his enemy, the Earl of Sussex in Dublin. Some say the MacDonnells killed Shane while he stupidly boasted of his past escapades against them; others say the MacDonnells had received a better offer from Sussex than what they could expect from Shane. Nevertheless, for the Elizabethan court, the death of Shane O'Neill was a welcome solution to an irritating problem. With his death, the O'Neill title was buried.

In 1567, the year of Shane's defeat, Hugh O'Neill was said to be in London where he had been educated and raised at court. Actually, here is where the story diverges a bit. One story states that Hugh was sent to London the year his brother

Brian had died while another states that he was sent there when his father Matthew was killed in 1559. Hugh himself said that he received "an education among the English," but this could have merely been an education received within the Pale. We do know that upon the death of Matthew, Hugh had been made a ward of the Crown which tended to his upbringing. What matters now, however, was that Hugh O'Neill was the second earl of Tyrone, and as far as the Elizabethan court was concerned this proper young gentleman was an able and loyal servant of the queen. He was sent back to Ulster in 1568. (Again whether from London or the Pale is arguable.) Such was Hugh O'Neill's allegiance to the queen that he even commanded a force for her against the Desmonds in their ill-fated rebellion in Munster. Yet, looking through the perfect hindsight of history, the young Hugh O'Neill seemed to be biding his time for some thing and some moment that offered much more opportunity.

Although the crown had granted Hugh the earldom of Tyrone, Turlough O'Neill, upon the death of Shane, claimed the O'Neillship for himself—a title that had been outlawed by Elizabeth. Turlough flexed his might while English attentions were focused on the Desmond revolt and at times threatened the Pale, but for the most part his claim was left unchallenged.

Because of his service in the Desmond revolt, the queen granted Hugh 600 soldiers—at her expense. Hugh took these men and trained them well. He continued gathering 600 men a year and giving them the most modern military training. So successful was his recruitment and retention that by 1593, Hugh O'Neill had a standing army of 15,000 well-trained soldiers. That potential power was certain to cause concern to Elizabeth and her court. It is also possible that this concern was due to the retirement of Turlough O'Neill, who the Elizabethans may have tolerated as a natural balance to Hugh O'Neill. The queen may also have been aware that by this time, Hugh O'Neill was in negotiations with Phillip of Spain—the chief Catholic adversary of Elizabethan England. Despite these fears, he still got permission to buy lead from Spain, purportedly to be used in repairing a roof but which was immediately used in making munitions.

If Elizabeth had reason to worry, the events of 1594 confirmed her fears. In that year, Hugh MacGuire, an Ulster chieftain, staged a small rebellion over the Crown's attempt to force a sheriff on to his lands. Hugh O'Neill refused to lead his army against the MacGuires. (With a force of 15,000, O'Neill could have easily stamped out the uprising.) When Hugh O'Donnell of Donegal joined ranks with MacGuire, O'Neill still refused to step in. Only when O'Neill learned in 1595 that the English were assembling a large army to send against MacGuire and O'Donnell, did O'Neill finally become engaged. But he entered not on the side of the queen but on the side of the Irish. He had dropped all pretense of loyalty and was now fighting for an Irish cause no matter how ill defined.

Now this is a good time to digress a bit from Hugh's actions in Ulster in order to set the stage in the rest of Ireland. For in many ways, it is the Irish reaction to Elizabeth's actions in the entire country that allowed Hugh O'Neill to unify the country behind his rebellion.

A few years earlier, in the Parliament of 1569–1570, Sir Henry Sidney, the Lord Deputy, immediately began affecting legislation that would satisfy Elizabeth's "forward policy" for Ireland. No doubt, the most drastic of these new actions were that he changed the terms of Irish tenancy and abolished the chieftaincies. Tenants now needed to pay money rather than offer services to occupy their land. And the Gaelic order of chieftaincies and tainists would no longer be recognized. (In a way this latter policy is what Elizabeth's father Henry tried to do by granting English titles to the Irish chieftains whose chieftainships he took away.) Also, through a process of plantation—taking Irish and Anglo-Irish lands and granting them to Elizabethan loyalists—Elizabeth hoped to take control of Munster, which she saw as dangerous, as in fact it was at that moment: a province that was a regular and valuable trading post with Spain and France and thus could become a perfect flash point for a Catholic revolt. She achieved her purpose in Munster after crushing the Desmond revolt and subduing and "planting" the province. Before long Elizabeth had also taken control of Leinster and Connaught.

Contrary to the fears of those who opposed Sidney's tenancy plans, Elizabeth's conquest policy drove the Anglo-Irish and the Irish closer together, for the old Norman families were having their lands seized as well, only to be given to Elizabethan adventurers such as Walter Raleigh and Humfrey Gilbert.

Elizabeth's worries about the religious issue were also well founded, for never was the Catholic issue more volatile. In 1570, the Pope excommunicated Elizabeth, and on the continent rumors of assassination plots and rebellion were rampant. Many of the Irish clergy, who had been dispossessed by the Tudor Reformation, had settled in Europe, and while they flourished there in universities in Spain, Portugal, the Netherlands, and Italy, they also kept the Church's attention focused on what was happening in Ireland and helped ignite a fervent desire to bring Ireland back to the Old Faith. Spearheading this movement were the Jesuits who came to Ireland as a counter-Reformation force to deal directly with Elizabeth's reformation in Ireland, and served as a "mini-crusade" to regain Ireland for the Catholic cause.

So against this background of Anglo-Irish anger at the loss of land, Irish anger at the loss of traditional chieftaincies and Gaelic order, and religious agitation in opposition to the Tudor Reformation came Hugh O'Neill—a Catholic Prince who was descendant from Irish High Kings yet who had been schooled in the politics of English courts. He seemed the very man to unite all these separate causes against England and Elizabeth.

So when Hugh O'Neill asked for pardon in 1596, pardon for aligning with

Hugh MacGuire and Hugh O'Donnell in their rebellion, he was granted it. Yet by his actions, O'Neill had firmly thrown his lot in with the Irish cause. He and O'Donnell had given refuge to 3,000 Spanish survivors of the ill-fated Armada against England—an action that was a capital crime in Elizabethan law—and shipped them to Scotland; he was bringing large amounts of ordnance from Spain; and he had even asked the European powers to set up the Archduke of Austria as the (Catholic) King of Ireland. In hindsight for Elizabeth, the pardon seemed ill advised, for Hugh O'Neill was becoming a bigger and bigger danger—much more powerful than any vacuum his absence would cause, which was the original reasoning behind Elizabeth's pardon.

Hugh O'Neill was simply too big for Elizabethan comfort, and in 1597, the Crown sent a force to attack. O'Neill won handily. The Crown regrouped and attacked again, and again O'Neill won rather easily. By now in 1598, O'Neill could boast of an army of 30,000 well-trained and capable men. Elizabeth's resources were spread thin—since 1585 she had been waging war with Spain. The Crown would simply have to negotiate with O'Neill.

O'Neill's demands were telling—for they defined an Irish cause that would echo down through the years. What he asked for was the removal of all English officials and forces; all lands restored to rightful (and traditional) owners; full pardon for himself; the designation of Ulster as a "county palatine"; and the right of the Irish to worship as they pleased. All these demands would have been hard for Elizabeth to bear, but the last was simply untenable to her within the sphere of European politics. For to give Ireland the right of worship would ally it to Elizabeth's most feared enemies.

Elizabeth answered O'Neill's demands by sending a force of 4,000 in 1598. O'Neill's army killed 3,000 of them and forced the remaining quarter into an indefensible position. By this point all of Ireland was united behind Hugh O'Neill and Ulster. Munster, Connaught, and Leinster sided with him, and even the English Pale pledged its support. Hugh O'Neill had united the country and had the English stymied.

And so Elizabeth, strained as she was for resources, sent the largest army yet deployed in Ireland—over 17,000 foot-and horsemen—led by her own favorite, Sir Robert Deveraux, the second Earl of Essex. Essex, who had captured Cadiz in the Spanish wars and risen as high as one could go in Elizabeth's court, was given the title Lord Lieutenant of Ireland. His order from Elizabeth was simple: march immediately against O'Neill. Once he arrived, however, he was dissuaded from doing so by the Irish Council in Dublin. Worried about their own landholdings in Leinster and Munster, they advised Essex to first travel south and west and later attack O'Neill in the north. While Essex attacked the southwestern provinces, O'Neill was left free to ravage the Pale undeterred, gathering strength like a mighty storm. On the other hand, Essex's forces, although successful in gaining back much land in Munster and Leinster, suffered enormous casualties, and when he returned finally to face O'Neill he had less than a quarter of his original force. Knowing he could not survive a military encounter with O'Neill, he agreed to a truce. O'Neill once again defeated the English forces. (In understanding the mind of Elizabeth and the fury she could summon up in regards to O'Neill that when Essex returned to London to tell Elizabeth about the truce with O'Neill, he was put in the Tower and beheaded. After all, even the queen's favorites have to follow orders or suffer the consequences.)

With the truce in place, O'Neill used the time to strengthen his forces and win back most of the lands Essex had taken. Throughout this period, he was in continuous contact with Spain, and was promised assistance in men and supplies. It was perhaps his trust in this aid that would ultimately lead to his downfall.

In 1600, Elizabeth sent Lord Mountjoy to Ireland with 20,000 men. Elizabeth wanted to crush O'Neill desperately. In her order to Mountjoy—and perhaps thinking of the opportunity that was wasted with Essex—she expressly denied him the power to grant "the pardon of the arch-traitor, a monster of ingratitude to her, and the root of misery to her people." Hugh O'Neill had traveled a far distance from his days as a ward of the Tudor court!

Mountjoy's strategy was to set up garrisons along Ulster's borders, thus separating him from the rest of the country. When O'Neill came out to attack the Pale, Mountjoy counteracted by attacking Ulster from two directions, destroying crops and ravaging the land. Little by little, Mountjoy calculated that he would either starve out O'Neill's base or alienate his people from him.

Aside from Spain, O'Neill was also in contact with James IV of Scotland (who would succeed Elizabeth as James I of England). O'Neill had reason to hope that James might favor his cause—a potential coup if James did succeed Elizabeth—or that after Elizabeth's death, England would fall into a war of succession thus weakening his Tudor enemies. Yet, O'Neill was wise enough to know that those matters were out of his control; he could begin planting seeds with James but would need to wait to see what they produced. In the meantime, he trusted in Spain.

Mountjoy's tactics were succeeding. He knew that attempting to defeat O'Neill at his own game, in the guerilla operations at which the Irishman's army was so skilled, was futile. Mountjoy had decided to create famine—to starve out O'Neill's men and destroy the alliances. Yet, O'Neill's military fortunes were turning also. Hugh Maguire—who with Hugh O'Donnell had been O'Neill's staunchest ally ever since 1595 when O'Neill first came to their aid—was slain in a battle near Cork, and a number of important leaders were captured and sent to London. Mountjoy's men were burning acres and acres of cropland, and with the smoke of burning fields, O'Neill's support was slowly drifting away.

Finally, however, the Spanish forces that O'Neill had been depending on arrived. That they landed in the least strategic location—the southern coast of Cork—and that they arrived in such small numbers boded ill for Hugh O'Neill's great rebellion, which was coming to an end. Much hung in the outcome of the Battle of Kinsale—probably more than O'Neill himself could have guessed.

The Battle of Kinsale

Today Kinsale is a lovely town, considered the "gourmet capital of Ireland." It is situated on a natural harbor off of what is now called the Celtic Sea and at the mouth of the river Bándon and is only a short sea voyage from Spain itself. Unfortunately, it was of little strategic use at the moment to Hugh O'Neill's cause—and it could be argued that in landing there, the Spanish forces served O'Neill poorly as he and his army were forced to travel the entire length of the country to join them, dissipating precious supplies and an already sagging morale.

In September 1601, 4,000 Spanish troops landed at Kinsale, under the leadership of Don Juan D'Aguila. Historians seem to agree that D'Aguila was perhaps not the best man for the job, for he had soon alienated the very men he had come to assist. Before long, the Irish realized that the Spanish were not there to help the Irish call to liberty, but were merely attacking an old enemy, England. O'Neill and his men traveled quickly from Ulster to Kinsale, while O'Neill's chief ally Hugh O'Donnell, the Earl of Tyrconnell, came from Sligo. (As has been often the case in the old Gaelic order, O'Neill had cemented his relationship with O'Donnell by giving him his daughter in marriage; thus the two leaders were father and son-in-law.) The various chieftains had to leave enough men at home to protect their local areas and then make the journey southward. While traveling, they encountered English troops whose plain purpose was to prevent the Irish from joining— and at this moment from relieving—their besieged Spanish allies in Kinsale.

For in less than a week of the Spanish landing, Mountjoy and 7,000 men had arrived at Kinsale and surrounded D'Aguila's men. The Irish cause was being sublimated into a distracting rescue mission.

Both O'Donnell and O'Neill caused the English forces much damage as they converged on Kinsale, but when they arrived, they found Mountjoy and his men garrisoned and laying siege to the Spanish. Now, it had never been O'Neill's strategy to attack walled forts or even cities; his guerrilla tactics had been successful so far because he was able to lure English forces into vulnerable positions and then have his forces attack. Mountjoy's success in Ireland could be attributed to his patient use of garrisons throughout his campaign, a method that frustrated O'Neill's guerrilla style of warfare.

In Kinsale, the Irish found themselves facing heavily armed fortresses, and so the siege began. Throughout a very severe Irish winter, Mountjoy and his English forces surrounded the Spanish forces in Kinsale while O'Neill and O'Donnell surrounded Mountjoy and his men. (If the cost was not so great to Irish freedom, one could argue that the entire venture with the Spanish was comical—a veritable burlesque of warfare.) The standoff lasted for months, with O'Donnell arguing to attack the English and O'Neill opting to wait and starve them out. Finally, on Christmas Eve 1601, the battle took place. What had been long anticipated was over by mid-morning; it had lasted a brief three hours. The Spanish forces that O'Neill and the Irish had long hoped for were unaware that a battle was even taking place, and did not know it had occurred until they heard the celebratory cannon shot announcing the English victory.

There was great hope hanging in the Battle of Kinsale. If the Irish had been victorious—and if the Spanish forces had engaged at all—Spain would have come in with greater enthusiasm and all of Ireland would have thrown its weight behind O'Neill. As it was, the Irish suffered a devastating defeat. For nine years, Hugh

O'Neill's rebellion had grown as success followed success. For nine years he had successfully challenged the sovereignty of Elizabeth in Ireland. And in three hours, most of that was lost.

Hugh O'Donnell quickly took flight on a ship to Spain, where he continued to press for assistance. He died mysteriously within a year, and was very likely poisoned by an English agent. For his part, Hugh O'Neill was able to return to Ulster, where he continued to defend Tyrone. O'Donnell's brother Rory did the same in Tyrconnell. But, it was the end. After Kinsale, the English forces stormed Ulster, destroying butter stores, slaughtering livestock and burning crops; before long famine was sweeping the province as it already had in Munster. The provinces were quickly becoming depopulated, and Mountjoy himself claimed to have seen 3,000 dead of famine in Tyrone alone. (This turned out to be a handy circumstance for Elizabeth's plantation policies, as war weary English soldiers were awarded the lands of the newly dead!) To add symbolic resonance to Hugh O'Neill's defeat and to the end of the Gaelic order, at Dungannon, Mountjoy's men captured the city and destroyed the ancient inauguration stone of the O'Neills. For the first time, England now controlled all of Ireland, from north to south and from east to west.

On March 30, 1603, Hugh O'Neill surrendered, laying down his arms and submitting to Elizabeth. And while Mountjoy was aware of events in London, Hugh O'Neill did not know that his enemy the Queen had died six days earlier. He had long thought that he might succeed if he could outlast her. But that was not to be. In surrendering, the great patriot gave up the title of "The O'Neill," disavowed alliances with foreign powers, gave up his lands and lordships, and renounced all authority over his armies. If he had known that James I—who had promised him such favor before—was now the King of England, he may have attempted to bargain for a better ending. And that better bargaining may have changed his later course of action for Ireland.

The Escape of the Earls

It would have been easy to call this section "the Flight of the Earls," for that is the term that has come down to us in history. But I have never liked the term "Flight of the Earls," for it implies a running away. And indeed, much of the tales surrounding the earls' years traveling across Europe depicted a broken band of men, sadly living out their days in exile. But the truth is far from that. For certain, O'Neill boarded that ship to avoid going to London where he more than likely would have lost his head. But foremost in his mind, then and throughout the rest of his life, was to get to Europe, to the courts with whom he had been in constant contact, and raise an army that would once more challenge the sovereignty of the English crown in Ireland. O'Neill's vision stayed firm, despite the disappointment he found in others. His "flight," if that is what we are forced to call it, was very much the quest of an extraordinary patriot, doing his very best to acquire the resources he needed to throw off the foreign government whose obvious aim now was to resettle his entire country.

Although Hugh O'Neill was able to retain his earldom and O'Donnell's brother Rory had been allowed to inherit the title of earl of Tyrconnell after the submission of 1603, things were hardly comfortable for the Irish earls, and English rule was more and more a difficult yoke to bear. Much of Tyrconnell's best lands in Donegal had been seized and given to the Church (the Protestant Church of Ireland, at that). The lands of Cuchonnacht Maguire, Lord of Fermanagh, was partitioned and given to two hundred freeholders. And Hugh O'Neill found that the guarantees he had won from James's court were no guarantees against encroachment from official Dublin and its wily officials. And besides, he was also sure that his very life—on which there had been such a hefty reward alive or dead—was still threatened by the forces of the Crown.

For the next several years, Dublin presented O'Neill with two formidable adversaries in the persons of Sir John Davies—who believed that O'Neill represented the largest obstacle to the complete Anglicization of Ireland and felt that as a traitor O'Neill had been dealt with too leniently—and of Sir Arthur Chichester, who had served against O'Neill in the Nine Years War and whose brother had died while also fighting against O'Neill. As his holdings and hereditary rights came under attack, O'Neill countered the antipathy and stonewalling he met with in official Dublin by addressing his complaints directly to the English court. For instance in June 1605, he complained that his fishing rights over Lough Foyle and the river Baan were in danger of being removed. In December of that same year, he wrote to the King again to have him simply outline exactly what were his rights as stipulated in the terms of the bargain that he had reached in his submission of 1602. When his appeals to the English court fell on deaf ears, he did what he had been doing for most of his life—he appealed to the king of Spain. O'Neill and O'Donnell's representative to Spain told the king that James's ministers in Ireland were reducing the earls' resources at an appalling rate, and asked him to send them secretly financial assistance so that they could at the very least still maintain their homes. (Still hoping for the support of Catholic European countries, Hugh O'Neill had continued to keep in touch with the continent.)

At the same time that his man was in Spain, O'Neill was continuing his torrent of requests to James himself. For his part, James did write to his ministers that all care should be taken to protect the earls' rights, but Davies, Chichester and their circle were hardly the people to oversee justice in regards to O'Neill. In fact, both men felt that King James was too generous with O'Neill and that this generous attitude was an obstacle in the final Anglicization of Ireland and, more importantly, their acquisition of his lands.

During this time also, one of O'Neill's sons-in-law, Donal O'Cahan, had offered his services to Chichester and Davies with the hope that they would arrange for his acquiring some of O'Neill's lands. The Dublin ministers were glad to oblige, for stirring trouble between the Irish clans was a successful ploy in taking land. Added into the turmoil was the newly appointed Bishop of Derry who also had his eye on much of O'Neill's holdings. The wrangling reached such intensity that finally King James himself became involved and ordered all parties to London after Michelmas 1607. James, however, might have had other intentions as well, and O'Neill was well aware of them.

In the early summer of 1607, Christopher St. Lawrence, the Baron of Howth, informed the King of the existence of a "league of Catholics" in Ireland which was planning a revolt to shake off the Crown and attach itself to Spain. Among those in the league were the earls of Tyrconnell and the Baron of Delvin. St. Lawrence had tried hard to find incriminating information on O'Neill but found none. But the court must have known that no association of such import could exist without O'Neill's influence. (And they were right, as O'Neill's memoirs make known!) Many people in the English court felt the summons to O'Neill over the O'Cahan-Bishop Montgomery affair was actually a death sentence for O'Neill, and if he came he would never see Ireland again. O'Neill himself was very aware of these dangers—as he had been for some while even writing to King Phillip of Spain earlier in the year that his life was in constant danger.

With the news of O'Neill's summons to London—which most of his followers were certain was a writ of execution—plans, which must have been long in the making, went quickly into operation. Cuchonnaught Maguire, who was in Brussels and who was reported to be a master of disguise, went to Brittany disguised as a merchant and bought wines and salts. In Nantes he hired a ship and fitted it with merchandise and nets under the pretense that he was going fishing in Ireland. (The pretense was well conceived for the ship was in fact stopped off the coast of Scotland and released when only fishing gear was discovered.) From

Dunkirk Maguire finally set sail and reached Lough Swilly in the first week of September 1609.

O'Neill in the meantime had come down to Dublin to speak with Chichester about his imminent departure to London. After the speech, however, O'Neill went to the house of Sir Garrett Moore and retrieved his son who had been placed in the Moore household to be educated. This action alerted Chichester who suspected that something was afoot.

O'Neill next gathered his wife and three-year-old son and some of his household and they traveled hard to Lough Swilly. There they met O'Donnell, Maguire, and O'Brien, O'Neill's "minister to Europe," Matthew Tully, and the ship's able captain, John Rath. These men were accompanied by wives and children as well.

About a hundred people boarded the ship that morning of September 14, 1607, leaving their horses standing by the shore, and set sail around noon.

The news of the earl's flight caused great consternation in London where it was believed they were going to Spain and that the pope would outfit the earls militarily for a war against the Crown. They were not altogether wrong, as Hugh O'Neill's plan was to return to Ireland with an army.

Unfortunately, the ship had bad luck at sea. Instead of the four or five days it normally took to reach Spain, the ship was buffeted by storms for twenty days, and ultimately landed near LeHavre. The French King, Henry IV, denied them permission to travel to Spain—although he did not arrest them as the English ambassador asked—but he did grant them permission to travel through France to Flanders, a Spanish territory.

When O'Neill and his entourage arrived in Flanders on October 18, they were feted as heroes, not only by the Irish community well entrenched in the European universities, but by the European powers as well. O'Neill's success during his nine-year-war with Elizabeth had made him a hero in Europe and his fame was wide—

the fame of an underdog who had tweaked a bully and gotten away with it. He was hailed as a hero who had devastated much of England's military and as a champion of the church who had fought bravely against the Protestant forces. One town gave O'Neill the keys to the city; at another, the papal nuncio, a marquis, a duke, and the Spanish ambassador met him and helped his party from their coaches; and the banquets in his honor were comparable to those given to the highest heads of state. (There is a somewhat malicious joy in reading Sir John Davies' prognosis in Dublin when he stated that O'Neill's group would be scorned and taken as "a band of gypsies." In fact, the English government was quite put out by the glorious reception the earls were receiving.)

Unfortunately, while all this feasting was going on and the earls' plans to travel to Spain were being formed, the English ambassadors were putting pressure on King Phillip, who, not wanting to offend England, wrote to his ambassador in Brussels with instructions for the earls to remain where they were and to give him a written account of their plans. Wishing to please the English court, Phillip then instructed the earls to go to Rome where they should look for assistance from the pope.

For the next seven years, this was to characterize life for Hugh O'Neill and his party on the European continent: promises and vacillation from Spain and from Rome, spying, danger, and disinformation from English agents, and ultimately, sickness and death of those they loved. Throughout, however, O'Neill kept steadfast in his dream of raising an army and returning to Ireland—and too often empty promises allowed him to believe that the dream was near fruition. He died in Rome on July 20, 1616.

The Flight of the Earls—despite its dream of amassing an army to repel the English in Ireland—actually had the exact opposite effect. With the aristocracy of Ulster completely gone—and Ireland's greatest leader in self-imposed exile—the

Crown had no obstacle to its plantation of Ulster. The O'Neills, O'Donnells, Maguires, all their lands were seized and handed over to loyal solders. Six of the nine counties were taken, to be settled by English and Scottish Protestants. It is a sad truth that the great O'Neill's hope to bring an army from Catholic Europe to liberate Ireland in a very real way laid the foundation of the religious divisions that have scarred Irish politics ever since.

CHAPTER XI:

Grace O'Malley—Granuaile

It was in the late summer when I was attending a wedding reception that I met again the three O'Malley sisters, Patsy, Margaret, and Mary-Jane. Somehow the conversation turned to this book, and the three yelled in unison, "Malachy! You have to do a chapter on Grace O'Malley!" Now, I never doubted that I would for one minute, for Grace O'Malley is one of the truly amazing women of the sixteenth century, if not of all time. And she has always been of keen interest to me. Irish history has tried to ignore her, for she was not in the mold of the traditional Irish heroine—the O'Malley sisters told me that their own father once instructed them to never mind about her, that they shouldn't be asking questions about such a woman in their past—but in recent years, her reputation has soared. Of late there have been several books, documentaries, a major movie screenplay, a symphony, countless songs and ballads, and even an educational center dealing with her life and times. And now her name, appropriated by both nationalists and feminists, is one in which the Irish are, after too long a time, quite proud. So here is that chapter the O'Malley girls requested. And to their two young nieces both of whom have been christened "Grace O'Malley," may they strive to reach the strength, character, and purpose of the extraordinary woman whose name they bear.

The O'Malley clan, or the Uí M haille in Irish, took for their motto the phrase *terra marique potens*—powerful on land and sea. And indeed they were. They were a sea-faring people who lived mainly along the west coast of Clare, and who made their livelihoods primarily from the sea. They considered the sea to be their own particular dominion, and were given rights by the King of Connaught to charge levies and tolls and sell fishing rights. The sea also gave them a mobility that other families did not have, and the O'Malleys traveled to and traded with foreign markets to a large degree. Irish traders—including the O'Malleys—were regular visitors to ports in Britain, France, and Spain. Yet while their sea-faring exploits were already becoming well known, the earliest reference to the O'Malley land actually came in a description of St. Patrick's ascent of Croagh Patrick (at least that's what the mountain is called now), which was located on O'Malley territory.

While the sea provided the O'Malleys with fishing and expansive trading, it also furnished them with the means of another venture—piracy. And while this "profession" was in the family for many generations, none succeeded at it or became more notorious at it than Granuaile.

Granuaile was born at the beginning of the Tudor expansion around the year 1530. The Earls of Kildare were still trying to arrest power from Henry VIII, but the west of Ireland was greatly removed from Tudor politics. It was a world where the Anglo-Irish had been assimilated largely into the Gaelic order, and governance was still yet primarily through the chieftains. Granuaile's father was one such chieftain: Owen Dubhdara O'Malley. ("Dubhdara" means black oak in Irish and one can imagine a towering figure with a broad back and jet-black hair.) Her mother Margaret was of the O'Malley sect of Moher. Bred with a double-dose of O'Malley blood, it should have been no surprise that Granuaile would insist at a young age on accompanying her father on his sea-journeys or that she would become such an extraordinary sailor.

Now, the status of women in medieval Gaelic Ireland was hardly a grand one; they were defined by their relationship to men—some man's daughter or some man's wife. They did, however, have certain rights that their counterparts in England and Europe did not, dealing with ownership of property. A married woman in Gaelic society retained her property—in most European cultures ownership was transferred to the husband—as well as retained her maiden name. This right of ownership would be the subject of some of Granuaile's greatest and serious battles.

When she was sixteen, Granuaile married Donal O'Flaherty, whose family ruled most of what is now Connemara. At the time O'Flaherty was the Baron of Ballinahinch and had been elected as tánaiste to the chieftain of all the O'Flahertys. This implied that Donal himself was next in line to one day be chieftain. Her father must have been pleased with the match—the O'Flahertys and the O'Malleys, unlike many Gaelic clans, actually got along together rather well, and were usually allies rather than adversaries in any of the many wars that plagued the area. The dowry that Granuaile brought with her demonstrated her father's pleasure in the match: cattle, horses, sheep, and household goods. The dowry also came along with "sureties" that if Donal died or the couple divorced—which was not that uncommon among the Gaelic aristocracy—she would be entitled to full restoration of the dowry she brought with her.

To Donal O'Flaherty, Granuaile bore three children: Owen, Murrough, and Margaret. Although motherhood and marriage no doubt curtailed her sea-faring activities a bit, they certainly did not cut them off entirely. For even at sixteen when she came to O'Flaherty as a bride, Granuaile was a well-seasoned sailor—not only in the ways of the ocean but in the ways of the men who worked upon it.

Soon she was using her husband's main residence, the castle at Bunwen, to launch her raiding parties. The ships coming into Galway City were particularly vulnerable and valuable to her.

Coming from the sea-faring world of relative equality—where a person's worth was measured by what he or she could do on board—Granuaile quickly took to her husband's work and soon had eclipsed him as a ruler among his clan. When Donal became implicated in a murder in 1549, Granuaile seemed to have assumed the cloak of chieftainship from him. Through strength of character and personal charisma, she won the loyalty of her in-laws the O'Flahertys, and by the mere tenacity of her personality she maintained the lands of her husband.

An example of Granuaile's extraordinary leadership qualities is her encounter with the Joyce clan, long time adversaries of the O'Flahertys. Once after Donal had seized a castle of the Joyces, the Joyces slew him in revenge. Thinking that they could now easily regain their stronghold they attacked the now "master-less" castle, only to be driven back by Granuaile. Indeed so fierce was Granuaile's defense that the Joyces gave it the name of "Hen's Castle" in respect to her stance, a name, by the way, by which it is still known today.

But with Donal's death, Granuaile lost any official connection to power. She traveled north to her father's lands, accompanied significantly by her O'Flaherty in-laws, and set up her base on Clare Island in Clew Bay. At Clare Island she maintained a fleet of at least three galley ships—a type of ship for which she became famous—and a number of smaller boats. As the daughter of an O'Malley and as the inheritor of all her mother's lands, she had more power than most men and women of her time. But if Brehon law—and the machinations of Elizabethan law—worked to deprive her and her children of O'Flaherty's title, she would earn her own sovereignty through courage, confidence, and character. She would become the "Pirate Queen" who would be renowned throughout the British Isles.

That Granuaile was her own person there is little doubt. She hardly fit the mold of the traditional Gaelic woman. She had a penchant for swearing, a reputation for being sexually adventurous, was known for her violent temper, and had an apparent fondness for gambling. She did not wrap herself in a pan-Gaelic/Irish flag—indeed that would have been impossible for it was the very independence and disunited nature of the Gaelic order that brought about its downfall. Like all those around her, Granuaile acted solely to ensure her own survival and the survival of her family, as long as the two did not interfere. When one of her sons joined with her archenemy Bingham, she quickly made war against him! In fact, the tales that have come down through tradition aver that Granuaile was often "warring" while twice in official English records it is calculated that by 1593 she had been "warring" for more than forty years. (I truly love this woman's boldness. What her enemies called "piracy" and "treason" Granuaile described to Elizabeth I herself as her "maintenance by land and sea.")

It is precisely because Granuaile was such an iconoclast that she is not mentioned at all in the Irish annals—the records of a hugely masculine, highly religious world, yet records compiled in the very locales where she was most active. On the other hand, English state papers refer to her innumerable times, her name continuing to appear in official documents as late as a quarter century after her death. And so, much of what is known of her—apart from the government papers of England—has been passed down orally and has entered the realm of legend and folklore. And from there, stories abound.

One of my favorite Granuaile stories is her encounter at Howth Castle. Granuaile and her fleet had sailed around the island and had stopped in Howth to restock provisions. She considered herself—and acted as if she were—a chieftain of the Gaelic order, and she expected the privileges of such a position. And so when she docked in Howth, she made her way to Howth Castle. Now as has been said many times before, hospitality is practically a matter of legal duty in the Gaelic world, and Granuaile expected hospitality from the Castle and the Lord of Howth. She did not get it! She was sent away and the castle gates were locked against her. Now again, this is a woman of fierce temper and great pride, so you can imagine her foul mood as she made her way back to her ship. However, on her way she encountered the grandson of the lord playing on the beach. (History does weave intricate webs, for this very boy is the self-same St. Lawrence who spied on Hugh O'Neill and reported the "League of Catholics" to Chichester and James I.) The highly insulted Granuaile saw her chance, kidnapped the boy, and set sail for home on the other side of the island.

St. Lawrence was understandably aghast at the loss of his grandson, and quickly traveled by land across the breadth of Ireland to Granuaile's home in Clare, willing to pay whatever ransom this "pirate queen" demanded. And there he received perhaps his biggest surprise. For Granuaile did not want money. She wanted the law of hospitality to be followed. And so she returned the boy with St. Lawrence's assurances that the gates to his Castle would never be locked and that an extra plate would always be set at table for any guest that might arrive. To this day, an extra plate is still always set at the table in Howth Castle.

In 1567, Granuaile married again. This time she chose Richard Burke who was chieftain of Ulick. No doubt, his land holdings, complete with excellent and protected harbors, were of keen attraction to Granuaile and her "maintenance by sea." The Ulick chieftainship was the second most important in Mayo and Burke himself was considered the likely candidate for the MacWilliamship upon the death of the current MacWilliam. Despite this prestige—and evidence of Granuaile's influence and renown—Burke is often in official records referred to as "the husband of Grainé Mhaile."

One story of their marriage claims that according to Gaelic custom the two were first wed in a "trial marriage," something that was certainly not rare in Gaelic society. In this trial marriage, after one year, if either of the parties were dissatisfied they could withdraw from the union. Legend states that when one year had passed, Granuaile installed herself and her men in Burke's castle. When her husband returned, he found that he had been locked out, and from the castle wall heard his wife claim that he was being dismissed. If the story was true, it seems typical of Granuaile who with little exertion had acquired a new castle without the baggage of a husband. Yet, if so, the divorce did not last, for Burke and Granuaile remained partners until his death in 1583.

Richard Burke and Granuaile had one son, Tibbot-na-Long, whose very birth reveals Granuaile's character. Tradition claims that Tibbot was born on his mother's ship while his mother was marauding along the southwest coast of Ireland. (In fact, his name in Irish *Tíboid-na-Long* means "Toby of the Ship.") On the day following his birth, Granuaile's ship was attacked by Algerian pirates. The battle was not going well for the Irish, and finally one of Granuaile's captains rushed below deck where Granuaile lay with her newly born son. The man pleaded with her to show herself in battle, so that her very presence might swing the direction of the fight. More than likely cursing under her breath, she wrapped a blanket around herself, went up on deck with a musket in her hands, and fired it into the oncoming Algerians, leading her men to victory. She was the leader, after all, and a "little" thing like childbirth was certainly not going to set her back.

For the most part, Richard Burke and Granuaile made a complementary team. Burke had strength and land while Granuaile had political savvy and grit. They combined these traits well in their attempts to survive in the world that bred them, but that world was quickly falling apart due to circumstances beyond their control. Despite their personal characteristics, the Gaelic order was facing its greatest foe . . . and it too was a woman of unequaled power: Elizabeth I.

Part of the Elizabethan strategy in Ireland was to "divide and conquer," to undercut the Gaelic chieftaincies through the granting of noble titles and parcels of lands to men who in the Gaelic system were not in line for governance. Granuaile had seen this happen to her first husband, who while he waited as tánaiste for the chieftainship of Connemara saw Elizabeth give that position instead to Murragh na dTuadh. She was determined to fight hard to prevent it happening to her present husband. Elizabeth was changing Gaelic heredity laws, and in doing so was causing great dissension among the Gaelic clans.

At the same time, Elizabeth was also actively encouraging the plantation of Munster, granting land to Elizabethan adventurers and loyalists. This was not only upsetting to the native Irish but to the old English families that had come over with the very first wave of Norman invaders and who had become part of the Irish culture and makeup. With her "old English subjects" riled and with European and Catholic adversaries looking at Ireland as a potential launching pad for anti-English rebellion, Elizabeth was very wary of Munster—and thus very severe in her dealings with it. Nevertheless small rebellions were cropping up throughout the west.

In 1577, Elizabeth sent her Lord Deputy Sir Henry Sidney to Mayo to quash a small rebellion begun by the sons of the Earl of Carrickford. Sidney was traveling with his son, Sir Phillip Sidney, poet, courtier, soldier, and by all accounts the epitome of the Elizabethan Renaissance man. On their way home, the two encountered Granuaile who boasted of her power—two galleys and two hundred fighting men—and offered them to Sidney's service. (She also offered to take the senior Sidney on a tour of Galway Bay, but only if he paid a fee. He gladly agreed.) The young Sidney—this paragon of learning and courtliness—was awed by Granuaile and the two spoke together for some time. One can only imagine the conversation, for although Granuaile might be a woman of the sea, she was also a woman of the world and her spirit and charisma were enchanting to many.

Despite the favorable impression that Granuaile had made on both Sidneys, she was earning a far more infamous reputation throughout Ireland. In 1578, the Earl of Desmond, feeling pressured by Elizabeth—as indeed all of Munster was—attempted to prove his loyalty to his queen and country and his opposition to the Irish by arresting the notorious Granuaile. She was placed in Limerick prison and stayed there for more than eighteen months. It is noteworthy of her importance—or of her perceived threat and danger—that the authorities later transported her to Dublin Castle where only the Crown's most notorious prisoners in Ireland were kept.

For one reason or another, Granuaile was released in 1579, having spent two years in prison. She was nearly fifty years old and had already lived a rough life in a rough world. On her release from Dublin Castle, Granuaile established herself at her husband's castle at Carraigahowley. There she was immediately besieged by soldiers sent out from Galway City. True to form, Granuaile and her loyal men sent the attackers packing! It was not just on the sea that Granuaile was a force to reckon with.

At the time, however, the situation in the west of Ireland was getting more and more dire. The MacWilliam had earlier submitted to Elizabeth—with Elizabeth's laws of heredity potentially cutting Granuaile's husband as tánaiste from his likely succession to that post—and Desmond was now in open revolt. For a while Richard Burke attempted to attach himself to Desmond's cause, but Granuaile, as always, saw more advantage in submitting to Elizabeth. She knew that by allying with Desmond, no good would come, and that submitting to the English queen would both buy her time and secure her husband's title. Her plan was successful and in 1581, Elizabeth marked Richard Burke the MacWilliam. (Elizabeth shrewdly played the Gaelic chieftains. She had earlier outlawed such titles, but still bestowed them anyway, considering the titles mere bones to toss out to the chieftains in exchange for a semblance of peace and control of their lands.)

Granuaile was now Lady Burke—an odd fitting gown if ever there was one. Yet within two years her husband was dead. (Granuaile immediately claimed a third of her husband's property.) Perhaps of larger import than her husband's death, however, her greatest nemesis had now arrived in Ireland.

Richard Bingham believed in justice by the sword. And if that did not work then he reverted to hanging, burning and ravaging fields, besieging strongholds, and destroying property. He had arrived in Ireland in 1584 and was appointed the governor of Connaught. And while the damage and ruination he caused was devastating, his actions were in fact tempered by the Lord Deputy, John Perrot, who was also appointed at the same time but who maintained a more conciliatory view towards the Irish. It is a scary picture to imagine what else the monster Bingham might have been capable of without the reining hand of Perrot. But, Perrot's Dublin was far from Connaught, and Bingham was ruthless.

In response to the Desmond rebellion, Munster was ravaged, the entire countryside destroyed. An accelerated system of "surrender and re-grant" was instituted and the "Composition of Connaught" put an end to the levies and taxes that clannish chieftaincies were privileged to, as well as to the clannish system of succession. For Granuaile and the Burkes, this meant the virtual end of their MacWilliamship. (Granuaile had already been working behind the scenes to assure that her son Tibbot and next her stepson, Edmund Burke, would inherit the title of their father.)

To make matters worse, Bingham captured Tibbot-na-Long and held him hostage in Sligo. The plan was to "Anglicize" Granuaile's son, a common component of Elizabethan plans for conquest in Ireland. (It certainly didn't work with Hugh O'Neill who at this very same time was going through the same

Anglicization process within the Elizabethan court!) Bingham might have also been worried about Tibbot, for he had allied himself with the Sligos by marrying Maeve O'Connor Sligo. The Elizabethan strategy was always to pull these families apart and this inter-marrying formed allies that they often needed to be concerned with.

In the summer of 1585, Bingham besieged Hag's Castle on Lough Mask where the Burkes of Ulick were established. These were stepsons to Granuaile, children to Richard from an earlier marriage. Bingham demolished the castle, and then, when the MacWilliam died, gave the title to MacWilliam's oldest son rather than to Edmund Burke who claimed it through the system of Gaelic election. The Burkes of Mayo revolted, and were joined by several clans, as well as another Richard Burke who was married to Granuaile's daughter. Indeed, among those taking part were O'Malleys, Burkes, and O'Flahertys—all families with close connection to Granuaile. When he was released Tibbot-na-Long also joined the uprising. At the same time, Bingham's brother John murdered Granuaile's oldest son, Owen. Granuaile now put all her resources behind her son and the Burkes' rebellion.

Granuaile was arrested—ignobly tied with a rope, she claimed—and Bingham continued to act in a barbarous manner. Hostages were executed, lands spoiled, cattle seized. Her son-in-law was able to get her released and Granuaile went to sea, where she felt the most protected from Bingham and where she could sail and get Scottish mercenaries to bring back to the fight. (It is noteworthy that while she was at sea she made port in Ulster to make repairs to her ships, and while there spent three months with Hugh O'Neill and Hugh O'Donnell who were plotting their own rebellion. It is always interesting to imagine the fascinating conversations that must have taken place when remarkable characters of separate, momentous times are thrown together for a short while.)

Granuaile—and western Ireland's—luck seemed to turn for the better, for in

1587, Bingham was recalled to England. Wasting no time, Granuaile sailed to Dublin where she met with the Lord Deputy to complain about Bingham's tactics. (You must remember, this remarkable woman is nearly sixty years old and is still commanding her ships as they circumnavigate Ireland in order to fight a difficult battle.) In Dublin, Granuaile was able to attain pardons for her, her sons, and her daughter. When she returned to Connaught, she took advantage of Bingham's absence to augment her fleet and return to her business on the sea.

When Bingham returned in 1588, England was in no mood to deal with the likes of the Irish chieftains in the west. Much of the destroyed Spanish Armada that survived had landed on the west coast of Ireland, and England was diligent in its search for Spanish survivors. The punishment for harboring a survivor was the loss of one's land. In his fanatic zeal, Bingham once again roused the Burkes and stirred the largest rebellion yet. So great was the Burkes' success that the Lord Deputy in Dublin stepped in and began negotiating with the clan. Their demands included restoration of the tánaiste and the removal of Bingham. During the negotiations, Bingham was charged with numerous acts of cruelty and murder. Elizabeth was livid with—and as always with Munster fearful about—the situation in Connaught. Bingham was brought to Dublin and tried. And this is where the Burkes' rebellion went wrong. He was acquitted and ordered to return to Connaught to put down the Burkes' once and for all. Bingham marched through Connaught slaying women, children, and livestock. When Granuaile escaped to the sea for protection, he destroyed her lands.

The world that produced Granuaile was rapidly being subsumed by an entirely different order. In many ways she was cornered; the sea coast with its coves and island-filled bays that had provided her with so much protection and cover was penetrated by English ships. Bingham had for too long been the source of much misery and loss of property. Granuaile needed a more powerful scheme.

The Meeting of
Granuaile and Elizabeth I

The legends and stories that surround this extraordinary meeting between the era's most exceptional women are marvelous. Time has painted quite a romantic picture of the scene, with Granuaile in traditional Irish dress and traditional bare feet meeting with the regal Queen Elizabeth. However Granuaile was much too confident and much too proud to be cowed by this meeting; she did consider herself both a chieftain and an equal to Elizabeth. It was that same woman who entranced Elizabeth's most refined courtier, Sir Phillip Sidney, some fifteen years earlier. Since Granuaile didn't—or wouldn't—speak English and Elizabeth didn't speak Irish, the two conversed in Latin. (Elizabeth was considered one of the finest Latin speakers of the day and for Granuaile, Latin was a common language among the Irish aristocracy when speaking to the English. Granuaile may have lived her life on the sea, but she was no fool.)

In a chess match of status, Elizabeth when offering her hand to Granuaile was forced to raise hers to the taller Irish woman. Another story states that Granuaile took a proffered lace handkerchief, used it and threw it in the fire. When Elizabeth showed surprise, Granuaile commented that she just assumed that the English were as fastidious about their cleanliness as the Irish. Another tale states that when Elizabeth—ruler to ruler—bemoaned to Granuaile about the difficulties of their lot, Granuaile chided her by saying that there were a lot of women in Mayo suffering a lot more than she. And still again it is told that Granuaile refused a title offered to her by Elizabeth on the grounds that an equal cannot grant a title to another equal!

Yet, although these tales are meant to portray an almost humorous gutsiness, a picture of a bold—and sometimes cocky—Granuaile within the refinement of Greenwich Palace, they do little to convey the actual rapport that the two women shared. Granuaile was there to complain about her lot as a widow, a mother, and a property owner who has been persecuted by one of Elizabeth's ministers. Her demeanor and her argument must have won over the queen, for Elizabeth ultimately ordered Bingham not only to release her son and elderly step-brother from jail, not only to set her up with property paid for by her collected taxes, but also for Bingham to protect her and ensure that she lives in "life's enjoyment." The queen's letters to Bingham were hand-delivered by Granuaile herself, and as one can imagine, he was furious and indignant. He, of course, took his time to implement many of these orders from his queen.

The meeting between Granuaile and Elizabeth was not recorded. There are plenty of state records, however. In fact Granuaile filled out in great detail an interrogation report with eighteen questions covering her life, her marriage, her children, and her "career." State records also show that she gained several influential friends in Elizabeth's court, not the least of whom was Sir William Cecil. But there can be no mistake about the reasoning for Granuaile's meeting. She was not fighting for an Irish cause—the existence of an Irish cause did not even really exist until O'Neill gathered the chieftains to him in the next few years and even then its reality is debatable. She was fighting for herself, for her family, for her lands, for her survival, for her way of life. And it is because of this, unfortunately, because she has too often been portrayed consorting with the enemy for her own benefit, that she has been deliberately ignored in the annals of Irish history. Yet while her male peers spent their lives fighting with, negotiating with, and submitting to the queen's deputies in Ireland, Granuaile went right to the top and spoke, bargained, and successfully argued her case with the queen herself. For that alone, she should be admired.

There is not much known about Granuaile's death. Tradition says she died at Carraigahowley Castle in 1603. The world she tried to maintain was collapsing around her: Kinsale had fallen, O'Neill's revolt was a thing destroyed, and English troops and English governors were more present and more brutal than ever. She may have even known that her equal across the Irish Sea, Elizabeth I, had died. Yet if a person's life is measured by what he or she does in the circumstances they find themselves, then Granuaile's life is truly a remarkable one. Powerful and charismatic, she attracted men who followed her loyally into battle and onto the seas. Shrewd and wily, she negotiated with, bargained with, and manipulated many of those men—and one important woman—who tried to curtail her world. And if the course of history was against her, she stood her ground.

Fiercely independent, strong and confident, inspiring and able, Grace O'Malley—the Granuaile of sixteenth-century Ireland—is surely a model for anyone to emulate. The resuscitation of Granuaile's reputation in recent years has been too long in coming and is truly most justly deserved.

THE SEVENTEENTH CENTURY:
DESTRUCTION, CHAOS, AND LOSS

CHAPTER XII:

RORY O'MORE
AND OWEN ROE O'NEILL

The "Flight of the Earls" left Ulster denuded of most of its leadership and much of the Gaelic aristocracy; by 1614, there were more than 3,000 Irishmen in the Spanish army and 300 Irish students in Spanish universities. This vacuum, combined with the systematic conquest of the western provinces, left England in position to begin a full-scale plantation. War and famine had greatly depopulated the country; soldiers who had been in the Irish campaigns as well as thousands upon thousands of English and Scottish settlers were given tracts of land. (To get an idea of how vast this influx of settlers was, in the twenty-five years between James I's initial plantations and Cromwell, all but Galway, Clare, Mayo, Roscommon, and Sligo were systematically planted by the Crown.) This plantation of Ireland—particularly of Ulster—would surely have long-term effects. Among the more immediate effects were the resentment of the Old English of the new settlers and the ensuing awkward alliance between the Irish and the Old English families.

But of even greater consequence, the plantation of Ireland and the ensuing wars and uprisings in the seventeenth century were played out against much larger events in England. And once again, it was religion that played the leading role.

Almost from the beginning, the Stuart kings, James I and later, his son, Charles I, were in opposition to Parliament. For one, they were seen as being too tolerant of Roman Catholics—for although the zeal of the original Reformation had waned, a new movement, driven by Puritan zealots, was particularly hostile to all things that smacked of "popery." It was also held that the Stuart kings too often took positions in direct opposition to the will of the people. In addition, both James I and Charles I alienated Parliament through a series of ill-conceived and badly managed wars embarked upon by their chief minister, the Duke of Buckingham. The money that the monarchy requested to fight these wars—and at times which they illegally went about raising—further alienated Parliament from its king.

And so it comes to religion, once more. In Ireland, it pitted the fiercely anti-Catholic "New English" against the Catholic Irish and the "Old English," who were either much more tolerant or who had remained Catholic. As events and Civil War unfolded in England, the effect was to make the Irish and Old English alliance fall on the side of the king, while the new settlers sided with Parliament.

Such was the divide that after a major uprising in 1641, a Confederacy of Catholics was initiated: an assembly of Irish and Old English who announced their support of the king, and who set themselves up as a unified government, forming four standing armies, minting money, collecting taxes, and running a printing press. It was an unusual assembly marred, of course, by the usual back-biting and politicking inherent in any assembly, but for about a decade, the Catholic Confederacy did maintain a unified power, and successfully or not, negotiated and bargained with those representing England. It was no accident that in the same year that the Confederacy formed, Charles I had set himself up in opposition to Parliament. The lines of confrontation were clearly marked; unfortunately the Irish cause was most closely aligned with the ultimate loser. The winner—in the person of Oliver Cromwell—would bring the greatest dev-astation Ireland had ever known.

Within these turbulent times, there were many great Irish men—men for whom the dream of an Irish nation still burned deeply, and who fought and worked to bring that dream into being. Some were men of great intelligence and political savvy; others, of great courage and military skill; and still others combined all of these qualities: Irishmen such as Rory O'More and Owen Roe O'Neill, whose names still resound through history, legend, and song.

RORY O'MORE

Do you ask why the beacon and the banner of war,
On the mountains of Ulster are seen from afar,
Oh this is the signal our rights to secure,
'Cause we trust in God and in Rory O'More.

The hope that surrounded Rory O'More, that gave birth to the sentiments evident in the long-lived phrase "God, Our Lady, and Rory O'More!," sprang from his bringing the Old English from the Pale into the cause of Irish independence, as much as from his victories on the battlefield. His marriage into the family of Sir Patrick Barnewell, an Old English Catholic who had become an Irish hero for his actions against the penal policies in force at the start of the seventeenth century, seemed to foreshadow Rory O'More's success in getting the Old English to ally with his rebellion. And as the nephew of the great Rory Óg O'More, his very name helped to attract many to his cause.

Rory O'More first stepped onto history's stage in the 1640s. Together with the Irish chieftains at home, with the Irish generals in continental armies, and with Irish exiles throughout Europe, O'More had been plotting and planning. In Europe, the Spanish and Austrian armies were a renowned training ground for

Irish soldiers, while Irish priests and friars kept the Irish/Catholic cause burning in the university towns of the Low Countries, Spain, and Italy. Finally, a twofold plan took shape: Rory's forces were to seize Dublin Castle in October 1641, while Sir Phelim O'Neill would instigate uprisings throughout Ulster. (The taking of Dublin Castle, besides its political and military significance, must have some personal significance for Rory. When his great uncle was killed in 1578, his head had been sent to Dublin and put on display in the castle!)

Yet as would happen so often in Irish history, too many people were in on the secret plans. On the night before the attack was to come, one Owen O'Connelly, having drunk too much, leaked the plans to the English. The plot failed; the castle remained secure. Rory was able to escape.

The other half of the plan took off wildly. Throughout Ulster small risings began. Unleashing an anger that had simmered for a century, the Irish put thousands of English planters to the sword under the guidance of Sir Phelim O'Neill. The Scottish planters, for the most part, were spared on the idea that after time they might side with the rebel forces. As news of these uprisings traveled east, the numbers reportedly killed grew exponentially. By the time the news reached London, the numbers were exaggerated. Thirty thousand innocent people, the Londoners were told, had been massacred by the barbaric Irish, which to the Puritan mind equaled "Catholics." The Great Massacre, as it came to be called, fanned an already raging fire, and Cromwell, when he landed in Dublin in 1649, would vividly remember its reported excesses.

Of course, the English could not bear such rebellion easily. Yet, even the decision to send an army could not escape political factors. If Parliament allowed King Charles to raise an army, what, they feared, would prevent him from using that same army against them? Instead, Parliament itself would call up a force, and to raise money for this army, they confiscated the land of the rebels, of O'Neill and

Maguire and O'More, and sold it to "Adventurers." To ensure the future legitimacy of these land-holdings, the ensuing "Adventures Act" forbade the king
from ever pardoning the Irish rebels. This legal bar to the king's pardon, in
hindsight, proves interesting. There later appeared accusations that Charles himself supported—if not encouraged—the rebellion of '41. In fact, he was accused
of such in the trial that led to his execution. Four years later, Sir Phelim O'Neill
was offered a pardon if he would validate a commission signed by Charles I
authorizing the rebellion. He refused and was, of course, executed. Someone
believed or wanted to believe that Charles had authorized the uprising. Forged
commissions and rumors of Catholic plots abounded in England and added to
the growing disenchantment with Charles. During all this commotion in
London, an MP (Member of Parliament) for Cambridge began amassing more
and more power and respect; his name was Oliver Cromwell, and this same
"Adventures Act" would serve him well as he burned a swath through history.

In the meantime, Rory O'More and his forces were having success in Ireland.
A few weeks after the failure of the Dublin Castle plot, he won an encouraging
victory over English forces at Julianstown. The vanquished English forces took
refuge in the garrison at Drogheda. News of O'More's victory, and of the "mas-
sacres" in the north, caused others to take refuge in garrisons at Derry, Bandon,
and Cork as well. As he successfully lay siege to Drogheda, he also met with representatives of the Old English, first at Crofty Hill and then at Tara. O'More won
them over by convincing them of a very difficult concept to hold, one that would
seem counterintuitive for the rest of Irish history. O'More's argument was that
fighting against the government forces was actually fighting for the king! And in
many ways, he was right. The hostilities between Parliament and the king, along
with the tangential growing hostilities between Parliamentary Puritans and Roman
Catholics, caused the Old English to side with Rory, believing that their best inter-

ests were with him and the royalist stance.

Rory's rebellion spread, reaching Munster and Connaught. England responded by sending a large force of Scotsmen in April 1642, which landed in
Carrickfergus under the command of General Munro. For the most part, war
now was general throughout the country and would continue in varying degrees
for the next ten years.

Roman Catholics were expelled from the Irish Parliament when it convened in
Dublin in August 1642—and since Charles I had officially set himself up against
Parliament in the same month, the Old English Catholics were driven into forming a confederacy with the Irish that was both royalist and Catholic. The old
cliché was never more accurate: politics was making strange bedfellows.

The Confederacy formally first met in Kilkenny in May 1642. It included clergy and laity, Anglo-Irish and Old English Catholics, Irish from the continent and
native Irish, and would later even include an emissary from the pope. With the
motto *Pro Deo, Pro Rege, Pro Patria Hibernia unanimis* ("Ireland United God,
King, and Country"), the confederacy set up an executive council with two houses
made up of representatives from each of the four provinces. And while a religious
veneer was put upon the entire alliance, close to the surface was the desire to
regain lost lands, re-establish lost traditions, and recover lost estates. The cause for
Catholic emancipation, while very much a priority in the confederacy, was also
serving serious ulterior needs as well.

Rory O'More was the presiding force of the Confederacy, and his first great
action was to call over Owen Roe O'Neill from Spain to lead the Ulster rebellion.
O'Neill's arrival underscored the European and Catholic interest in Rory's rebellion. With O'Neill's arrival, Catholic leaders such as Cardinal Richelieu supplied
arms and money and encouragement for O'More's expedition.

While O'Neill commanded forces in Ulster, Rory O'More led his armies in

Offaly and Laois. The Confederacy was gaining legitimacy and the guerilla warfare of O'More's and O'Neill's forces were winning battles. These guerilla tactics initially repulsed Munroe, the general who had landed at Carrickfergus. In reprisal, he went on what can only be called a "scorched earth" campaign: Ireland's soil was becoming a repository for a great number of dead on both sides. Confusion and chaos seemed to rule the day.

The greater part of this confusion sprang from the overall chaos enveloping England. Because of it, in Ireland, there were basically four separate armies involved in war: the Irish Confederacy's army which supported the king, the King's Army which was of course loyal to him, Munro's Scottish army which had been raised by the anti-monarchial Parliament, and Parliament's own army. Charles needed the insurgents—because they were loyal to him—and yet he could not support them because they were revolting against his government. To add to this mix, the strange alliances formed in the Catholic Confederacy were beginning to show strain. Irish nationalism was grating against royalist leanings and European involvement was frightening Old English sensibilities. The cracks in the confederacy proved most fatal for its military operations. Momentum after decisive victories—as well as the strategic advantages that could have been gained— was dashed by disagreements within the confederacy. Rory O'More worked diligently as O'Neill's mediator, trying to negotiate with the Protestant general Inchiquin—who like Owen Roe O'Neill had been trained in the Spanish military—and with Ormond, the Lord Lieutenant who argued fiercely with the Confederacy that loyalty to Charles must define their alliance.

At the end of it all, after ten years of war, there was much waste and great destruction. In England, the monarchy was overthrown and Charles was beheaded. In Ireland, countless men, women, and children were put to death— Cromwell's reprisal for the Great Massacre of 1641. In 1652, fifty-two of the men who had plotted with Rory O'More, men such as Sir Phelim O'Neill and Sir Walter Bagenal, were executed.

But Rory had escaped that particular fate. It is believed that he died on Inishbofin, an island off the coast of Galway. He must have seen the course that events were taking and sought refuge on the island. Others report that he escaped to Scotland, perhaps to gauge the mood there which had so greatly vacillated between king and Parliament. One report has the great soldier disguised as a fisherman and escaping the island of Inishbofin. Nevertheless, he left the stage on which Ireland's history was unfolding. There is a sense of relief in knowing that he might have died before he saw it all collapse, before seeing his friends and comrades executed, and before seeing the dire repercussions that were to follow. One hopes he died before learning of the bloody repercussions that would ensue following his rebellion.

The name of Rory O'More, a name shared by three great Irishmen, is a glorious reminder of the nobility and courage, the strength and dedication to purpose that remained unvanquished in such men. It is in the worst of times that such men as Rory O'More rise to give hope to the hopeless, to hold out the possibility of a better world to those for whom such a possibility seems out of reach.

OWEN ROE O'NEILL

When Owen Roe O'Neill accepted the call to lead the Ulster rebellion in August of 1642, he had already served in the Spanish military for thirty years. He was not alone; the Spanish army was replete with Irishmen, with as much as 30,000 swelling its numbers following the flight of the earls, and it was renowned throughout the world as an estimable training school of highly skilled soldiers and officers. In addition to this military expertise, Owen Roe O'Neill—like Rory

O'More—had a name that resounded in the hearts of Irishmen. He was the nephew of the great Hugh O'Neill whom so many Irishman followed to Europe in search of funds and arms to battle the crown.

His years in Europe had given Owen Roe the reputation as a great figure and a legendary soldier. He had the aristocratic bearing and subtle mind that moved easily through the nuances of politics. (Although, whether any mind no matter how nimble could maneuver through the maelstrom that was English politics at the time is not an unreasonable question!) Like many on the continent, he was also filled with a certain Catholic zeal that he would use to his advantage once he returned to Ireland.

In April 1642, Owen Roe O'Neill accepted the offer from Rory O'More and the Catholic Confederacy to lead the Ulster rebellion. His arrival gave great encouragement to the Irish cause, for not only was the great O'Neill back on Irish ground but he had come with one hundred officers, with arms and money, and with many messages of encouragement from European powers. The continental assistance that the earls had left Ireland for at the beginning of the century seemed finally now to have appeared, and momentum and morale was high.

When O'Neill reached Ulster, he was devastated by what he saw. It looked like no place on earth, he exclaimed, but like hell. He used the summer of 1642 to build his army; rather than one army, the Confederacy had decided on four separate forces. One such army was headed by Thomas Preston, an Old English Catholic who, like O'Neill, had been in the Spanish military. It was this unsteady alliance between O'Neill and his Irish proponents and the Old English that would bring down the Confederacy. Despite its in-fighting, nevertheless, in November of that year, Owen Roe O'Neill swore allegiance to the Confederacy. He couched his uprising in language that stated he was not setting himself up against the king, thus placating the Old English, but was fighting for Catholic emancipation. Being an O'Neill, however, there was no doubt that he was also acting out of a familial ambition to see the old titles restored.

On November 12, 1645, the papal nuncio, Giovanni Battista Rinuccini, arrived in Kilkenny, the seat of the Confederacy. Before long, Rinuccini's policies would collide with the less Catholic concerns of the Old English, and soon there were three distinct factions: Rinuccini who wanted full restoration of Catholicism on one side, the Old English who supported Charles on the other, and a moderate middle-ground.

The Confederacy had brokered a deal with the Crown which had been intended to reconcile Old English Catholics within the Confederacy by defending the king who had been defeated and deprived of his army in June. But the process imploded. Charles, needing an army, had offered the Confederacy religious concessions if it would provide him with an army. The arrangements, however, were leaked before they could be implemented, and Charles found himself in the unenviable position of seeming to parley with the Irish insurgents and worse—to the Puritan minds in his Parliament—with the Catholics. He of course denied that such a plan had ever been made.

On June 5, 1646, General Munroe marched on O'Neill. His plan was to come from the northeast while the "Lagan army" commanded by two Scottish settlers, the Stewart brothers, came from the northwest. Together these two armies would squeeze O'Neill's force. But O'Neill had not trained thirty years in the Spanish army without learning something about military strategy. He was known as a patient man, and, as a soldier, he was no slouch. O'Neill prevented the two armies from meeting, and on the Blackwater River (close to the very site where his uncle had won the legendary battle of the Yellow Ford), he destroyed Munroe's army. Over 3,000 English and Scottish soldiers fell that day. Such a victory for the Confederacy—coming at such a time—should have led to a great conclusion. But the different factions working within the Confederacy were never as united as they might have wished, and the momentum of the battle was left to wither.

O'Neill's Catholic zeal may have grated against the more conservative Old English royalists in the Confederacy, but Rinuccini's rabid Catholicism truly threatened them. Two months after the victory at Benburb, a treaty was offered, called the "Ormond Peace." It rescinded the Oath of Supremacy for officeholders (which would allow Catholics to sit again in the Irish Parliament), repealed religious penalties, and restored landtitles. The majority of the Old English supported it. Rinuccini and the clergy did not. Again, unlike their Old English allies, the clergy were not as interested in appeasing Charles as they were in completely restoring Catholicism.

As all this unfolded, Rinuccini staged a coup, excommunicating anyone who favored the treaty. He was backed by Owen Roe O'Neill, who had traveled quickly to the south to denounce the treaty. For the moment, the Confederacy was under Rinuccini's control, but it was O'Neill's support that gave him power. O'Neill, who had just won what would be the most important victory of the time, had the strongest hand. Rinuccini would win the day—the agreement was rejected in February 1647—but his divisive tactics would bring about the end of the great Confederacy.

As Charles's reign grew more and more tenuous, Ormond unfortunately handed over Dublin to the Parliamentary army and left for England. (Eight thousand Roundhead soldiers had arrived in July.) The Confederate armies were being routed in battle after battle. When Ormond returned to Ireland in September 1648, even more staunchly supportive of the beset monarch, much of the Confederacy joined him as he led the royalist cause. His hope was to unite the various Irish armies, O'Neill's, Inchiquin's, and his own, and present a defense against the Parliamentarians. However, the time was too late. Charles was executed in January 1649. A month later, Rinuccini departed from Ireland, at the request of the Confederacy. The great dream of O'Neill and O'More, the hope embodied in the creation of the Confederacy, seemed to be crumbling. For all intents and purposes, there was no English king—that figure against whom Irish forces had for so long fought was no longer an entity. And in the vacuum came Oliver Cromwell.

He arrived in August 1649 and commanded an army of 20,000 zealous and highly skilled men. He had abolished the monarchy in England, and he was here now to take Ireland for England, once and for all. He was also bent on revenging the "Great Massacre" of 1641. Within a month, he stormed Drogheda, killing 3,500 soldiers, men, women, and children. He continued on to Wexford where he repeated the same. After that, it seemed, towns surrendered readily.

In the midst of Cromwell's nightmarish campaign, Owen Roe O'Neill died mysteriously in November 1649. There are some who say he was poisoned in Cavan as he made his way to join his forces with Ormond's and to challenge Cromwell. His death, no matter what its cause, removed from Ireland perhaps the only man at the time who might have successfully faced the great butcher. As the poet Davis wrote:

Did they dare, did they dare, to slay Eoghan Ruadh O'Neill?
Yest, they slew with poison him they feared to meet with steel.
May God wither up their hearts! May their blood cease to flow!
May they walk in living death who poisoned Eoghan Ruadh!

History had delivered many great heroes by the name of O'Neill, men who had fought more successfully against the English crown than most others. And with the death of Owen Roe, it seemed that the great line was crushed at last. But as I have said many times before this history is a great ironist and always has the last word. In the two years that Cromwell was in Ireland, he suffered only one defeat and that came at the hands of one of Owen Roe's nephews, another hero named Hugh O'Neill.

Chapter XIII:
A Short Biography of an Odious Gatecrasher of Irish History

I have a friend Tom McGuire who is an historian by trade, and a fine one at that. Now, when it came time to write about Oliver Cromwell, I was in a bit of a quandary. If I was writing a history of Ireland, which I surely was, wasn't it incumbent upon me to write a chapter about this man who carved out such an indelible gash on the historical landscape of the country? Yet, the nonhistorian in me, the proud man with proud Irish ties, couldn't bear to give such a man space in my slim volume of Irish lives. He wasn't Irish, heaven knows, so did he belong in this book? Yet, could one truly have a history of Ireland without giving this man space in it? So I ask my friend, the aforementioned McGuire, for his opinion.

Much of it I won't repeat, though the words "fanatic," "madman," and "megalomaniac" come to mind. He did give me one phrase that I liked very much. He said that he "out-Heroded Herod." Says I, "we'll leave it at that."

So here you have it, your chapter on Cromwell:

"He out-Heroded Herod!"

Chapter XIV:

Patrick Sarsfield, the Wild Geese, and the Penal Laws

When Oliver Cromwell came to Ireland in 1649, he was a man driven by a sense of religious fervor and righteousness, by racial intolerance, and by a sense of revenge for the Great Massacre of 1641. He was fiercely anti-Catholic (in England he granted tolerance to Jews and non-Anglican Protestants, but not to Roman Catholics), and the Catholics in Ireland rightfully feared the future with him in it. Indeed, after his campaign in Ireland, the total population had sunk to below a half-million. His desire was to make Ireland a second England, and once he quelled the rebellion, his goal was to make a lasting peace. This he would do, not by legal niceties with the Gaelic Order and the Old English as had been done in the past, but by simply confiscating the land. The ensuing Act of Settlement confiscated two-thirds of the land for plantation (11 million out of 20 million available acres were newly taken). And the Irish who remained were forced to move to the barren land of Connaught. "To Hell or to Connaught" was his decree. Although he spent less than a year in Ireland (he left his son in charge when he returned triumphantly to London), the damage he caused was irrevocable. He arguably caused more death and destruction than any man before or since on the island.

Cromwell, having rid England of its Anglicans, Scotland of its Presbyterians, and Ireland of its Catholics, was named lord-protector of England, Scotland, and Ireland in 1653, but his rule was not to last. He died in 1658, and while his son Richard was named his successor, this new Cromwell could not maintain the iron rule of his father. In 1660, the son of the executed Charles I, who had been in exile in France during Cromwell's rule, was restored to the throne. This period of Oliver Cromwell became known in history as the Interregnum, for it was a short space between the reigns of two monarchs. But in that short space, he left a mark of which all good men of feeling and justice should be ashamed, though Richard Harris, a fellow Limerick man, gave a flattering portrayal of him in the film *Cromwell*.

While the country was for the most part relieved that the monarchy had been restored, Charles II was not a particularly effective king. His stay in France, his critics claimed, had dandified him, and he—again—seemed too tolerant of Catholics. This fear of catholicity reached its pinnacle when his brother, James II, took the throne upon Charles's death. James II was a Catholic, and his zeal for the faith and his desire to impress it upon his subjects left many in Parliament anxious—as well as the Protestants who had settled Ulster. Within days of his ascension, there was an unsuccessful plot to have his nephew, Charles's son, placed on the throne. In 1687, James signed the Declaration of Indulgence that granted tolerance to Catholics and non-conformists. It was too much for even his allies in Parliament. With the birth of James's son the following year, Parliament set about to find a Protestant replacement. They invited James's Protestant daughter Mary and her husband, William of Orange, to London, and James fled, understanding the situation fully.

To try to gain back his throne, James raised an Irish army. It was a rallying cry for the Catholics in Ireland who had suffered so greatly since Cromwell, and who had already seen such great turnaround since James had come to power. Many placed their hope in the Catholic king. It was not, however, to be. James II was defeated by William of Orange at the infamous Battle of the Boyne on July 12, 1690. It is a date that still resonates through Irish politics today.

One of the Irish soldiers who followed James II was Patrick Sarsfield. A grandson of the great Rory O'More and a soldier well trained in the European armies, Sarsfield is known not only for his military successes for the Jacobean cause, but also for his retreat afterwards, a retreat known as the flight of the Wild Geese—an Irish diaspora, if you will, that sent Irish men to countries around the world.

PATRICK SARSFIELD

You have to love a fellow whose dying words on a battlefield in Belgium were, "Oh, if only this were for Ireland." But that was not to be. Indeed, Patrick Sarsfield was just one of many Irish men—the Wild Geese—who have fallen in foreign wars after 1691.

Patrick Sarsfield was born around 1650, near Dublin in Lucan. His mother was the daughter of Rory O'More who had started the great rebellion of 1641. Like many young wealthy Irish sons, he was trained on the continent in the armies of foreign powers. He studied at the French Military College, where he was noted for being more daring than strategic, and then served first in Luxembourg and then, from 1671 to 1678, in the army of Louis XIV of France.

With James II's ascension to the throne in 1685, Sarsfield took a position in the King's army in Dublin under the command of Richard Talbot, the powerful Earl of Tyrconnell. With Tyrconnell, Sarsfield went about organizing and modernizing the Irish army. Times, however, were turbulent in England—James had never been able to temper his Catholic zeal with practical politics, and he was making enemies even of the friends who had once approved of him. Consequently, when James fled to France, with him he took Patrick Sarsfield.

In France, an army of Irish and French soldiers with Sarsfield among them was formed with the purpose of returning the throne to James. In 1689, Sarsfield and his King landed in Kinsale with a sizeable force, and with the knowledge that in Ireland, there would be many more whom they could enlist.

The year 1689 was a momentous one for Sarsfield. He won important battles in Sligo and Connaught, and his prowess was rewarded in his moving up the ranks, first to cavalry commander and then to major general. In this same year, Sarsfield married Honora de Burgo, a truly extraordinary woman. That same year also saw him named as MP for County Dublin. In January 1690, the King made Sarsfield Baron Roseberry, Viscount of Tully, and Earl of Lucan. James's creation of titles for the men loyal to him seems somewhat puzzling as he was no longer on the throne and in exile from England. But nevertheless, Patrick Sarsfield was made the first Earl of Lucan. Meanwhile, William of Orange had landed in Ireland with a sizeable army. The legitimacy of the English monarchy was going to be settled on Irish land.

On July 12, 1690 (July 1 on the old Julian calendar), William of Orange's forces met the Irish/Jacobite army of some 25,000 men along the River Boyne. James's Irish army also included French, Dutch, German, and English soldiers. (The rest of Europe saw these wars in Ireland as an adjunct to the wars that William was waging in Europe against Louis XIV.) William had 36,000 men, and like James, his army was a *mélange of* continental soldiers. The battle lasted all day, and William's forces ultimately crossed the river Boyne and routed the Irish.

It is said that when the fleeing James II arrived in Dublin, he complained to Lady Tyrconnell that his Irish soldiers had all run away. His hostess, a woman with as sharp a tongue as mind, is said to have replied, "But your Majesty, you won the race!" James would leave Ireland entirely within the month, renouncing his claim to the throne.

The Battle of the Boyne is one of those moments that carry more weight in history than the actual actions warranted. It is seen as the moment when the Gaelic/Old English aristocracy was finally crushed and the Protestant aristocracy established itself fully in Ireland. It is still a date of contention, and each July there are great confrontations—political and social—when the Orangemen of Ulster celebrate the day that William of Orange routed the Catholic James II.

Now James II liked Sarsfield and admired his military abilities, yet he felt that his tendency to jump into a fray, his undaunted spirit, one might say, was also a liability. And thus, on this fateful day, he kept Sarsfield and his cavalry at the back of the forces to protect the rear for escape. We can never know what the outcome might have been if Patrick Sarsfield—who was nominally in command of the king's forces—and his men were at the front of the battle.

While James II gave up on his own cause, the Irish armies did not. They continued moving westward in front of William's pursuing armies. As he moved, William took city after city: first Dublin, then Clonmel, Kilkenny, and Waterford. The Irish army had garrisoned in Limerick, a Catholic city and an important stronghold. As William neared the city, disagreement broke out among the leaders whether the city could be defended. Tyrconnell and the French commander Lauzun believed they should surrender and evacuate. Sarsfield and the Duke of Berwick (who would later marry the widowed Honora de Burgo, Sarsfield's wife) believed they should not submit. The army was split, and Tyrconnell and Lauzun took the French troops and ordnance and evacuated the city for Galway and then to France.

Meanwhile, William made a costly mistake. Instead of besieging the city immediately, he decided to wait until his convoy of provisions, munitions, and supplies caught up to him. He and 40,000 men camped a bit southeast of the town, while those within the city wondered why they were delaying their attack. A deserter from William's army informed Sarsfield as to the reason of William's wait. And Sarsfield had a plan.

On the night of August 10, 1690, Sarsfield rode out of Limerick with a company of 600 handpicked men. Muffling their horse's hooves, they rode north of the city, through Clare and across the Shannon. They camped that night in the

Silvermines Mountains. Guided by one "Galloping Hogan," the leader of the Wild Rapparees, the force was able to navigate through the thick countryside and creep closer and closer to the train bringing William's supplies. Meanwhile, the convoy, feeling perhaps a bit over-confident, struck camp at Ballyneety. Horses were set out to graze, wagons were brought in close to a ruined castle wall, and only five or six men—who quickly fell asleep—were on guard duty. To add to Sarsfield's advantage, one of his men came across a woman going to Ballyneety to meet her Williamite husband. Unwisely, she gave the man the "password" to get into the camp—the password was "Sarsfield"!

As the Irish soldiers came upon the camp, they entered one by one. The first man got through with the password "Sarsfield." The second man was Sarsfield himself, and tradition records that he entered the camp with the words "Sarsfield's the word and Sarsfield's the man." (You should all know by now that a thing is verifiable or not, the fact that it's a great story is all that matters.) Sarsfield's men were now in the camp, and they routed the force protecting it. Half were killed and the rest escaped. But men were not the attraction of this particular sortie.

Sarsfield gathered all the wagons—150 of them filled with powder and ammunition, cannons, mortars, and pontoons—and heaped them into a pile. The cannons he filled with gunpowder, and their muzzles he stuck into the ground. The rest of the supplies and wagons were placed on top. With a thin line of gunpowder leading away from the pile, the Irish soldiers got safely away. The gunpowder was lit, and in a matter of minutes came the greatest explosion ever to rock the heavens over Ireland. The Irish made an easy escape, with Sarsfield's men first going to Portumna—the family estate of Sarsfield's in-laws—and then making their way to Limerick.

Consequently, William could not attack at the moment, and the Irish in Limerick were given time to regroup. Sarsfield's bold ambush had invigorated morale, and news that assistance from France was soon to arrive and knowledge of the coming bad weather (more to the English disadvantage than to the Irish advantage) gave the Irish hope. Finally, on August 17, William began his siege. He was not prepared for the resistance he met from Sarsfield and his men.

The siege of Limerick lasted only for two weeks. William lifted the siege and left Ireland. But his Irish wars were by no means over. In the summer of '91, when William's forces lay siege at Athlone and Aughrim, Sarsfield and his men rode out to defend the town. But as before, disagreements, politics, and personal jealousies divided the Irish commanders. The commander at Aughrim, a French general named St. Ruth, for some reason, allowed Sarsfield and his elite cavalry no active part in the battle. A battle, by the way, in which St. Ruth literally lost his head. By the time that Sarsfield learned of St. Ruth's death, the day was already lost. A strict military leader, whose men were disciplined, Sarsfield saved many lives in his orderly retreat from Aughrim. Other troops were not so lucky, as many perished in their chaotic escape.

Once again, Sarsfield was headed back to Limerick, and once again the Williamite forces lay siege to the town. This time Sarsfield would not be as successful in defending the garrison.

Controversy surrounds the capitulation of Limerick. The Irish soldiers far outnumbered the English, and the town itself could be taken only if attacked at once on all four sides. Food supplies were not an issue, winter was setting in, and a prolonged siege in winter would be unwise for the English. But capitulate Limerick did. On October 3, 1691, the Treaty of Limerick was signed. The Irish had made seven proposals, points that for the most part ensured Catholic liberties. None of these were agreed to. What was finally deliberated was a two-part treaty: civil and military. The civil part dealt with Catholic tolerance and the security of Catholic estates. The military treaty concerned how to deal with the Irish soldiers. The first part led in many ways to the establishment of the Penal Laws; the second part, for the flight of the Wild Geese.

As evidence of Sarsfield's character, after he had signed the Treaty of Limerick, a large number of French reinforcements arrived to support the Irish cause. Although he was counseled to tear up the treaty, he stated that by signing it, he had pledged his honor and would not go back on it. Unfortunately, the English who signed it were not so honorable. An important clause in the treaty had been left out of the "fair copy" sent to William. To his credit, William reinserted the missing clause and sent it back to be ratified. But the Dublin Parliament refused to allow William's insertion and abandoned many of the articles of the treaty. William should have known the limits to his power. He had been "invited" to the throne of England by a Parliament much stronger than the monarchy itself, a Parliament that could depose the sitting king at will. With the Treaty of Limerick, he had little power to insist on his word of honor that the treaty implied. For all practical purposes, the Treaty of Limerick was null and void.

The Wild Geese

As part of the military treaty, Patrick Sarsfield was allowed to go to France, and on December 22, 1691, he left Ireland with twelve ships and many men. (I have read differing accounts that put the number of soldiers between 2,600 and 20,000. Eleven thousand was the number that was most often quoted.) Like the earls who left with O'Neill at the beginning of the century, this second wave of Irish exiles left the country much poorer in spirit and heart. The Wild Geese, as they came to be known, proved themselves well in foreign affairs: in European, American, and African wars, as well as in the great expansion of the American West. And yet, as Sarsfield alluded to in his dying words, this bravery and sacrifice was sadly not for an Irish cause.

When Sarsfield landed in France, he was made captain of the second troop of the Irish Brigade. James II was there in exile, and together they organized the Irish troops with the purpose of attacking England. But a major defeat of the French at La Hogue proved fatal to their plans. The Irish were then subsumed into the French army, and continued to fight against William with their French counterparts, though now it was for the cause of France. Finally, while leading an attack in Flanders at the Battle of Landen, Patrick Sarsfield was mortally wounded. He died three days later, in the village of Huy in Belgium, his wife and son—named James Francis Edward after the Prince of Wales—by his side.

An interesting side story is that after Sarsfield's death, his wife and son were utterly impoverished, and for several years lived by the graveside where he was buried. Two years later, by a stroke of luck, the young Duke of Berwick came through the town of Huy. This was the man who had stayed with Sarsfield during the first siege of Limerick. He met with Sarsfield's wife and child, and was apparently very moved by their condition, for he married her and promised to look after and protect the son of the great Patrick Sarsfield.

Between 11,000 and 20,000 able-bodied men left Ireland in 1691 with Patrick Sarsfield. As had happened with the flight of the earls, their absence created a gaping abyss that was quickly filled by the Protestant aristocracy. Much of the land left behind was appropriated, and the increasing strength and breadth of the Protestant aristocracy could be directly linked to the loss of so many men. This loss of the native population would continue in waves throughout the coming centuries—primarily through famine and emigration. It would not be until the last decade of the twentieth century that that trend would be reversed.

THE PENAL LAWS

It was said that while the military portion of the Treaty of Limerick gave flight to the Wild Geese, the civil part would ultimately lead to the Penal Laws. Ever since the Protestant Reformation, the English crown had been imposing laws in Ireland that would segregate the Catholic population. It was this very segregation—of both Irish and English Catholics in Ireland—that led to many of the uprisings in the 150 years since Henry VIII's initial Oath of Supremacy was ordained. And it was against this type of legislation that the civil part of the Treaty of Limerick was addressed. Yet not only were the proposals made by the Limerick Irish never accepted, but the Treaty itself was soon abandoned and a strict code of laws put in its place. These laws were meant to make Ireland an all-Protestant nation and to rid the country of Catholicism once and for all.

While commonly known as "the Penal Laws," the formal name was "The Laws in Ireland for the Suppression of Popery." In general, the laws dealt with education, immigration, intermarriage, voting rights, employment, land holdings, family relations, criminal law, weapons, civic life, practice of religion, and the taking of oaths. Like apartheid in the twentieth century, their purpose was to disengage the Catholic majority from the political and economic power of the country. In effect through much of the eighteenth century, the Penal Laws began to unravel in the late 1700s. But their dismantling would be a slow process, and not until the Catholic Emancipation Act of 1834 would the Penal Laws be truly challenged.

Earlier, despite widespread and legislated anti-Catholicism, the Old English Catholics were still able to influence policy and maintain a measurable economic clout. Now, the Penal Laws were passed primarily to keep that from happening again, to separate the Catholic population entirely from the political system. Children were not to be educated at home and could not be sent to foreign schools. Only Protestant-run institutions were allowed for their education, if they were to be schooled at all. Intermarriages were forbidden, and for those that already existed, all property reverted to the Protestant mate and his family. Most positions were forbidden to Catholics: the legal profession, the army, civil service, and local corporations. Elected office was, of course, out of reach. No land owned by a Catholic could be bequeathed in a single block, but had to be divvied up among male heirs—thus effectively diminishing the land holdings of individual Catholics after several generations. Most holdings were on tracts of land suitable for subsistence farming only. And no Catholic could own a horse worth more than five pounds! Penal laws could be summed up with a couplet: "Catholics could not read nor teach, plead nor preach."

The laws were effective, and the Catholic population was demoralized and emasculated. There was no resistance. Ironically, the only resistance available to them—besides emigration, which further exacerbated the situation—was their religious observances, which continued through the services of the many clergy who remained, despite the Law in 1697 banishing all Catholic clergy from the country.

CHAPTER XV:

OLɪᴠᴇʀ Pʟᴜɴᴋᴇᴛᴛ

The Catholic Church in Ireland seems to have always traveled a different path from the rest of the world. And the seventeenth century was no exception. While anti-Catholicism was rampant and fierce in England during the 1660s and 1670s, with accusations that the Stuart kings were too lenient, with memories of the "atrocities" of 1641, and discoveries of "popish plots" everywhere, in Ireland it was not entirely the same. First of all, since the majority of the population was Catholic, simple economic logic necessitated to some degree "looking the other way," and Catholics by their sheer numbers made up a large part of the workforce. Secondly, while the mendicant friars went underground during the excesses of the Cromwellian era, working as tradesmen and laborers, they reemerged in the general relaxation of the 1670s under Charles II's reign. Indeed, such was the situation in Ireland before the Jacobite wars that the Protestant aristocracy was quite friendly with the Catholic bishops of their area.

One such bishop was a man named Oliver Plunkett. Born in Meath in 1629, Plunkett came from Old English heritage, with wealth and powerful family connections, and was in fact related to the Earls of Fingall and Roscommon. When he was sixteen years old, he went to Rome to study at the Irish College. He was ordained there in 1654, with a doctorate in both canon and civil law. (In Ireland at the time, as he was sure to have discovered, civil law was a much more powerful weapon than canon law.) He remained in Rome as a professor of theology at the College of Propaganda Fide, which was in charge of educating missionaries to Protestant and non-Catholic countries, and which also acted as the center for handling Irish affairs. (It would remain such until 1908.) In Rome, he also acted as a solicitor to the Vatican for Irish causes.

In 1670, Plunkett was sent home to Ireland as the Archbishop of Armagh. Such was Plunkett's spirited mind that for the next eight years he debated with the Archbishop of Dublin as to what was the true seat of primacy in the country. He argued that Patrick, after all, had made Armagh the center of Irish Catholicity, and Dublin's status came only from the influx of invaders who inflated its importance. Indeed, Plunkett's feistiness—and the firmness with which he held to his convictions—also made him many enemies. For example, in a dispute between the

Dominicans and the Franciscans, he sided with the Dominicans, and later he founded an order of Jesuits in Drogheda. The Franciscans were so outraged by his obvious preferences that in Rome the head was smashed from a bust of him in the Irish Franciscan House. Plunkett's Old English sensibilities often clashed with the native Irish among the Franciscans. In the end, it would be a Franciscan who would bring about Plunkett's downfall.

Yet Plunkett's most dangerous enemies were never to be his co-religionists, although a few would come back to betray him. Although the restoration brought Charles II to the throne, it did not abate the anti-Catholicism in England. And to many, Charles seemed too inclined to tolerate Catholics. Charles did seem to modify some of the measures enacted during the Cromwellian period, but his actions were always more political than religious. In 1661, Charles introduced the Law of Remonstrance. This law demanded that the Catholics of Ireland acknowledge Charles II as king "under pain of sin" and despite any contrary claims of the pope. (An attempt to modify the law came later, an oath negating any claim of temporal power that the pope might have.) The act, for whatever reason it was instituted, served to reignite the religious loyalty question that had inflamed the Confederate Wars twenty-five years earlier.

Always a firm believer in papal authority, Plunkett naturally opposed the Remonstrance Law, and he and a few others had to go into hiding. The Remonstrance issue, however, was simply a single symptom of a greater anxiety that England felt about the Catholic population.

In 1678, a disgraced Anglican clergyman named Titus Oates—who had spent time in a Catholic seminary—"uncovered" a plot instigated by the pope to assassinate King Charles. As a chaplain, Oates had been expelled from the British navy for misbehavior. He then entered the Jesuit school at Saint-Omer, where he was again expelled on the same vague charge. He also claimed to hold a doctorate from the University of Salamanca, but once more, that was a lie.

One day, for whatever reason, he met with a friend Israel Tonge, a rabid anti-Catholic. Oates unfolded some forged papers that looked very much like papal documents. The papers, he claimed, were from Don John of Austria, and the confessor of Louis XIV. In them was revealed a plot to assassinate the king, murder thousands of Protestants, and place the Duke of York on the throne of England. Tonge, a gullible audience if ever there was one, seized the papers and took them to show the king and members of Parliament. The plot was pure nonsense, yet the aftermath was brutal. In England, eighteen priests and several laymen were executed. The Queen's own secretary and physician, who were Catholics like her, were both executed. In Ireland, Catholic churches were closed in cities and towns, bishops and clergy banished, and several high-ranking bishops arrested.

Oliver Plunkett was arrested on December 6, 1679, charged with planning a French invasion and with inciting 70,000 Irish people to rise up, massacre the Protestant population, and found a Roman Catholic Ireland. Several priests, particularly one John Moyer, the vicar of the Armagh Franciscans, testified against him. Yet by the time the trial began in June in Dundalk, all the witnesses had recanted their testimony. So Plunkett was transferred to London, tried, and convicted.

The hysteria that had surrounded the "popish plot" had fizzled out, but the mood in London was not one of tolerance. The case against Plunkett was all but non-existent; the three priests who accused him were discredited; and there was nothing but hearsay to convict him. Yet convict him they did. The lord chief justice, Lord Pemberton, pronounced a sentence that seems cruel even for the most depraved criminal. Plunkett was to be hanged. Before he was dead, he was to be cut down and disemboweled, his bowels burned in front of his face. He was then to be beheaded and his body to be cut into four quarters. In an act of kindness, perhaps, the authorities allowed the king to decide what to do with the quartered body.

England was appalled. The case had proven to be such a travesty that even many English Protestants had come to side with Plunkett. The Earl of Essex, the very man who had had Plunkett arrested, pleaded with the king for Plunkett's pardon, assuring him that the man was innocent. Apparently, as the story goes, Charles lost his temper and asked why Essex did not appear during the trial. Plunket's blood, the king replied, would seem to be on Essex's hands and not on his.

Yet Charles was certain he could not risk pardoning this Irish bishop. Despite the reaction to the severity of the sentence, Charles knew that in his subjects' eyes, Catholic and Irish were the same thing, and both were to be mistrusted and feared. If he were to maintain his crown, he could not risk the smallest hint of leniency to this Catholic bishop. So on July 1, 1681, Oliver Plunkett was executed according to the judicial institutions.

A woman named Elizabeth Shelton, from a good Catholic family, petitioned the king to be allowed to gather the head and quartered remnants of Plunkett's body. She got permission and buried much of the body in the graveyard by St. Giles Church. The head and the two forearms she sent to the Sienna Nuns in Drogheda. They remain on display in St. Peter's Catholic Church to this very day.

In 1920, Oliver Plunkett was beatified, and in 1975, he was made a saint. He was the last Catholic martyr to be executed in England.

THE GREAT PATRIOTS

The eighteenth century is often referred to as the time of the Protestant Ascendancy in Ireland. What this really was about was a double-sided program that established and empowered the Protestant class, while at the same time disenfranchising and emasculating the Irish Catholics. The Ascendancy was the intended result; the Penal Laws codified those intentions. Its success can be measured in several ways. In 1703, for example, Catholic land ownership had fallen to a mere 14 percent of the country. Within fifty years, that had sunk further to a pitiful 5 percent. Poverty had so blanketed both urban and country Irish by mid-century that the dire descriptions of Ireland's poverty were readily recognized by English readers of Jonathan Swift's savage satire "A Modest Proposal" in 1745. Added to this legislated devastation were nature's own slaps; Ireland suffered crop failures and famines throughout the century, with four major failures in 1728, 1740, 1744, and 1756.

And while the Penal Laws increasingly were relaxed or ignored as the century stretched on, they had established a new spin on the traditional Irish/English enmity. No longer were the two sides identified as Irish/Old English versus New English. The Protestant Ascendancy had now segregated the country into two camps: the Anglican and the Catholic/Presbyterian. In many ways, it was these new divisions that would result in organizations such as the United Irishmen and in the emergence of such great patriotic men as Wolfe Tone, Robert Emmet, and Daniel O'Connell—two Protestants and a Catholic, respectively.

Yet there was also something else in the air of the eighteenth century. The American and French Revolutions of the last quarter of the 1700s had a profound effect on the Irish mind. Emigration from Ireland to America had been great—by 1790 nearly a half-million people of the American population were from Ulster alone—and sympathies with these fellow countrymen against their British foes ran high. Interestingly enough, these sympathies attached themselves more to the economic and tariff changes that were enacted between the New World and England than to any larger sense of liberty. On the other hand, the French Revolution proved to the Irish people that a mobilized populace could unseat a monarch—and for years the Irish celebrated the anniversary of the fall of the Bastille. The writer Thomas Paine, whose early works gave such encouragement to General Washington's troops (Washington was said to have printed copies of Paine's *Common Sense* to distribute to his cold and hungry troops at Valley Forge) was also a figure in the French Revolution. His *Rights of Man* became a tract well known and beloved by the Irish by the end of the eighteenth century. (As a matter of fact, Thomas Paine is still well-known in Ireland. I was sitting in The Mad Monk, a pub in Kinsale, in the summer of 2003 when this young man to whom I had just been introduced—Florin McCarthy—began lecturing me on Tom Paine, linking Paine's philosophy to the turmoils of the twenty-first century.)

With the stark contrast between elegant Georgian Dublin and the poverty of Irish Dublin and the rest of the Irish countryside, with the spirit of liberty proclaimed by the American and French Revolutions, with the increasing influence of newspapers and broadsides, and with the emergence of a newfound sense of unity and nationality among Irishmen, the last quarter of the seventeenth century seemed ripe for revolution in Ireland. Yet in the end, the century's uprisings and invasions, its well thought-out alliances and ambitious organizations, its hopes and dreams were crushed by forces beyond control. England had lost one great possession in the seventeenth century, and was determined not to lose another.

CHAPTER XVI:

WOLFE TONE

If you enter Stephen's Green in Dublin at the northeast corner, a little above Lower Baggott Street and before Kildare Street, you will see a modern sculpture of the great Irish patriot Theobald Wolfe Tone.

Theobald Wolfe Tone was born in Dublin in 1763. He was the oldest of sixteen children in a relatively prosperous Protestant family, though they would soon face dire economic woes. Ironically, Tone was born in a house behind Dublin Castle, the seat of Anglo-Irish government. Education was emphasized for all of the Tone children. Thus when he was eight years old he was accepted into the school run by the prestigious and liberal scholar Sisson Darling. So greatly did the young boy impress Darling that he recommended that the young Tone be sent to a preparatory school in Dublin that trained students for Trinity College. (At the time, Trinity College was called Dublin University.)

The school was a "classical school," and Tone became proficient in the Greek- and Latin-laden curriculum. (So proficient that after a while he decided that he could meet all expectations in two days rather than five, and spent a good time larking about Dublin on his self-appointed days off. In later life, he regretted these days of wasted opportunities.) It was at this school, however, that Tone first showed his interest in politics, and formed a debating society at the lower school. Perhaps it is noteworthy that around this time, when Tone was thirteen, the American Declaration of Independence was proclaimed. The politics of liberty was in the air.

His grades suffering from his lack of effort and his observation of the lure exerted on women by a military red coat, Tone at seventeen decided to join the British Army. Fortunately, his schoolmaster interfered and wrote Tone's father, who dissuaded his son. (In the most damning of ironies, Tone would ultimately be tried and convicted in a "court martial," never having served in the British Army.)

As hoped, Tone continued his studies and entered Trinity in 1781. The world that Tone entered was in many ways a rarified one. There was much privilege and status for a university student, and Tone took his part in it. But he also was a voracious reader, and the curriculum of the university fed his mind. This was the very literature of the Enlightenment. John Locke's treatises on government and liberty, the republican philosophies of Cicero and Demosthenes, these were the writings studied and discussed at the time, classical studies to be sure, but to the Irish student an extraordinary lesson in revolution and oratory. And more importantly for Tone, the ethos of the Enlightenment was not mere erudition, but action supported by thought and understanding.

Tone's mind may have been radicalized by the required readings, but his style was tempered in the great College Historical Society into which he was initiated in 1783. The society was the first debating society in all of the British Isles, and it had acquired a status in Ireland second only to the Irish Parliament. Since membership continued after graduation, and since so many of its members had gone on to political careers, it was not unusual for meetings of the society to be attended by current MPs, college faculty, and other professionals. With such a make-up, debate in the society tended to reflect the politics of the day, the concerns of the Irish Parliament itself. Throughout the 1780s, Tone would prove himself an invaluable, thoughtful, and respected member of this esteemed institution, and there he would meet friends whose influence would remain with him for the rest of his life.

Wolfe Tone was now a barrister—he had passed the bar in 1789—and his politics were with the Whig party, the opposition party in the British government. (He would sign his early writings simply, "a Northern Whig.") A minor crisis had developed when news of George III's madness broke. The English government wavered on giving power to the Prince of Wales, so the Irish Parliament suggested that the Prince of Wales be designated King of Ireland and George remain King of England. This proposal was quashed, as it seemed to separate the two countries more than England desired. It also had the consequence of creating a separate Irish Whig party—an official entity whose purpose was to argue against undue influence of the English crown. Tone grew enamored with their positions, and soon began attending sessions of Parliament regularly. Apparently, others were of Tone's mind, for in the 1790 election, the Whigs obtained control of the city government in a landslide vote.

It is, however, Tone's interest in the workings of Parliament itself that assumed importance at this time. Tone saw the Irish Parliament as an Irish institution more ready to serve British interests than Irish interests. The fact that three-fourths of the Irish people were forbidden to vote and had no representation in this Parliament was also a slap at the republican ideals he had discovered in the Roman and Greek writers of his education. And those same writers had insisted that a certain activism was required in such a republic. It was time for Tone to put his education to the test.

The first part of this action was political pamphleteering, and as he had done in his debates in the Historical Society, his writings were logical, well researched, and cogent. His first attempt, *A Review of the Conduct of the Administration During the Last Parliamentary Session* reflected his fascination with Parliament; his second, *The Spanish War!* separated him from Whig politics and revealed an astute and mature political mind. It also revealed a nascent sense of national Irish identity. This sense grew even more robust with Tone's next essay, *An Argument on Behalf of the Catholics in Ireland.* In it Tone stated that Ireland should be "free from Britain and free from religious oppression" and insisted on the common interests of both Protestant and Catholic in Ireland.

It is surely this sense of national identity that brought around the next step in Tone's political activity. On October 18, 1791, in Belfast and on November 9, 1791, in Dublin, Tone, along with Sam Neilson, Tom Russell, and Napper Tandy, founded the Society of United Irishmen. In Dublin, the organization was made up of both Protestants and Catholics, in Belfast, primarily Presbyterians. Both, however, were founded with the purpose of reforming Parliament and excising English control of Irish affairs. The greater purpose, however, was to unite all Irishmen, Catholic, Protestant, Dissenter, and Presbyterian.

Earlier, Tone and Russell had started up a newspaper, *Northern Star*, and this publication acted as the mouthpiece for the United Irishmen. Through discussion of foreign and domestic politics, *Northern Star* tried to educate its readership, which at its peak reached 4,000 people, and which was larger than any other contemporary paper. (*Northern Star* was closed in 1797 after its offices were wrecked by the militia. If anyone ever doubts the truth of the adage "the pen is mightier than the sword," think of all the times in history that absolute rulers and governments have tried to stifle writers. Those who write well are dangerous to those who try to stifle freedom.)

In 1792, Tone was made secretary of the Catholic Committee, which, although founded in 1756, had grown increasingly radical in the 1790s. In 1792, the committee held a convention in Dublin. The stated purpose was to petition the king for formal relief from the Penal Laws. What it revealed, however, was the ability to politicize, assemble, and organize a substantial mass of people. Tone was one of 231 delegates—including 48 members of the United Irishmen—who traveled to London to petition the king directly. (This was a deliberate snub of the Lord Lieutenant in Ireland and the Irish Parliament. Tone was not alone in realizing that this executive force too often acted with British interests at heart!) The petition was successful, for in 1793, the Catholic Relief Act became law.

How many times is the momentum of Irish history stopped by betrayal and loose lips? The United Irishmen were making inroads, particularly within the Volunteers. The latter were locally raised militias instituted in the second-half of the eighteenth century, when British forces pulled out of Ireland in order to fight the colonists in America, and could not be replaced afterward because of economic straits. By 1782, there were over 60,000 men; by this time they were also increasingly radical. Having a large force of armed men associating with patriots, radicals, and the freethinking of the French Revolution was a threat to Britain. In the meantime, the Protestant Wolfe Tone was using his legal expertise to defend Catholics throughout the country, to defend them in cases in which the Catholic Relief Act had finally armed them with legislative teeth. In fact, such was Tone's dedication that he had begun to move away from the United Irishmen, which he felt were devolving into something apart from their original intentions and losing much of their impetus.

In 1794, William Jackson, an Irish-born Anglican clergyman turned radical writer, had come to Dublin to get a reading on the will of the Irish people to a French invasion. His companion was John Cockayne, a spy for the government. Jackson and Cockayne joined the United Irishmen, and the two began to visit Hamilton Rowan, a fellow radical and United Irishman, who was in Newgate prison for a seditious speech he had given to the Volunteers the previous year. Rowan's prison, however, was more like a political salon, and he entertained visitors, including Tone. In the discussions between Tone and Rowan, Jackson noted that the two agreed that the Irish population would support a French invasion, and together they asked Tone to draw up a statement demonstrating such support and outlining the pros and cons. Tone did and sent it on to Rowan, but soon realized the danger of such a report, and asked for his original back. But Rowan had already made copies. Throughout all this political discussion, Cockayne was relaying intelligence back to England.

It is hard to give any traitor credit, but Cockayne, through cowardice or a newly found sense of honor, refused to sign anything that "named names." The only evidence was Tone's paper in Rowan's hands, and that, as one deputy told the Prime Minister, was short of proving any treasonable designs by the two.

Somehow Rowan escaped to France, and Tone was left to bargain with the English. They had little concrete evidence against him, the papers were all in Rowan's hand, and with Rowan having escaped and Cockayne refusing to testify, their case was thin. Nevertheless, Tone was exiled, and shortly after, the Dublin society of United Irishmen was suppressed. For his part, William Jackson was found guilty of treason and hanged.

Exile

Before Tone left for America, he traveled to Belfast, where he and his family were feted, a large subscription raised for their expenses, and plans made. With his friends Russell, Neilson, Simms, and McCracken, Tone swore never to stop their work until England's authority over Ireland was no more and Ireland had won independence. All the men believed at that time that any chance of this occurring lay in bringing the French into Ireland. They all agreed that as England was at war with France, the time was right; Ireland's opportunities were tied to England's troubles with France. And so on June 13, 1795, Wolfe Tone, his wife, his children, and his younger brother Arthur set sail on the *Cincinnatus* for America, although, as had been planned in the hills surrounding Belfast, his final destination was France.

On the trip across the Atlantic, their ship was stopped by three English frigates. A recruiting party boarded the ship of emigrates and for two days caused havoc on board. Finally they left, but only after "recruiting" all the deckhands but one and forty-eight of the passengers into the British navy. On August 1, the *Cincinnatus* arrived in Wilmington, Delaware, and Wolfe Tone and his family made the short trip north to Philadelphia, the new capital of the United States. Quickly, Tone discovered that Hamilton Rowan was in Philadelphia, having recently arrived from France. His friend Napper Tandy would arrive soon after. He also found that the political partisanship in America was similar to the divisions in Ireland: the Federalists who were in power were pro-British, while the Democratic Republicans were pro-French, as was the majority of public opinion. To Tone, this was no different from the divide between the Irish aristocracy and the Irish people. But most importantly in Philadelphia, he was introduced to the French minister in America, Pierre Adet.

To Adet, Tone made the following proposal: he had been authorized by his fellow countrymen to tell the French and the Americans of Ireland's plight and to ask for their assistance in detaching itself from England's chains. Logically he set out the premises for success. England was France's most powerful enemy; two-thirds of her navy was manned by Irish sailors; English military might in Ireland had dissipated greatly since the American Revolution; and almost 90 percent of the Irish population would support a French invasion. The time and situation, he concluded, was right for France to invade. Adet's initial reaction was anything but warm. But within months, the situation had changed.

France was upset with the pro-British attitude of the Federalist Party and was actively supporting the Democratic Republicans and their candidate James Monroe. Adet realized that Tone was valuable and even had a coded message sent to Monroe introducing Tone as a trustworthy ally.

In the meantime exile in America was proving difficult on Tone; he suffered the heat and humidity, was exasperated by the expense of living in Philadelphia, and moved several times looking for lodging, finding the American people to be greedy, unlettered and uncouth, and worrying about his wife and children. This unhappiness solidified Tone's identity with Ireland, and by extension his republicanism. Finally, Adet came through; he was to leave for France. He spent his last day in Philadelphia with his Irish friends, Reynolds, Rowan, and Tandy, and traveled to Princeton to make arrangements with his wife. (Matilda, his wife, was pregnant at the time, but did not tell Tone in fear that it might dissuade him from leaving. She would inform him later when it was too late to change plans.) He moved on to New York, where he bought a ticket to France aboard the *Jersey*. He was now a republican agent and no longer Wolfe Tone; he had been given a new passport under the innocuous name of James Smith. On January 1, 1796, the *Jersey* set sail.

In France, Tone was backed by James Monroe, although as an American, Monroe's favor was running thin, as the French grew increasingly frustrated with the American government's pro-British stance. Monroe had also helped in getting the release of Thomas Paine, who was now a long-termed if unwelcome guest in Monroe's home. To be in conversation with such a republican luminary as Paine must have been encouraging to Tone's republican hopes for Ireland. Tone noted that Paine was much wittier in person than on paper, and the two enjoyed many conversations about the relationship between religion and government—a relationship which was anathema to Tone, but less so to Paine. Tone was not confident speaking French, so Monroe served as linguistic support when Tone needed to negotiate with French officials.

Yet despite his own insecurities, Tone was a creditable agent in France, and finally he negotiated a sizable invasion force for Ireland. To head this invasion was France's most illustrious general, General Louis Lazare Hoche. (In fact, in 1796, the only man who rivaled Hoche was the diminutive Bonaparte, who was beginning to make a name for himself in Italy.) Always impressed by military men— remember his own youthful desire to enlist—Tone idolized Hoche. Yet despite Hoche's eminence, there were problems. The plans for the invasion changed numerous times, causing delays. Tone argued for a northern landing, where a sizeable Ulster force would augment their impact. Hoche was wary of the Irish Sea, and insisted on a southern landing. Secrecy was also tantamount, but foiled uprisings in Ireland seemed to warrant some message to the rebels that aid was forthcoming. In November 1796, many of Tone's friends in Ulster—including McCracken, Russell, and Neilson—were arrested. Finally, on December 15, almost a year to the day since Tone left Philadelphia, an impressive French Armada set sail from Brest. Hoche was commanding forty-three warships and 50,000 men. There were more guns, ammunition, and ordnance than had ever before headed to Ireland.

Oh, when one thinks of missed opportunities! Bad weather and poor sailing separated the fleet; only seventeen of the original forty-three stayed together. One ship had foundered and lost most of its 1,300 men. The *Felicite*, the ship Hoche personally was commanding, was missing, through a mistake in naval signals, and because of his insistence on secrecy, none of his other commanders knew their destination. Finally, on December 20, the commanders of the remaining ships opened their sealed packets to learn that they were headed to Bantry Bay.

When the ships finally arrived in Bantry Bay on December 21, many of the commanders were already assuming that the expedition had failed. The fleet now numbered thirty-six ships. Seventeen entered the bay, and nineteen remained just outside, but once again severe weather played havoc, and by the next morning, the ships were all separated again. A mere 6,400 men, four pieces of artillery, no horses, and a paucity of supplies, remained of the grand plans for the invasion. Despite this, a desperate optimism seemed to rise and argue for continuing with the inva-sion. Once again, raging weather ruined their plan. Ship after ship began cutting anchor and sailing home to France. On New Year's Day, Tone's ship and seven others entered the port of Brest. Three ships had already arrived, and four more showed up a few hours later. Of the forty-three that had embarked with such hope on December 15, only fifteen had made the journey home to France.

The great invasion had failed through bad luck and incompetence. Referring to 1588, Tone himself noted that once again England had survived a seemingly invincible armada. (An interesting sideline to this ill-fated adventure: one ship that never made it back to France, the *Surveillante*, had been scuttled off Whiddy Island off Bantry Bay. It was not discovered until 1982.)

Tone felt himself a defeated man. He assumed that he would never be able to induce the French once more to invade, and there was no chance of his ever returning to Ireland. So he resigned himself to spending the rest of his days in France. But the French—and particularly Hoche—did not lose interest in the Irish situation. Tone was made an adjutant general in the French Army.

As new plans were drawn, new obstacles arose. France's wars on the continent were a priority for the Directory, and the man most involved in these was Bonaparte, for whom Ireland played a small role, if any at all, in his own plans for empire. Tone's family had now settled in Hamburg, while Tone was stationed with Hoche along the Rhine. Communication with his countrymen at home was hard when it existed at all, and much of the news Tone received was from fellow Irishmen on the continent or newspapers. The United Irishmen were getting impatient with France and were considering open revolt without French aid. The possibility of a French-Englandish peace treaty also necessitated the rapid deploy-ment of a French invasion, for it was believed that if such a treaty were broached, France would lose interest in Irish affairs. A two-pronged Dutch/French invasion was planned and nearly embarked upon, but was crushed when Hoche marched on Paris to counter a royalist attempted coup. The great general, so admired by Tone, would die shortly after, a broken man in spirit and body.

Meanwhile, as plans for a French invasion wavered, a series of uprisings occurred in Ireland in late May and early June 1798. In Dublin, Kildare, Meath, Wexford, Ulster, and Connaught, small bands of rebels, loosely tied to the United Irishmen, struck out. Undermined by a lack of coordination, the insurrection of 1798 resulted in an estimated 30,000 deaths on both sides and a horrifying orgy of savagery and butchery. One report, for example, describes lines of peasants attacking cannons with pitchforks. In Wexford, the rebels set up an interim government, which maintained control for nearly three weeks. In Ulster, separate armies of 4,000 and 7,000 men fought in Antrim and in Down. The rebellion of 1798 had been effective, and with French help, might have successfully routed the English. Instead, it revealed to the government the tinderbox it was sitting on, and draconian measures followed.

The need for French action had never been more immediate, and on September 6, 1798, another "French armada" set sail for Ireland. It too, like the invasion of Bantry Bay three years earlier, was buffeted by severe weather and incompetent seamanship. When this second invasion finally arrived off the north coast of Ireland on September 16, the British were waiting. In fact, the fleet was actually about two months too late, for the uprising of '98 had come to an end with the defeat at Vinegar Hill. By September, much of the rebels' momentum had been lost.

The French navy had rarely been a match for the British navy, and this invasion stayed true to form. After a short naval battle near Lough Swilly, the British captured all of the ships and all of the men. As an officer in the French Army, Wolfe Tone sailed aboard the French ship *Hoche*, named after the man he admired and with whom he had plotted so long. Captured, he should have been treated as a prisoner of war, for the English were unaware that this officer James Smith was actually Tone. (Indeed, throughout the entire French exile, the deception that Tone was still in America had remained intact to all but the innermost circles of British government. When Fitzgibbon pilloried Tone in Parliament in connection with his involvement in the Bantry Bay invasion, it was news to most of the sitting members.) Tone most certainly knew that if he was discovered, French officer or no, he would be treated as a traitor to the Crown.

Capture, Trial, and Death

Old enemies seem to have good memories, and Tone was done in by a loyalist lawyer against whom he once argued. On November 3, 1798, Wolfe Tone stepped off a prisoner boat in the town of Bunkrana in Donegal. The old legal opponent, Sir George Hill, recognized him and England discovered the great prize they had inadvertently snared. (There are other stories that claim that the British knew all along of the identity of their captive.) Despite never having served in the British Army, a court martial was set up in order to try Tone. And to make matters worse, the Lord Lieutenant of Ireland overseeing Tone's case was General Cornwallis. This was the same Cornwallis who twenty years earlier had had to surrender to General Washington in Yorktown. He had come home humiliated, having been defeated and forced to surrender to what he saw as a band of lawless rebels. Cornwallis had been cowed once by rebels; he would make sure it would never happen again to him. Consequently, Cornwallis ran the court martial without any regard to legal procedure and precedent. There was to be only one outcome in this trial and that was to be Wolfe Tone's execution.

Tone was brought to Dublin in irons and under full military guard. Just outside of the city, Tone changed into his full military uniform, for he was always a man concerned with his own sense of dignity and honor. On November 10, he was tried by seven military officers and a judge advocate and the charge of treason was read out to him. Tone asked for—and was given—permission to read out an explanation of his actions and his only disagreement with the charges was that he wanted the word "traitorously" removed from the charges. It was testimony to Tone's honest belief that his actions were guided by the noblest and most enlightened reasoning. A member who felt that the speech itself was incendiary stopped him once in the middle of his speech, but he was allowed to continue after being warned. At the end of his speech he also asked that he might be given the dignity of a soldier and shot by firing squad. This was not promised, as it was entirely in Cornwallis's hands.

The following day, November 11, Tone spent writing letters to the French government and arranging financial assistance for his wife and family. He wrote to several of his old friends, to his father, and to his wife. He also learned that day that he was to be publicly hanged at Newgate at 1 P.M. the following day, at the request of his Dublin enemies.

That night Tone cut his throat with a penknife, severing the windpipe. Four separate surgeons stitched the wound and saved him from dying—so that he could hang the next day.

On that following day, a challenge to the military court was successfully filed, and the sitting judged ordered a writ of *habeas corpus*. When made aware of the impending execution, the judge sent word to the barracks where Tone was held to suspend the execution. The commander in charge refused to obey the court's order, saying that his ultimate duty was to Cornwallis, the Lord Lieutenant. The judge ordered Tone to appear in court, and that is when the court learned of Tone's attempted suicide. It was told that removal of Tone would kill him instantly.

Tone's worsening condition postponed the execution, and during the week, his health deteriorated greatly. The wound was infected and his lungs were inflamed. Rumors said that he had been placed in restraints to prevent another suicide attempt.

The story goes that Tone's surgeon, while examining him, ordered him not to move his head in a certain way, as it would kill him instantly, and Tone supposedly thanked the doctor for the kindest words he had ever received. He moved his head precisely the way that he had been warned about and died. Whether the story is true or not, no one knows, but on November 19, 1798, Wolfe Tone was a corpse.

His body was taken to the house where his parents were staying. There a death mask was made. On November 21, he was buried in County Kildare, in the family plot at the Bodenstown Churchyard Cemetery. The grave itself would remain unmarked for the next fifty years.

If Cornwallis had created an Irish martyr in Wolfe Tone, then Tone's wife Matilda ensured that that martyrdom would be honored and well publicized. She and her son carefully edited Tone's memoir—which to this day is a masterpiece limning the development of a political mind and the ideals of the enlightenment—and she zealously guarded his name. She was twenty-nine at the time of her husband's death, and the promises from friends that Wolfe Tone had wrangled to support her rarely materialized. She did receive a pension from France, garnered after much campaigning on her part and the personal involvement of Napoleon. Yet she was wary of the Irishmen in France and their hope of appropriating Wolfe Tone's name to their various causes. Ultimately, she married an old family friend and moved to America, living in the Georgetown neighborhood of Washington, D.C. She much preferred the American-Irish to the French Irish, and allowed Tone's name to be used by the different organizations that were rising around a growing Irish-American identity. Her success in guarding the legacy of Wolfe Tone

and her own identity as the great patriot's widow was evidenced by her funeral,
which was attended by military officers, members of Irish societies, and the French
ambassador to America. She had ensured that the name of Wolfe Tone outlived
the Dublin acrimonies and the scandalized reactions to his suicide. In its stead, the
name of Wolfe Tone became synonymous with the righteousness of the fight for
Irish independence.

CHAPTER XVii:
RObERt EmmEt

Bold Robert Emmet, the darling of Ireland,
Bold Robert Emmet will die with a smile,
Farewell companions both loyal and daring,
I'll lay down my life for the Emerald Isle.
—"Robert Emmet" *by Tom Maguire*

Ironically, I know this song primarily through a recording by an Irish folk group
called the Wolfe Tones. They are a talented band famous for their straightforward
republicanism, and in times of peace talks and accords, their songs of past republican heroes have irked not a few. But they play well, and like the bards of old
Ireland, they maintain for us memories through song of many a hero who might
otherwise be forgotten. For in Irish history, the poetry and the drama of a man's
life are often as important—if not more so—than the events that he precipitated.
Never is this more evident than in the case of Robert Emmet. His bold speech

from the dock just before his execution and romantic verses of his life by his friend, the poet Thomas Moore, ensured Robert Emmet's memory as one who made the ultimate sacrifice for his native land.

Robert Emmet was born in 1778 into a respectable Protestant family, with his father serving as doctor to both the Lord Lieutenant and the British Royal family whenever either of them deigned to visit Ireland. His brother was Thomas Addis Emmet, a leader of the United Irishmen and a good friend of Wolfe Tone when the two were at Trinity College together. Emmet also attended Trinity, but by then Ireland was a much more volatile place. As an undergraduate in 1799, Robert Emmet was expelled from Trinity for his membership in the United Irishmen during the repercussions that followed the 1798 insurrections and narrowly avoided arrest by fleeing to France. His brother Thomas had been active in the original United Irishmen, and in fact, in 1795, had publicly taken the United Irishmen's oath defying the Act of Insurrection. He was now one of its leaders, despite the fact that the organization was splintering, both from its Belfast counterpart and within itself.

Yet other forces were at play besides the unsuccessful rising of 1798. For a while, the Act of Union had been a contentious point of political debate. The Prime Minister, William Pitt, supported it, for he believed that Ireland's union with England would defuse any animosity of the Irish toward England. Irish Protestants were against it, for they felt that if the two countries were united, English lawmakers would not protect their interests as well as they were protecting them at home. For the exact opposite reason, the Act was supported by the Catholics. As these lines became drawn the focal point of Irish resistance moved away from the republicanism of Tone and towards Catholic emancipation. It was Robert Emmet who would continue in Tone's path, a middle-class Protestant fighting for a united Ireland's independence.

The Act of Union was enacted in 1800. It had been rejected by the Irish Parliament in 1799, but bribes, sinecures, and promises of Catholic emancipation were enough to turn the vote the following year. At the beginning of 1801, Ireland officially became part of Great Britain.

In the meantime, Thomas Addis Emmet was in Paris, as an emissary of the United Irishmen. It was a difficult time for Ireland, for France and England had signed a peace treaty in 1802, and France, despite its failure to deliver on several occassions, was still a tangible hope for the United Irishmen. As a leader of the United Irishmen, Thomas Emmet was busy negotiating with Napoleon. Both Emmet and Napoleon knew that the fragile peace with England could not be maintained (they were right; it lasted a little more than a year), and the Irishman was urging Napoleon to use Ireland as a launching point for an invasion of England. The outlook for a successful uprising looked bright: France had promised troops; revolutionary societies in both England and Scotland had pledged support; and many Irish were committed to the rebellion.

Robert Emmet—never as circumspect and careful as his older brother— returned to Ireland as soon as the French and English had started fighting again. His job was to coordinate activity throughout the country, particularly in Dublin, Wexford, and Carlow, gather and amass weapons, and wait for the French to arrive. When one of his weapon caches exploded in a house on Patrick Street, Emmet believed that his plans were soon to be discovered. And so he decided on his own to move up the rising, without waiting for the French.

The plan had always been to attack Dublin Castle, which would be a signal for other flare-ups across the city and throughout the country. Emmet's early implementation of the plan verged on the farcical. The usual culprits—informers, lack of communication, and poor coordination—wrecked what was a hastily thrown together, piece-meal uprising. On July 23, 1803, Emmet and eighty men, in broad daylight, marched out against the castle. Bystanders joined in and the attack resembled more of an urban riot than a military incursion. The only success was taking control of James Street and Thomas Street, but even this glory lasted only a few hours before being retaken by soldiers. Another aspect that went according to plan was the printing up and distributing of Emmet's *Proclamation of the Provisional Government.* In it, he wrote, "we war not against property—we are against no religious sect—we war not against past opinions or prejudice—we war against English dominion." Stirring words, but the uprising was squashed, and Robert Emmet escaped into the Wicklow Mountains.

Now this is when the story takes on its mythic and romantic shadings. Emmet had a girl, the "bright love" of his life, Sarah Curran. On the run he stayed in contact with her, writing letters describing his dream of an independent Ireland, declaring his love, and asking her to elope with him to America. When he was captured on August 25, he was carrying unsigned letters from her in his pocket. When pressed to reveal who they were from, Emmet reportedly answered "a delicate and virtuous female." He kept her name completely out of the court proceedings, stating that he would rather give up his own life than injure another. The thought that Emmet had stayed in the area and risked arrest because of a woman increased the romanticism of his story.

Surely the poetic and romantic lines Emmet spoke to his captors were instrumental in building the mythology, but even if he had never spoken them, his words of farewell, spoken in the dock, were sure to enshrine him in the pantheon of Irish martyrs. On September 19, 1803, Robert Emmet was tried for treason, and on the following day, he was hanged and beheaded along with twenty-one others. The emotional speech he gave after the reading of his sentence was interrupted by the court seven separate times, because the wording was so powerful, so moving, and, to the English mind, so incendiary. "Let no man write my epitaph," he announced. "When my country takes her place among the nations of the earth, then shall my character be vindicated, then may my epitaph be written." And no epitaph was written for Robert Emmet. Always powerful with words, he was even more so in silence.

The Irish, accustomed to defeat, have a soft spot for their failed heroes, and will have a song or poem written to cover lack of success.

For Emmet's deeds were not great; greatness lay in his hopes, his dreams, and his ideals, and above all his words, which could inflame hearts and fill them with vision. In this, he would prove an inspiration to later nationalists, to men like Padraig Pearse, who saw in Emmet's death a "sacrifice" that was "Christ-like in its perfection."

CHAPTER XVIII:
DANIEL O'CONNELL

To this day, the most Irish part of the country is in the west. It is where the language is spoken more than anywhere else and where the rocky countryside is a far cry from the European-like cities of the east. For this is where Cromwell drove the remaining Irish Catholics in the early seventeenth century. And it is from the west, from County Kerry, that Daniel O'Connell emerged.

O'Connell was raised in a thoroughly Gaelic world. Irish was O'Connell's first language, and he later spoke English and French as well. And as in the ancient Gaelic tradition, O'Connell was sent to a peasant family to be fostered, and stayed there until he was four years old. When he returned, he and his brother (O'Connell was the oldest of ten) were adopted by their uncle Maurice, who had the intriguing nickname "Hunting Cap."

One wonderful story goes that after sending his child to the peasant family, O'Connell's father, Morgan, came across the young boy playing in the fields. Wondering about the boy's nutrition, the man asked his unknowing son if he ever was given meat to eat. "Certainly," replied the boy. "My father just stole one of Morgan O'Connell's sheep, and we have dined mightily." This was the world from which O'Connell emerged.

Now it was not only the farming out of children or the Irish language that came straight out of the past, but also the O'Connell's main source of income—a source that dated well before Granuaile herself. The O'Connells were smugglers, and Hunting Cap was the manager of all their enterprises. West Kerry was a hard land, and Kerrymen were hard men, but for Daniel O'Connell, the world of County Kerry would always be a peaceful haven for him, a remove from the intrigues and bustle of the larger world.

The O'Connells were also one of the few remaining Catholic families that retained significant property after all the confiscations, plantations, and forced settlements of the previous centuries. They lived well and maintained a cosmopolitan worldliness—primarily with their "trading" enterprises throughout the world—that would have surprised any visitor. Hunting Cap even became a Justice of the Peace after the Catholic Relief Act in 1793. O'Connell was raised to believe he was as good as any man; hence his passion for equality.

When he was fifteen, Daniel and his brother Maurice were sent to France to receive a classical education. O'Connell's talent, drive, and determination were such that after only one year, his headmaster wrote to Hunting Cap to say that if O'Connell did not become something remarkable, he would be surprised. In 1792, the two boys moved from the school at St. Omer to the English College at Douai, but the French Revolution interrupted their studies, and the two returned home on the day the king was executed. (It has been suggested that the excesses of the French Revolution played a role in O'Connell's non-violent philosophy.)

O'Connell went to London, where it was decided he should try for the law. In 1794, he enrolled in Lincoln's Inn—Catholics were now admitted to the profession of barrister. More importantly, he also set out on a course of reading and self-education that would radicalize him, moving him away from the conservative politics of his prosperous Irish Catholic upbringing. His reading was wide, and the writers that most influenced him were Godwin, Locke, and Paine.

In 1796, O'Connell returned to Dublin in order to be eligible for the Irish Bar. Like Wolfe Tone a few years earlier, he began attending debates in Parliament and participating in the Historical Society. For the next few years, as his political development proceeded, O'Connell joined the Volunteers, worried about the effects of the Bantry Bay invasion, debated with the United Irishmen, but primarily stayed on the peaceful resolution side of the fence. If he acted otherwise, he believed, all he had worked for could come to naught. Indeed, it was rumors of his association with the United Irishmen that caused him to leave Dublin in 1797 and return to Kerry. He probably was a member, but as the United Irishmen began more and more to accept the necessity of violent rebellion, O'Connell grew disenchanted.

In 1800, Daniel O'Connell stepped onto the stage of Irish politics. (The stage is a metaphor he himself used in outlining his plans to his uncle.) It was a debate on the Act of Union, an argument divided pretty evenly between Protestant "nays" and Catholic "yeas." O'Connell was in the minority of Catholics who were against the act. O'Connell's speech is notable for enunciating a running theme in his life: that he was being forced to speak as a Catholic, when in fact he was speaking as an Irishman. The promise of emancipation that the pro-union voices had offered was an empty one, he told his listeners. Dramatically, he stated that given the choice, he would rather have the old Penal Laws than the new Act of Union. He would fight against this Act—even after it was passed—for the rest of his life.

In his speech, O'Connell went against the politics of his Kerry family and particularly of Hunting Cap, who were all pro-Union. He countered him again two years later, when he secretly married a penniless cousin, Mary O'Connell. Hunting Cap had wanted his adopted son to marry a moneyed heiress, and he never forgave this. When Hunting Cap died in 1825, he had reduced the portion of his estate previously bequeathed to O'Connell.

After the 1800 debut speech, O'Connell—like Wolfe Tone before him—spent much of his time defending Catholic interests in the courts. However, it was in the courtroom that O'Connell earned the sobriquet that would stick on him forever: "The Counselor." One contemporary stated that Daniel O'Connell might be the finest counselor in all of Europe. He was certainly the best in Ireland.

This success, in a way, also fed his passion for equality, and his proven skill in the courtroom would not allow him to permit a Protestant colleague to claim superiority based solely on his Protestant background. For O'Connell, trained in the spirit of the Enlightenment, the equality of man was more than just a high-flying phrase.

O'Connell was an Irishman, and a Kerryman at that. He knew the Irish people, and this knowledge aided him in the courtroom. His dramatic flair, his quick temper, his mastery of language, and his many victories soon made an O'Connell courtroom session a spectacle for the local folk. One story goes that in a case involving the testimony of a dead man, O'Connell noticed that each of the witnesses answered the question as to the man's life or death with the same phrase: "There was life in him." Again, O'Connell knew his people, and after hearing the same words repeated, he understood what was going on. When he asked the next witness if he had put a live fly in the dead man's mouth in order to be able to speak a truthful statement—there was life in him—the man crumbled at O'Connell's perspicacity. O'Connell won the case and amazed the onlookers.

O'Connell was gaining renown as a barrister. It would be almost a decade after his first speech that he would draw notice as a political leader. In 1809, O'Connell again spoke out against the Act of Union, an act that had been in force since 1801. This time, he spoke not to Catholics but to the Dublin Corporation, a group of Protestant businessmen, whose enterprises had suffered since Union had been enacted. Again O'Connell harped on the same theme he had introduced in 1800: that Irishmen—of whatever religion—were bound by nationhood. The Act of Union, he insisted, exacerbated religious differences to the detriment of all Irishmen. And again, he claimed that the draconian Penal Laws were preferable to the devastation of the Act of Union.

From this speech, O'Connell was catapulted into political action. Soon afterwards, he organized the Catholic Association (not to be confused with the much larger Association he founded in 1823). What is noteworthy about O'Connell's organization is that its members did not come from the upper level of Irish Catholics, but from the poor. O'Connell rightly believed that similar previous organizations had failed because their upper-crust members had too much at stake to lose. As one American singer would say some two and a half centuries later, "When you've got nothing, you've got nothing to lose," and so O'Connell reached out to the poor, to the people who had the most to gain and the least to lose.

O'Connell was a tough Kerry man, and once he entered into political activism, he was like a bulldog. He organized associations in various towns throughout the country. In 1811, he convened an assembly in Dublin of all the delegates from the outlying towns. The government deemed these actions as illegal under the Convention Act, and swooped in to arrest many attendees. O'Connell held another meeting six months later. More arrests. Three months later, he held another assembly. One of the men arrested went on trial. O'Connell defended him and won. His fame and influence were growing more and more.

At the time, a political issue was coming to the forefront after having been bandied about for several years, and that was Catholic Emancipation. Such a law would remove many of the barriers imposed on Catholics by the Penal Laws, particularly those barring Catholics from entry into particular professions and official positions. And while Emancipation seemed to be perfect for the plight of Irish Catholics, it was being bundled with a more nefarious bill: the Veto Act. This legislation gave the British government the power to veto any church appointments, as well as the power to appoint commissioners to examine and regulate all correspondence from Rome. Worst of all, Rome agreed to it. (Coziness with the British Parliament, apparently, was more important for Rome at the time than its Catholic flock in Ireland.)

O'Connell's fight against this was difficult, for he was essentially fighting against Catholic Emancipation, but he saw the Veto Bill as a Trojan horse that would cause more ills than emancipation would cure. The Bill met defeat, but in taking his stance, O'Connell lost many Catholic supporters.

Here's a story of how determined O'Connell could be when attached to an issue. The Secretary of Ireland at the time was a man named Robert Peel, a fierce anti-Catholic who, to O'Connell, represented everything wrong with the Protestant Ascendancy. Indeed, he had already dissolved the Catholic Board in Dublin. O'Connell, who was known for having a blistering tongue, once stated that Peel would never say in public the things about O'Connell that he said in the safety of Parliament. Peel took up the dare and challenged O'Connell to a duel! Both men's handlers were nervous, of course, and the duel was moved to England. O'Connell was arrested on his way to the fight, and the affair lost wind. But O'Connell's readiness to duel with the very Secretary of Ireland must have made for some great stories in the streets of Dublin. It certainly enhanced his reputation with the common people.

In 1821, a new relief bill—giving Catholics everything they dreamed of—went before Parliament, but, as with the Emancipation Act, the Veto Bill had been attached to it. O'Connell stood firm and brought the Irish clergy onto his side, and the bill was again defeated in the House of Lords.

O'Connell realized the latent power of the poor Catholic population, and with that power, he was establishing democracy in Ireland. First, he began to court the clergy, the small town priests, who, since Catholics had no elected official they could trust, held enormous sway with the common people of their parishes. In 1823, he founded the Catholic Association of Ireland—and he invited the poor to join in. He began what were known as the Catholic Rents: a penny a month. People laughed at the paltriness of such a "rent," but the action worked in two ways: One, there were an extraordinary number of Catholics paying the rent, and the monies added up. And two, symbolically and morally, it gave the poor Catholics some sense of participation, some dignity and some hope in the system that had so long ignored them. (Remember, past "Catholic" organizations were run from the top up. O'Connell's associations included the more numerous bottom and middle.) The monies were used not only to help finance the needs of the Association, but to help impoverished men take their claims to court.

How effective were he and his association? In 1826, a Parliamentary election in Waterford pitted a liberal Protestant against Lord George Beresford. It was a foregone conclusion. The Catholics voted as their landlords told them (on pain of eviction), and Beresford was assumed to be the winner. But, O'Connell told them, the landlords could not evict every peasant, and the peasantry voted in the liberal Protestant. O'Connell shocked the governing establishment by showing how he could organize and get out the vote.

The next voting success was even more impressive. In 1828, Vesey Fitzgerald—a pro-Catholic MP from Clare—was placed in the new Prime Minister's cabinet.

The law required that in order to be in the cabinet, he had to go home and contest a new election. Like the one in Waterford, this was considered a *pro forma* affair, and Fitzgerald was well liked even by the Catholics of Clare. But O'Connell's forces took an interest in the contest, and after fruitlessly searching for a viable candidate, they decided to run O'Connell himself. His victory was an awakening call to London. King George IV was furious, Prime Minister Wellington flummoxed, and the entire English government wondering where this was leading. The Emancipation Bill was passed on April 13—but there were consequences. Voting rights grew more stringent for Catholics. (One now had to be a ten-guinea free-holder as opposed to a forty-shilling freeholder. This shrank the Irish Catholic voting block from 700,000 to 26,000. O'Connell felt that in allowing this to pass, he had failed his constituency.) The Catholic Association was dissolved, and O'Connell's election was deemed illegal, as Catholics could not hold office without swearing the oath that declared the king head of the church and the mass "impious and abominable." The Emancipation Bill, which would have excused him from such an oath, was not retroactive, he was told. After a dramatic stance in the Parliament, he returned to Clare and was re-elected. Daniel O'Connell had won the day, again—and the stature of his enemies was getting greater.

At this point, O'Connell began to fight vigorously to repeal the Act of the Union, but he was stymied at every turn. The Catholic Association had been shut down. (In a speech, O'Connell had praised the revolution in Bolivia—to which his son had gone to fight with his father's blessing—and wished for a similar Bolivar to assist Ireland. He was arrested and tried but he was acquitted.) He founded the Friends of Ireland Society, which was suppressed by the government. He next founded the Irish Volunteers for the Repeal of the Union. That was closed down. He organized breakfast meetings to argue against the Union. They too were shut down. He kept organizing; the government kept closing down the organizations. (When the breakfasts were banned, he threatened to have lunches, teas, and suppers!)

Yet he fought on. His time as an MP was effective, particularly after George IV died and Victoria ascended the throne. As a true son of the Enlightenment, he fought and argued for equality and liberty, and not just the Irish cause: he fought for Jewish rights, for the abolition of slavery, for the end of capital punishment. So great had O'Connell become in the eyes of his Irish people that the Church (and he) organized what became known as the O'Connell tribute—a subscription that paid O'Connell to do the work he felt he must do. Part of this was to protest the hated tithe—a tax by any other name—that all Catholics had to pay to the Protestant Church. O'Connell refused to pay and, of course, was arrested. But his people followed; thousands upon thousands refused to pay. (O'Connell's tactics here and in the Waterford election seem to prefigure Gandhi's methods of civil disobedience against the British. And the British handled it the same way.) For six years, between 1830 and 1836, the Tithe War raged, pitting Catholic dissenters against the soldiers the government had amassed. Finally, the tithe was changed—there was a still a tax, but it did not go just to the Protestants.

As political parties gained and lost power within the government, O'Connell tried to make alliances which would continue his push for repeal of the Union. To this end, he formed the Repeal Association and began convoking mass meetings to deliver his message. In August 1843, Daniel O'Connell called a meeting at Tara—that legendary seat of Irish kings, a place more wrapped in the glory of old Ireland than any other site. O'Connell knew the historical impact of such a place. The meeting was enormous; reports estimate between 500,000 and 750,000, three-quarters of a million people. Never before in the history of Ireland had so many Irish people gathered in one spot. The government was understandably concerned. O'Connell was gaining power, so he planned yet another mass meeting, this one at

Clontarf, where Brian Ború had defeated the Ostmen. The government would have none of it and cancelled the meeting just hours before it was to begin. O'Connell had to tell the hundreds of thousands who were gathering to go home. And they did, peacefully. To be able to control such an enormous crowd, to disappoint them yet have them behave responsibly, was evidence of O'Connell's power—and to many in government, this power was frightening.

Undoubtedly, these meetings and O'Connell's influence were too dangerous for the government to abide. O'Connell and eight others were arrested. O'Connell was found guilty of conspiracy and trying to change the government, sentenced to a year in prison, and fined £2,000.

When he had first started out in public life, O'Connell was a robust figure. He had a great presence—known for his humor, his wit, his temper, and his vitality. These qualities had carried him through most of his career, had gained him loyal supporters and made him great enemies. But in September 1844, when he got out of prison after serving four months of his sentence, he was noticeably a weaker man. He was nearly seventy, after all, and his innate vitality and characteristic energy was diminishing. At the same time, there were large cracks appearing in the Irish unity he had tried to forge. The Young Irelanders had walked out on the Repeal Association—as much in disagreement with its priorities as with the old-school politics embodied in O'Connell. Despite his own pride and self-confidence, he was shrewd enough to see the ebbing of his power and influence.

Believing he was dying, O'Connell decided on a trip to Rome—to the spiritual center of those Catholics he had spent a lifetime defending. He never made it, but died in Genoa on May 15, 1847.

Daniel O'Connell, the Great Liberator, the Counselor, the uncrowned King of Ireland, was gone. His funeral was said to have drawn even more people than his gathering at Tara. In the end, he left behind a legacy that would be long disputed—argued over by each new group of "liberators" grappling with the daunting task of Irish independence. But his unwavering dedication, his steadfast principles, and his unshakeable belief in an Irish nation undivided by religious sects made him a man who transcended national politics, and who became an inspiration to all people for whom liberty and freedom are sacred. In reaching out to the lower orders of the Irish population, in amassing the poor and the disenfranchised, in organizing them and empowering them, Daniel O'Connell was the font of Irish democracy, and in that alone his legacy is intact.

IRELAND AFTER
THE GREAT HUNGER

It is an odd thing for a country to benchmark a crop failure as a major moment in its history, but the "Great Famine" of the late 1840s in Ireland did more than any other event to shape and define the history of its people. The very word "famine" is controversial, for technically it was not a general famine, but a blight of the potato crop on which a large majority depended. For over two centuries, the Irish peasant was dependent on the potato. It was easy to grow, needed little land, and provided better nourishment than more costly grain. Indeed, the Irish peasant's diet consisted almost exclusively of potatoes and milk or buttermilk. So it was not a famine in the general sense; during the worst years in the 1840s, Ireland export-ed more beef than any other part of the British Empire. What is called the Great Famine was simply the failure of a single crop, but one, however, on which the majority of the peasantry depended.

Hindsight is always easy, and through its perfect vision, one can see that the potato blights of 1817 and 1822 foreshadowed the damage a larger blight could bring. However, the blight of the 1840s had a greater impact than anyone could have ever imagined. To put it into perspective, the census of 1845 counted the population of Ireland at between eight and nine million. Six years later, it was six and a half million, and by 1881, the number had dipped to five million. Three million people had died or emigrated in thirty-five years; one third of the native population was gone.

It is always difficult to speak of the "Great Famine," because everything one says seems an understatement. There were, of course, many repercussions besides the loss of population that had an enormous impact on Ireland in the nineteenth century. The Irish language, for example, all but vanished. Those who spoke

Irish—the poor and the marginalized—for the most part had emigrated or died, save in a few small pockets of the country. Those who emigrated needed to speak the new language of their adopted lands, and those lands—for the most part England, America, and Canada—were English-speaking. At one point, the Church of Ireland tried to convert the native Irish through a proselytizing campaign in the Irish language. This had the reverse—and damaging—effect of putting the Catholic Church in opposition to the Irish language.

One other effect of the famine was that in cities throughout America and industrialized England, "little Irelands" arose. The emigrants, like emigrants everywhere, settled among their own, with people who shared the same history and background. Those emigrants who were now working, at wages far beyond those they had known at home, sent money back to Ireland, and the money had two purposes. One was to book passage for the loved ones who had remained behind, further intensifying the depletion caused by emigration. The other purpose was support of revolutionary societies. For the Irish may have left their native home, but many did not leave behind their hopes for an Irish nation and their hatred for the English, whom they blamed for the dire situation of their country.

Thus, during this time, various insurrection movements arose. The two most notable were the Irish Republican Brotherhood and the Fenians. Created through a web of American-Irish and Irish patriots and often by colorful able men such as John O'Leary, Jerimiah O'Donovan Rossa, John Devoy, and John O'Mahony, the organizations wielded increasing power—latching onto the land agitation issue that had grown out of the famine, and preaching the necessity of complete independence from England. Indeed, the overriding dogma of these societies was that parliamentary and constitutional agitation had failed over the past centuries, and that the only way to right Ireland's situation was through the violent overthrow of England. Yet while these groups fostered violence as the primary means of gaining independence, and held some sway over the politics of the day, it was a strictly non-violent man who overshadowed them all—a quiet, aristocratic, London-educated, Protestant land-owner who perhaps, to this day, was the greatest hope that Ireland ever had. The man's name was Charles Stewart Parnell, and his story—like so many tales of great Irish leaders—has all the marks of a Greek tragedy.

CHAPTER XIX:

CHAᴙʟᴇs Sᴛᴇwᴀᴙᵗ PᴀᴙⅡᴇʟʟ: ᵗHᴇ UⅡᴄᴙᴏwⅡᴇᴅ KⅈⅡG ᴏF IᴙᴇʟᴀⅡᴅ

For many people who have never read a word of Irish history, the first they hear of Charles Stewart Parnell is through James Joyce. His missing presence haunts the men and women in the later stories of *Dubliners*, as the country tries to grapple with the demise of the "Uncrowned King of Ireland." In Joyce's first published novel, *A Portrait of the Artist as a Young Man*, the hero, Stephen Dedalus, envisions Parnell's funeral as he lies feverish in his school's infirmary. Then at Christmas dinner, there is a scene, a violent dispute among the hero's relations about the tragedy of Parnell's fall and the church's turning on him from the pulpit, which many people saw as a betrayal. The scene is typical of the conflicting contemporary feelings on Parnell: passionate, loyal, hurt, or angry. The Irish people called him "Chief"— and his fall, coming when Home Rule seemed so near, seemed to many like a knife in the heart of their dream of independence.

Given the devastated condition of the country mid-way through the nineteenth century, the ever-growing resentment toward England and English policy in Ireland, and the rise of various insurrectionist movements, Charles Stewart Parnell would seem to be the least likely person to emerge to lead the people, to be the primary figure in the Irish Catholic national moment. He was reserved and soft-spoken, a tall man with aristocratic bearing, who seemed to embody the very Protestant Ascendancy that Ireland's frustration was vented against. Yet, he proved to be principled and inflexible, energetic and intelligent, unwaveringly dedicated to Ireland's poor and disenfranchised, and remarkably able to manipulate the treacherous chambers of British politics.

Parnell was born in 1846 in Avondale, County Wicklow. He was a child of the Protestant ascendancy: schooled in England and raised at home by nannies. A headstrong child, he was expelled from his English boarding school for "disobedi-ence," and one of his nannies was so overwhelmed by his stubbornness that she is said to have declared that Charles "was born to rule." After the school incident, his father arranged for Parnell to be educated at home at Avondale. This beautiful estate in the eastern part of the county would soon be Charles Stewart's own, for his father died early in 1859, making Charles Stewart the squire of Avondale.

His paternal great-grandfather had been an opponent of the Act of Union throughout his life, and his maternal grandfather was a hero in the American War of 1812. However, it was the Parnell women who were the most radical in the household, sometimes embarrassing Charles Stewart with their passion. His moth-er, an American, was fiercely anti-English. His sister Fanny was a poet whose nationalism and pro-Fenian leanings informed her verse. Her most famous poem, "Hold the Harvest," was called "La Marseillaise" of the Irish peasantry by Michael Davitt, and her prose writings were likewise an inspiration to the impoverished masses. And his other sister, Anna, founded the Ladies Land League of Ireland, which was to become a formidable force, keeping up agitation and political action while Parnell himself was in jail. Some hold that Parnell might have never entered politics if he had not been urged on by his mother and sisters.

Schooled in England and the proper squire of a handsome estate, Parnell impressed the leading Irish parliamentarian at the time, Isaac Butt, who had become radicalized after defending a number of Fenians in court. The son of a Church of Ireland clergyman and a graduate of Trinity College, Butt seemed to the government to be an affable, middle-class man who would not cause problems. Indeed, he was often embarrassed by the roughness of his fellow Irish MPs, who were laughed at by their British counterparts, and felt that their demeanor was a hindrance to using Parliament for Irish needs. Parnell's quiet, handsome, well-mannered appearance, Butt thought, was the perfect antidote to his countrymen's boisterousness. (Having gradually attained more and more suffrage over the past century, the Irish people often voted in men with more character than political savvy. The secret ballot meant they no longer had to answer to a landlord for their votes. Tipperary, for instance, elected O'Donovan Rossa even though he had been arrested in September 1865 and was heading to jail for planning an armed insurrection in Dublin.)

Butt had formed the Home Rule Party in order to achieve a limited form of Irish self-government, and in 1874, the Home Rule Party won 59 of the 103 Irish seats in the House of Commons. The next year, however, would mark the end of business as usual in Parliament, for in April 1875, Charles Stewart Parnell was elected as MP for County Meath on the Home Rule ticket.

From the beginning, it seemed Parnell was a master politician. In his opening speech, he aggressively argued for Irish concerns, stating Ireland was not a "fragment of England," as it had been referred to in Parliament, but a nation. He pressed these Irish issues continually, and when Parliament ignored them, he and Joseph Biggar—a clever, hunchbacked butcher who represented Cavan—would disrupt all Parliamentary business through a tactic called "obstruction," similar to the American filibuster. (One story states that when Biggar first started these tactics, he read from government blue books. Once, after several hours of Biggar merely reading from the book, an irritated MP shouted that he could not hear. Biggar apologized and started again from the beginning!) Biggar's obstructionism flummoxed Parliament; he certainly made it recognize the Irish MPs. Biggar would joke that before he was through, England would grant Ireland Home Rule if only to get Biggar out of its government!

Parnell's embrace of Biggar's tactics disappointed Butt, who was always concerned with propriety, and after he admonished Parnell publicly on the floor of the House of Commons, the two became political opponents. The argument was waged through letters in the press, and Parnell's stance, that British Parliament itself was an antiquated institution, endeared him to the militant leaders who usually disassociated themselves from all political channels. Such was the open nature of the argument between Butt and Parnell that in August 1877, Parnell was elected president of the Home Rule Confederation of Great Britain. Up to now, Isaac Butt had always been its president. A new star had appeared in the Irish firmament.

In December of that year, Parnell traveled to County Mayo to speak at a Home Rule rally. Mayo was as poor a county as one could find in Ireland. The potato crop was failing once more, American competition was bringing down prices at market, and evictions were growing rampant. (In 1880, nearly 2,000 Irish Catholic families were evicted from their homes.) Parnell's speech is noteworthy, for he combined the land question and nationalism for the first time. He also stated that he would be willing to fight for a self-determination that was more than what was offered by the Home Rule agenda.

With speeches such as this and with his obstructionist tactics in Parliament, Parnell was being noticed not only by the government, which detested him. The Fenians and the Irish Brotherhood both began to consider Parnell's strong influence, and both tried to bring him into their line of thinking. But Parnell, after a

meeting with John O'Leary and William Carroll where he was derided for working within the government rather than against it, noted that violent movements
had never succeeded in Ireland. Land reform was the issue that would ultimately
lead to Irish freedom.

One of the Fenians who particularly took to Parnell was Michael Davitt, and
Parnell took to him. Davitt grew fiercely loyal to Parnell, remaining so until a
scandal years down the line. Believing at first that he could convert Parnell to
Fenianism, he instead quickly grew to become a strong supporter of land reform.
(Typically, the militants believed that independence should come first and then
land reform. Parnell argued—and nearly demonstrated—that the inverse was
true.) In the summer of 1878, Davitt sailed to America to explain Parnell's positions to the Irish-American journalists and leaders of the various Irish-American
organizations. In October, John Devoy, leader of the *Clan na Gael* in America,
sent Parnell an agenda that spelled out conditions under which the Irish
Nationalists in America would agree to support him. The conditions included
declaring himself for "self-government" and "agitation on the land question."
These were issues that Parnell had already broached, and he needed to make no
formal acceptance of Devoy's message. It seemed as if the insurrectionists were
coming to Parnell rather than vice versa. The Fenians, on the other hand, were not
pleased with this compromise with constitutional government.

Ireland, however, was once again rushing toward ruin. Evictions were on the
rise, and with them the reprisal agrarian crimes. Hunger was rampant and memories of the Great Famine were still vivid and frightening. In the summer of 1878,
Michael Davitt began to organize protests in his native Mayo, and this led to the
foundation of the Land League. Starvation was not localized in Mayo, but ran
throughout the country, and within months, the Land League had been reformed
as the National Land League. Charles Stewart Parnell was its first president;

Michael Davitt its secretary. To the protesting and starving tenants, Parnell out-
lined the vision of the Land League: "Show your power and make them feel it."

As starvation seemed more and more apt to engulf the country, Parnell went
on a fund-raising tour of America. That the plight of the Irish peasantry had
become a mainstream issue in America is evidenced by Parnell's giving a speech to
the House of Representatives and being invited to the floor of the Stock Exchange.
His fund-raising had a two-fold goal: relief for the starving Irish and support for
the Land League. An American Land League formed while he was there, and it
ultimately boasted more than 200,000 members.

It is noteworthy that all this political involvement, all the grand speeches and
noble alliances, were against Parnell's natural temperament. He was a very quiet
man, never in the best of health, and one who preferred his own company. His
public demeanor in the political arena, his boisterous attacks, his rabid villifica-
tions, his charming camaraderie, were as alien to his personality as could be. But it
was the role necessary for a politician.

The charity of Americans may have reduced the devastation of famine, but it
could not stem tenant evictions. The Land League tried to legislate equable rents
through the courts; it protested against hard-headed landlords, and it watched as
the countryside grew increasingly militant. The favorite tactic of the Land League
was the boycott.

(The very word "boycott" comes from Captain Charles Boycott, a land agent
in Mayo who was ruthless in his eviction policy. To show their unity with
Boycott's evicted tenants, the Irish refused to help Boycott with his harvest. They
"boycotted" the work, and a group of outside Protestants had to be brought in to
do it. Boycotts began springing up throughout the country, and many landlords
had to bargain with their tenants on rent issues.)

The countryside was armed and Parnell knew it. He was gingerly balancing the

militant dreams of the Fenians with the legislative workings of the Parliament and
the civil agitation of the Land League. In the meantime, he had amassed the
largest united force of people since the days of Daniel O'Connell—and to Britain's
concern, some of these people were armed.

It was also at this time, in October 1880, that Parnell took a mistress. Kitty
O'Shea, the wife of one of his colleagues, would become not only his lover, but his
advisor, and the cause of his ruin.

Britain responded to the agitation in the same way that it had for three centuries, through increased force. Parnell and his cohorts in Parliament ratcheted up
their obstructionist tactics until the issue—the Coercion Act—was addressed. (At
one time, the obstructionists kept parliament sitting for forty-one hours straight—
the longest session of the House of Commons to date!) Davitt spoke out vehemently against the rising British force, and countered with the threat that Irish-
American power was being mobilized to help free Ireland. He was promptly arrested. Parnell refused to let the Prime Minister speak in the House, and was forcibly
removed from the floor. The rest of the Parnellites in the House of Commons
were likewise removed.

At this time, with tension at a breaking point, the Prime Minister, William
Gladstone (who was more sympathetic to the Irish cause than any English Prime
Minister before or since), responded with a stroke of political genius. Gladstone
offered an enormous Land Bill that was far-reaching and seemed to address Land
League issues such as fair rents and tenant security. The introduction of the bill
caused much debate and concern within the Land League. It separated Home-
Rule, independence, and self-government from Land Reform—now a united issue
that Parnell and Davitt had worked carefully to forge. And it was going to play
into the fears of the militants who had grudgingly come along with the
Parliamentarians.

When it came time to put the bill to a vote, Parnell and six of his followers abstained. Parnell then set upon giving a real tongue-lashing to the Prime Minister, in a blistering speech that warned the Irish of the duplicity of Gladstone's bill. Gladstone charged Parnell with sedition, and placed him and six others in Kilmainham jail. From jail, the Parnellites issued a manifesto telling farmers to stop paying rents altogether.

While Charles Stewart was in jail, his sisters Anna and Fanny, who had founded the Ladies' Land League, kept up Land League agitation. The Land League itself had been suppressed. The Church, of course, had to get involved, and it condemned the Ladies' Land League for allegedly placing shame on the modesty and dignity of their sex. Before long, it too, like the Land League itself, was suppressed. In a way, it was a sign of the effectiveness of Anna and Fanny's Land League that the government felt that it must be squashed as well. It is even more telling that so vociferous were the demonstrations Anna organized after the league was suppressed that the government did not enforce its ban, but allowed the league to function as normal.

Despite the promises of Gladstone's Land Bill, there was little relief for the Irish farmers. Evictions hit more than 16,000 in 1881, and over 26,000 in 1882. (Gladstone had provided a loophole for landlords that stated they could evict tenants who were deeply in arrears.) Yet the Ladies' Land League agitation was having its effect—and anarchy was spreading throughout the countryside. The Ladies Land League had proven more militant that its male counterpart, and now there were more and better organized boycotts, more rent strikes, as well as more agrarian crime and more outrages. The government concluded that its security was better served with the male leaders free than in prison.

In a cruel irony, Captain William O'Shea, whom Parnell had been cuckolding since 1880, was in charge of the negotiations to attain Parnell's release. He got out on May 2. The terms of his release are known as the Kilmainham Treaty, and actually stated that all agrarian agitation—the rent strikes, the boycotting, etc.—would end. In return, Parnell and Davitt and the other Parnellites would be released. Land reform was promised, so Parnell could now concentrate on Home Rule.

This momentum, however, would be interrupted by a brutal murder. The new Chief Secretary of Ireland, Lord Cavendish and his under secretary, Thomas Butler Burke, were attacked in Dublin's Phoenix Park by members of a group called the Irish National Invincibles. Using surgical knives, the gang hacked the two to death. Parnell, who had nothing to do with it, nevertheless offered to resign his chairmanship. In a formal statement, he spoke of Ireland's revulsion at such barbarity. (Yet his sister Anna wrote a letter to the *London Times* that seemed to justify the murders. She also stated she had no intention of easing agrarian agitation just because some politicians such as her brother made a deal saying to do so.)

The Phoenix Park murders nullified the repeal of the Coercion Act, which had been negotiated within the Kilmainham Treaty, and, in fact, harsher measures were passed in the guise of the Crime Bill. The Invincibles were arrested, tried, and executed. They denied complicity with Parnell, although some whiff of responsibility continued to cling to him. Despite this—or perhaps even because of it—Parnell's popularity was growing larger than it had ever been before. He had stood up to government, had served his time in prison, and had still managed to effect land reform.

Gladstone, who was never a supporter of the Crime Bill but had succumbed to popular opinion, was allowing it to run its course and die on the books, when in early 1886 militants simultaneously detonated dynamite packets at the Tower of London, Westminster Hall, and the House of Commons. These bombings—the dynamite war as it became known—were a continuation of a campaign from two years earlier, when the American *Clan na Gael* set off a series of bombings in

London subways and even at Scotland Yard. Outrage took over political sense, the bill was renewed, and Gladstone—whose Liberal party had lost when the Home Rulers had sided with the Tories—resigned. During the interim between Gladstone's resignation and the next general election, the Crime Bill was revoked and an important bill, the Ashbourne Act, was passed. This act provided a fund of five million pounds for farmers to borrow in order to buy their farm when they were behind on the rent.

With the next general election, Gladstone's Liberal Party was returned to office and Parnell's party was greatly reinforced. In December 1885, Gladstone introduced a Home Rule bill that was struck down by the Conservatives, who felt it did not address sufficiently the concerns of the Orange Protestants in Ulster. (Parnell had spoken eloquently to his supporters in Ulster, arguing for tolerance and consideration for all members of the Irish nation.) In its stead, Gladstone introduced the Land Bill, which would have bought out the landlords and given over the land to the tenants. Gladstone's bill traveled far in the House but again was defeated. With this Gladstone dissolved Parliament and once more began campaigning throughout England on Irish issues. The Irish themselves began to recognize how much this English prime minister had done for Ireland and how much his hopes coincided with theirs. A new, although unlikely, hero, his picture was soon hanging in many Irish homes.

Parnell was having difficulties balancing land agitation with the threat of the Coercion Acts and the Crime Bill. If he supported agitation, the government would react with the harshness of the Coercion Act and Crime Bill. If he did nothing, he would fail his people. He drew up a plan, funded by the Irish National League of America, that would allow tenants to organize and decide the rate of rent they should pay. They would offer this amount to the landlord, and if he refused, they would use the funds to support the evicted tenants. The genius of the plan was that it circumvented the strictures of the Coercion Act. The plan was effective, and while Parnell never took credit, the Tories in Parliament blamed him for it.

The Crime Bill was up again for consideration, and it was an angry and frustrated Parliament that was voting on it. Yet a matter outside of the House of Commons altered the impetus of the Bill. The *Times* of London began running a series of articles entitled "Parnellism and Crime," with accusations that Parnell, as head of the Land League, encouraged the murder of landlords. Most damning, however, was a forged letter supposedly from Parnell stating he had approved of the Phoenix Park murders and that his public condemnations were an act. A Parliamentary investigation—delving into Parnell's connections with the Irish-American militant organizations as well as with the Phoenix Park murders—resulted in the revelation that the incriminating letter was indeed a forgery. The letter had been written by Richard Pigott, a journalist who had once championed the Fenian cause and alerted the world to the mistreatment that Fenian prisoners such as O'Donovan Rossa had undergone at the hands of the British. At this point, though, he was a man down on his luck, and he was willing to do anything for money.

Parnell was vindicated, the *Times* and the attorney general who led the investigation were humiliated, and Parnell ultimately won a suit against the paper and received five thousand pounds. (Although a member of the landed class, Parnell was never good with money. In 1882, after he had put his beloved Avondale up for sale, T. D. Sullivan wrote an article in the *Nation* asking the people to organize a monetary tribute to their "Chief" so that he could retain his home. At first, the reaction to such a tribute was quite tepid, but under English pressure, the pope got involved and counseled the people not to give their hard-won money. This of course had the opposite effect, and the tribute garnered more than double what had been originally asked.)

With Parnell's victory over the *Times* and Parliament, and with the impression that the "Chief" was being persecuted, Parnell's popularity grew even greater than before. No Irishman before had ever held out such possibilities for nationhood, for a united Ireland, as Parnell did at this moment. Yet, all was to be dashed. Like Icarus falling from the sky, Parnell's descent was quick and devastating, caused by his devotion to and love for Kitty O' Shea.

Parnell and Kitty O'Shea

As stated before, Parnell met Katherine O'Shea in 1880 at the height of the land agitation. She was an intelligent woman—no other could have attracted the attention of Parnell—and like the women in his family, she was political and independent. Throughout the next decade, she became Parnell's closest ally, and often, she was an intermediary between Parnell and Gladstone.

How they met is a circuitous tale, running from London to Clare back to London. Her husband, Captain William O'Shea, a man of no great character— having failed at a variety of projects and living off the regular income that his wife's rich Aunt Ben provided as well as in the London house she bought for them—decided suddenly that he would run for election in Clare. He was elected to Parliament (where one of his first acts was to vote for Parnell as leader of the Home Rule Party), and it was here in London that his wife met the great Parnell. When the two became lovers, their actions primarily went unnoticed, for Parnell was an intensely private and somber man and few took note of his absences. The two were often together, and when he was sick, Kitty nursed him. That O'Shea knew nothing seems to be belied by the rages he would fly into (he once sent Parnell's suitcase to London when he found it sitting in the hallway of his own house), and ultimately his challenging Parnell to a duel. Perhaps, O'Shea's reluctance to admit the affair stemmed from his desire to use the great man for his own ends, or it was because he himself was hardly blameless when it came to marital infidelities. Only once during the course of their affair did Parnell act atypically concerning O'Shea. Against all the advice he was receiving from his friends and supporters, Parnell backed William O'Shea as MP for Galway. Warning him against supporting such a man, his friend Biggar, who must have known the situation, told his friend that the O'Sheas would be his ruin.

When Parnell was arrested in 1881 and placed in the Kilmainham jail, Kitty O'Shea was pregnant with his child. It was a difficult pregnancy, made more so by the fact that her husband Captain William O'Shea believed the baby to be his. At the time, O'Shea was deliberately ignoring his wife's affair. Kitty O'Shea claimed that her husband had always known of the affair; there was little enough passion in their own marriage. But nevertheless, he may very well have believed the baby to be his.

Ironically and poignantly, it was O'Shea who initiated negotiations for Parnell's release from Kilmainham, negotiations that he had to put aside in April, for the child born to William and Katherine O'Shea had died at two months of age and was buried on April 25 at Christchurch, Dublin. Parnell, however, had been able to see his first-born when he had been given parole to attend a nephew's funeral and had gone straight to the new mother and child.

Negotiating for Parnell's release put O'Shea in contact with Gladstone and Joseph Chamberlain, which augmented O'Shea's sense of self-importance. O'Shea's relationship with Chamberlain would continue long after Parnell was released, and there are those who believe that when O'Shea finally did come out against Parnell, it was at the suggestion of Chamberlain, who saw it as a way finally to destroy him.

In the year of the *Times*'s "Parnellism and Crime" fiasco, Kitty O'Shea's aunt died, leaving her niece a goodly amount of money. For Kitty, this meant that she would finally be able to buy off her boorish husband. By this time, she had already given birth to two more of Parnell's children, so she packed the children up and bought a house in Brighton. Parnell bought the house next door. When Kitty's cousins contested Aunt Ben's will, William O'Shea joined them in their suit. And then he dropped the bomb. He sued his wife for divorce and named Charles Stewart Parnell as co-respondent. On December 30, 1889, the newspapers carried the story—the *Times* was going to get its revenge.

When the story broke, the people and his political allies initially stood behind Parnell. Yet Parnell seemed not to recognize the magnitude of the charges among his Catholic constituency. To him it was a private matter and did not affect his ability to lead, and so, in November, when the case was brought to court, Parnell and Kitty O'Shea offered no defense. The divorce proceedings went against them, with Parnell named the cause of the marriage's dissolution. Parnell quickly married Kitty O'Shea, but the storms were just beginning to brew.

Gladstone suggested that Parnell resign—Parnell himself had never considered it. Indeed, it was Parnell's acting as if nothing had happened that infuriated the common people. Disapproval grew rapidly among the English, particularly by the lower middle class. This disapproval spread to Ireland, and ultimately to the Catholic Church. The Church preached from its pulpits that Parnell was not morally fit to lead Catholics. (It is this politicizing of the pulpit that so outrages one of the guests at Stephen Dedalus's Christmas dinner in *A Portrait of the Artist*.)

But it was his own men, his own partners that turned on him most fiercely. Michael Davitt became an ardent opponent and called Parnell a "cold sensualist," which was truly unfair, for Parnell had had only two loves throughout his life: Ireland and Kitty O'Shea. The journalist Thomas Healey, the man who years before had given Parnell the title of the "uncrowned king of Ireland," was particularly rabid, and remained so even after Parnell's death. Even the Irish-American organizations that had once given him so much support voiced their opposition and demands for his resignation. Parnell was adamant; he would not resign.

Finally, on December 1, the party met to discuss the situation. Parnell would not give up the chair, while members argued and debated his removal in front of him. Finally, after a vote, Parnell was removed from the leadership. In his removal, the party was split, and, in many ways, from that moment it ceased to exist.

Although he lost the leadership, Parnell continued to work as an MP, but that too would soon come to a close. In the next general election, he lost his seat. He ran in three more elections and lost each time. The people were so vehemently against him that at one campaign stop, a woman threw lye in his face. With his health failing, Parnell caught a chill and died in Brighton in the arms of his wife.

The power of great tragedy lies in the greatness of the character that falls. It is no coincidence that Hamlet and Macbeth, Oedipus and Agamemnon, are all powerful, noble, and much-admired men; the weight of tragedy is in direct proportion to the degree of descent. In Charles Stewart Parnell, this was never more evident, except in this case, the tragedy is not his alone, but the fate of an entire country. He was a Protestant who gave his life to the Catholic cause; he was a landlord who spent his career fighting against landlords; he was the most able man for the Irish cause at a given time. Even his long-time political opponent Gladstone, when asked about him later in his life, stated that he was the most remarkable person he had ever met, and he was sure that if the divorce had never surfaced, Parnell would have brought Home Rule to Ireland once and for all.

And in that lies the greatest tragedy.

The Drombeg Stone Circle, known locally as the Druid's Altar, is a Bronze Age mystery located near Glandore, County Cork. Of the original 17 pillars of smooth-sided sandstone, only 13 remain.

DEATH OF BRIAN BORU.

Vol. I, p. 38

H.Warren.

J.Rogers.

BrianBorú is known in legend as the last of Ireland's great High Kings. This nineteenth-century engraving depicts his death at the battle of Clontarf.

The Cross of the Scriptures at Clonmacnoise, County Offaly. Founded in 545 by St. Ciarán, Clonmacnoise was a major religious center. This tenth-century cross intertwines Pagan and Christian symbols. The west face, pictured here, depicts scenes from the life of Christ.

Study portrait of Jonathan Swift, an eighteenth-century oil on canvas, by Charles Jervas. Jonathan Swift, best known as the author of *Gulliver's Travels*, was a savage satirist with a heart of gold and true compassion. Poverty had so blanketed both urban and country Irish by the mid-eighteenth century that the dire descriptions of Ireland's poverty were readily recognized by English readers of his work *A Modest Proposal*.

Robert Emmet (1778–1803), Irish orator and patriot, led an unsuccessful rebellion in 1803. He was hanged and beheaded. His last words earned him a place in the pantheon of Irish martyrs: "Let no man write my epitaph. When my country takes her place among the nations of the earth, then shall my character be vindicated, then may my epitaph be written."

"THE BATTERING RAM HAS DONE ITS WORK". 1772 W.L.

Charles Stewart Parnell in a cartoon by Amand, Brussels. The woman in the picture represents Ireland. Parnell (1846–1891) is known as the "Uncrowned King of Ireland," a term originally coined for Daniel O'Connell. Under his leadership, the Irish Parlimentary Party became one of the first professionally organized political parties in all of Britain and Ireland. He is remembered as a fighter of freedom and remains an Irish national hero.

Portrait of Nobel Laureate William Butler Yeats as a young man, in an 1898 lithograph by Sir William Rothenstein.

ABOVE

Photograph of the General Post Office and O'Connell Street, Dublin after the Easter Rising 1916. The rebellion began on Easter Monday, April 24, 1916, with an estimated 1,000 to 1,500 armed Irishmen and Irishwomen attempting to seize Dublin with the ultimate goal of creating an independent Ireland. This week-long war for independence resulted in an overwhelming desire for freedom among the Irish.

RIGHT PAGE

Who Fears to Speak of Easter Week?: The Irish Rebellion of 1916 and its Martyrs (1916), by Francis Joseph Rigney. Portraits: Roger Casement, Padraig Pearse, James Connolly, Thomas MacDonagh, Michael O'Hanrahan, F. Sheehy Skeffington, Joseph M. Plunkett, Sean Heuston, Michael O'Rahilly, Countess de Markievicz, Thomas Clarke, Edmond Kent, Edward Daly, Sean McDermott, John MacBride, and Cornelius Colbert. All were executed, assassinated, or killed by the British, with the exception of Countess de Markievicz.

POBLACHT NA H EIREANN.

THE PROVISIONAL GOVERNMENT
OF THE

IRISH REPUBLIC
TO THE PEOPLE OF IRELAND.

IRISHMEN AND IRISHWOMEN: In the name of God and of the dead generations from which she receives her old tradition of nationhood, Ireland, through us, summons her children to her flag and strikes for her freedom.

Having organised and trained her manhood through her secret revolutionary organisation, the Irish Republican Brotherhood, and through her open military organisations, the Irish Volunteers and the Irish Citizen Army, having patiently perfected her discipline, having resolutely waited for the right moment to reveal itself, she now seizes that moment, and, supported by her exiled children in America and by gallant allies in Europe, but relying in the first on her own strength, she strikes in full confidence of victory.

We declare the right of the people of Ireland to the ownership of Ireland, and to the unfettered control of Irish destinies, to be sovereign and indefeasible. The long usurpation of that right by a foreign people and government has not extinguished the right, nor can it ever be extinguished except by the destruction of the Irish people. In every generation the Irish people have asserted their right to national sovereignty; six times during the past three hundred years they have asserted it in arms. Standing on that fundamental right and again asserting it in arms in the face of the world, we hereby proclaim the Irish Republic as a Sovereign Independent State, and we pledge our lives and the lives of our comrades-in-arms to the cause of its freedom, of its welfare, and of its exaltation among the nations.

The Irish Republic is entitled to, and hereby claims, the allegiance of every Irishman and Irishwoman. The Republic guarantees religious and civil liberty, equal rights and equal opportunities to all its citizens, and declares its resolve to pursue the happiness and prosperity of the whole nation and of all its parts, cherishing all the children of the nation equally, and oblivious of the differences carefully fostered by an alien government, which have divided a minority from the majority in the past.

Until our arms have brought the opportune moment for the establishment of a permanent National Government, representative of the whole people of Ireland and elected by the suffrages of all her men and women, the Provisional Government, hereby constituted, will administer the civil and military affairs of the Republic in trust for the people.

We place the cause of the Irish Republic under the protection of the Most High God, Whose blessing we invoke upon our arms, and we pray that no one who serves that cause will dishonour it by cowardice, inhumanity, or rapine. In this supreme hour the Irish nation must, by its valour and discipline and by the readiness of its children to sacrifice themselves for the common good, prove itself worthy of the august destiny to which it is called.

Signed on Behalf of the Provisional Government,

THOMAS J. CLARKE.
SEAN Mac DIARMADA.   THOMAS MacDONAGH.
P. H. PEARSE.   EAMONN CEANNT.
JAMES CONNOLLY.   JOSEPH PLUNKETT.

Proclamation of Independence. Padraig Pearse read the Proclamation of Independence outside the General Post Office in Dublin on Easter Monday, 1916. This proclamation is addressed to Irishmen and Irishwomen, forward thinking for 1916.

Portrait of Eamon de Valera, c. 1914–23 photograph. Valera, or DeV as he was popularly known, spent three-quarters of his life fighting for the dream of an independent Ireland. He was the last commander to surrender in the Easter Rising, spared execution because of his American birth.

LEFT PAGE
Portrait of James Joyce in Paris at age 20, c. 1902 photograph.

ABOVE
Brendan Francis Behan in a 1959 photograph by Ida Kar. Behan was a prolific author and playwright who was known for his powerful political views and satirical works. He was one of the most successful Irish dramatists of the twentieth century.

TOP
Photograph of Bloody Sunday in Derry, January 30, 1972. The loss of life caused shock and revulsion at an international level. Thirty years later, investigations are still being conducted to find out who was responsible.

BOTTOM
Photograph of Bernadette Devlin, February 1972. Devlin, a civil rights activist for Northern Ireland, who at 21 was the youngest MP ever elected to the British Parliament, survived an assassination attempt in 1979 by Loyalist paramilitary. She has been called "the Irish Joan of Arc."

CHAPTER XX:

Michael Davitt

Sometimes it is hard to understand what turns one man towards violence and not another, why one man might see parliamentary agitation as a viable weapon, while another would seek out sticks of dynamite and the Tommy gun. The arming of the Irish peasantry in the late 1800s is understandable against the backdrop of famine, starvation, eviction, and government inaction—and in the case of Michael Davitt, there was even greater motivation.

Michael Davitt was born in the village of Striade, County Mayo, in the same year as Parnell. While Parnell's landlord father died when the boy was only thirteen, Davitt was just four when his family was evicted from its farm. Without a home, food, or work, the family sought refuge in a workhouse. There they were told that Michael was too young and needed to be housed separately, a decision by which his mother, Catherine Davitt, would not abide. They were given shelter by a local priest, Father John McHugh, before setting off for England and the textile town of Haslingden. There the Davitt family—father, mother, and four children—was again evicted, in the depth of a winter in which young Michael nearly died. Fortunately, another Irish emigrant—and there were plenty in the world in 1850—rescued the family and allowed them to stay with him until the young boy recovered.

That another Irish emigrant lent them a hand was not uncommon. For as the industrial revolution made its sooty way through Victorian England, the industrial cities became hosts for an underclass of disenfranchised Irish. And as emigrants are wont to do, these Irish brought much of their culture with them, their music, their dance, their storytelling, and their memories. Martin Davitt, the boy's father, worked as a teacher of Irish music and language. Thus, Michael was raised among the joys of music and dance, pride in his native language, and appalling memories of famine-ravaged Mayo. The poorest of counties, Mayo was hard hit, and Michael's mother told her impressionable son of the horrors. She certainly would have told him of the mass grave right outside the workhouse where they were turned away. Into this grave, 300 corpses had been dumped.

If the stories of his mother and other emigrants in the Irish ghetto impressed the young boy, yet another moment would solidify his resentment of English rule. At the age of nine, Michael was sent out to work—a twelve-hour shift, six days a week in a textile factory. When he was eleven, he was told to take over on a piece of equipment, which he was too young to operate. Within an hour the boy's arm was mangled in the machinery; after two weeks it was amputated.

It takes the passage of time and history for one to decide which events in a person's life were beneficial and which were detrimental. The factory accident for Michael Davitt when he was eleven years old set him on another life's path. No longer fit for factory work—where he would have been subsumed into the faceless underclass of Irish workers in industrial England—he instead was sent to school. Perhaps it was because his mother could neither read nor write, but whatever the reason, Davitt applied himself assiduously to his schoolwork. What was not assigned in the schools, Davitt supplemented at the local library. There he began devouring books on Irish history. At the age of sixteen, while working for the local postmaster, he began taking evening classes in Irish history.

It was no surprise then, given the evictions, the family history, the tales of the famine, the horrors of child labor, that Michael joined the Irish Republican Brotherhood when he was nineteen, in 1865. Haslington's Irish ghetto was a hotbed of Fenianism, and the young Davitt was a perfect recruit. He became organizing secretary for the Fenians in Northern England and Scotland. He also assisted in smuggling arms to Ireland, and for this, he attracted the government's attention. In 1870, he was arrested in Paddington Station with a shipment of arms, and sent to Dartmoor prison for fifteen years.

In prison, the one-armed Davitt was forced to do hard labor, breaking stones. He was sickly throughout his prison stay and lost twenty percent of his body weight in little more than a year. (On his release, one man mentioned that he looked more like a starving poet than a dangerous revolutionary.) Yet his letters revealed an intelligence that would belie his upbringing. He had sworn that after prison, he would be more dangerous than before—and that the Home Rule issue was inexorably wrapped around the land issue. This was counter to the standard Fenian dogma, and it was this belief that would bring him and Parnell together.

When Davitt got out, he met Parnell, whom he had heard about in prison. The man fascinated Davitt, for he was so different from the Irish he knew, more English than Celtic, but tenaciously dedicated to the Irish cause. From the first, the two men—as different as two men could be—were steadfast friends. Nevertheless, when asked, Davitt informed Parnell that he was returning to the IRB, compromising Parnell as a member of Parliament by admitting so. Davitt did as he said, and was immediately elected to the Brotherhood's supreme governing body, but in accordance with the conditions of his parole—he had served only seven years of his sentence—he left immediately for America where his mother was now living.

In America, Davitt spent much time talking land reform to his friends, and suggesting that Parnell was the man to bet on. The Fenians had never agreed with parliamentary change (primarily because sitting in Parliament involved taking an oath of allegiance), but Davitt was sure of Parnell. Through his connections with editors of the *Irish World* in New York and the *Pilot* in Boston, Davitt was able to spread the message of land reform while at the same time bringing Parnell's name to the general public.

When he returned from America, Davitt went to Mayo, the county of his birth. The county was suffering: evictions were on the rise, crops were selling at low prices, and another potato blight seemed to be threatening. A month later, he organized a protest against unfair rents, which more than 10,000 people attended—the first of many protests that Davitt would organize, the raw beginning of the Irish Land League.

Davitt met with Parnell in June, and the "Chief" agreed to attend one of Davitt's meetings in Mayo. The next week, he was the speaker at Davitt's biggest demonstration, where he told the listeners to show the landlords that they would hold on to their homesteads, that they would not be disenfranchised as their ancestors had been.

In October 1879, Davitt founded the National League of Ireland, in which he acted as secretary to Parnell's presidency. The league and its actions were well received by the farmers, so much so that when Davitt was arrested in Sligo for incendiary language, so many people turned out to demonstrate that the case was dropped. Thousands of people were showing up for each of the demonstrations that Davitt organized.

The Land League was so effective that it won the attention of the British government, which acted in typical fashion, sending in the armed military. When the league was suppressed and Parnell and the others lodged in jail, Davitt encouraged the use of the Ladies' Land League. Davitt was proved right in trusting the women with the land agitation, for they were forceful, organized, and tenacious—so much so that the government chose to release the leaders rather than continue with the anarchy the women caused.

In 1881, Davitt was arrested for seditious language. He had spoken to a crowd in Cork with the argument that England's brutality was an embarrassment to the civilized world, and that no one would condemn the Irish when their American cousins came over in force—because it would be England's cruelty and insensitivity that were to blame.

His release in 1882 was a result of the Kilmainham Treaty, whereby Parnell and others also got out. Davitt once again sailed to America accompanied by Fanny Parnell, and there he deviated from his friend's direction, preaching to the American societies the need for government seizure of the land and land nationalization.

It was also on this trip that Fanny Parnell died—some suspected suicide; others thought it was heat exhaustion. Davitt had been with her that afternoon, walking in the hot July weather. Davitt was always fond of the Parnell sisters and often took their side against their brother. This may have had to do with the Parnell women being more radical than their brother and, so, closer to Davitt's way of thinking.

After Davitt's release, he became more eclectic in his causes and argued on the side of Jews in Russia, the working class in Britain, the Boers in South Africa, and of course always the poor in Ireland. On one of his American trips, he met a California woman named Mary Yore, whom he married in 1886. (When the couple returned to Ireland, the people presented them with a house—the Land League Cottage in Dalkey—as a wedding present and in gratitude for his work.) Davitt's frequent widespread human causes took him not only to America, but also to Russia, South America, Australia, New Zealand, South Africa, and the Holy Land—always seeking out the Irish diaspora to better understand the burden of the working class. And, of course, he traveled to every part of Ireland. He always was a great organizer and a dedicated Home Ruler.

It was this very dedication and ferocity that surely broke his heart when Parnell fell from grace. For his part, Davitt was appalled. He felt betrayed and believed Parnell had misled them all. As to his knowing of Parnell's affair earlier, Davitt—always loyal to the movement—said that before William O'Shea filed divorce proceedings, what Parnell did was his own business. But it was the ruination of the movement. With this, he and many others abandoned their leader. With Parnell's fall, momentum waned. The Home Rule movement withered without the "Chief."

In 1892, the year following Parnell's death, Davitt won a seat in Parliament representing Mayo. But he was disheartened by the machinations and compromises of politics and resigned four years later, his experience solidifying his Fenian belief that only physical force could bring about change. He continued to organize, but there was a palpable loss of steam in Irish nationalism. The push for independence was being taken up by a younger crowd and Michael Davitt found himself on the fringe.

On May 30, 1906, Davitt died in hospital in Dublin. He had arranged that no public funeral should take place, and so his body was quietly taken to the Carmelite Friary on Clarendon Street, Dublin. Despite his wishes, on the next day, more than 20,000 people came to the friary to pay their respects. When his body was brought by train to County Mayo, a huge crowd—similar to the ones he had successfully organized to protest the inequities of landlordism—attended his funeral. The funeral was held in Straide Abbey, not far from where his family had been evicted and where his political education had begun.

CHAPTER XXI:

DOUGLAS HYDE

Douglas Hyde straddles the Age of Parnell and the Coming of Independence. He was fifteen years old when Charles Parnell first took his seat in Parliament, and he was seventy-seven when he was unanimously elected to the newly created office of president of Ireland. He served in the latter role for eight years. In the interim,

Ireland went through Land Reform and almost gained Home Rule; it experienced
a cultural revival, a revolution, and a bitter Civil War. And in the end, it finally
gained a modicum of independence—although partial independence at best.

While the famine may have caused devastating harm to the Irish language, it
was Douglas Hyde who tried to revive it. And as with many such stories, much of
Hyde's interest in the Irish language began through serendipity.

Douglas Hyde was born on January 17, 1860, into the household of Reverend
Arthur Hyde, rector of Tibohine, Frenchpark in County Roscommon. When he
was thirteen, Hyde was sent to boarding school in Dublin, but within the first few
weeks, he contracted measles and had to be sent home. He never returned to
school and was educated at home. Hyde continued his studies and was an extraor-
dinarily successful student: At Trinity College, he won awards for English verse
and prose, for theology and for modern literatures, and was fluent in Latin, Greek,
German, French, and Irish. He received his LLD in 1888, and spent a year as a
professor of languages at the University of New Brunswick in Canada.

More importantly, though, it was that first convalescence at home in
Frenchpark that would shape his future. Hyde was surrounded by native Irish
speakers, the last generation of such, and he was fascinated by these country people whom he got to know and who got to know him. Hyde also kept a diary—an
activity he continued religiously for the rest of his life. His diaries, which offer a
remarkable insight into those remarkable times in Ireland, were begun in English,
but before long, Hyde was writing almost exclusively in Irish. And in them, he
early espouses his lifelong vocation: stemming the disappearance of the Irish language and unearthing and celebrating the rich cultural past of the Gaelic world.

A large part of this interest in the glories of the Celtic past came as a logical
"second-step" to the land reform and Home-Rule movements of O'Connell and
Parnell. Granted, Ireland had achieved some respite from its years under the heavy

boot of English rule, but the Irish Revival tried to instill a special pride in the country's past. And although this movement may have been derided by the hard-line politicos and militants who still saw much to be done, it nevertheless was essential in defining Ireland's identity. People such as William Butler Yeats, Lady Gregory, John MacNeill, and John Millington Synge were integral in reawakening a national pride that had heretofore only found expression in opposition to government. The difference was that most of these artists revived Irish culture in their native tongue—English. Douglas Hyde worked in Irish, and believed it was a truer rebirth.

In 1889, Hyde published a collection of folktales that he had culled from the country-folk surrounding his home in Roscommon. This book, *Beside the Fire*, was followed by *Love Songs of Connacht* in 1892, with verse translations by Hyde himself. (Soon after, Yeats and Lady Gregory combed through the tales of the peasantry for their own materials.) His poetry in the Irish language was published under the pseudonym, *An Craoibhín Aoibhinn*, which translated into "the delightful little branch."

At Trinity College, Hyde joined the Society for the Preservation of the Irish Language. He argued that in forsaking the Irish language and culture, the Irish abandoned their national identity. If, he argued, the English were the antithesis to all things Irish, why then did the Irish imitate them so in the English language and dress? Hyde first made these points in a speech in New York City, which he delivered in Irish, and in which he stressed the need for the emigrant population to retain its hold on its native language and to take pride in it. (It is an almost indisputable—and understandable—phenomenon that emigrants retain and embrace their cultural identity more fiercely than those they have left behind. This can be seen by the very fact that Hyde was able to speak in Irish to a packed lecture hall in New York.) When he returned to Dublin, he gave a similar speech on

November 25, 1892, to the National Literary Society, a new organization to which
he had been named president. The inaugural speech, entitled "The Necessity for
De-Anglicizing Ireland," is noteworthy because while the Gaelic revival was estab-
lished and the nationalist movement had been around since at least the days of
Wolfe Tone, this was the first instance where the two joined into one mission—
Hyde equated the revival of the Gaelic with opposition to England. In both his
Dublin and New York speeches, Hyde argued that if England, in conquering
Ireland, had tried to wipe out all things Irish, then it was now incumbent on the
Irish to preserve their native identity and to prevent their ever-increasing assimilation into English-ness. This was the true rebellion. He argued that by allowing the
Anglicization of Ireland, the Irish had "thrown away" their identity, had severed
their connection with the likes of Brian Ború, the O'Donnells, the O'Neills, and
even the men of '98. Despite his continued insistence on separating culture from
politics, in this speech, Hyde had, for the first time, linked the Gaelic movement
inextricably with the nationalist movement. (Later, Yeats would note that he had
overheard someone in the audience say that Hyde's speech was the most important
"utterance since '48.")

In July 1893, Hyde and John MacNeill (who later Gaelicized his name to
Eoin) founded the Gaelic League. Attempting to energize Irish culture, the league
organized classes in Irish and encouraged Irish dances and games. It was a successful venture, and before too long, the league could boast over 100,000 members in
900 chapters. This de-Anglicization was also encouraged by an earlier organization, the Gaelic Athletic Association (the GAA), which was founded in 1884, and
which encouraged the people to take up Gaelic games such as hurling and Gaelic
football camogie and to foreswear such English sports as cricket, lawn tennis, polo,
soccer, and rugby.

The Gaelic League's greatest success was in education. By 1903, it had seen to it that the Irish language was part of the curriculum in 1,300 national schools, and within five years, had made Irish mandatory for entrance to the newly instituted National University. There were certainly pockets of resistance—to this day it is still called "compulsory Irish"—yet Hyde and his followers had been able to bring the language forth from the rapidly disappearing *shebeens* and cottages of the west and into the more mainstream population. Hyde served as president of the Gaelic League from its inception in 1892 until 1915, when he resigned. As president, Douglas Hyde was adamant about separating politics from his organization—a task that grew more difficult as the league grew more influential. The epitome of the Protestant Ascendancy, he sought cultural revival, not national revolution. Nevertheless, given the nature of the league's goals—to rid Ireland of Anglicization and to revive a native Irish spirit—it was inevitable that many of its members would take the next step toward revolution. And his desire to keep the league apolitical caused confrontations with those who wanted more. Arthur Griffith, for example, who founded the Sinn Fein League at the time, regularly urged Hyde to use the influence of the organization for political ends. Padraig Pearse, himself one of Hyde's friends, would ultimately resign from the league, believing that it had run its course. Pearse would go on to lead the uprising of 1916.

In 1909, Douglas Hyde became the first professor of Modern Irish at University College, Dublin. He remained in that position for twenty-three years. During the civil war of the 1920s, however, he supported the Free State, and consequently, with its establishment, was made one of its senators along with William Butler Yeats. Yet Hyde's tenure as senator was short lived. The following year, the office was changed from an appointed position to a countrywide elected one. Hyde stood for the office, but was the target of a vicious smear campaign by the Catholic Truth Society. (Once again, the Church's name was used in mucking things up.) The Catholic Truth Society, a far-right organization, harped on Hyde's

Protestantism and stated that he was pro-divorce, which he was not. After the
Catholic Truth Society began barraging the newspapers with anti-Hyde letters,
Hyde's good name was tarnished and his chances for election lessened. Upon losing the election, Hyde was able to return to his one true love—the Irish language—and once more took the chair of Professor of Modern Irish at UCD.

In April 1938, three years after Hyde had retired from the university, the
taoiseach, Eamon de Valera, recalled Hyde to the Senate. It was a new world in
Irish government: The Irish Free State was now *Éire*, and a new constitution had
been hammered together in 1937. This constitution had created the office of
President, and de Valera (along with the leader of the opposition party) wanted
Douglas Hyde as president. Appointing him to the *Seanad Éirean*—the upper
house of the government—was a means of making Hyde eligible to be appointed
to the presidency. As the government went about selecting its first president of the
nation, all political parties unanimously selected Douglas Hyde.

In June 1938, Douglas Hyde was inaugurated as the first president of Ireland.
Fittingly, he gave his inauguration speech in Irish.

There were various reasons for Hyde's selection, in addition to his being the
choice of de Valera and the opposition party leader W. T. Cosgrave. He was seventy-seven years old and an affable and gentlemanly figure, whose warm personality
quelled any fears that the framers of the constitution had had of an overbearing
president who might become a despot. Franklin D. Roosevelt, after meeting with
Hyde, called him a "fine and scholarly old gentleman." That he was non-Catholic
was also important for the government, which wanted to underscore the fact that
this new nation was not a Catholic state. But most importantly of all, the presidency of Douglas Hyde was meant to be a recognizable tribute to the role that the
Gaelic League played in achieving Irish independence. For it was the Gaelic
League and the pride that it instilled in its young members that was the impetus

of the men who carved out their nation's destiny.

Not even two years into his presidency, Hyde suffered a massive stroke. Everyone assumed that the old man would not survive, and plans for a state funeral were made. But Hyde surprised everyone and recovered. He was partially paralyzed, and confined to a wheelchair, but he served capably for the next five years.

In 1945, Hyde retired as president. His health poor, he did not return to his family home in Roscommon. Instead, he took residence in the site where the former Secretary to the Lord Lieutenant had once lived, on the grounds of the presidential residence. It was there that he died quietly on July 12, 1949.

As a popular Protestant president of a primarily Catholic country, Douglas Hyde's state funeral revealed the problems of contemporary religion in politics. Hyde was buried in St. Patrick's, the Church of Ireland's cathedral in Dublin. Religious rules at the time forbade Catholics from going into Protestant churches. (The one God must have had a good laugh at that bureaucratic nonsense!) The result was that the entire cabinet—including de Valera—could not go into the Protestant church for the funeral, but had to wait outside to join the funeral procession. Douglas Hyde was buried in Roscommon, at his familial home. The house today is a museum dedicated not only to the history of Ireland's first president, but also, fittingly, to the cause of the Irish language itself.

De Valera's selection of Hyde as Ireland's first president was indeed a tribute to the Gaelic revival and the importance of the Irish language. For although Hyde worked incessantly to keep politics out of the Gaelic League, the pride it instilled in Irish men and women had the exact opposite effect. For if it were the writers of the Enlightenment—writers such as Thomas Paine and John Locke—who lit the nationalist flame within Wolfe Tone and Daniel O'Connell, it was Douglas Hyde's revival of the Celtic cultural past that fired hearts in Ireland's early twentieth century. The men who forged the new Irish nation at the beginning of the twentieth century, that next generation of rebels who would select Douglas Hyde to be the nation's first president, these men were raised on the principles of Hyde's Gaelic League and nourished by a new national pride in Ireland's Gaelic past.

A TERRIBLE BEAUTY IS BORN:
PROCLAIMING THE REPUBLIC

Charles Stewart Parnell's death meant more than the loss of the one individual who was most capable of bringing Home Rule to Ireland. With him, to a large degree, died the belief that Home Rule could be won through parliamentary means. Consequently, the necessity of armed insurrection and civil disobedience seemed more and more logical. Secret militant societies sprung up throughout Ireland, England, France, and the United States; organizations of every sort supporting nationalists, workers, and land reform arose; and when these societies acted out—violently or through mass meetings—England struck back with ever more draconian measures.

There had long been an adage in Ireland that "England's difficulty is Ireland's opportunity," and at the end of the nineteenth and beginning of the twentieth centuries, England had enough woes to offer Ireland plenty of opportunities. Amongst these were the Boer War in South Africa and World War I in Europe. (World War I was particularly ironic as England's fight was supposedly "to make small nations free" at the very time that England was shelling Dublin with its big guns.) Exacerbating this was the fact that for England to fight these wars, it needed Irish men, many of whom fought and died bravely. (In 1917 alone, 14,000 Irish men had volunteered to fight in World War I in a British uniform. England's Prime Minister, Lloyd George, himself asked how these men could be expected to fight for the principles of freedom and self-determination when these same principles were denied them at home.) Yet an undercurrent of dissatisfaction was swelling that argued that England's use of Ireland's men on the battle lines was one more facet of England's rape of Ireland. And thus a countermovement began. From the time they were young, boys were encouraged not to volunteer, although for many, economics alone would force them into the British military—it was, after all, a paying job when none other could be had. In South Africa, a separate Irish Brigade formed to fight against the English. It was led by John MacBride, who later would take his place among the martyrs of 1916.

England—whose fighting forces were becoming depleted by the carnage of World War I—had the gall to attempt a conscription law in 1918, at the very moment when Ireland was fighting England in its own War of Independence. The "carrot" offered to have the law enacted was the promise of a diluted form of Home Rule when the war was over. The attempt was condemned roundly, and had the effect of uniting many of the quarreling factions of Irish politics. In no small way, George's proposal, in uniting Sinn Feiners, labor, the Irish Parliamentarian Party, and even the Catholic Church, did much to distance Irish politics from Westminster and to settle it in Dublin. Nationhood was only a few years away.

Against the backdrop of all this, there rose a large number of social organizations: programs that fed school children and spread Irish culture and literacy, organizations to assist workers and secure them rights, prisoner societies dedicated to stopping the abuse of prisoners, literary groups from which a national literature was born, efforts to assuage the devastation of evictions. If England would not take care of the people it claimed were part of its kingdom, the people themselves would do so. And in doing so, a fervent nationalism spread.

Yet ultimately it was a failed insurrection—and England's heavy-handed reaction—that perhaps cemented Irish nationalism among the largest percentage of the population. On April 23, 1916, a group of teachers, poets, soldiers, and intellectuals proclaimed an Irish Republic from the General Post Office in Dublin. Plans had gone badly, and it was a small army of men and women who were determined to overthrow the British government. The big British guns reduced

Dublin to rubble, civilian casualties were high, and after a week of bloody fighting, Padraig Pearse and the other leaders surrendered.

The British acted heavy-handedly and executed most of the leaders—Countess Markievicz was reprieved because she was a woman and Eamon de Valera because he had American citizenship. James Connolly was so badly wounded that he had to be strapped to a chair in order to face the firing squad. The world was aghast—and the Irish dream of nationalism had become an international issue. What this small group of men and women had done was to offer the supreme sacrifice—themselves—to the Irish cause, and their martyrdom was successful in ways they could never have imagined.

Some of their names are well-known, many of them less so. They emerged from a nationalism founded by Douglas Hyde's pride in the Irish language and the Irish past, out of a militarism fostered by years of political frustration and English brutality, and out of a social consciousness fostered by the inequities of Victorian industrialism, and together they strove to bring about the ideal they believed in. Of course, no ideal can ever be realized, and there would be many, many horrors and troubles ahead. But this particular moment—and these particular people—was indeed extraordinary. They were Protestant and Catholic nationalists and Marxists. They rose from Irish slums and English drawing rooms. They were poor teachers and free-thinking nobility. They were radical thinkers and conventional patriots.

Three of the more unique characters at this time were Maud Gonne, Padraig Pearse, and James Connolly. One probably could not meet three more disparate characters, and yet their names are forever bound in that historic moment when, to quote the poet Yeats, "a terrible beauty was born."

Chapter XXII:

Maud Gonne

The course of Irish history is filled with marvelous, spirited women who were more than just the meets of their male counterparts, which is more often the case than usually recorded in national histories. In Ireland, perhaps, this is the outgrowth of the ancient Gaelic order in which women wielded a more powerful force than they did in other societies. Whatever the cause, it is true from Brigid, who was Bishop of Kildare, to Grace O'Malley, who controlled the seas surrounding Ireland, from the women who fought mightily in the uprising of '98 to Anna and Fanny Parnell, who agitated so successfully for Land Reform. The end of the nineteenth century and the beginning of the twentieth century featured an impressive list of likewise remarkable women: Countess Constance Markievicz, Hanna Sheehy-Skeffington, Kathleen Clarke, and Maud Gonne. Perhaps a measure of these women's import to the Irish cause was the number of times that England felt it necessary to throw them in jail, deny them travel rights, and raid their homes. In truth, a great number of Irish women made their mark on the course of Irish history in those dramatic times.

And in Maud Gonne's case, she not only made her mark on history, but on literature as well. A committed and tireless worker in the cause of relief for the poor and dispossessed, a staunch fighter for the rights of the imprisoned, a dedicated proponent of independence and of a role for women in the creation of the new nation, and finally a fierce guardian of the principles on which the Republic was proclaimed, she was also the inspiration for William Butler Yeats, the muse for much of his best poetry. (Yeats was so enamored—actually "enamored" is too weak a word—that he proposed marriage countless times to Maud and was rejected. Years later, he asked if he could marry her daughter!)

Like so many in the past who fought for Ireland—Wolfe Tone, Robert Emmet, Charles Parnell—Maud Gonne was born into a Protestant family. She was born in England in 1865 or 1866. Her father, Thomas Gonne, was an English soldier who brought his wife and two daughters with him to Ireland when he was garrisoned there in 1868. Maud's mother died when Maud was six years old, leaving the soldier father to raise his two daughters alone. He raised them to think for themselves, and he gave Maud a bit of advice that she lived by throughout her life: never be afraid of anything.

It does not always serve history to talk about a figure's physical beauty, but in discussing Maud, it is pertinent. For she was an extraordinary presence, with a beauty that entranced most who came upon her. Men and women commented in their diaries and letters, having met Maud for the first time, about her stature, her grace, her flair, and her beauty. By the time she was fourteen years old, Maud was already five-foot ten and a formidable young girl; she would grow to be a commanding six feet tall. And in her father's household, she strove to be both daughter and hostess; in this dual role, she forged her own character.

At one point, her father moved Maud and her sister Kathleen to a house in Howth, looked after by a governess. There the two sisters rambled through the mountains and met with Irish children, whose homes they often visited. It is perhaps these early visits to homes where the stark conditions were in such contrast to the relative abundance of their own home, but where hospitality nevertheless was plentiful, that Maud had her first inklings of the inequality between Irish and English in Ireland. She also discovered, contrary to what she had been trained to believe, that many of these Irish children were better than she and her sister at several things: simply being English, she learned, did not make her superior.

Because of weak lungs, which would trouble her the rest of her life, Maud with her sister was sent to southern France to recuperate while her father was stationed in Eastern Europe. The girls traveled through France and to Rome—and finally returned to Dublin with their father. The day they returned was the day after the infamous Phoenix Park murders. (In a classic bit of understatement, in her memoirs, Maud simply states that they arrived the day after the Lord Lieutenant left!) For three years, from 1882 to 1885, her father had no post and remained in Dublin. Maud spent three years of relative privilege, and served as the woman of her father's house, a young woman with responsibility and independence and the support of her father. Her beauty was indeed remarkable; she was a statuesque six feet tall and possessed a sophistication that caught the eye of Oscar Wilde as well as the attention of the Prince of Wales! Later, when Maud's father learned that the Prince of Wales happened to be in the same town in Germany where Maud was staying, he quickly packed her up and brought her back to Ireland.

Yet Tommy (which is what Maud always called her father) would not be able to protect his daughter's interests much longer. He died in 1886, when Maud was only twenty. A maternal uncle, William Cook, deceived the Gonne girls into thinking that their father had mangled his financial affairs, but in a perverse way Maud saw this as a positive sign, as a signal for her to take control of her own destiny. Which she promptly did. She was hired to perform in a play in London, and received star billing. When Uncle William learned of this, he was aghast and ordered her to desist. She of course refused—it was her life, after all. Worried that she would cheapen the family name by pursuing a career on stage and concerned when Maud once again became sick thanks to the effect that dusty and cold rehearsal halls had on her lungs, he informed Maud and her sister that he had lied. Their father had, in fact, left a trust for the two girls, adequate to supply them with an income for a great while.

It was during these times, also, that Maud Gonne met and fell in love with a Frenchman, a married man named Lucien Millevoye. Their political discussions

undoubtedly served to radicalize her own developing politics, and Millevoye ultimately involved her in his own plans. (At one point, she crossed Europe by train,
illegally carrying secret documents intended for the Tsar and asking Russia to support Millevoye's French cause.) Yet it was not Millevoye's ideas for which Maud
had set out to fight. In Russia, she had met a journalist who told her that if she
wanted to do something for Ireland, she must go and listen to Michael Davitt,
who was sitting then as a Member of Parliament. Maud returned to England, sat
in the House of Commons, met with Davitt, and was disappointed. (Davitt felt
that she, with her ingenuous questions and her enthusiasm, was a spy.)

So she moved back to Dublin, where she was introduced to Charles Oldham,
who in turn brought her to a meeting of the Contemporary Club. This gentlemen's club was founded in 1885, and at the time included the famous Fenian
John O'Leary, whom Maud had expressly wanted to meet. Maud told him out-
right that she wanted to work for Ireland.

In Dublin, Maud took lessons in nursing, some rifle practice, and began organizing meetings throughout the city. Her first, an all-Irish night to support the
Dublin Hospital, was noteworthy for Maud's insistence on ending the night with
the song "Let Erin Remember" rather than the traditional "God Save the Queen."
The notoriety that this earned served notice that Ireland had a new force to reckon
with. Soon she was hosting a "salon" where such luminaries as Douglas Hyde visited, and which more often than not ended in the wee hours. Politics and literature
were the topics of the day, and many a new poem or newly hatched plan first saw
light in Maud's Nassau Street flat.

When Maud Gonne went to join the National League, she was again told that
women were not permitted to join—never a good thing to tell Maud. Though
arguing heatedly with the men in charge that Ireland needed all its people to fight
for freedom, she nevertheless could not sway them. However, these men were not

so blind or thickheaded as not to know that in front of them was an extraordinary woman, whose background, dramatic bearing, and passion could be put to good use. While she could not join the National League, she could help them. They gave her introductory letters and told her to travel to Donegal, where evictions were still a problem. Surely, such a woman would bring some publicity to the situation.

Her trip to Donegal in 1889 was enlightening. She met and comforted the poor and evicted. She visited with Fenian priests who had despaired of anything but the use of force. She attended court sessions, invited journalists in, and called in builders to construct huts to house the evicted. Also, the dire condition of Donegal instilled in her a life-long hatred of landlords and of the futility of parliamentary "reform." Before Donegal, Maud Gonne was a spirited young woman; Donegal transformed her into a rebel.

She left the west of Ireland to meet Millevoye in France, excited about the work she had done and eager to share her excitement. On the way, she stopped in London to make other contacts in the Irish nationalist community. One of these men was William Butler Yeats. On January 30, 1889, Maud Gonne visited the Yeats household in London. While neither Yeats's father nor his sisters were much impressed with the passionate young woman, Yeats himself was enthralled. He dined with her every evening afterward while she was in London. During this time, she mentioned to Yeats—already celebrated for his poems on the Celtic twilight—that she would love to have a play to perform in Dublin. Yeats immediately offered to write one for her.

This trip to Paris and to her lover would prove eventful for Maud Gonne as well. Millevoye's man had won an important election (although he fled the country when threatened with arrest and committed suicide), Millevoye himself was elected to office, and in January 1890, Maud Gonne gave birth to a son, George.

When Maud returned to Donegal in 1890—alone, for she could not bring nor admit to an "illegitimate" child in Ireland—she found that she had become a celebrity to the poor of the region. The people spoke of her as a goddess, as a spirit of the Sidhe who brought victory to the people. And this trip served to strengthen that impression. One story tells how, when visiting a family about to be evicted, she met an MP from London who had fallen in love with her and had followed her to the west of Ireland. (That he was not there to bring relief to the destitute must have rankled Gonne.) He proposed marriage to her, there on the spot in the simple hut, and gave her an enormous diamond pendant. Maud handed over the diamond to the poor woman, saying that the MP had brought it for her to help and shelter others. The MP was infuriated, but Maud's reputation soared higher than before—she was a woman who showered diamonds on the poor.

At this time, she also made her first political speech in a campaign against the government. As her name spread through the west, it also reached the ears of the British Government—they had received their first report on her after the all-Irish concert in Dublin that had ended with "Let Erin Remember." There was now a warrant out for her arrest. With her weak lungs damaged by the cold, damp conditions of Donegal, and with arrest imminent, she returned to France, where she always went to regain her health. It was on this trip that she realized her relationship with Millevoye was disintegrating, and her young son, George, died of meningitis. He was one year old.

Maud Gonne was crushed—years later, on her own deathbed, she asked for little George's baby booties to be placed in her coffin when she died. Dressed in mourning black—which she would retain for the rest of her life—she left France once again for Ireland.

In times of heartbreak, Maud turned to Yeats, who was always pleased to offer her any solace she would accept. In this instance, she had told him that in France, a child "she had adopted" had died and that her heart was rent. In one of history's many ironies, she sailed to Ireland on the same ferry that was bringing back the body of Parnell. Her fellow passengers—and indeed all who knew her—assumed that her mourning was in memory of Parnell. Her own heartbreak was silent.

Such was Maud's resiliency that before too long—and not without much support from Yeats, who arranged for all sorts of people to involve her in all types of activities—she was back in France lecturing on the evils of the evictions in Ireland, on the Irish fight for independence, and on the injustices Britain had showered on the Irish people for centuries. With her flare for the dramatic, Maud brought her audiences to tears as she recounted tales of the Great Hunger. The lecture tour was an embarrassment for England: over 2,000 articles appeared in French papers alone about the dire situation of British/Irish relations; what had up until now been a dirty secret of England's was in the international press.

It was also at this time that Maud grew involved with prisoners' rights, particularly those who had been jailed under the Treason-Felony Act—a duplicitous piece of legislation that allowed jailing political prisoners as felons. Indeed, she threw herself into every sort of committee and organization. In London and Ireland there were the Amnesty Association and the National Literary Society; in France, she was urging clothiers to buy Donegal tweed; and she was once again pregnant. (Having dabbled in the occult arts which so fascinated Yeats, Gonne hoped that she could reincarnate the spirit of her beloved George. Thus, the story goes, she and Millevoye coupled on the boy's tomb, and Gonne always claimed she conceived there.) In August 1894, Iseult Gonne was born.

In 1897, a committee formed to celebrate the centenary of the 1798 Uprising of the United Irishmen. It was also the year of Queen Victoria's Jubilee. The committee decided to hold its convention on the very day of the Jubilee. It was in preparing this convention that Gonne first met James Connolly. He would remain a faithful and loyal partner—as interested in the social causes that Gonne embraced as in the establishment of Irish independence. One story goes that Connolly wanted Gonne to give a small speech at an open-air rally, but when she saw posters advertising her as the main speaker at a socialist rally, she hesitated. Yeats smoothed things over, and Gonne went to visit Connolly in his tenement home. She had been in the poorest huts and cottages of western Ireland, but this was her first visit to an urban tenement. Its abject condition was enough to make her decide, and the next day she gave a speech on Dame Street to an enormous crowd, and even Yeats—who believed he knew her better than anyone—was awestruck.

Another coup that Gonne arranged during the Jubilee year was the Patriotic Children's Treat Committee. When Victoria visited Dublin for her Jubilee Year, a staged picnic for 5,000 children was presented in Phoenix Park to show the world that a majority of Irish backed the queen. Gonne and several of her friends arranged a counter-production. They organized a "treat" for all those children who refused the queen's largesse. A woman of many talents, Maud Gonne was a magnificent organizer. She gathered donations from all over the country: one thousand oranges twenty tons of sweets, forty thousand buns, casks of ginger beer, bags full of sandwiches. When the children gathered in Clonturk Park, they numbered more than 25,000. Aside from the treats they received that day, the children also heard a speech from the famous Maud Gonne, who urged the boys never to join the English army and the girls to work for the Irish nation. She then told them that by the time they grew up, Ireland would be free. The day was an enormous success, and Maud got due credit.

From the Patriotic Children's Treat Committee there emerged another organization, *Inghinidhe na hÉireann*, the "daughters of Ireland." Founded by Maud Gonne in 1900, it was a women's organization that held classes in Irish history and language and put on plays and tableaux celebrating the Celtic past. Openly nationalist, the *Inghinidhe na hÉireann* promoted buying Irish-made goods, discouraged young boys from volunteering for the army, and was instrumental in organizing one of Gonne's favorite causes—meals for schoolchildren. (Incredibly, the Church was against feeding schoolchildren, as it believed it smacked of "socialism." Maud's arguments were not only fierce—as usual—but cogent and well founded.) The organization thrived, and soon had spread from Dublin to Ballina, Cork, and Limerick. But the small plays that *Inghinidhe na hÉireann* put on for its students were nothing compared to the historic one that they would soon help mount, and which would become a landmark in Ireland's national literature: *Cathleen ni Houlihan* by William Butler Yeats. Of course, the title role was played by Maud Gonne. Indeed, Yeats had given the play to the organization *on the condition that Maud would play Cathleen.* It had, after all, been written for her.

It had often been said that Maud Gonne had a strange power over people. On the stage, that power affected everyone. The worst that people said of that night was that Maud did not act the part of Mother Ireland, but became it. Faint criticism, to be sure. Others called her the most beautiful woman in Ireland, the very muse of the revolutionary movement, the embodiment of Ireland itself. Appearing as an old woman in the first half of the play, when she removed her old woman's cloak to reveal the statuesque beauty, it was as if the chains of Ireland's bondage had fallen aside with the old woman's rags, and its glory had come back to life right there on stage. After all the political speeches, all the late discussions, all the passionate arguments, perhaps nothing inspired the people of Ireland as Maud Gonne's portrayal of Cathleen ni Houlihan. Yeats himself worried that his simple play sent too many men out to be shot down by England. Throughout her life, many people would claim that they had either heard her speak at the Patriotic Children's Treat or had watched her on stage as

Cathleen. For many, she was bigger than life, an undeniable force in Ireland.

On February 21, 1903, Maud Gonne married John MacBride in France. MacBride had been celebrated in Ireland as a hero for fighting against the British during the Boer War, yet because of this, he could not enter Ireland, where he would have faced arrest for treason. In order to marry him, Gonne converted to Catholicism, and as with all things spiritual, she immersed herself in the religion. (Though to Yeats, she once said that she had always felt restrained as an outsider from attacking the clergy in her speeches, but that now that she was a member she would be able to go full throttle!) Typical of her independence, she insisted on keeping her own name—it was only after MacBride's death in the aftermath of the Easter Uprising that she began using the name Maud Gonne MacBride. She telegrammed Yeats, who was, of course, devastated. In their occult days, the two had tried a spiritual marriage where they would meet on "astral planes"; and he had believed her protestations against physical love. But here she was, married, and once again Yeats was heartbroken.

But the marriage was not successful—she was fiercely independent and he was stubbornly traditional—and within months, she was in London, again with Yeats consoling her. Politics would soon make her forget her troubles. Her success in defying Victoria's visit had emboldened her to disrupt Edward VII's visit in 1903. She publicly questioned the intentions of the mayor, her old friend Tom Harrington, in what one paper described as "one of the most sensational incidents" ever in Irish history, and she rallied public opinion so that when it came to a vote, the Dublin Corporation voted against officially acknowledging the king's visit. When the vote was announced, Maud Gonne was feted as a hero. On the day of the king's visit, Maud flew her black petticoat out of her bedroom window. When her neighbors—who were Unionists all, proudly flying the Union Jack—saw it, the police were called to remove it. Immediately, she flew another petticoat, and this time, she, a friend, and her housekeeper fought off the police attempting to remove this second "black flag." The police then called for reinforcements. In the meantime, someone had run to *Inghinidhe na hÉireann*'s offices to tell everyone to meet on Gonne's street; Arthur Griffith had also sent around people from *Cumann na nGaedheal*. By the time the back-up police came, they were obviously outnumbered, and so returned to their stations and allowed Maud Gonne's petticoat to fly. It was a silly and trivial stunt, but the story garnered more attention than the king's visit itself. And it continued to build the legend of Maud Gonne.

More importantly to Maud, who always thought of the children, another Children's Treat was organized. Although nowhere as successful as the first, it still claimed to have fed 15,000 children in the pouring rain.

On January 26, 1904, Maud Gonne gave birth to Jean Sean MacBride. It was a child whom Maud could show off proudly, as she was now a married mother, and she doted lavishly on the boy. Such was the excitement throughout Ireland of this new Gonne/MacBride son that one man sent a telegram to the pope announcing that the king of Ireland had been born. (As an aside, Sean MacBride would grow up to join the IRA, and often argued with his mother in politics. As the son of John MacBride and Maud Gonne—and with John O'Leary as his godfather—it was no surprise to find him in the leadership of the IRA as well as in English prisons a number of times. What was surprising was that this man of militant parents later turned to peace, anti-discrimination legislation, and world disarmament, for which in 1974 he received the Nobel Peace Prize. Sean MacBride died in 1988.) However, the birth of a child was not enough to save the faltering marriage, and a little more than a year after Sean's birth, Maud Gonne filed for divorce. The scandal and all its details took over the papers, and for once Maud Gonne's politics were not what kept her in the public eye. Indeed, the amount of stress and attention that the divorce proceedings demanded left little time to do her work. Worst of all, MacBride had friends in Dublin, the same as Maud. The city split. And while Maud herself had many supporters, one man in particular stayed by her side. That man was, of course, Yeats.

Amid all the publicity and rancor, Maud Gonne returned to her home in France where she lived for ten years with her children, her menagerie of pets, and a steady stream of visitors. When World War I broke out, Maud did what she knew how to do best; she cared for the needy. Working for the Red Cross, she tended to the increasing stream of casualties returning from France. It was this experience, this first-hand knowledge of the horrors of war, that softened Gonne's attitude about armed conflict, although she never lost her conviction that it was necessary in shaking off Britain's hold on Ireland.

That armed conflict would come soon enough, yet when it occurred, Gonne was in France. On April 23, 1916, the Irish Citizens Army took over the General Post Office and proclaimed an Irish Republic. The British Army responded with force, and soon the city was in rubble. John MacBride, who was one of the few who had real battle experience from his time in the Boer War, knew nothing of the plans for the uprising, and was actually coming home from a friend's wedding when the fighting broke out. He joined Thomas MacDonagh, who was posted at Jacob's Biscuit Factory, and he proved to be an exceptional leader in the fighting. When the leaders were executed, John MacBride was among them—not because he had been a leader of the uprising, but because the British had long memories. They had wanted this man since the days in Transvaal, and now that they had him, they were not going to let him escape the firing squad.

World War I censorship curtailed the amount of information that reached the continent, so Gonne was frantic for news. As usual, Yeats stepped in and sent her the English papers every day. She learned that many of the people she knew had been executed, that the city she loved was destroyed, and that the husband who had treated her and her family so poorly had proven himself honorable in the end. Indeed, when John MacBride was shot, he refused a blindfold, stating that it wasn't the first time he had faced British guns.

Given her reputation, however, the British Consulate in France was not eager to issue her a passport, and when they did, it permitted her to travel to England only—she was forbidden to travel to Ireland. In England, Gonne gave several lectures to a suffragette organization on the topic of Sinn Fein, in which she attacked the British government for not allowing her son to visit the grave of his father, and which were covered by the press. Finally, fed up with government regulations, she disguised herself and set sail for Ireland.

Gonne was not in Ireland long before she and Kathleen Clarke, along with seventy-three Sinn Feiners, were arrested and sent to English jails. Actually, Gonne and Clarke were not prisoners—they were charged with nothing. They were detainees, but the conditions were dreadful nevertheless. While in jail, she learned of the death of both Millevoye and of her sister Kathleen. Her health began to fail so in October 1917, she was released.

Things in Ireland were going from bad to worse. The War of Independence was raging; the Black and Tans were brutal; and Irish men and women were being sent off to jail in unimagined numbers. Gonne kept up her work for prisoners' rights—no doubt intensified by her own experience—and, as part of Sinn Fein's publicity department, she worked to bring international opinion on the side of the Irish cause. Part of this publicity was getting American and British organizations to form an international committee of inquiry into the state of Irish political prisoners. At the end of the investigation, both the American commissions and the British organizations soundly condemned British policy.

(An odd insight into the revolution that Sinn Fein wished to effect was the court system. In order to separate themselves from the British system—which had proven to mete out justice so niggardly to Irish appeals—Sinn Fein opted for a system that harkened back to the old Brehon laws. And in that system, women were judges. So for a while Maud Gonne acted as a judge, in secret in an outlawed organization.)

On December 6, 1920, five men who had been sent to negotiate in London, including Michael Collins and Arthur Griffiths, signed a treaty with Lloyd George ending the war. (Maud's son Sean was Collins's *aide-de-camp* in London at the time.) The treaty was a compromise. Ireland was to be partitioned, with the six northern counties remaining part of the Union while the Free State—the twenty-six counties in the south—would attain some form of self-rule. Members of the Free State Parliament, however, would still be required to take the hated Oath of Allegiance to the Crown. The treaty did do more than divide the country geographically; it irrevocably split the republican movement and caused a civil war.

At first, Maud Gonne accepted the treaty as a stepping-stone to a broader republic. It was not all that she had wished for, all that she and Willie Yeats had dreamed of, but it was a start. And she—and several other prominent women—tried to negotiate a treaty between the republicans and the Free Staters. But to no avail. In fact, as the Free Staters became more and more intolerant of the republicans and their methods became more and more totalitarian, Maud soon embraced the republican cause. Her home was made into a make-shift hospital for IRA wounded; she and her coworkers tried to bring clothes and food to republican prisoners held in Mountjoy prison; she formed the "Mothers" to protest the detention of these republican prisoners—prisoners, she argued, now being held by an Irish government. Indeed, despite laws preventing mass demonstrations, the "Mothers" met every Sunday as the pro-Treaty forces acted more and more draconian. As protests fell on deaf ears, she helped form the Women's Prisoners' Defense League. In her weekly demonstrations, she faced gunshots and arrest. Her home was continually raided; it was once set afire, and a bomb was discovered in the outhouse. She was a dangerous person to the government, and for the first time in Maud's life, it was not a British government who feared her tactics. It was an Irish government.

When William Butler Yeats was made a senator of the Free State, a serious breach was created between the two long-standing friends. It was one that would not be healed for more than a decade.

She continued making speeches—in lecture halls or on street corners—and demonstrating for prisoners' rights. When de Valera's Fianna Fail government took office, he released the prisoners as he had promised, but he quickly fell from her favor. The IRA was deemed an illegal organization, and the yearly trip to ceremonies at Wolfe Tone's grave was banned. Maud Gonne's work was still not finished. Even one of her earliest causes, the role of women in the work of the Irish nation, seemed to be set backwards by a clause in the new 1937 de Valera constitution. The article set out that the Irish woman would best serve the country by staying in the home. Gonne, naturally, was incensed—for it flew in the face of what she and James Connolly had mutually agreed upon and what had drawn them together, and it contradicted the spirit of the Proclamation that Pearse had read from the General Post Office.

And it was against de Valera and his government, as it slouched toward nationhood, that Maud Gonne fought the remainder of her battles. Prison conditions, the plight of the poor, the role of women, freedom of expression, and the freedom of all Irish men and women: these were the causes that she dedicated her life to, and now, in her seventh decade, she continued fighting these same battles. There must have been times in those years where she wondered whether she had effected any change at all.

She was eighty-six when she died on April 27, 1953. By that time, she had become a legend—the last of the great Republicans. Yeats's fame as a Nobel Laureate added to her renown, and she was often visited by Yeats scholars who wished to meet the woman who had inspired some of the world's greatest poems, as well as by historians in search of an eyewitness account of the birth of a nation.

When she died, she left a legacy of unwavering principle, of untiring dedication and political activism, of a life lived with drama, passion, and intensity. She had often spoken about the role of women in Ireland's destiny, and like Cathleen ni Houlihan herself, she came to be the embodiment of what she spoke.

CHAPTER XXIII:
PADRAIG PEARSE

I first met Colman Welby in 1977. He was an old man by then, and had forgotten his English completely, although he had spent some four or five years during the twenties as a steel worker in Pittsburgh. He had a lovely wife, Brigid, and a full pot of tea, and I spent a good afternoon with the two of them, Brigid trying to translate my English and his Irish. It was the first and only time I was in his company, for he died soon after.

I visited Brigid again about twenty years later. She was no longer the young woman looking after an elderly husband whom I had first known, but had grown old herself. She was as spry as always, however, still offering a full pot of tea and a plate of biscuits, although now she probably wouldn't have been able to translate her husband's Irish as easily as she had that first time. For she, too, was beginning to lose the English.

It was a gray afternoon that day I sat in her cottage, the rains moving in and out by the quarter hour and the lake behind her small cottage looking like a tarn in a landscape of desolation. That description is not overly written, for the area around Rosmuck, County Galway, is one of the most remote and most beautiful on earth. There are rocky pastures, winding lanes, and bracing lakes. And a fellow setting out there alone might not see a human face for several days walking if he were not sure what he was about.

But as I said, the weather was changing rapidly, and by my second cup of tea, the sun had come out and was showering the lake behind with golden rays, changing the dark water to a crystalline blue. What had been so foreboding a half-hour before had become a slice of heaven. This is Rosmuck's nature.

But Brigid Welby's was not my only destination that day. I was there to see the cottage of Padraig Pearse.

About two miles down the road from Brigid Welby's, there is a simple cottage—now run by the National Trust—in which Pearse once lived. It is a perfect retreat from the bustle of modernity, where one can look out on a soft valley and a small lake by sitting in the front room and looking out the door. It is the cottage of a man who thinks with his heart and feels with his mind, the cottage of a poet, a teacher, a revolutionary. The landscape of Rosmuck perfectly reflects the man: the hard rocks of Connemara capture the steely resolve of the man slated to be the president of the Provisional Government, who would bravely face an English firing squad, and the green valleys and blue lakes reveal the poet within, the optimistic teacher who founded a bilingual school in order to preserve the best of Irish culture.

Indeed, the men who signed Pearse's Proclamation of the Irish Republic on April 13, 1916, were not by nature a fierce bunch; on the contrary, a more intellectual and artistic bunch of revolutionaries could not be found. Pearse was a poet, as was Joseph Plunkett and Thomas MacDonagh; de Valera was a schoolteacher, a mathematician; Connolly was an intellectual, a socialist writer; Eamonn Ceannt, while he worked as a clerk, was a uileann piper and a contributor to Pearse's Irish-language newspaper, *An Barr Buadh*. With Thomas Clarke and Sean MacDiarmada, these five men put their names on Pearse's eloquent document, from which Irish independence would ultimately spring.

Padraig Pearse was born in Dublin in 1879. His father was an Englishman who had converted from Unitarianism to Catholicism and who moved to Ireland to work as a stone carver. His mother was from County Meath. As a stonecutter, Pearse's father enjoyed a brisk business—primarily in building Catholic church-es—and the family lived in relative comfort. In a prescient gesture, Padraig—the second of four children—was named not after the patron saint, but after the American patriot Patrick Henry.

When he was eleven, Pearse with his younger brother Willie began learning the Irish language as part of the curriculum at the Christian Brothers school in Westland Row. The Irish language was to become a lifelong avocation for Pearse, and in many ways propelled him into the fire of Irish nationalism. For the rest of the curriculum, Pearse later had little good to say, and, at the time, he wrote an essay called "The Murder Machine" on the deplorable state of Irish education.

Along with the Irish language, Pearse was regaled with tales of ancient Ireland and stories of the great patriotic heroes such as Cúchulainn, Brian Ború, Wolfe Tone, and Robert Emmet by a great-aunt who often visited the Pearse house in Dublin. These, too, he kept close throughout his life. His father, though an Englishman, was fiercely political and a strong proponent of Parnell. Pearse would always remain loyal to the name of Charles Stewart Parnell, even when among his fellow militants who had grown disenchanted with any form of Parliamentarian participation.

A serious student more comfortable in the classroom than on the playing fields, Pearse graduated from the Royal University in 1900 and studied at Trinity

College for the bar. And though he passed the bar at King's Inn, he never practiced the profession but once, and that was to defend the Gaelic League in court. A man of Pearse's idealism would never have fared well in the corrupt and compromising world of British trained lawyers.

Fresh out of school, Pearse was thrown into a role of unexpected responsibility. His father died shortly after he graduated, and Pearse found himself the head of a household that included his widowed mother, his brother Willie, and his two sisters, Margaret and Mary-Brigid. It was a responsibility that he proudly accepted, and one that he kept for the rest of his life, as neither of his sisters ever married or found work. (One of my favorite stories of Pearse's mother is that when, on Easter morning, her adult sons Padraig and Willie were setting off to begin the Easter Uprising, she told the boys not to do anything rash.)

Undoubtedly, Douglas Hyde's Gaelic League was a most important influence on Padraig Pearse. One of the earlier members, he joined the central branch in 1895, and was soon spending summers in the west to perfect his knowledge and use of the language by studying with native speakers in Connemara. While still attending university, he started teaching Irish at the Westland Row School. His zeal for the language—and his complementary disdain for English—so infuriated one student that the boy left after one class. That student was James Joyce.

While in the Gaelic League, Pearse was appointed to the editorship of the League's official journal *An Claidheamh Soluis*. He was still young, only twenty-four, for such a visible position, but he improved the paper greatly.

Steeped in ancient Irish literature, folklore, and poetry, and working within the literary influences of the Gaelic League, Pearse himself became a fair poet and playwright in his own right. His work, while placed firmly in the Celtic revival of Hyde's Gaelic League, was written in English as well as in Irish. He edited an Irish-language literary journal, contributed articles to Arthur Griffith's *The United*

Irishman, and, in 1912, began his own Irish-language newspaper, *An Barr Buadh*— "The Trumpet of Victory."

Earlier, after a trip to Belgium where he visited a bilingual school, he started his own bilingual school, St. Edna's—*Scoil Eanna*—in 1908, giving up the rather cushy position of editor at *An Claidheamh Soluis.* He invested all his savings; his brother Willie invested as well and left his stone-cutting business to teach at the school; and his friend Thomas MacDonagh became headmaster for the first three years, before taking a position at the National University. (All three of these teachers would be executed by the British following the Easter Uprising.) The school was Pearse's answer to "the murdering machine" that he saw ruining so many young Irish minds. Yet St. Edna's was not purely academic; for Pearse, it was to be a source of national pride, a place where young boys would be introduced to the greatness of the Irish past, of its culture, language, and history.

This full immersion into the Gaelic League, into the celebration of Irish identity, could not help but make one nationalistic, and Pearse was not alone in his jump from Douglas Hyde's classes and lectures to full-blown nationalism. Indeed, it was Pearse who told Hyde that the Gaelic League had become ineffectual in the growing militancy of the times.

The year 1913 was a seminal one in Irish revolutionary history and in Padraig Pearse's own history. The successful Dublin Lockout had nevertheless produced Connolly's Irish Citizens Army; in the north, the Ulster Volunteers were preparing to fight against any passage of Home Rule; and the Irish Volunteers were training in order to defend Home Rule if civil war did break out with the Unionists. By the end of the year, the Volunteers had evolved from a defensive organization to a force intending to wrest independence from Britain's hands.

Pearse had been one of the founding members of the Volunteers, but by the end of the year, he had been brought into the Irish Republican Brotherhood by

Thomas Clarke, one of its organizers. The proselytizing and speechifying that so turned off the young James Joyce in the classroom were what attracted Tom Clarke! And if there had been any second feelings about Pearse's role—and there were such grumblings by hard-bitten men who were unsure of this scholarly romantic—they were squelched by his eulogy at O'Donovan Rossa's graveside in August 1915.

The story of O'Donovan Rossa's funeral itself demonstrates the pull of the IRB toward armed revolt. Jerimiah O'Donovan Rossa had died on Staten Island, New York, on June 29, 1915. At one time he was a fierce agitator, but now he was an old man, often confused and bereft of his senses. When he died, John Devoy sent a message to Tom Clarke asking what to do. Clarke told him to send the body over—a proper Fenian funeral could be the very match to light the powder keg that was Ireland in 1915. Clarke deliberately chose Pearse to give the funeral oration, and there surrounded by Irish Volunteers, James Connolly's Citizen Army, Countess Markievicz's paramilitary youth group, the *Fianna na hEireann*, Pearse proved Clarke's confidence right on. In the gray drizzle, Pearse held the onlookers—and not a few government witnesses spellbound. If there were a few uncomfortable glances among the gathered when he told his listeners that "we pledge to Ireland our love, and we pledge to English rule in Ireland our hate," by the time he finished his speech, he had driven his meaning home. The closing words, "Ireland unfree will never be at peace," were a warning shot across the bow of English politics. The battle itself would come in less than a year.

The rest of the year was taken up with planning. By early 1916, it had been decided that the uprising would take place on Easter Sunday, April 23. The following day was a holiday and the British contingent in Dublin would be smaller since many of the soldiers would be on leave at the Fairyhouse Races. (British forces were at low levels anyway, as casualties piled up in the fields of France and reinforcements continued to sail over to Europe.) Also a prime objective of the IRB at the time was to rein in James Connolly, who seemed to be planning an insurrection of his own. Poet Joseph Plunkett had planned an assault on Dublin with 5,000 troops seizing particular strongholds in the city and using the General Post Office as headquarters. A similar number of troops would rise in the country-side. In the meantime, guns and ammunition would arrive from Germany as arranged by John Devoy in New York.

What the planners could depend on was what they themselves were in control of—the seizing of Dublin strongholds. The German aid fell through on Good Friday night, and Eoin MacNeill countermanded the order to assemble the Volunteers in the countryside on Sunday morning. Nevertheless, the leaders went on with their plans.

It has been commented on that these leaders foresaw that their deaths would unify the Irish people, for as they marched through the Dublin streets on April 24, 1916, each one of them must have known for certain how it would all end. They were aware of MacNeill's countermand; they knew that the German guns were beyond reach and they saw their own raggle-taggle muster of men march out to take on the might of the British Army. On Easter morning, Pearse argued to pro-ceed to the west and regroup; Connolly wanted to stay on in Dublin and bring the fight to the streets; Clarke argued that the plans should stay as written. They decided to go forward with the original plan, but on Easter Monday rather than on Easter itself.

Padraig Pearse, in the full uniform of the Irish Volunteers, bicycled to Liberty Hall where the leaders were meeting. He was Commandant in Chief of the Army of the Republic. While others took posts throughout the city, Pearse, Connolly, and Clarke marched to the General Post Office on Sackville Street (now O'Connell Street). They moved the customers and staff out and turned the post office into a military encampment. Then, with a sword by his side, Padraig Pearse stepped outside and read the proclamation to a gathering of somewhat confused citizens.

By Tuesday, the British forces were at full strength, and attacked with fury. The uprising lasted until Saturday, and in the end sixty-four rebels and more than 300 civilians were dead. Dublin was a smoldering mass of rubble. On Saturday, April 29, Padraig Pearse, as president of the Provincial Government, surrendered unconditionally. His reason, he stated, was "to prevent the further slaughter of unarmed people and in the hope of saving the lives of our followers."

Pearse had predicted that the Irish people of Dublin would turn on them, and indeed, they did; jeers and threats accompanied the rebels as they were marched to jail. And yet, he also predicted that given time, the people would come around and see their actions for what they were—a blow for freedom. Britain, by its heavy-handed reprisals and its summary execution of the leaders, helped bring that change about more quickly that Pearse could have imagined.

At his court-martial, Pearse—in the spirit of Wolfe Tone and Robert Emmet—delivered a rousing speech from the dock. Such was its effect that the judge himself stated his regrets in having to send to death "one of the finest men he had ever come across." On the morning of his execution, unaware that his brother too was sentenced to death—for simply being Padraig's brother; he had not been a leader—he wrote two final poems: one to his mother and one to his brother.

On May 4, Padraig Pearse went before a firing squad.

The change in heart in the Irish people that Pearse had predicted came fast. Not only was the Irish public more and more revolted by the British reprisals, but the world in general was sharing in the feeling of revulsion. While militarily the uprising was in many ways a fiasco, as a bloody, symbolic protest, it was enormously successful.

CHAPTER XXIV:

James Connolly

A man I know tells a story of when he was in Dublin in the late 1970s. He had been spending the evening in Slattery's—an altogether different place from what it is now—and listening to a *sean nois* singer and a political band. He himself was wearing a T-shirt with a portrait of James Connolly on the front and the words "For an Irish Socialist Republic" underneath, and he admits to feeling a little squeamish. Well, anyway, after several pints, it was time for him to visit the jacks, when who should sidle up next to him but the singer who had just finished his set. The singer—a thin man full of hair and beard—took a glance at the shirt and shook his head. "It's a pity, you know," said he. Now my friend, preparing himself for what was sure to be a lecture on the commercial appropriation of a revered figure and the crass modernity of placing Connolly's face on a T-shirt, merely nodded in agreement. "To think the bastards strapped him in his chair before they shot him," continued the singer. It wasn't the fact of his wearing the T-shirt in 1976 that was the pity; it was the details of Connolly's execution sixty years earlier. More than half a century had passed, but the atrocities that followed the botched Easter Uprising still seemed fresh. Your man left the loo and bought the singer a pint. They raised their glasses and toasted "To an Irish Socialist Republic."

Few people could have had a more different upbringing than James Connolly and Maud Gonne, and yet the two worked well together, both committed to the plight of the poor working classes and universal suffrage, and both aware of their ability to rouse a crowd. While Gonne was born into relative ease and, upon her maturity, was the recipient of a trust fund, Connolly was as poor—perhaps poorer—than many of the workers he fought for.

James Connolly, born in 1868, was the third son of Irish emigrants who had moved to Edinburgh in the mid-1800s. There were many Irish in Edinburgh at the time, and the section called Cowgate could be termed an Irish ghetto. His father at one time had been a farm hand and had followed the harvest like many Irish men in Scotland, but before long, he and his family were staying in the same tenement house, which indicates that he had found town work. And indeed he did. The tenements threw their sewage into a common close, and Connolly senior worked as a "night-soil collector," gathering and removing human waste and animal dung from the streets. James Connolly himself would later work in this profession, but only after having been a printer's devil at the age of eleven, a baker's assistant at twelve, and a worker in a mosaic factory (from which he was fired for being too old at the age of fourteen). After this, he forged documents about his age and joined the British army.

A precocious reader, James had read much by the time he had joined the army. It was said that the squint he had as an adult came from his reading by the light of dying embers when he was a child. He had read many of the Land League publications, and in the army, spent his free time reading history, economics, and politics. He received another type of education in the army as well. Despite his wearing a British uniform, he was still Irish, and prejudice was rampant in the British military. At the time, the Phoenix Park murders were still fresh in people's minds, which led to an even heightened anti-Irish feeling everywhere. This prejudice against him—in addition to his reading—served to forge in him a fierce nationalism and a radical political sensibility.

Having lived with the abject poverty of the Cowgate ghetto, the childhood spent working in stultifying jobs, the general animosity directed toward all Irishmen, and his determined and directed reading, it is little surprise that James Connolly's keen political mind embraced the tenets of socialism. For socialism offered hope to the working man, far beyond the dreams that pure nationalism could hold out.

In the army, Connolly was stationed for a time in Dublin, for which he maintained a life-long affection. There he also met Lilly Reynolds, a servant girl for a
Unionist family. The two became engaged in 1889, but plans were accelerated and
altered when Connolly heard that his father had had an accident, lost his job, and
been rehired at half his already meager wages. Concerned about his father and
sickly mother, Connolly went AWOL from his unit and resurfaced in Perth.
There, in 1890, Connolly and Lilly married. They took up residence in the West
Port section of Edinburgh. Like his father before him, he had taken a job as a
"night soil" carter.

In the army, Connolly had educated himself in socialist thinking, and in
Edinburgh he quickly gravitated toward the Scottish Socialist Federation and the
Independent Labour Party. He became a voracious student of socialism, not only
of modern texts, but of the classics of socialist literature as well. Connolly's sharp
mind, his broad reading, and his encompassing intelligence allowed him to merge
his two preoccupations: Irish nationalism and social inequality. He opened his
small tenement flat to socialist meetings, attended three classes a week, and soon
developed a reputation as a bright, plain-speaking orator and a persuasive writer.

In 1892, Connolly became secretary of the Edinburgh SSF, and his published
reports soon garnered the attention of prominent socialists throughout England
and Scotland. He organized lectures and spoke at wherever he was asked. He ran
twice, unsuccessfully, for office—but was encouraged in the votes that a lowborn
socialist was able to garner in those elections. And yet, despite his dedication to his
socialist ideals and his status among his socialist friends, he was still a husband and
a father who had to provide for his family. When the private company for which
he worked lost its contract with the Edinburgh corporation, Connolly was out of
work. Influential friends wrote in socialist papers for anyone who could provide a
job for this remarkable young man. There were no responses. Finally, the Dublin

Socialist Club offered him £1 a week to become a "salaried" organizer. With a subscription got up by his friends, Connolly and his family booked passage to Dublin.

In Dublin, Connolly moved his family into the tenements on Claremont
Street. If Edinburgh had been tough, Dublin was much harder, with filth,
disease, stench, and death competing with drunkenness and prostitution. It gives
one some idea of the squalor of their Dublin neighborhood when one considers
that Lilly Connolly always looked at life in the slums of Edinburgh as the happi-
est times in her life.

It was this very tenement flat—home to Connolly, Lilly, and their three children at the time—that Maud Gonne visited when she had second thoughts about
speaking at the rally Connolly was organizing. Gonne was so aghast at the conditions that greeted her—and this from a woman who had seen rural poverty in
Donegal—that she set aside her reservations and agreed to speak.

Maud Gonne and James Connolly became great partners, and when fears of
another famine were growing in the west, they produced the manifesto "The
Rights of Life and the Rights of Property," in which they argued there was no
human law that should prevent a starving person from attaining food.

Later, during the preparation for Queen Victoria's Jubilee, Connolly and
Gonne coordinated their efforts to mount a counterdemonstration. In support
of Connolly's organization, Gonne had black flags made with the dire statistics
of the famine emblazoned on them; she projected slide images of the famine
horrors on a big screen against a public building; and she and William Butler
Years accompanied Connolly's Irish Socialist Republican Party marchers
through the streets of Dublin. The marchers carted along a coffin draped in
black with the words "British Empire" written on it. As the crowd grew in
numbers, the police came. Rather than have the coffin confiscated, Connolly
ordered the marchers to throw the coffin into the Liffey. He spent the night in

jail before Maud Gonne paid his fine and had him released.

Yet another time, when Connolly and Gonne were protesting the Boer War—for Connolly, it was always a matter of young laboring boys on both sides dying for the profit of the moneyed classes—they were traveling to an open-air rally with the Fenian John O'Leary and the MP Pat O'Brien when the police stopped their coach. The driver was pulled down from his seat, but Connolly, who had been sitting next to the driver rather than with the passengers behind, grabbed the reins and crashed through the barricade. When they got to their destination, they met with tumultuous applause. Gonne remembered that when Connolly drove the coach past Dublin Castle, he suggested that the four of them take over the castle, seeing that there were only two guards on duty. Whether he was serious or not is a matter of conjecture.

Soon after his arrival in Dublin, Connolly disbanded the antiquated and ineffective Dublin Socialist Club and formed the Irish Socialist Republican Party (ISRP). The party's goals, he announced, were Irish ownership of the land, the tools of production, and the system of distribution. He argued for pensions for the sick, the elderly, widows, and orphans. He saw the need for free education, free maintenance of children, universal suffrage, a minimum wage, and a forty-eight hour workweek. And most importantly, he stressed that the Irish Socialist Republican Party saw the need for the establishment of an Irish Republic before any of these goals could be met. He also argued that traditional Marxist determinism was not relevant in Ireland, since the English had so ruined the course of the nation's natural economics. With his intelligence and understanding, Connolly had shaped Marxism to fit the needs of an individual country. (The same wouldn't be done again until Mao gave the Chinese version of Marx.)

At the same time, Connolly began contributing articles and pamphlets to socialist journals in Ireland, England, and America. He founded the *Worker's*

Republic, as the party's official newspaper, and he began several useful debates through his contributions to the Belfast paper, *Shan Van Vocht*. He argued that all religious prejudices, regional jealousies, and mutual distrust had to be eradicated from Irish politics, for he believed they were encouraged by the ruling classes in order to keep the working class and peasants divided. The American socialist newspaper, *The Weekly People*, hired him to write articles on the current famine in Kerry and Mayo—where he saw firsthand the inherent problems in small farming out in the west. He was a formidable writer, and his articles and pamphlets ensured his reputation among fellow socialists; the tough part was getting the common man to listen.

However, once again, socialist politics alone could not feed his family, which seemed to grow each year. Connolly took a job as a manual laborer—having to pawn much of his family's possessions to buy suitable shoes and clothes—yet that didn't last long as his long stretch in organization had left him little prepared for the rigors of manual work. In the summer of 1901, Connolly went on a lecture tour of England and Scotland. He had already alienated many of the British socialists by combining Irish nationalism with socialism, and these lectures were conceived to further argue his point. They were also a source of much-needed money, as Lilly had recently given birth to their sixth child. The lectures were successful, in that they fostered lively debate. One became so lively that Connolly had to shove four men from the stage using a flagpole. And they established Connolly once and for all as a powerful orator.

Connolly's talent as a speaker is indicative of his drive and personality; it did not come by itself. He was a short man with bowed legs—probably a result of rickets as a child. He had a pronounced squint and a stammer. And his low-Edinburgh accent was anything but endearing to his Irish audiences. Yet through sheer force of will and a passionate belief in the truth of what he was saying, he became a remarkable orator, noted for his ability to make complicated issues understandable to the common man. For instance, in explaining his frustration and distrust of governmental reform, he compared such reforms to workers who wanted a baker's shop. The baker, he explained, will gladly throw out loaves in order to appease them, but he will never give them control of the shop. It was this folksy manner, wedded to a brilliant mind, that served him well on the speaking trail.

In August 1902, Connolly set sail for America to raise money for the struggling ISRP and the *Worker's Republic*. While the tour was a success, it was also draining. Connolly crossed the country from New York to California and up to Canada, speaking at stretches at a time in a different city each night. What was maddening to him—and he did have a fierce temper—was that the staff he had left behind in Dublin was remiss with its work and misspent much of the American funds he had raised. When he returned to Dublin, he resigned from the ISRP, although he did rejoin a while later. But the ISRP was fractured, and Connolly was fed up. In Scotland, he arranged for the *Socialist*, a leading socialist journal of the day, to replace the American subscriptions which the *Worker's Republic* could not fulfill. Disgusted with and alienated from the Irish socialists, on September 18, 1903, James Connolly emigrated to America. When his family finally joined him, Connolly met with sad news. His oldest daughter—for whom he believed America would be a great opportunity—died the night before she was to embark. She had died when her dress accidentally caught fire. Some say it changed Connolly forever, and the man who returned to Ireland seven years later was not the same affable, gregarious chap who had left.

In America, work was as hard to find as it had been in Scotland and Ireland. He worked for a while for Metropolitan Life, selling insurance on commission. But his territory was going through a huge labor strike, so people naturally were not buying insurance. He got a job working a lathe for the Singer Sewing Machine Company, but he was uneasy and unsatisfied. A steady income did not guarantee happiness, and even his faithful Lilly was "mad to get out" of America.

While in America, Connolly worked for the Socialist Labor Party. Frustrated with the inroads he was making within the Irish community, he set his sights on the Italian emigrants who already had some grounding in socialism from their homeland, and among whom young recruits might be found. Connolly taught himself Italian, and was soon translating articles from the Italian periodicals into English for *The Weekly People*. He spoke at Italian Socialist functions and at times even gave his speeches in Italian. His socialist activities and union organizing soon lost him his job at the Singer Sewing Machine Company. Fingered as a troublemaker, he resigned in 1907 rather than cause problems for a foreman who had been kind to him.

For three more years, Connolly struggled in America, in dire poverty, while he formulated his socialist program for Ireland. (He was also quite active in the American socialist organizations, being elected one of three national organizers—which also paid a regular salary of $21 a week.) From abroad, he wrote articles analyzing Arthur Griffith's new Sinn Fein party, examining it to see what the socialist response to "ourselves alone"—the meaning of the party's name—could be. Connolly argued once again that nationalism, individualism, and even the Catholic Church could co-exist within socialism. What emerged from his writings and his conversations with his socialist friends who remained in Ireland was the new Socialist Party of Ireland (SPI). (Connolly was always a prolific letter writer, as well as a pamphleteer and journalist. In 1909, a collection of his articles appeared in the States, and later came out in Ireland, Britain, and Australia.)

On June 14, 1910, James Connolly sailed for Ireland in order to run the SPI. His first task was to organize the Irish Transport and General Workers' Union in

Belfast, where he was successful in organizing dockworkers, and in 1911, he formed the Irish Textile Workers' Union. He also helped negotiate raises for Belfast firemen and seamen.

But overall, these were not good times for organized labor. In 1913, a group of business owners tried to break the Irish Transport and General Workers' Union by compelling their workers to withdraw from the union or face dismissal. Connolly and other leaders organized a massive movement that within a month involved over 25,000 workers being locked out by their employers or striking in support. Connolly was arrested on sedition charges, and the strike itself stretched into the start of 1914. The action was not successful, for the workers—unskilled laborers for the most part—were forced to return at reduced terms. However, the action, which pitted workers, intellectuals, militants, and nationalists against employers, Parliamentary politicians, and the Catholic Church, did achieve the result of uniting nationalism and socialism. A further result was that Connolly began organizing the Irish Citizens Army.

Upon release from prison, Connolly campaigned against World War I. His feeling always was that these grand wars did little but bring profit to the rich and death to the poor. He was not, however, against war itself. In fact, he was impatient with all the talk about revolution in Ireland when so little action went with it. Acting primarily on his own, he, of course, had little knowledge of the plans that the IRB were developing. The headquarters of the Irish Transport and General Workers Union of which he was head was in Liberty Hall in Dublin. Outside the hall, there hung a banner that read: "We Serve Neither King nor Kaiser, but Ireland." More political words to be sure, but inside the hall there were more potent materials: Connolly had amassed a cache of arms in the basement of Liberty Hall.

Connolly may have been unaware of what the IRB was doing, but it was certainly aware of him, and worried that he might call for armed rebellion prematurely and negate its own plans. In January 1916, the IRB's Military Council informed Connolly that Padraig Pearse wished to meet him. Taking him into their confidence, they revealed their plans for an uprising on Easter Sunday, April 23. The meetings were intense, but the result was what Connolly had been working for all along. After three days, he was sworn into the Irish Republican Brotherhood and appointed to its Military Council. Connolly had finally fused his labor movement with the nationalist movement.

For the next three months, the plotting was intense. John Devon in New York frequented the German embassy, which promised the rebels arms. By April 8, a German ship disguised as a Norwegian vessel entered the North Sea with the armaments; unfortunately for the rebellion, the British had already become aware of the plot. On Good Friday, the British navy accosted the ship and the German captain scuttled her. The weapons slated for the Irish rebellion sank to the bottom of the sea.

The loss of the German ship was not the only drawback; in fact, by Easter Sunday the plans had splintered so badly that many of the leaders knew that what they were doing was making a sacrifice, simply offering their lives for the cause of Irish freedom. But the plans were not to be jettisoned; they would merely be held up for one day. Padraig Pearse had drawn up a document that proclaimed the Irish Republic, and on Easter Monday, they were in Connolly's Liberty Hall printing up a copy. (When you look at a copy of this proclamation [see photo insert], you might be struck by its distinctive typesetting. The Irish Transport and General Workers' Union's typesetting supplies being sparse, a combination of fonts had to be used. Its look came not from graphic design but necessity.) Connolly was among the seven men who signed the document.

In the afternoon, James Connolly led his Irish Citizens Army on a march through Dublin. With him was his second in command, Countess Constance Markievicz, an extraordinary woman who had turned her back on her aristocratic upbringing to become one of the heroes of independence. She took her troops to Stephen's Green, where ultimately they were fired upon by soldiers in the Shelbourne Hotel. (When Markievicz's death sentence was commuted because she was a woman, she was furious. It greatly offended her sense of equality.) Connolly had been named Commandant-General of the Dublin Forces, but as he left Liberty Hall, he knew that the chances of victory were nil. He also knew that in their dying, ironically, Ireland's chance of winning was great.

With a ragged group of soldiers, armed with rifles, pistols, shotguns, shovels, picks, and pikes, Connolly entered the General Post Office. His experience as a British soldier rose to the fore, and he quickly took command of the situation— for which Padraig Pearse was grateful. The tricolor flag was raised over the post office (plus a second flag that Markievicz had made from a green bedspread), and Connolly and Pearse stepped outside where Pearse read the proclamation. And although the document was Pearse's creation, the proclamation contained many of the goals Connolly had spent his life fighting for: ownership of land by the people, women's suffrage, equal rights for all citizens, and religious and civil freedom.

Connolly's military ability shone throughout the week of fighting. Michael Collins, who was just a young soldier at the time, said that Connolly's leadership was such that he would have followed him to hell. For two days, the fighting was sporadic, and those in the post office were mainly the targets of sniper fire, as the British army concentrated on rebel outposts elsewhere. However, on Tuesday night, the British began bombarding the city, and artillery fire pounded the post office. (Connolly had erred in believing that English capitalists would never use large guns on the city because of their intrinsic worship of property.) Soon the GPO was surrounded by British army troops. Buildings along the street were set ablaze, and artillery fire was heavy. Connolly was hit once, but it was minor; a second shot shattered his ankle. From a bed, he continued to command, trying to keep up his soldiers' morale. When the GPO was set ablaze, Connolly and Pearse evacuated their men to a nearby house. It was from there that the rebels finally surrendered.

By now Connolly's ankle was gangrenous, and he was unable to stand. He was placed in the infirmary in Dublin Castle and court martialed on May 9. On the day that he was to be executed, he was visited by his wife Lilly and his daughter Nora—who had acted as a courier through much of the planning. After saying goodbye, he was taken to Kilmainham Jail. Because he unable to stand, he took the bullets sitting down, strapped to a small table. Before the firing, a priest asked him to pray for the men who would shoot him. His socialist conscience still strong, he said he would pray for any brave men who were doing their duty.

Fifteen rebels had been executed in all, and it had the effect of turning the Irish citizenry and world opinion against the British. The Irish people, for the most part, had been apathetic toward the uprising, but the executions created in them a nationalistic fervor. And the image of the British shooting a seated Connolly was particularly horrendous and barbaric. It was probably the outraged reaction to Connolly's death that caused the British to forgo executing the remaining convicted ninety-seven prisoners.

In all, Connolly had perhaps the best mind of those fallen leaders—the most acute political sensibilities and understanding. He was also one of the best military men in Dublin on that Easter Sunday. But because of his socialism, his name was for a long time handled gingerly thanks to the fiercely anti-communist stance of the Catholic Church; the repute of the man who had brought Marx to Irish nationalism had to be carefully vetted, his socialist writings pushed into a dark corner far from the glow of his patriotism.

Yet wiser minds and less church-ridden minds ultimately prevailed, and James Connolly, who before he died in 1916 had fought so hard for the Irish worker and the Irish poor, had by the 1960s gained the reputation he deserved. More than just a symbol of British barbarity, he was a powerful thinker, an insightful writer, a fervent patriot, and an unflinching champion of civil rights. He was an Irish hero whose name stands beside those of Tone, Emmet, and Parnell.

A CENTURY OF IRISH VOICES

It should come as no real surprise that the majority of the leaders of 1916 were writers and poets, for Ireland has had a long tradition of elevating writers. This literary inclination goes all the way back to the Gaelic custom of maintaining bards, whose creations were both celebrated and feared, or perhaps more simply to a long-standing oral tradition which gave such eminence to a finely told tale.

And when one takes into account the fact that English was forced on the Irish people—and not including those who wrote (and write) in their native Irish—the list of masterful writers is even more impressive: Jonathan Swift and Laurence Sterne, Oliver Goldsmith and Richard Sheridan, Sean O'Casey, George B. Shaw and Oscar Wilde, Frank O'Connor and Sean O'Faoláin, Flann O'Brien and Elizabeth Bowen, Bram Stoker, Samuel Beckett, W. B. Yeats, James Joyce, and Brendan Behan. (Take a survey course in British literature some time and you will be amazed at the number of authors who claim Ireland as their native land. For some, their inclusion in the British canon is a point of political contention.) And today, that tradition seems to be as strong as ever, with poets such as Seamus Heaney and Eavaan Boland, playwrights such as Brien Friel and Hugh Leonard, and novelists like William Trevor, Patrick McCabe, John Banville, and Colm McCann, and memoirist Frank McCourt.

I knew a university professor once who, at the risk of sounding chauvinistic, used to claim that Irish writers were the dominant twentieth-century force in literature written in English. His argument stated that modern poetry began and was defined by William Butler Yeats, that the modern theater was born with Samuel Beckett, and that no one would ever supplant the genius of James Joyce's fiction. And to be honest, the man was right. (In a bizarre way, it might be a measure of an author's relevance when his or her name is generally known by a non-reading public. There are numerous people, to be sure, who know the names of Yeats, Joyce, and Beckett, yet who have never read one of Yeats's lyrics or cracked into Joyce's *Ulysses* or witnessed the delicate absurdity of Beckett's theater. But they know the names, for they are part of the culture of the twentieth century, which in many ways they helped to create.)

That professor did have a point. For the achievements of Yeats, Joyce, and Beckett stand apart in twentieth-century literature. Their works have inspired many a hopeful writer, and they have greatly changed the way that we look at the English language, at ourselves, at Ireland, and at the world in general.

CHAPTER XXV:

William Butler Yeats

Seamus Heaney, the Nobel-winning Irish poet, claims that the troublesome divide within Ireland—the long-standing division in its politics, its heritage, its people— is embodied in the person of William Butler Yeats. He was descended from the Protestant Ascendancy, yet he was an important part of the Celtic revival and the ensuing nationalism; he was a fixture of London and Dublin society, yet most comfortable in the wild beauty of his grandparents' Sligo or Lady Gregory's Galway; he was mystical and spiritual, yet underwent at the end of his life controversial operations to revive his physical vigor and increase his longevity. To say that he was a man of many masks is an understatement, for Yeats spent much of his life creating and re-creating himself. This lifelong seeking can be anticipated in an early poem, "The Song of Wandering Aengus," in which the speaker, having been visited once by a magical "shimmering" girl, spends the rest of his life searching

for her elusive vision. And in many ways, for Yeats, that vision that he sought—
and worked for—was a particular sense of Irish nationhood.

William Butler Yeats was born in Dublin on June 13, 1865, into a Protestant
Irish family. His father, J. B. Yeats, was a lawyer who left the law to become a
painter. His mother's people, the Pollexfens of Sligo, claimed that their name
could be traced to Pollex, the brother of Helen of Troy. (This perhaps gives new
resonance to Yeats's continual comparison of Maud Gonne to Helen.) Whether
the ancient Mediterranean linkage was true or not, J. B. Yeats knew something of
the spirit of his wife's family, for he said that in marrying a Pollexfen, he had given
voice to the unruly cliffs of Sligo. And in a way, his children did give voice to
those western cliffs: William Butler in drama and verse and his brother Jack
(named John Butler) through paint. Indeed, it was his sons rather than he who
would reveal true artistic genius, and consequently the senior J. B. Yeats kept the
family in relative insolvency and transition for most of their young life.

When Yeats was two, the family moved to London, where they stayed for sixteen years before returning to Dublin. During that time, the Yeats children spent
their summer with the Pollexfens in Sligo. Yeats senior was against contemporary
education, and much of Yeats's education was erratic and in the hands of family
friends in Sligo or J. B. Yeats himself. When Yeats was finally enrolled in the high
school on Harcourt Street, he was not a good student. One year, among his classmates, he ranked last or next to last in classics, math, language, and English.
Science, however, was his strong point—he was self-taught in that through voracious reading—and his father would boast that once when he was thirteen, he
won a science competition against eighteen-year-old boys.

When the family moved back to Dublin in 1881, they stayed in several
houses, in Howth where Jack Yeats kept rooms and a studio in Dublin city.
These were explosive times in Ireland; Land League agitation was proving

successful; Home Rule seemed more and more possible; nationalism was rampant; and the Phoenix Park murders had everyone on edge. The young Yeats, when visiting his father's studio, was certain to hear lively discussions and radical new ideas from the artists who visited.

Because of poor grades, Yeats was unable to get into Trinity College, so instead he joined his siblings at the Metropolitan School of Art. (He was never happy with the realism of modern art, which was so foreign to the romantic, mystical world that was the foundation of his readings and of the folk tales he grew up with in Sligo.) He soon forswore the plastic arts for literature.

In 1885, he published his first poems in the *Dublin University Review*. He placed more poetry and two verse dramas in the next three issues. (Yeats was always talented at self-promotion—in this he was truly his father's son. The verse play *Mosada* was published as a stand-alone booklet. The senior Yeats insisted that the cover feature a portrait of W.B.Y. rather than a scene from the play. If it was a bold gesture, it nevertheless acted as an announcement that a new writer had appeared.)

The *Dublin University Review* opened up other avenues for Yeats as well. It had been founded by Charles Oldham, a professor with strong nationalist and Home Rule leanings. In the 1880s, he established the Contemporary Club, which Yeats joined. The membership at the time included the Irish-language proponent and future president of Ireland, Douglas Hyde; Parnell's lieutenant and future MP Michael Davitt; the legendary old Fenian, John O'Leary; and Yeats's father's and Yeats's friend, the writer George Russell. The club was noted for its heated debates and arguments, pitting Unionist views against Home Rule aspirations. Here, Yeats came under the influence of O'Leary, who more than anyone else guided Yeats into his Irishness. Within months of his publication in Oldham's *Dublin University Review* and his visits to the Contemporary Club, Yeats had joined the

Young Ireland Society—a nationalist organization leaning more and more to armed uprising. He may even have taken the Fenian Oath at this time as well.

In addition to Irish nationalism, Yeats was also becoming immersed in another trend sweeping through young Ireland—the occult. (Some argue that this fascination with spirituality and the occult among the privileged class of Dublin stems from the feeling of helplessness that many Irish Protestants subconsciously might have had as they watched their privileged world sink slowly.) Throughout much of his life, Yeats joined these spiritualist movements with great enthusiasm, and in a large way they led him to the mythical, fairy world of ancient Celtic tradition that so inspired his verse and drama. For Yeats, the spirit, the emotion, the connection to a world behind our own was an essential part of the Ireland he knew in Sligo. And so in 1886, he was able to publish an essay that called for a "passionate Irishness" as opposed to what he termed a "bloodless English rationalism." In this essay, he was claiming a distinct "Irishness" for himself, which became his life's work: making an Irish literature that could stand proudly on its own.

The Yeats family, however, was on the move again, and in 1886, they were back in London, in the bohemian neighborhood of Bedford Park. From here, he published "The Lake Isle of Innisfree" in 1888, as well as a study done with George Russell and Douglas Hyde entitled *Fairy and Folk Tales of the Irish Peasantry*. In London, he visited Madame Blavatsky and joined the Esoteric Section of the Theosophical Society. (Yeats was so enthusiastic about his mysticism that the letters of others at the time often include condolences for those people who had suffered through Yeats's protracted conversations on the subject at tea or dinner. Perhaps, it was this endless proselytizing and discussion more than anything else that ultimately make Blavatsky kick Yeats out of the society.)

In 1889, Yeats published his first book, *The Wanderings of Oisin*. A narrative conversation in verse between St. Patrick and the bard Oisin, the work was anchored in ancient Celtic and Irish themes, and, considering it was the first collection by a relative newcomer, it received fairly good reviews.

Yet, the most important event of the year 1889 for him was not the publication of the book, but the arrival of a woman who would cast her shadow on Yeats and his work for the next three decades, if not the rest of his life: Maud Gonne. The vibrant, dramatic woman had been introduced by Oldham to the Contemporary Club, had sought out John O'Leary for his advice on helping the Irish people, and now, on her way to France, stopped in London to seek out William Butler Yeats. Yeats's romantic obsession is one of the most fascinating and productive in history. And while his love was never reciprocated the way he had always hoped, it did inspire some of the finest poetry in the twentieth century. Yeats would remain loyal to Maud Gonne throughout his life—despite breaches in their relationship—and he was an important friend and support during her most troubled times.

In 1891, Yeats published two novels: *John Sherman* and *Dhoya*. At the time, his intention was to become known as an Irish novelist, and these two works combined the mystic occult that he had so immersed himself in (he had joined the Theosophical Society, the Rhymers Club, and the Hermetic Order of the Golden Dawn) with the Irish myth and legend that he had gathered with Hyde and Russell. It was a marriage of themes that would long serve him well in his art.

Yeats returned to Ireland in 1896, with both his literature and politics growing entwined as he tried to create a uniquely Irish literature. (This goal had been behind his study done with Russell and Hyde a decade earlier.) Toward this aim, he founded the Irish Literary Society, the National Literary Society in Dublin, and worked to promote the New Irish Library. In that same year, he also met another woman who—in a different way from Gonne—would affect the rest of his life.

Isabella Augusta, Lady Gregory, was a forty-four-year-old widow from Galway when she met William Butler Yeats. Her husband, Sir William Gregory, had died four years earlier and her widowhood freed her to follow the literary pursuits she had always desired. After a visit to the Aran Islands, she soon began learning Irish, as well as the particular English-Irish dialect spoken around her native Kiltartan. The rhythm of this local language would find its way into both her and Yeats's drama. At Kiltartan, with Yeats, she also began collecting the folk tales that circulated in the countryside surrounding her home in Galway. In fact, her residence at Coole Park became a second home to Yeats, ultimately supplanting Sligo as his chosen retreat. In 1917, he bought Thoor Ballylee, the tower and attached outbuildings that were on Gregory's property, as a summer house for his wife and family.

In 1899, Lady Gregory and Yeats founded the Irish Literary Theater that would ultimately become the Abbey Theatre, perhaps one of the most famous theaters in all of the twentieth century. Yeats wanted people to support the theater for patriotic reasons, for he believed that Irish drama was an affirmation of Irish identity, though at the same time he was having heated debates with leading nationalists who felt that Yeats's theater was too avant-garde, too "spiritual," and not nationalistic enough.

When the Abbey Theatre opened on December 27, 1904, the group that had been an essential part of the Irish Literary Theater was quite changed. Yeats was still the director, and while he wrote several plays, more were coming from Lady Gregory herself, John Millington Synge, and Sean O'Casey. The plays were not as "nationalistic" as some had anticipated—in fact, Synge's *Playboy of the Western World* famously caused riots as an insult to Irishness, and O'Casey's *Juno and the Paycock* seemed to many to be an insult to the men of 1916—and yet the Abbey Theatre did provide a national Irish theater that mounted dramas that were to have an influence far outside of Irish politics.

But one could not live in Ireland at the time and be outside of Irish politics, and during this time, Yeats—encouraged by Maud Gonne—was revealing his allegiance to the more radical politics of the day. In 1897, he had traveled through northern England to organize a celebration commemorating the centenary of the 1798 uprising, had marched with Gonne and Connelly in protest of the queen's jubilee, and in 1899, shared a platform with Douglas Hyde, where he lectured on the necessity of fighting Anglicization. He also at this time had published a new collection of poems, *The Wind Among the Reeds*, influenced by his frequent visits to Coole, his mysticism, and his difficult relationship with Maud Gonne. However, at the moment, it was drama rather than poetry that defined his literary career.

Some see this period in Ireland—working with the theater and involved in Gonne-inspired political agitation—as a middle period in Yeats's life. He had left behind the youthful arrogance and fin-de-siècle affectation that had been so much a part of his "poetic mask," and he had dedicated himself to his dream of Irishness. He and Gonne had together imagined an ideal Ireland, peopled with heroes and noble hearts, toward which he worked, but which had even less chance of fruition than his love for Gonne.

In total, Yeats proposed marriage to Gonne on five separate occasions (1891, 1899, 1900, 1901, and 1916). Not all of these stemmed from the same sort of love; Gonne always surprised, shocked, and sent Yeats reeling into depression as she confided in him little by little those pieces of her life of which he—and the rest of the world—had been unaware. By the time of his proposal in 1916, although still devotedly in love with her, he was also acting as her protector. He had long been both protector, confidant, and supporter, but these roles had intensified when the Dublin friends of her husband, John MacBride, harassed Gonne so fiercely following their divorce. Following her rejection of his final proposal in

1916, he proposed marriage to her daughter Iseult.

When Easter 1916 came around, Yeats was in London. Like many others, he was surprised and angered by the events, particularly because so many of the men and women who had died were known to him. Pearse had been a supporter of his theater, and Yeats had allowed the boys in Pearse's bilingual school to perform his plays for free; MacDonagh had dedicated a book of poems to Yeats; and MacBride, who had hurt his beloved Maud Gonne, even he had redeemed himself in Yeats's eyes. Of course, his most notable response to the uprising was through poetry—more than half of the poems in the volume *Michael Robartes and the Dancer* were concerned with the events of Easter week. His poem, "Easter 1916," although on closer reading it seems a somewhat ambiguous reaction to the week of fighting, still gave an artful, public gravitas to the sacrifice and martyrdom of those who had died. Ironically, Gonne did not like it at all.

On October 20, 1917, Yeats, then fifty-two, married George Hyde Lees. George was a young woman—she had just turned twenty-five three days before her marriage—who had been raised among the literary salons of London. She was a bright woman with a talent for languages, literary scholarship, and art. But perhaps most attractive to Yeats, she was a spiritualist, a medium through whom the spirit world spoke. (During their honeymoon, George revealed her gift for what was known at the time as "automatic writing.") For the rest of his life, she was the perfect wife, helpmeet, manager, and inspiration for Yeats, and after his death, she was the guardian of his legacy.

As the violence of Easter week gave way to the atrocities of the Black and Tans' keeping the peace, Yeats bought and restored the Norman tower and outbuildings on Lady Gregory's estate and named the place Thoor Ballylee. "I, the poet William Yeats . . . Restored this tower for my wife George," wrote Yeats in his dedication. He saw it as a symbol of his own life—the synthesis of the Anglo-Irish divide. For

Yeats, the tower itself—built originally by the de Burgh family in the 1500s—represented his Anglo-ancestry and the role that the Anglo tradition had in shaping the new nation; the Irish peasantry and laborers who helped him restore it represented the ancient Ireland from which he derived his artistic life. In 1928, he would publish a book of poems entitled *The Tower*, which dealt not only with the restoration of the tower, the building of its furniture, and the involvement of the local workers, but also with the Civil War, his son, and old age—of which he was becoming more and more aware.

The treaty brought back by Michael Collins, Arthur Griffith, and the others delegated to negotiate with Lloyd George violently split Ireland's independence movement in two: the anti-treaty IRA and the Free Staters. Yeats sided with the latter—which caused the worst rift ever between him and Maud Gonne, who was fiercely anti-treaty. On December 1, 1922, he was rewarded for his support of the Free State when he was asked to consider nomination to the Senate, in a role concerned primarily with education, literature, and the arts. Yeats took to his job wholeheartedly and even went outside the realm of his supposed influence. In January, he was already negotiating secretly with the British Government to modify the treaty so that the oath of allegiance—which was such an obstacle to the anti-treaty forces—might be abolished.

In 1923, Yeats was awarded the Nobel Prize for Literature. His was an extraordinary poetic career, unique in that unlike most poets who have a surge of passion and fire—usually when they are young—and then fade away like dried leaves, Yeats continued to produce poetry of ever-increasing subtlety and power throughout his old age. He was sixty-three now, and still had some of his best work in front of him. As a young man, Ireland was an old and ancient muse; now, in his senior years, Ireland had become a young nation. For nearly forty years, he had known, worked with, debated with, and influenced practically everyone involved in creating the new Irish nation. And he had argued—vehemently with Pearse and Hyde—that Ireland could have a unique literature in the English language; his Nobel Prize validated his argument.

Yeats had been at the forefront, had been a leader of Irish intellectualism from the earliest days of the Celtic revival, and this continued well into nationhood. He had helped take the wonder and beauty of the past to recapture an Irish identity, and he memorialized forever those who took that new-forged identity into battle in order to achieve Irish independence. At the same time, he fostered creativity and Irish artistry in those he came across: John Millington Synge, Sean O'Casey, Lady Gregory, and George Russell among others. In 1932, he founded the Irish Academy of Letters as a forum for the Irish literary world that he had sought to establish throughout most of his life.

During the last years of his life, Yeats continued to publish poetry—some of it the most powerful he had ever created. He also worked closely on the last version of *The Vision*—the mystical treatise that he had begun in cooperation with George's automatic writing. He was still capable of causing controversy: his *Oxford Book of Modern Verse* was a scandal among reviewers and fellow poets, on account of whom he admitted and whom he left out, and his poem on Roger Casement caused a reaction in the press that Yeats enjoyed thoroughly. He was also still involved with a variety of different mystical sects, seeking as always the secrets behind the veil.

In October 1938, Yeats and George left Ireland for France with a stop off in London. He had been suffering with the flu and was bothered by Ireland's damp, but remained busy in both London and France. Always working, he finished his last play *The Death of Cúchulainn* by the end of December. He also completed what was to be his final poem, "The Black Tower." On January 28, 1939, Yeats died at a hotel in France, so fittingly named *Hotêl Idéal Séjour*. For a long while,

Yeats lay buried in a temporary grave in Roquebrune, France—he had asked his wife to bury him there until the inevitable publicity died down, and then bring him quietly back to Ireland and to Sligo.

It took nearly ten years for Yeats to return. World War II (which I have always believed Yeats anticipated in the poem "The Second Coming") had delayed his removal, and the municipality of Roquebrune had—unknown to all concerned—moved the body from the temporary grave. On September 6, 1948, his body was transferred to the Irish navy escort *Macha*. The ship anchored in Galway, and then the journey was undertaken to his beloved Sligo. Along the route, the Irish people came out in great numbers to show their love and respect for the poet, the man, and the legend. Yeats had asked that there be no state funeral, and there was none; yet there were enormous crowds of the plain people whom he loved and who inspired his poetry.

Yeats was buried in Ireland on September 17th. His grave looks out at the majestic Ben Bulben, the Sligo mountain, which towered over the scenes of his early Sligo summers. By the time William Butler Yeats was returned to Ireland, the world had claimed him as the foremost poet in the English language. At his funeral—nearly a decade after his death—the Irish people claimed him as their own.

CHAPTER XXVI:
JAMES JOYCE

Perhaps no man has ever been more successful in marking an anniversary than the Irish writer James Joyce. On June 16, 1904, he had his first date with a young chambermaid by the name of Nora Barnacle. Nearly twenty years later, Joyce published what would become the most influential novel of the twentieth century—a long, circuitous novel that bent the norms of fiction as it went through the streets of Dublin. The entire novel takes place on that very day, June 16, 1904—a day that has become known throughout the world as Bloomsday. Such is this renown of Joyce's *Ulysses* that all over the world there are annual celebrations of Bloomsday; in many cities there are staged performances and readings; in Dublin itself, people, many of whom are in period costume, retrace the steps of the novel's two heroes, Stephen Dedalus and Leopold Bloom.

And while he spent the large majority of his life away from Ireland in self-imposed exile, he never really let go of it. For Ireland—and particularly Dublin—is the backbone of all his works. It is always his subject. No other writer has ever portrayed the entirety of a city like Joyce captured Dublin, mapping out the individual buildings and businesses, the various streets and alleyways, the people, the nuances, the voices, and sounds that gave a city its very character.

James Joyce was born on February 2, 1892 in the Dublin neighborhood of Rathgar. His paternal grandmother was a second cousin of Daniel O'Connell, and the Joyces were quite fervent in their support of the Home Rulers and of Charles Stewart Parnell in particular. Unfortunately, Joyce's father was as passionate about his politics as he was about his drink, and the family moved continually during Joyce's childhood. (I count nine separate addresses in the first fifteen years of Joyce's life.)

As a young boy, Joyce was nicknamed "Sunny Jim" because of his pleasant disposition and general cheeriness. As he grew older, however, he became increasingly more serious, more sensitive, and somewhat nervous, although he always retained his love of life and his humor. When he was six years old he attended Clongowes Wood College, forty miles from his home at the time. He was the youngest boy in the school, the next in age being two years older. Clongowes Wood College was the type of Jesuit-run school that Padraig Pearse had leashed out upon in his essay "The Murdering Machine," yet Joyce was plucky enough at the age of seven to walk the long corridor towards the administrative offices to complain about what he considered an unjust punishment. Much of Joyce's school experience—as well as his experiences at home—is thinly disguised in *A Portrait of the Artist as a Young Man.* Indeed, his sister complained when the novel finally was published that everyone was embarrassed about the family details that Joyce had included.

He nevertheless was precocious young child, and when he was nine years old wrote his first known poem, "Parnell," in memory of the fallen hero. The time of Parnell's fall, however, was also a time of decline for the Joyce family. After Joyce's father had been suspended, then fired from the Civil Service, and then fell into arrears with Joyce's tuition, Joyce was enrolled in the Christian Brothers-run Belvedere College. It was there that Joyce believed for a time that he had a vocation to the priesthood, and indeed in 1895 was elected to membership into the Sodality. Two years later he was elected as its prefect. And like so many Irish sons before and after, his mother encouraged this religious direction.

A serious student with a wry sense of humor, Joyce won several monetary prizes through his performance on certain exams, and in 1898 he entered University College, Dublin. At the same time, he began attending meetings and presenting papers to the Literary and Historical Society. Once such paper—on James Clarence Magnan—was noticed by the *Freeman's Journal* which deemed it the finest paper of the night. Another entitled "The Day of the Rabblement" was reviewed in the *United Irishman* by none other than Arthur Griffith. His essay on the Norwegian dramatist, Henrik Ibsen, even received acknowledgement from Ibsen himself. Joyce was making a name for himself for his cleverness, his willingness to take a stance, and his interest in the world outside Ireland.

At the same time he was meeting the important people in Ireland's literary—and nationalist—circles. He dropped out of Padraig Pearse's Gaelic League classes after one meeting and attended a party for the National Theater with Lady

Gregory, Patrick Colum, and William Butler Yeats in attendance. (Dublin would remain a small-village-like city for much of the twentieth century where local celebrities were frequently encountered and easily recognizable.) Joyce's first private meeting with Yeats, however, was marked by the younger artist's arrogance and confidence, both of which nevertheless impressed Yeats. For Joyce, Yeats's fascination with the Irish peasantry was peculiar at best and condescending at worst, and he saw little use for it in his own art.

In 1902, Joyce left Dublin for Paris, ostensibly to study medicine. Before he left, he dined with Lady Gregory and Yeats. He was writing poetry at the time, and was publishing reviews in the *Daily Express*. He also began writing what he called "epiphanies," short passages of sudden clarity and insight. These would become a basis for his early fiction—and through his use of them would become a common term in the English language.

In 1904, a young woman named Nora Barnacle arrived in Dublin from Galway and took a job as a chambermaid at the Finn Hotel. Joyce was back in Dublin, having arrived for his mother's funeral, and had taken a teaching job in Clifton so that he could live in Dublin on his own. He was also making a name for himself singing in public. (Actually, he was a very fine tenor and once came in second to the great John McCormack in a musical competition.) On June 10, he spied Nora Barnacle walking along the street and approached her. The two struck up a conversation, and he asked her to meet him a few days later, but although she agreed, she did not show up. Undaunted, he wrote to her asking again. They finally met on June 16.

It was during that summer that Joyce began living in the Martello tower on the Irish Sea in Sandymount. (The tower is the opening setting of *Ulysses* and today is a museum dedicated to Joyce.) He also began seeing some of his poems as well as the stories that would be collected in *Dubliners* published: "The Sisters" in July,

"Eveline" in September, and "At the Races" in December. But by that time, Joyce and Nora had already left Ireland and were living in Italy.

Joyce and Nora stayed in Europe pretty much for the rest of their lives. He returned to Ireland only a few times. Once in 1909 he returned to start up what would be the first movie house in Ireland, the Volta Cinema. It lasted less than six months and Joyce and his partners sold it at a £600 pound loss. Always strapped for money—and seldom seeing a return on his writings—he often was involved in business propositions that came to nothing. A year before the Volta Cinema project, he had been exploring the possibility of exporting Irish tweed. In 1912, Joyce went again to Ireland for a month in Nora's Galway and to check the status of the publication of *Dubliners*. When he left Dublin for Trieste on September 11, 1912, it would be his last time in Ireland.

Like his father before him, Joyce moved his family through a series of homes living primarily in Trieste, Zurich, Rome, and Paris, and throughout his life they moved to a variety of locations in these cities. (Also like his father, Joyce had a fondness for the drink.) In Europe, he supported his growing family through teaching, reviewing, lecturing, and journalism. His facility with language was astounding—the family spoke Italian in the home; he was adept at German, learned Norwegian because of his admiration of Ibsen, knew Latin through his Jesuit education, and French from his years in Paris. It is said that his last novel, *Finnegans Wake*, contains more than sixty different languages. He translated John Millington Synge's *Riders to the Sea*, Oscar Wilde's *Soul of Man Under Socialism*, and Yeats's *The Countess Cathleen* into Italian, as well as other works from the Irish canon, and for the journal *Piccolo*, he often wrote articles on such aspects of Irish culture as Home Rule and Fenianism.

One of the more obvious reasons for the Joyce family's continued poverty was his problems with publishers—and his were legendary. While his short stories were published, they were published individually in small papers and journals, rarely a source of great income. Having the stories published in book form was a nightmare that Joyce would suffer through for nearly a decade. Joyce first offered *Dubliners* to Grant Richards in December 1905 who accepted the manuscript within two months. Two months later Richards demanded changes in three of his stories. Joyce refused, but suggested other alterations. When these were refused, he withdrew the manuscript. In 1907, *Dubliners* was rejected by Elkin Matthews who had previously published Joyce's book of poems, *Chamber Music*. Finally, in 1909 the publisher Maunsel accepted the collection of stories, though in 1911 the company postponed publication. In late August of the following year, Maunsel rejected the manuscript in fear of libel and obscenity laws and destroyed all the plates already set for printing. It was not until 1914 that Grant Richards—the publisher who had originally accepted the manuscript—published *Dubliners*. The work must have seemed old to Joyce by that time, for by then, Joyce's novel *A Portrait of the Artist as a Young Man* was being serially published in Ezra Pound's *The Egoist* and Joyce's master work, *Ulysses*, had been started.

Joyce was often the beneficiary of men who recognized his genius. The American poet Ezra Pound—and by association Yeats himself—is notable for this. In 1913, Yeats had, unsolicited by Joyce, told Pound about the young Dubliner now living in Trieste. Pound had written asking for material, and on February 2, 1914, his magazine published the first chapter of *A Portrait of the Artist as a Young Man*. (Joyce, who was man obsessed with numbers and dates, must have loved the coincidence of the magazine coming out on his birthday.) For the next year and a half, *The Egoist* would publish the novel chapter by chapter in its pages. And although Grant Richards rejected the entire manuscript, another benefactor came to Joyce's aid: Harriet Shaw Weaver. The editor of *The Egoist* offered to publish the novel, and would continue to support Joyce financially and artistically throughout most of his life. In 1916, the novel was published in the United States.

Joyce's woes in publishing *Dubliners*, which had been held up nine years for fear of obscenity (the use of the word "bloody") and libel (a swipe at the Prince of Wales and the mention of actual place names), were nothing compared to what he would face with *Ulysses*.

The novel *Ulysses* follows a middle-aged man Leopold Bloom from 8:00 A.M. on June 16, 1904 until a little after 2:00 the following morning. It traces not only his actions, but his every thought, his opinions, his lusts, his worries, his regrets, and his insecurities. On the same day, his wife, Molly Bloom, is having a sexual tryst with a music impresario. When Bloom returns home late that night and falls into bed, he unwittingly wakens his wife who lying in bed allows her mind to race—in a stream of conscious monologue that will never be equaled. As her soliloquy concludes, she affirms the ordinariness of her husband, and—since he is Everyman—of humanity in general.

Published serially through the efforts of Pound and Harriet Shaw Weaver, and finally by a Paris bookshop run by an expatriate American named Sylvia Beech, the novel was unlike anything the literary world had seen before. Told in various styles that ranged from typical narrative to newspaper journalism to dramatic dialogue to a chapter echoing the growth of the English language, the novel was difficult and challenging and extraordinary. Joyce had worked on the novel steadily for eight years, from about 1914 to 1922. Once again, on his birthday, the novel was published in 1922. And while it did not make Joyce a rich man, it very much made him a famous one.

The novel was banned in England and the United States under their respective obscenity laws until 1933, when Judge John M. Woolsey of the United States District Court handed down a monumental decision in favor of the novel. The judge's written decision itself was a thoughtful critique of Joyce's methods, his

intentions, and his story, and, in handing down his decision, gave affirmation
to Joyce's genius. Like Molly Bloom herself as she lay awake with thoughts
careening madly through her mind, Judge Woolsey answered with a resounding
"Yes" to Joyce's work. (The British would not publish *Ulysses* until three years
later in 1936.)

Throughout this time—the creation of work, the reading of proofs, and the
struggle for publication—Joyce was also suffering from extreme eye problems. A
number of various surgeries were more or less successful, but as time passed, Joyce
lost more and more of his vision. (Looking at the manuscript of Joyce's next work,
Finnegans Wake, one notices that the letters are nearly six inches high. For much of
it, he was forced to dictate to an amanuensis—one of who was Samuel Beckett.)
In addition to his own problems with his eyesight, Joyce was also trying to cope
with his daughter Lucia, whose mental instability caused her several times to be
institutionalized and once even analyzed by Carl Jung. Lucia's condition worried
and disturbed Joyce greatly, so much so that at one time he stole her out of one of
the sanitariums where she had been staying.

As his reputation and his concern for his children Georgio and Lucia grew,
Joyce decided that he and Nora should be legally married. On July 4, 1931, the
two were wed in a civil service in London. That same year saw his first grandson
born. The child was named Stephen—in tribute to Joyce's semi-autobiographical
hero, Stephen Dedalus, who appeared in both *A Portrait of the Artist* and *Ulysses*.

In 1922 Joyce began what would ultimately be titled *Finnegans Wake*. He had
told Harriet Shaw Weaver that he had wanted to write a history of the world, and
Finnegans Wake is that attempt. It is an extremely difficult work, inaccessible to
most readers, which attempted to connect the history of mankind to the cycles of
Irish history through a single night in the family of a Dublin pub owner. It has
been said that as *Ulysses* followed the daytime travels of Leopold Bloom, *Finnegans*

Wake is a dreamscape, a subconscious night-novel that tests the very nature of language itself. (Joyce famously—and correctly—remarked that *Finnegans Wake* would be a puzzle that academics would spend a lifetime unraveling.) While chapters of *Finnegans Wake* were published as separate books throughout the course of composition, the book itself was published on May 4, 1939, in London and New York. Four days later, Joyce's face appeared on the cover of *Time* magazine. (It had appeared there previously in the aftermath of the Woolsey decision.)

Yet despite the ever-growing fame and reputation, in 1939, the Joyces were more concerned with the ever-worsening situation in Europe. In September of 1939, Joyce, ever the singer, led British and French soldiers in singing the "Marseillaise." So thrilled were the soldiers that they hoisted him up onto a table—this frail, practically blind man—to sing it again, which he did. But such joy was rare and short-lived. The Germans were approaching and Joyce's fears were not only for moving him and his wife, but on assuring that there would be a place for Lucia when she needed it.

On June 14, 1940 Paris fell to Hitler. Joyce spent the next six months attempting to flee France. The United States offered him asylum but nothing came of it. Instead, he pestered the Swiss embassy to provide him with visas; it was Switzerland, after all, where Lucia's *maison de santé* was being transferred. In the second week of December, he and Nora left France, arriving in Zurich on December 17th. Within a month, Joyce was hospitalized with stomach pains; he had been complaining of such pains for a month or two, though most of his friends associated it with nerves made worse by his worries. The doctors, however, diagnosed a perforated duodenal ulcer in his stomach. He died in the Zurich hospital on January 13, 1940 and was buried the next day in the cemetery at Fluntern.

It is difficult to state here what Joyce did for modern literature—that is a job for men much more capable than I. Joyce was correct in stating that his writing would forever provide work for academics, for Joyce scholarship today is a full-time business. He was a serious, brilliant man, who also liked a drink, a good song, and good company. And he left us with a portrait of Dublin that is for the most part gone forever. But enough of it still remains, and that is why it is indeed a bittersweet endeavor to retrace the steps that so many of his characters followed, to visit Joyce's own "dear, dirty Dublin": the Martello Tower and the forty-foot swimming hole (where I last saw people swimming on a snowy St. Stephen's Day, the morning after Christmas), the pubs named in *Ulysses*—Davy Byrne's and Barney Kiernen's, the Gresham Hotel where Gabriel Conroy had his aching epiphany as the snows fell generally over all of Ireland. One could go on and on— and many do—retracing the stories of Dublin that Joyce so beautifully and explosively gave to the public.

In many ways, it is a shame that Joyce's name is so associated with high-minded scholarship and esoteric writings, for that is not true of most. The stories of *Dubliners* are beautiful and delicate and humorous and realistic. *The Portrait of the Artist as a Young Man* is an insightful look into a clever Irish boy's upbringing at the end of the nineteenth century. And *Ulysses* is more than worth the effort. Full of humanity with all its vices and virtues, it too is both funny and tragic, thought provoking and puzzling. But most of all it is wonderfully alive, and it is that to which Molly Bloom voices her resounding "Yes." And as for *Finnegans Wake*, (no apostrophe, mind you) even those readers who cannot make it through its entirety should pick out sections just to hear the pure musicality of the prose. For in a large way that was what James Joyce was—the man who captured the very music of the language and sang it so masterfully upon the written page.

Chapter XXVII:
Samuel Beckett

It used to be my contention that you always remember the first time you attend a production of a Beckett play, for it never coincides with any preconceived ideas you may have had about theater or storytelling. I am not so sure that is completely true now. The risks Beckett took in his drama have now become part of our age's repertoire, and what must have seemed so avant-garde at the time, is less so to an increasingly jaded audience. Yet, I still want to believe that no one can leave the theater after seeing a production of *Waiting for Godot*, or of *Krapp's Last Tape*, or of *Endgame*, and not feel profoundly affected. Perhaps there is not the flash of clarity that Joyce's epiphanies sought to produce, for Beckett's insights come at a much slower crawl, but there is the unmistakable understanding that one has witnessed something very rare in theater indeed.

I remember one production I saw in the mid-1970s. It featured the talented Hume Cronyn and Jessica Tandy, who were good interpreters of Beckett's work. Two plays were on the bill: Cronyn in *Krapp's Last Tape* and Tandy in *Not I*. I can still see Cronyn as Krapp, old and haggard and eating banana after banana, listening to a stodgy tape recorder playing tapes of a younger and less defeated man. But it was Tandy's performance that affected me most, and she never appeared on stage at all. Actually, part of her did appear, but it was only her mouth. (Surely there are times where some people you meet seem to be nothing but yapping maws and blathering gobs.) Yet, Tandy's performance—and Beckett's play—is not a joke but a harrowing text about confinement. The production itself was extraordinary. Tandy was perched, I believe, on a high ladder and shrouded in black cloth with only a hole for her iridescent mouth. A spotlight from beneath and within the shroud stayed focused on that floating mouth, and Tandy, in a remarkable,

and what must have been an excruciating, performance, presented her edgy monologue. It was a night where we all stayed up very late, for Beckett had jolted our
minds, and with my friends I tried to make sense of what we had just witnessed. I
still fondly remember that late night talk with the people who had accompanied
me. It was a good example of what the Irish call *craic*. And it was the power of
Beckett's plays that brought it on.

Samuel Beckett was born on April 13, 1906, in Foxrock, County Dublin, at
his father's estate, Cooldrinach. His father was the manager of a surveying firm,
and Samuel Beckett and his older brother Frank lived in the relative comfort that
a middle-class Protestant family could enjoy, far enough away from the social
unrest and physical squalor of what Joyce called "dear Dirty Dublin." Indeed, in
1916, as Dublin burned and the rebels barricaded themselves in the General Post
Office, Beckett's father took his two sons up upon a high hill where they could
watch in safety.

When he was ten, Beckett was enrolled in the Portora Royal School, the same
school that Oscar Wilde had attended. It was there he began studying French. And
while a studious young man, he was also a fairly gifted athlete at school. He
excelled in tennis and cricket—the very sports that the Gaelic Athletic Association
railed against—as well at boxing.

Between 1923 and 1927, Beckett attended Trinity College, where he majored
in French and Italian. There he also was able to get a taste of the intellectual scene
that was thriving in Dublin at the time. The theater—particularly Lady Gregory
and Yeats's Abbey Theatre—was an important part of a young student's life, and
Beckett saw the premiers of O'Casey's *Juno and the Paycock* and *The Plough and
the Stars*, as well as Yeats's versions of Sophocles's Oedipus plays. He was, however,
most taken with Synge's plays that were being revived at the Abbey. Yet, it was not
only serious theater that attracted Beckett; he loved the light theater and music

hall revues, and most importantly, the cinema. (Joyce too was very fond of the cinema, and had in fact opened the first cinema in Ireland nearly twenty years earlier.) In the cinema, Beckett was introduced to the films of Buster Keaton and Charlie Chaplin, two actors who would greatly influence his own plays, and to Laurel & Hardy. (In fact, in 1964, Beckett flew to New York to make a film with the great—though now elderly—Buster Keaton.)

After Beckett graduated from Trinity with a degree in Italian and French, he took a teaching position in Paris at the École Normale Supérieure in 1928. In that same year, he met Joyce. Soon the two would become friends, and Beckett was a frequent visitor to the Joyce home, helping the nearly blind writer with his work on *Finnegans Wake*. (There is an apocryphal story about Joyce dictating pages to Beckett. Apparently, someone knocked at the door and Joyce said, "Come in." The story goes that Beckett copied it down and the phrase entered *Finnegans Wake*.) Joyce thought highly of Beckett and considered him the most talented of the young men who gravitated toward him. At the same time, Beckett began a relationship with Joyce's daughter Lucia that lasted for about two years. It was not unusual for Joyce and Nora, Beckett and Lucia, and Joyce's son Georgio and his date to go out together as a group. Yet Beckett was not interested in an amorous relationship; he was simply happy to act as an escort when the Joyces went out together on the town, but he wanted nothing more. When he finally told Lucia the truth, it caused a terrible rift for some time with Joyce, who was always very protective of his daughter.

In 1930, Beckett had his first short story, "Assumption" published in the journal *Transition*, as well as the essay "Dante . . . Bruno, Vico, Joyce," for a symposium on Joyce. He was becoming acquainted with the Parisian literary circles and also gaining a small amount of fame and confidence. His poem "Whoroscope" won ten pounds in a literary competition, and his book-length study *Proust* was considered an important analysis of the recently deceased French novelist. By 1932, he was working on a novel *Dream of Fair to Middling Women*, which would not be published until 1992, three years after his death.

Despite these minor literary successes, he was out of money. He returned to Ireland, where he lectured at Trinity for a while, moved to London, where he worked on his novel *Murphy*, wandered about in Hamburg, Dresden, and Berlin for a short while, returned to Dublin, and in 1937 moved back to Paris, which would—with few interruptions—remain his home for the rest of his life. (The novel *Murphy*, however, shows that Beckett had an extraordinary knowledge of London's streets and neighborhoods.)

Soon settling in Paris, on January 6, 1937, Beckett was attacked and stabbed by a Parisian pimp. Beckett was taken by ambulance to the nearest hospital, where he fell into unconsciousness. It was also big news in Paris and Dublin. Friends from all over arrived at the hospital. Joyce used his influence to arrange for a private room. (Beckett claims that Joyce was the first thing he recognized when he regained consciousness.) In truth, Joyce was very solicitous about Beckett, taking care of all the expenses and gathering friends to come visit. (Joyce could be quite generous in his own way. Later that year, Beckett helped correct proofs of *Finnegans Wake*, and for the work Joyce not only paid well but threw in an old overcoat and five neckties.)

Another positive result of the stabbing was that Beckett's mother, with whom he had been estranged due to his very un-Protestant situation of not having an actual job, rushed over to Paris, and the two were reconciled. But perhaps more importantly to Beckett's life was the arrival in the hospital of a young French woman named Suzanne Deschevaux-Dumesnil. Suzanne had met Beckett ten years earlier, when he was at the École Normale Supérieure, and now when she heard about the attack, she attended to him with tenderness and care. When he was released, the two continued to see each other frequently, attending galleries and concerts together. Suzanne Deschevaux-Dumesnil was his life-long companion and in 1961 they were wed.

Beckett's novel *Murphy* was published in 1938, and Beckett immediately began translating it into French. This was a technique that he would employ throughout his life. At first he wrote in English and translated his works into French. Later, after the war, he wrote primarily in French and translated into English.

The late 1930s, however, was not a time to be in France. Two days before Hitler marched into Paris, Beckett and Suzanne fled with little food and less money. They met the Joyces in Vichy, who were staying in Maria Jolas's language school, and Joyce gave Beckett a letter of introduction to Valery Larbaud. Larbaud lent Beckett 20,000 francs, and he and Suzanne set off to the west of France and the sea.

In 1941, Beckett joined the Gloria SMH cell of the French Resistance, and worked within the Resistance for three years. Somehow and somewhere the cell was betrayed, and Suzanne and Beckett fled their apartment just hours before the arrival of the Gestapo. After a brief stay in Paris, the two went underground in the country village of Roussillion, where Beckett did farm work in exchange for room and board.

When the war ended in 1945, Beckett and Suzanne moved back to Paris, trying to continue life as they had left it. On a visit to his mother in Ireland, Beckett suddenly began doing all his writing in French, which he would continue for the rest of his life. This period from 1945 to 1953, when he was writing in French, was particularly prolific. Most of what he was writing at the time was fiction, except for one dramatic piece entitled *En attendant Godot (Waiting for Godot)*.

On January 3, 1953, Roger Blin mounted a production of *En attendant Godot* at the Théâtre de Babylone in Paris. It was his first great success; it brought both fame and financial reward. It also changed the history of modern drama.

Godot is the story of two tramps—perhaps Laurel & Hardy—who are waiting for someone or something named Godot. They while the time away, and are met by a man and another fellow whom the man treats like a dog and a servant. The two leave and the tramps remain and wait. The first act ends with no sign of Godot. During the second act, the tramps are still waiting, still visited by the man and his dog/servant, and still Godot never arrives. The play was a brilliant combination of existential angst, vaudeville slapstick, and Brechtian theater. Its success was worldwide.

In London, the Royal Court Theatre presented *Fin de Partie* and *Krapp's Last Tape* while the BBC broadcast his radio plays. His fiction—in both English and French—were produced regularly. Always fascinated with movies—and the consequent growth of television—he began writing for that media as well, although he was always careful that the things he did for the stage were not indiscriminately filmed for television or cinema.

Beckett was a literary celebrity, a difficult thing for an intensely shy and quiet man. In the theater, he knew exactly the vision he was looking for, and could be quite commanding just by his very presence, but the glare of fame was too much for him. (It is not without reason that the best biography of him is entitled *Damned to Fame*.) It was even more abhorrent to Suzanne. In 1969, they would try again to dodge the spotlight that would be focused upon him.

In 1969, Beckett and Suzanne traveled to Tunis for a vacation. At his hotel, he received a telegram from a friend, Jerome Lindon, stating that the Swedish Academy had awarded him the Nobel Prize for literature. His friend, who knew him well, advised him to go into hiding, that the press would soon be descending upon them. Suzanne and Beckett were sincerely horrified—the attention that this would bring to their privacy was frightening and the interruption to his work would be maddening. Four days after the announcement, Beckett telegrammed Stockholm to say that he was honored to have received the award, but that he was unable to attend the ceremony. Acting in his stead would be his friend, Jerome Lindon.

It is argued that Beckett accepted the award—when others had famously refused it—out of generosity. The money attached to the prize was given out by Beckett to a wide variety of people and places. The library at Trinity College was the recipient of a sizeable sum, but so also were a large number of individual writers, directors, artists, and others who had supported Beckett when he was unknown and to whom he expressed his gratitude. Importantly, Beckett also wanted to reward the publishers who had stuck by him despite the low bottom-line that his works always presented. Having "Nobel Laureate" on their book jackets was sure to increase their sales.

Even before the Nobel Prize, Beckett had become a literary phenomenon. His plays and writings were performed and produced all over the world. His works were the focus of spirited academic research, and the volume of books and articles critiquing the works was sizeable. Just the articles claiming to know who or what Godot stood for were formidable! Perhaps, at the time, only his old friend James Joyce was the focus of more academic criticism. (It is a cruel irony that Beckett also suffered through painful cataract operations at this time, reminding him much of his early mentor.)

In 1986, Beckett was diagnosed with emphysema. In the hospital, he wrote what would be his final piece, the poem "What is the Word." Surprisingly, it was also discovered that he was badly malnourished. The years on the run in the Resistance had made both him and Suzanne very frugal with food, and his condition was a result of simply not eating enough. After several falls outside and inside his apartment, he was moved into a nursing home, where his health was so bad that he could no longer write. He focused his attention therefore on translation. While he was there in the nursing home, Suzanne, his loyal and faithful companion for fifty years, died on July 17, 1986. He was well enough to be allowed to attend her funeral, but her death brought deep sadness. He did not live much longer, dying on December 22, 1986.

Samuel Beckett was a fascinating man who gave the world a great body of work. Although he spent most of his life in Paris and even wrote in a language that was initially his second one, he was formed during the intellectual resurrection of post-independence Dublin. Befriended by the literary genius of the century and blessed with an Irishman's odd mixture of wit, morbidity, humor, and scholarship, he changed the modern theater forever.

Yeats, Joyce, and Beckett make up a triumvirate that is unparalleled in any century. As artists, they rose above—and were inspired by—the political upheaval at home and abroad that surrounded them and the excruciating physical and psychic pain that accompanied their lives to create art that defined a century. Always a literary nation, most of Ireland reveres them as much as their fallen heroes and great warriors. They are an essential part of the Irish fabric.

To understand the import of literature in Ireland, I will leave you with a final story. I was in a very small pub in County Kerry, miles from anything but sheep and stone walls. Behind the bar, there were three books on a shelf. One was a book of sporting records—to settle arguments, I suppose—and the others were *The Collected Poems of Yeats* and *Ulysses*. These very modern men were very much part of this ancient tradition.

BIRTH PANGS
OF A NEW NATION

In the first decade of the twentieth century, William Butler Yeats was founding the Abbey Theatre, Joyce was writing his epiphanies and eloping to Europe with a Galway-born chambermaid, and Beckett was but a mere boy. Yet cataclysmic rumblings were brewing in the movement towards Irish independence. In the 1890s, Gladstone had introduced his second Home Rule bill which passed in the House of Commons but was defeated in the House of Lords. When the bill again passed in the House of Commons in 1912, one of the immediate results was a strengthening of Ulster Unionism, the resurrection of the Orange Order, and the formation of the Ulster Volunteers. The Ulster Volunteers were dedicated to preventing Home Rule, even if it meant by force. (It is a perverse irony that the volunteers were willing to commit treason against Britain—to battle against British troops enforcing a Home Rule act—in order to stay loyal to Britain.) Led by Sir Edmond Carson, this revived Unionist movement set up drafting a separate Ulster constitution as well as launching a petition that was signed by more than 200,000 people. The petitioners stated that they would use all means necessary to prevent the establishment of a Home Rule parliament in Ireland. Carson's belief was that the Irish Party would never accept Home Rule for part of the country, so if Ulster opposed forcefully enough the plan would have to be abandoned.

Neither Carson nor John Redmond—the main force behind Home Rule in 1912—could have anticipated how events would ultimately be played out: after a brutal War of Independence, a treaty would be negotiated that offered, in fact, partial Home Rule; Ulster became a separate entity and the debate about such a partition resulted in a cruel and bloody Civil War.

As in any time of war, of negotiating, of debate, when a country is taking its first steps towards nationhood, there are scores of men and women whose names have come down in history—for noble and ignoble reasons. And the list of Irish heroes, martyrs, politicians, and firebrands is quite lengthy, two of them being Michael Collins and Eamon de Valera. Comrades during the 1916 uprising, partners during the War of Independence and the subsequent negotiations, they fell out over the Treaty and became enemies during the Civil War. One died in 1922 when he was thirty-two years old and Ireland was still suffering the pangs of birth. The other continued on until 1975 when he had become the elder statesmen of Ireland. The two, so different in temperament, were extraordinary individuals who were united by their passionate dedication to Ireland but whom the forces of history contrived to set against each other.

CHAPTER XXVIII:
MICHAEL COLLINS

In 1996, the Irish screenwriter/director Neil Jordan released a major motion picture on the life of Michael Collins. Filled with glamorous stars and beautiful landscapes, it created a controversy among historians of the era, who worried about many of the film's historical inaccuracies. Yet, for all its faults, it brought the name of Michael Collins out from the history books and into the general culture. (One fellow I know in Cork, Collins's home county, claims with obvious disdain that no one but Cork people cared about the "Big Fella" until the release of the movie. I don't know if that is altogether true. I do know that this particular Cork man and his wife were passionate about him; the woman claimed her granny ran a pub where Collins used to stop, and after a long night the two wanted to drive me to *Beal na mBlath* where Collins had been assassinated. I was wise enough not to drive out that night, but I wished I had gone the following day, for Collins—long before the Jordan film—had always intrigued me.

Michael Collins was born on October 16, 1890, in the tiny village of Sam's Cross in West Cork. The town is just east of Skibbereen—a place associated with both the most horrible accounts of the Great Famine and the reprehensible inaction of the British Government during that time. A local boy, Collins would surely have absorbed the bitterness of Skibbereen's starvation less than half a century before, and some biographers claim that the heart wrenching song "Skibbereen" was Collins's own party piece. (To this day still in Ireland, men and women usually have a "party piece," the song that they sing at gatherings when they are inevitably asked to. Singing a solo piece at parties is much more common in Ireland and in Irish communities than it is in America.)

Michael Collins was the youngest of eight children, and his father—who had married when he was sixty-three years old—was seventy-five when Collins was born. He died when Collins was six, and on his deathbed is said to have predicted that his young son would one day do great things for Ireland. Collins would recall two men in particular who helped to make him the man he became. One, Denis Lyons, was his schoolmaster at the national school in Lisavaird and a secret member of the Irish Republican Brotherhood; the other was the local blacksmith, James Santry, a proud Irishman and a Fenian. Lyons probably introduced Collins to the nationalist poet Thomas Davis, whom he read voraciously, and to Arthur Griffith's paper the *United Irishman*. Both men helped shape Collins's political and nationalistic beliefs, and Collins credits them for forging his pride in being Irish and his determination to end British rule. He also was greatly influenced by his sister Mary, who on returning from school in Edinburgh during the height of the Boer War regaled Michael with stories of the brave Boer farmers fighting against the British army. It is probable that Mary's stories—of laboring Boers ambushing

British soldiers and then melting back into a crowd of civilians—were the seminal influence in Collins's guerilla strategies during the War of Independence.

A big child with a streak of wildness, Collins was sent from his home at Sam's Cross to live with his sister in Clonakilty where he took the Post Office exams and where he worked for his brother-in-law who owned the newspaper, *West Cork People*. He learned how to typeset and was given the opportunity to write some articles, primarily on local sports. He was thirteen at the time. Almost two years later, he moved to West Kensington in London where his sister Hannie lived. He had passed the postal exams in Clonakilty so was able to get a position at the Post Office in West Kensington. Soon after arriving, he was involved with the London Irish community, playing hurling with the Gaelic Athletic Association—and with his best boyhood friend and cousin Sean Hurley who was in London at the same time. He also was becoming more and more politicized.

In 1909, Collins read a paper condemning the Catholic Church's anti-national-ism stance at a political rally. He had been invited to read the paper by Arthur Griffith's newly formed Sinn Fein party. That same year he was sworn in as a member of the Irish Republican Brotherhood. His legitimate occupation in the Post Office provided him with a growing understanding of financial matters and before long he was the treasurer of the London and South of England branch of the IRB, as well as treasurer of the GAA.

Still a great reader, Collins taught himself enough about agriculture to win an agricultural scholarship in 1910—although he financially could not make up the remaining necessary fees to attend. Although he read widely and broadly—Hardy, Synge, Swinburne, and Yeats—his reading continued to be heavily based in the nationalist literature of the day.

On April 25, 1915, Collins and his cousin joined the London unit of the Irish Volunteers. The Irish Volunteers had been formed by Eoin O'Neill, the Gaelic scholar and associate of Douglas Hyde, in response to the Ulster Volunteers who had pledged to fight against any implementation of Home Rule. (Ireland had been promised Home Rule—as an incentive to get Irish boys to volunteer for the British Army strained by the bloodbath of World War I—but its enactment was postponed until after the war when the promise was then rescinded. Thus, at the time, the Volunteers believed they were a necessary defense if the Ulster forces kept good to their word.) The Irish Volunteers also contained a large number of members of the Irish Republican Brotherhood, whose intentions were not merely to defend against the Ulster Unionists.

In January 1916, Collins sailed for Ireland. He had been told by the IRB in London of the encroaching uprising in Dublin and he wanted to be part of it. Upon arrival, Collins was made Captain and given an Irish Volunteer's uniform. When the uprising occurred he was second in command to Joseph Mary Plunkett, the poet and one of the signers of the proclamation. Of the leaders, Collins was closest to Sean MacDiarmada, whom he liked and trusted greatly. The two spent much of Holy Week together, and Collins would remark later that it was MacDiarmada's realism—much like that of James Connolly's—that attracted him much more than the poetic idealism of Padraig Pearse.

Collins was stationed in the General Post Office during the uprising, spending much of his time in the operations room. His extraordinary sense of organization and his commanding presence—they didn't call him the "Big Fella" for nothing—was especially useful in sorting out the ever-changing orders and the minor rows that surfaced as the rebels' plans seemed to be going up in the flames that were enveloping Sackville Street. When the rebels had to evacuate the burning GPO, Collins led his men across the street to a grocery shop. There they waited for the end. On Saturday, April 29, Pearse surrendered; Collins learned that his cousin Sean Hurley had died; and the dreams of an independent Ireland seemed very far away.

Following the uprising, Britain imposed martial law on Ireland, and more than 17,000 men were imprisoned in English jails or interned in Frongoch in Wales. Collins was sent to the latter. The apathy of the Irish people towards the uprising had been turned to spirited nationalism by the barbarity of its leaders' executions, and one tangential result of this brutality was the growth of Arthur Griffith's Sinn Fein party.

In the meantime, Frongoch in Wales acted—as internment camps and prisons acted for so many of the men—as a "Republican University." It was in such camps that new plans to bring down British rule were formulated and refined. Here, the tactics of guerilla warfare were solidified; here the cells of the IRB were devised as the necessary organization of the next uprising; and here, amid great fears of conscription into England's army—to die for England in its foreign war—the prisoners developed a means to fight the system. (One way that Collins foiled the threat of conscription was to organize a system where the prisoners had given false identities to the authorities. They could not be drafted because the government did not have their real names.)

Frongoch was a filthy abandoned distillery, where the conditions were horrible and the food scant and inedible. The British authorities tried to treat the Irish prisoners as criminals rather than as prisoners of war, and against this Michael Collins fought hard. Refusal to do hard labor was met with rescinded privileges and lock downs. Collins then developed a very Gandhi-esque strategy: complete refusal to cooperate. On November 2, 1916, two hundred prisoners went on a hunger strike in Frongoch internment camp. Doctors refused to assist those who would not give their real names. The strike continued and—as the hunger strike would do often in Irish politics—public and international opinion swung against the British. Collins wrote an article describing the situation and had it published in the *Cork Free Press* and the *Manchester Guardian*, which further shaped public opinion, particularly in America. On December 21, 1916, a general amnesty was declared for the political prisoners and Collins was home in Cork for Christmas. But Collins had learned many invaluable lessons in prison and internment; not the least was the value of meticulous organization and the importance of gathering all kinds of information. He would rely on both of these in his war against Dublin Castle and the British intelligence within its walls.

Meanwhile the strength of Sinn Fein was becoming greater and greater. In February and May of 1917, Sinn Fein won majorities in the bi-elections making John Redmond's Home Rule Party practically ineffective. Later that year Eamon de Valera won the MP seat for East Clare and Collins took over as director of organizations for the Volunteers. In an extraordinary misreading of the public mind, early the following year, Britain attempted to pass a conscription act that would draft Irish boys to fight for England in the European war. The attempt united every faction of Irish life against the proposal: the Church, the Home Rulers, the city laborers, the country farmers, the Fenians, the IRB, and the Volunteers. The result was, in a very large way, the first rip in Britain's control of Ireland.

Sinn Fein, in protest, ordered a one-day national strike. The Home Rule Party MPs withdrew from Westminster, and England as always played a heavy hand. On May 17, 1918, Britain began arresting Irish leaders. Arthur Griffith and Eamon de Valera were among those arrested. Only Collins and Cathal Brugha among the leaders remained at large. (In 1919, Michael Collins and his friend Harry Boland personally went to Lincoln jail in England and organized Eamon de Valera's escape from jail. De Valera went almost immediately to America to raise money for Sinn Fein, and Collins—one of the most wanted men by the British government—attended to not only political business in Ireland but personal business as well. Throughout de Valera's absence, Collins risked his life regularly to visit de Valera's wife and children. In stark contrast to his brutality in the arena of war, Collins was always noted for his kindness to the elderly, the poor, and to women.) The arrests however did not deter the nationalist movement. In December that year—after World War I had ended—another election was held. Seventy-three Sinn Fein members, twenty-six Unionist members, and only six Irish party members were sent to Parliament. However, this election meant more than just a victory for Sinn Fein; the party had always operated under an absentee policy, refusing to sit in Westminster, which they did not recognize as a legitimate government of Ireland. Thus with a majority of seats, on January 21, 1919, Sinn Fein assembled the first *Dáil Eireann* in Dublin. "Ireland's Assembly" was sitting regardless of whether Britain approved or not. The assembly ratified the republic that Pearse had proclaimed on Easter 1916; it drafted a provisional constitution and a declaration of independence; it sent a message to free nations of the world; it announced a socioeconomic plan for Ireland; and it selected delegates to attend the post-war peace conference in Paris. On the same day, the IRB attacked an explosives convoy in Tipperary. Like that other country that had announced its Declaration of Independence from Britain, 150 years earlier, Ireland now had to win that independence through a war. And Michael Collins was the prime director of that war.

What had been known as the Irish Republican Brotherhood was now renamed the Irish Republican Army, the official arm of the assembly that had met in Dublin. The guerilla tactics that Collins had learned from his sister and her stories of the Boer farmers, from John MacBride—who had fought in the Boer War and during Easter week had told his men that never again should they let themselves be locked in a building against superior military might—and from all the planning and conversations in Frongoch internment camp now came to the fore. Munitions and armament depots were regularly attacked. Both the police and the military were fair targets of the republican army. Britain was at a loss as to what to do. Their policy of "containment" was costing the British taxpayer twenty million pounds a year. The British Prime Minister Lloyd George believed it was time for negotiations. A truce was called after two years of fighting. (Collins later admitted that at the time the IRA could not have lasted more than three weeks more at most.)

Lloyd George would not negotiate with Collins, whom he considered no more than a gangster. He also insisted on an unconditional surrender of the IRA before negotiations could be started. He might have won in his insistence on keeping Collins out of the negotiations, but no unconditional surrender was put forth. De Valera, who seemed more of a reasonable politician to Lloyd George, stood firm on his principles. (Collins claimed he had no ability in diplomacy and had no desire to become involved in it—a truth that would serve him poorly in 1921. He also knew that if he appeared in public negotiations he more than likely would be arrested—or worse.) But British capitulation of any sort was a moral victory. The great empire had been forced to negotiate with the republicans.

In the negotiations, Lloyd George proposed the creation of a six-county separate entity called "Northern Ireland." To the republicans who had fought and suffered for the better part of six years this was an insult, and was refused. The result again was a landslide victory for Sinn Fein, which won 124 of 128 seats and the south and again refused to sit at Westminster. The second *Dáil Eireann* was assembled.

England responded to this political obstinacy by sending over a new group of military police known as the Black and Tans. (They actually got their name because there were not enough uniforms to go around so that some had dark police uniforms and some had khaki soldier uniforms.) They were a brutal bunch of ex-soldiers more suited to warfare than civil policing, and their brutality was met head-on by Michael Collins and his troops. And once again, the savagery and brutality of the British changed public opinion. Initially, the people were revolted by the IRA's killing of police, but the atrocities committed by the Black and Tans turned them once again against the British, reinforcing their belief of England as the cruel and brutal oppressor.

Collins knew enough about organization. He knew Irish history enough to know the pitfalls of informants and betrayals. And so, he organized his own system of spies and informants. And he believed that the only way to fight terror was with terror. By the middle of 1919, he had been appointed President of the Supreme Council of the IRB, he was the Minister of Finance in the Dáil government, and he was the commander of the IRA. He had created an intelligence network to subvert the system that Britain had operating in Dublin, had organized an arms-smuggling operation, had created an elite assassination squad (known as "The Twelve Apostles"), and even organized a national loan to fund the rebellion. With de Valera in America and Arthur Griffith still in prison, he was also acting President of the Republic. And he was the most wanted man by the British with a 10,000 pound price on his head.

On November 21, 1920, Michael Collins decided to rid Dublin of British intelligence once and for all. His special squad went about and assassinated fourteen British officers; in one day, the entire British Secret Service in Ireland had been destroyed. Britain naturally responded with force. The Black and Tans invaded Croke Park where a Gaelic football match was being played and fired indiscriminately into the crowd of onlookers, killing thirteen and wounded scores more. Once again, news of the atrocity circled the globe and Britain was once more trying to stem a bad propaganda crisis. Also, it has always been Britain's unwise policy to think that brutal reprisal would break the spirit of the Irish, and always it seems it had the opposite effect, instead tempering their resolve like steel in a fire.

At this time, the British assassinated the mayor of Cork, arrested his successor Terrence MacSwiney for possessing seditious documents (and then allowed him to die during a hunger strike in prison), and finally set fire to Cork itself. Certainly Michael Collins, being a Cork man, played no small part in location of the British reprisals. However, the resolve of the Republicans was unwavering. Finally, it was Lloyd George who had had enough, and who began talks with de Valera. (Now here is where it all gets complicated. De Valera had spoken with Lloyd George, and he knew the prime minister would never agree to an independent Irish Republic. The Republican Army had the British on the run—a guerilla army had outmaneuvered the British forces. But guerilla tactics were a small strength at the negotiating table. De Valera sent a commission of four to negotiate the treaty. Michael Collins was among them. Collins argued correctly that he was not a politician, and that indeed de Valera was the most able politician in Ireland and should be there at the table. Yet hindsight is perfect, and de Valera's decision to step away seems unwise at best given the history that would ensue.)

The negotiations were difficult. The Irish delegation wanted nothing but an independent republic; Lloyd George refused to consider anything but dominion status for the twenty-six counties and Ulster to remain part of Britain. Collins was smart enough to know he could never expect Ulster to be brought into the Republic then and there, but he hoped that a border commission might redraw the lines of Ulster and bring Catholic Fermanagh and Tyrone into the Free State. (He was wrong.) There was also the ever-present problem of the Oath of Allegiance. Collins believed they could reword the oath to pass through the Dáil, and once British troops were withdrawn they could seek other alterations. But the general feeling of the Irish delegation was not one of joy. Collins himself—who believed the treaty was an initial step that could be improved upon without further loss of life—stated, all too tragically prophetic, that in signing the treaty he had signed his own death warrant.

When Michael Collins returned from London with the 1921 treaty, there was small reason for celebration, for it involved a partitioned island and dominion status for the twenty-six counties under the auspices of the UK. A long debate on the treaty followed in the Dáil, and on January 7, 1922, a vote was taken. Those who supported the treaty claimed a narrow 64 to 57 victory. The Irish Free State had been born and Michael Collins was appointed commander. But de Valera walked out of the assembly and resigned his presidency. And while England handed over Dublin Castle to Michael Collins, and though British soldiers withdrew and handed over barracks and supplies to the Irish Republican Army, all was far from right in Ireland. For the anti-treaty forces, under the leadership of de Valera, would challenge the government and ultimately send it spiraling into a brutal Civil War.

There is a great story about England's handing over Dublin Castle to Michael Collins. Moods were high despite the breach with de Valera, and Collins took a cab to Dublin Castle for the formal ceremony. There he was met by his British counterpart who promptly shook Collins's hand and said, "I am glad to see you, Mr. Collins." Collins laughed aloud and said, "Like hell you are." Michael Collins, the man who had been the most wanted man in the British Isles, who was hated ferociously by the British Government, was accepting for Ireland the keys of Dublin Castle—so long a hated symbol of British domination.

In June 1922, after a general election was held and de Valera's Fianna Fail party had taken only a small percentage of feats, hostilities between the Free State and the anti-treaty republican forces broke out. Michael Collins was now the official opposition to the Republican forces—many of whom had been his comrades-in-arms through a long, hard struggle—and when the Republicans took control of the Four Courts in Dublin on June 28, 1922, it was he who had to make the difficult decision to fire upon it. Irish men were now fighting against Irish men.

The IRA itself was split. Those who sided with de Valera were called the Irregulars and the soldiers of the Free State were formed under Collins's old friend Richard Mulcahy as the Free State Army. Collins, still believing in a united Ireland, began arming both anti- and pro-treaty IRA forces in the North in order to defend the Catholic population in Ulster. This led, in a way, to further resistance to the treaty in the South. The state of things was truly a mess, and in July, the government appointed Collins commander-in-chief of the national army.

The Civil War would last only ten months, but in those first months, it was brutal, bitter, and deadly. The superior government forces soon wore down the Irregulars in the cities and towns, but they remained active in the countryside, particularly in the south and west, in Michael Collins's "Rebel Cork."

On August 20, 1923, eight days after Arthur Griffith died of massive hemorrhage, Michael Collins traveled to his beloved Cork to visit troops there. He had been sick and some claim depressed, and wanted to end the warfare that pitted Irishman against Irishman. On the trip he even visited with anti-treaty men. On August 22,1922, his convoy set out from Cork to West Cork, the world of his youth. The convoy passed through Bandon, and through Clonakilty where he had first been sent to live with his sister and where he worked on the *West Cork People*. He then stopped in Woodfield. There at the Four Alls pub, in sight of the house where his mother was born, he treated his family and his escorts to the local brew. They returned the way they had come, and passed once more through Bandon. East of Bandon in a place called *Beal na mBlath* ("the mouth of flowers"), Michael Collins's convoy was ambushed. Only one person was killed—Michael Collins. He had been shot cleanly in the back of the head, dying only a few miles from the place where he was born.

To those who knew him, Michael Collins had seemed invincible. At the height of his notoriety, when Britain had a sizable price on his head, he refused to go into hiding and rode along the Dublin streets on his bicycle. "The Big Fella" had always seemed to be beyond the reach of death. His men were stunned. They brought the body back to Cork where it was then shipped to Dublin. There Michael Collins's body lay in state for three days. (I have a good friend, Tom McLaughlin, who's a descendant of the second wife of the great Belfast painter Sir John Lavery. When the Irish delegation was in England for the treaty negotiations in 1921, it was at the Lavery home at Cromwell Place in South Kensington that the delegation stayed. In gratitude, the Irish government later commissioned Lavery to design its currency, and it is the portrait of his wife—my friend's relation—which used to grace the Irish pound note until the 1970s. Lady Lavery also allowed people to believe she had had an affair with Collins and had to be dissuaded from wearing widow's weeds to Collins's funeral. Nevertheless, Lavery had painted Collins in life and now as the Big Fella lay in state in Dublin, he painted his portrait once final time.) Tens of thousands of people filed past the casket, and all of Dublin seemed to line the streets as his funeral procession wound through the city towards the cemetery in Glasnevin. Michael Collins was dead, and Ireland had to go on without him.

Michael Collins, Miceal O'Coileain, the "Big Fella," Mick. Many had a name for him, and the name seemed always to be given with respect and love. No doubt he was a ruthless soldier, but he had brought down the British intelligence almost single-handedly. Yet he was also well known for his kindness—kindness to a widow, a young orphan, the poor prostitute on the street, the out-of-work laborer. A physical roughhouser who loved wrestling with his mates even as an adult, who enjoyed a good laugh and loved a good song, he was fiercely loyal to those he loved—and he loved all of Ireland. There have not been many like Michael Collins either in life or in death. If he had lived, Ireland would have surely seen a different future.

CHAPTER XXİX:
Eᴀᴍᴏɴ ᴅᴇ Vᴀʟᴇʀᴀ

I have a friend in London, a very creative, energetic Dublin man, who was telling
me about a radio play he was working on. He had read somewhere about an
encounter between Eamon de Valera and Winston Churchill during World War II.
Churchill supposedly had offered de Valera the whole of Ireland—partition be
damned—if de Valera would bring the Republic into the war. (Ireland's official
neutrality was causing supply and logistic problems for England.) The radio play
was to be entitled *Blink*—I don't know if he ever got around to finishing it—but
it sounded like a perfect title for this high-stakes card game that the two leaders
were playing.

And a card player is not a bad metaphor at all for de Valera, for his entire
political career seemed one gamble after another, and for the most part he
played his cards exceedingly well. He came up to the table in the Easter Rising
of 1916 and remained throughout most of the twentieth century, surviving jail,
political defeats, civil war, and the birth pangs of a new nation. But in his stead-
fastness, he led the country as it evolved into a modern republic and took its
place among the nations of the world. As *The New York Times* stated in his obituary when he died in August 1975, "De Valera dominated Irish life as a fighter,
hero, leader and statesman."

(Another thing I've learned, Dev's name was never spelled "Dev"; it was always
spelled "DeV." I like this spelling—it sort of gives it the grandeur of the Roman
Republic . . . and there are some who would say that DeV would have fit well in
Caesar's senate.)

Perhaps the most important fact of Eamon de Valera's early life was that he was
born in New York on October 14, 1882. The importance of this fact would

appear later when his American birth would work in commuting his sentenced execution with the other leaders of the Easter Rising of 1916. His mother was an Irish immigrant and his father a Cuban who died within the first two years of de Valera's life. Upon the death of his father, de Valera's mother sent him in 1885 back to her people in Limerick. The young boy was alone; his mother remained in America. There in a small one-roomed thatched cottage, de Valera was raised, digging potatoes and milking cows, and growing in his understanding and appreciation of the Irish peasantry and Irish life.

A lifetime of digging potatoes was not among de Valera's ambitions. He graduated from Blackrock College and the National University in Dublin with a degree in mathematics, and in 1904 he began what would have normally been the quiet life of a mathematics teacher. However, at the time his interest in the Irish language directed him towards the Gaelic League. But it was not only Ireland's language and pride that brought him frequently to the Gaelic League classes; he had also fallen in love with one of the teachers, Sinead Flannagan. He married her in 1910.

In 1913, de Valera joined the Irish Volunteers. Before long he had also joined the Irish Republican Brotherhood—which by that time had infiltrated the Volunteers and was actively planning an armed uprising. De Valera rose quickly through the ranks of the IRB, and when the Easter Rising occurred on April 13, 1916, he was the commander of a troop of soldiers outside the center of town. Indeed, it was a point of pride among de Valera's men that they had successfully held off the British troops who were advancing towards the city's center. Not many Irish soldiers could brag of such during those catastrophic six days.

There is a picture of de Valera before his court martial in 1916, guarded by a pair of British soldiers. He is a big man, easily six or seven inches taller than either of the guards; he stands tall in the picture, his arms folded behind his back, his

face wearing an expression of proud dignity and defiant acceptance of whatever
would be his lot.

His lot, however, was not to be executed like the other leaders. His American
birth prevented that. (In 1916, England needed the United States very much to
enter the war in Europe, and did not want to risk the chance of enlisting their
help by executing a native born citizen.) He was not sent to the internment camp
in Frongoch either. Instead, he was rotated through five separate prisons in the
course of less than a year. Yet, in prison—like Collins at Frongoch—de Valera agitated for prisoner rights, organized work stoppages, and hunger strikes. When he
ultimately was released—under a general amnesty brought about to a large degree
by the prisoners' strikes and the consequential public pressure—the authorities
were much aware of this serious-minded, stern mathematician. He would continue
to be a thorn in their side for many years more.

When de Valera was released he was made president of the Irish Volunteers. A
month earlier he had taken over the leadership of Sinn Fein from Arthur Griffith.
Yet it was not the internal politics that would weigh so heavily at this time, but
forces from outside the party. In 1918, when its political clout seemed to be wan-
ing, the Sinn Fein party was given an unintended gift by the British government.
The British attempted to pass a conscription law for Ireland (promising to give
Home Rule to Ireland when the war was over). The mere idea was an insult, the
words of explanation even more so. To exacerbate the situation, the British arrested a number of Sinn Fein leaders, claiming they were plotting with the Germans.
Among those arrested was de Valera. Countess Markievicz, who had also escaped
execution in 1916 because of her being a woman, was also taken in, as was Arthur
Griffith, and Kathleen Clarke, the wife of Thomas Clarke, one of the signatories
of the 1916 Proclamation. The arrests, the conscription idea, the death of prisoners on hunger strikes, it all combined to make Sinn Fein the most popular party in

the south. In June, Arthur Griffith, who was in prison, was elected MP on the slo-
gan "Put him in to get him out."

The elections that immediately followed produced an even greater win for Sinn
Fein. World War I was over—England had fought it so that "small nations might
be free." Now, the one small nation that England had denied freedom to for so
long was going to take its independence once and for all. In the general election,
seventy-three of the hundred and five seats were won by Sinn Fein. The majority
of Irish MPs now wanted an independent Ireland. Most amazing of all, of the seventy-three that had been elected, forty-six of them were in prison or exile. And, as
was always part of their formal position, Sinn Fein was not going to sit at
Westminster. Ireland's Assembly, the Dáil Eireann, was going to sit in Dublin.

During this time, de Valera was in Lincoln Jail in England. Always a devout
Catholic, de Valera assisted the priest at daily mass. But his prison devotions were
not solely motivated by spirituality. Seeing the chaplain left his key to the inner
doors and gates of the prison out in the open in the sacristy when he said mass, de
Valera made an impression of it in the soft candle wax, and then drew an exact
replica of the key. The drawings were sent to Michael Collins, and a newly manu-
factured key was sent to de Valera in a cake. Three times, the key failed to work,
but on the fourth time it fit perfectly. On February 3, 1919, de Valera made his
way through the cell doors, through the gate of Lincoln jail, and into a car driven
by Michael Collins and his friend Harry Boland. It was a bold, audacious, and
magnificent escape—and it was front-page news around the world.

When he returned to Ireland, he took his elected place on the Dáil Eireann
and was elected Prime Minister, or Taoiseach. Yet Ireland was no safe place for de
Valera at the time, and besides the party needed money. He stowed away on a ship
bound for America and there he raised over six million American dollars. But he
failed at what he most desperately wanted: American political support for the Dáil.

While he was gone, Michael Collins and his IRA had caused devastating harm to the British power in Ireland, so much so that Lloyd George had secretly been in contact with Arthur Griffith—de Valera's surrogate in Ireland while he was away—about negotiating some sort of truce.

When de Valera returned to Ireland, it was very different place than when he left. The British government, by the very fact of their communicating with Arthur Griffith, seemed to be recognizing the Dáil's legitimacy. Sinn Fein had just won another spectacular victory, taking 124 of the available 128 seats in the south. And Michael Collins was inflicting serious damage on the British forces in Ireland. Despite the success of Collins's tactics, de Valera never liked guerilla warfare. So, on May 25, he ordered a traditional battle where a troop of one hundred men attacked and burned the Custom House. In a decades-long war, where symbolism always played a very large role, the siege on the Custom House was impressive. It was a fiasco; for of the hundred men involved, eighty were captured and eight killed. As Collins knew, captured troops were always a liability in a war of intelligence.

On June 22, 1921, de Valera was arrested, while King George V was in Belfast presiding over the formal ceremonies partitioning the island. Embarrassed, Lloyd George had him immediately released—one reason was, to the surprise of his own cabinet, he was about to invite de Valera to a conference in London.

If Lloyd George's communications with Griffith had seemed to bestow a form of legitimacy, the invitation to de Valera was more so. Added to that, a formal truce between the Crown and the IRA was signed. Through political boldness and military audacity, the Irish had raised themselves to a degree where Britain was now asking them to come to the negotiating table.

The day after the truce was signed, de Valera and his aides went to London to begin talks with Lloyd George. They were not successful—they could not be.

Lloyd George would not hear of an independent Irish Republic and de Valera refused to give on the issue of partition. The talks broke down.

When de Valera was elected president of the Irish Republic in September of that year, he suggested that he once again negotiate with Lloyd George, but this time as a representative of a sovereign state. Lloyd George refused. For him Ireland would only exist as a part of the British Empire. De Valera's next decision—and one that people have argued about ever since—was to send a delegation to London. The delegation included Arthur Griffith and Michael Collins—two men whom the British hard-liners and the Ulster unionists considered no more than terrorists. (When the makeup of the delegation was voted upon in the Dáil, it was de Valera's deciding vote that sent Collins and Griffith to London.)

What the delegation brought back, after weeks of intense bargaining—though Britain never had considered giving up much—was a divided Ireland that was still part of the British Commonwealth. The contentious "Oath of Allegiance" also remained. The treaty met with great opposition at home—de Valera called the treaty a "sell out of the Republic" and felt it came nowhere near what had been hoped for—and so it was put to a vote. On January 7, 1922, the treaty was narrowly ratified by the Dáil Eireann.

De Valera immediately resigned. And on January 10, he took his opposition party with him. Politically and symbolically they represented a powerful bunch: Countess Markievicz, Kathleen Clarke, the mother of Padraig and Willie Pearse, and the sister of Terrence MacSwiney—the mayor of Cork who had died in prison on a hunger strike.

As the new government, termed the Irish Free State, went about setting itself up, de Valera was in the countryside giving speeches to IRA members who joined him in his opposition to the treaty. On April 14, 1922, an anti-treaty force occupied the Four Courts building in Dublin. In the North, warfare was the order of the day. A showdown between de Valera and Collins was necessary, and the two met and decided upon a general election to be held on June 16. To de Valera's dismay the pro-treaty forces won seventy-three percent of the vote. From an electoral standpoint, the people seemed to be behind the treaty. On June 28, twelve days after the election, Michael Collins made the decision to fire upon the Four Courts where the anti-treaty forces were still ensconced. The Civil War had officially begun.

It is a truism in world history that no wars are as brutal as civil wars. It is accepted by many that the Irish Civil War was brutal and bitter as any. There were numerous casualties—both human and political. Arthur Griffith died of a brain hemorrhage. Michael Collins was assassinated in his home county of Cork. Relatives of Free State officials were murdered. Anti-treaty IRA men were executed; 13,000 anti-treaty forces were imprisoned. Enough was enough, and de Valera called a halt and ordered an end to resistance. Following the cessation of hostilities, de Valera was arrested and imprisoned. In 1924 he would be released. The Civil War did not break his spirit and there was much yet left for him to do.

When de Valera was released—despite the continued violent attacks that his IRA Irregulars carried out—he decided to use parliamentary measures to gain support for his beliefs. In 1926, he convinced enough of his Sinn Fein supporters to follow him into a new party—Fianna Fail ("the soldiers of destiny"). In an early election in 1927, Fianna Fail and de Valera gained a number of seats, but not a majority, in the Dáil. And now the old obstacle arose again.

One of the contentious articles of the 1921 Treaty was the "Oath of Allegiance" to which de Valera was adamantly opposed. Now in 1927, de Valera and his party had two options: refuse to take the oath and walk away from government or take the oath and present the first opposition party that the Free State had ever faced. They chose the latter, saying that the oath itself was meaningless. Once in power the problem of the oath could be addressed.

In the general election of 1932, Fianna Fail won forty-four seats out of forty-seven. It had taken over the government and de Valera was now Taoiseach, or prime minister. (History is always perverse in my eyes, as this would have been de Valera's position ten years earlier when he walked out after the treaty ratification. It would have meant a lot less bloodshed and a lot less bitterness.) The rise of Fianna Fail was a testimony to Ireland's belief in democracy—it brought about a two party system, albeit a system divided on the same lines as the Civil War.

Once in power, de Valera and the Fianna Fail abolished the oath of allegiance, stopped payment of land annuities to Britain, began developing modern industries, and took up genuine social reform. The withholding of the land annuities, however, caused a damaging economic war with Britain, which more or less amounted to a trade blockade. Punitive tariffs made Irish farming and textiles noncompetitive. (This economic war would last for many hard years, until the land annuities situation was settled by the government paying Britain a lump sum.)

Another result of de Valera's victory was the collapse of the pro-treaty party, the *Cumann na nGaedheal*. In its place there rose an organization, the Army Comrades Association, who were nicknamed the Blueshirts. Claiming to be protectors of the pro-Treaty forces that were now in the opposition, they set themselves up against the IRA whom de Valera had released from prison and had decriminalized. De Valera feared the military—and political—potential of the quasi-fascist Blueshirts and curtailed their activities greatly. He worried they would evolve into the same sort of threatening organizations that were supporting Mussolini in Italy and Hitler in Germany. But they just faded away.

In 1937, de Valera also set about creating a new constitution for the Republic of Ireland. It was through this constitution that Douglas Hyde was made the first president. Always a devout Catholic, de Valera also included a clause in the constitution that designated a "special position" for the Catholic Church. For someone who was as dedicated to the idea of a united Ireland, this type of language was hardly what would encourage rapprochement with the ever increasingly anti-Catholic North, and in many ways helped to solidify the divide between the North and the twenty-six counties of the Free State. (In this same way, it was not until de Valera lost power that present day Ireland became a nation independent of Britain, for de Valera would settle for nothing less than a united Ireland, including the six counties to the north. He was true to what he believed in—an independent Ireland that included the entire island—and he never backed down on his principles.)

To understand how far de Valera took the Irish nation, one only needs to look at the appointments given to de Valera in the 1930s. In 1932, de Valera was made head of the Council of the League of Nations and in 1938 he became president of the Assembly of the League. What is remarkable about this is that de Valera had gone in the 1920s to ask the American president, Woodrow Wilson, for political support for the emerging Dáil. Wilson not only refused but was rather appalled by the entire Irish independence movement. The League of Nations was Woodrow Wilson's child. Now the "rebel" whom he had snubbed was head of that very institution. And Ireland was a leading player on the world's stage.

As World War II approached, de Valera boldly—and controversially—kept Ireland neutral. And while some termed the position as "neutral on the English side," this status nevertheless worried England greatly. Britain remembered vividly Ireland's relationship with Germany previous to the Easter Rising of 1916, and, aware of the devastating potential of a German-Irish alliance, pressured de Valera often to formally ally Ireland with Britain. But de Valera stood firm and insisted on neutrality during the course of the war. (Neutrality would remain a formidable tool for Ireland throughout the century.)

De Valera's austere personality, his serious-mindedness, and his past—wrapped in the Republican flag and the heroism of the Easter Rising of 1916—created a particular cult of personality about him, and the Irish people—particularly those in the rural areas—responded readily. He was re-elected until 1948 when the Fianna Fail lost the majority in the Dáil. (It was at this time that the new majority party withdrew the Republic of Ireland from the British Commonwealth—something that de Valera had always avoided in hope of eventual unification of the thirty-two counties.)

De Valera returned as Taoiseach in 1951, and again in 1957. But by 1959, his worsening blindness was curtailing his effectiveness. When he was forced to retire as Taoiseach, rather than leave politics, he ran for president—the post he had created for Douglas Hyde through the 1937 constitution—and won two consecutive seven-year terms. He was ninety-one years old when the second term was finished. By then, he knew it was time to retire from Irish politics.

Eamon de Valera retired to a nursing home near Dublin and lived quietly until August 29, 1975. The quietness of his final years stood in contrast to the frantic activity of his life. From the moment he arrived in Limerick at the age of two, Ireland began to shape the young de Valera; by the time he was in his twenties de Valera helped shape Ireland. Few men in any country at any time have had such a long and lasting effect on their nation. A brave soldier and heroic commander, an intelligent thinker, a principled politician, de Valera was all of these. And throughout his life—indeed throughout three-quarters of the twentieth century—de Valera deployed these skills towards one purpose: to bring about an independent Ireland. There are few men, if any, who have done more in that regard.

IRELAND IN
THE MODERN WORLD

Ireland's journey towards nationhood was bloody, divisive, dramatic, and memorable. In 1948, what was known as the Irish Free State, a dominion within the British Commonwealth, became the Republic of Ireland. But nationhood is always an on-going process and the health of a country depends on a variety of forces: economic, political, social, and human. Ireland, like all democratic countries, weathered economic ups and downs, political change, and the frenetic rush of modernity. Unlike most countries, however, it also had the potential powder keg of the six counties to the North. A separate country, a separate history, it raised fierce passions, the partition of the 1920s never fitting comfortably in the South and seeming too tenuous in the North. It was a situation that loomed large over much of the century and one that shaped identity, divided allegiances, caused much bloodshed, and more hatred.

While Eamon de Valera, who came to power in 1932 and remained for forty years with few interruptions, dominated all of Irish politics, there were also a number of other able, passionate, and towering figures. Among them are Jack Lynch, Conor Cruise O'Brien, and F. H. Boland. These men, in their different ways, brought the fledgling nation into the modern world, directing the nation on the international stage, and maintaining its dignity and identity at home. Now, it is the very nature of political and public men to please some while infuriating others, and judgment on these three is still fresh and still divided. Indeed, some of them elicit passionate disagreement still. Nevertheless, they were there as Ireland stretched out from under Britain's thumb and proved itself in the modern world.

CHAPTER XXX:

Jack Lynch

I have never met Jack Lynch, though there were a few Irish politicians at the time with whom I did get chummy when the Irish delegation to the United Nations began spending their non-working hours at Malachy's, the eponymous New York City tavern where I once held court. Anyway, as I said, I hadn't met Lynch. But everyone who did always said what a "nice fellow" he was. (We Irish have a penchant for that "fellow" sobriquet. Collins was the "Big Fellow," de Valera was the "Long Fellow," and Lynch was the "Nice Fellow.") Even his political rival, Liam Cosgrave, called him the "most popular Irish politician since Daniel O'Connell." But if the blood carries much of our heredity and character—as the DNA scientists all claim it does—then the easy-going personality of Lynch rings true to me. For every single person I have known of that name—from a now deceased New York firefighter in the Bronx to a young woman who teaches the handicapped— every one was exactly the same: one of the nicest people you could meet.

John Mary Lynch was born on August 15, 1917, in Cork City. He was three years old when the Black and Tans set fire to the city center. His father, Dan Lynch, had come from West Cork and found work in a tailor shop where he met Nora O'Donaghue, the woman he would marry. And though the father was always employed, often it was on short time, and Nora supplemented the income by taking in seamstress work after the children were born. They were not poor, nor were they well-off. They did well enough however, considering the overall scarcity of material goods across the entire country at the time.

The Lynch family—five sons and two daughters—were a sporting family, and Jack's father played Gaelic football with a city team. The children were avid athletes as well. Jack, the youngest of the seven Lynch children, was always regarded as the wild boy of the family, but from the beginning he also showed great talent as an athlete—and his father encouraged and helped him. His particular passion was for hurling, his skills finely tuned by playing in the small family cellar with his brothers when the weather was wet, but he also played Gaelic football like his father as well as rugby and soccer.

As the youngest child, the baby of the family, Lynch was also quite close to his mother, and her sudden death in 1932 when Lynch was fifteen was a shattering segment in his life.

Lynch received his education at the North Monastery Christian Brother School, and sat for his Leaving Certificate in 1936. Those years, however, would not be marked necessarily by his educational attainments but by his growing prowess—and local fame—on the hurling pitch. When Lynch sat for the Leaving Certificate exams, he did well enough to qualify for teacher training or the Civil Service. Lynch chose the Civil Service.

Now, the trouble with writing about a famous sports figure—and before politics that is what Jack Lynch was—is that everyone has their favorite story. Whether it was first seeing Lynch as a schoolboy playing for North Monastery, or watching him in the Limerick and Cork match in 1940, which one sportswriter called the greatest match ever in the greatest game on earth, or watching him captain the various All-Ireland championship teams in the 1940s, everyone seems to have their favorite Jack Lynch story. Suffice it to say that Jack Lynch had become a legend, first in Cork and then across the country. In 1939, he was made captain of the Cork football team. He was also captain of the All-Ireland championship hurling team that same year. I don't know if it's been done since, but he was the first man ever to captain both the football and hurling teams in the same season. (One of my particular favorite Jack Lynch football stories is about a football match against Cork and Clonakilty where the teams only possessed two footballs, one of which was punctured. When the only usable ball was kicked into a stream, Jack Lynch dived into the water and swam to retrieve it. He returned to the pitch, dripping wet in the cold November afternoon, and led his team to its second consecutive championship.) The scope of Jack Lynch's athletic skill—and the talent of the teams he played for—can be measured by the success of the teams he played for and captained. In 1939, 1940, and 1942, he was the captain of the Cork Hurling team. He was an integral player on the team when Cork won the All-Ireland Finals in 1941, 1942, 1943, 1944, and 1946. In addition, he also played on the Cork football team that won the All-Ireland Football Final in 1945.

Yet, sports were sports and work was work, and beside creating a reputation on the pitch, Jack Lynch needed to begin a career. Having passed the Civil Service Exams in 1936, Jack began working Cork Circuit Court Staff as a clerk. It was this experience that pointed him towards the law, and in 1941, he began studying for the Bar, completing his studies at King's Inns in Dublin and qualifying as a barrister. He returned to Cork and began his own practice. That same year he married Marion O'Connor.

If any one person is responsible for Lynch's entry into politics, it would have to be de Valera. Lynch had always admired the man, ever since he was a boy and walked beside de Valera's carriage during the campaign of 1932 in Cork, the campaign that brought de Valera and Fianna Fail to power. But by the 1940s Fianna Fail was actively looking for young men to enter politics—the old order, those who had actual experience in the War of Independence and the Civil War was becoming ossified—and Lynch seemed the perfect candidate. He was approached by both Fianna Fail and Sean McBride's newly formed opposition party, Clann na Poblachta, to run in the 1946 election, but he refused, primarily because his friend Pa McGrath was also running and he didn't want to run against him. In 1948, Lynch was approached again by Fianna Fail. It was during this campaign that he

met de Valera for the first time; apparently the two men developed a mutual admiration, for Lynch remained with de Valera for the rest of the elder statesman's
career, and de Valera used the young sporting politician in a series of important
roles. (A tale of Lynch's entry into politics goes that on the day he was to file his
papers, his wife Marian was still arguing against the decision. She had not been
excited about his being drawn into public life. As they drew closer to the party
office, Marian finally suggested they toss a coin for it. Lynch won and he began a
career in politics. How fragile history sometimes seems that a different side of the
coin might have changed the course of Irish politics.)

Lynch's first election was successful for him personally but not for Fianna Fail,
which lost its majority. In the opposition now, Lynch spent his first few years as
speechwriter and research assistant for de Valera, who also made him secretary of
the party. Locally, Lynch kept very close with the people in his constituency. Back
in Cork he employed his good friend Séamus O'Brien as a conduit for his district's
problems. O'Brien was a shoemaker and was known and trusted by everyone;
Lynch used O'Brien's information wisely to learn what his constituents needed and
what were their concerns.

After two years, Fianna Fail once more gained the majority, and in 1951, de
Valera was once again made Taoiseach and offered his young assistant the new
post of Parliamentary Secretary to the Government. Yet the 1950s would see
Fianna Fail go in and out of power again for a period of three years, and while
in the opposition party, Lynch took on the job of developing and speaking for
the Gaeltacht areas of the country. A dutiful party man, Lynch served the
Taoiseach well—both de Valera and Sean Lemass who replaced him in 1959.
He was appointed to several minstries (Minsiter of Industry and Commerce in
1959 and Minister of Finance in 1965) and carried out his duties with vigor
and dedication. In 1966, however, Lynch would be catapulted far beyond the

scope of a simple government minister.

The Taosieach, Sean Lemass, retired in 1966. Lemass trusted none of the several candidates who were expected to take over. In fact, he wanted Lynch. And for the first time in the history of Fianna Fail there was jockeying to see who would succeed the Taoiseach. (The party had been around for forty years and had had only two leaders: de Valera and Lemass.) On November 10, 1966, Lynch, who had been somewhat reluctant to run for the position, soundly beat his opponent. He was now the fourth Taoiseach and the third leader of Fianna Fail. Lynch was a popular politician and his actions during several crises served to enhance him in the public eye.

During his first years as Taoiseach, the "troubles" in Northern Ireland were reignited. The partition of Northern Ireland had been a niggling fact of Irish independence since the beginning of the century, but in the late 1960s, emphasis moved from politics and nationhood to civil rights. As the Catholic minority sought for redress of the legitimized social and economic injustices they suffered in the Protestant North, they were inspired by the civil rights movement of African-Americans that was reaching its zenith in the United States. Unionists in the North feared that any call for Catholic rights was in reality a disguised movement for reunification with the South. Battle lines were clearly drawn. Throughout the summer of 1969, police and demonstrators clashed often and violently. On August 12, a traditional Protestant parade in Derry—aimed at reminding the Catholics just who was in charge and what the situation was in the Protestant North—devolved into a rock and bottle throwing melée as the parade wound through the Catholic ghetto of the Bogside. Police were called in, tear gas fired, and the Catholics manned their barricades for three days. This demonstration led to a similar situation in Belfast, where police fired machine guns into a crowd of unarmed citizens. At the end, six were dead, hundreds wounded, and many left homeless as their houses were burned to the ground.

In the Republic of Ireland, tensions were also high. It had been general government policy to keep out of the business of Northern Ireland, yet something had to be done—at the very least something had to be said. In a national televised speech, Jack Lynch spoke to the Irish people. The Government of Northern Ireland, he remarked, evidently could no longer control the situation and could no longer protect its own people. He then stated that his government would not sit and watch innocent people being killed and injured. For that reason, he was deploying the army to be ready at the border. These were alarming and powerful words. Nothing like this had been thought—or at least been said publicly and officially—since the 1920s. Jack Lynch was showing the fortitude that he had displayed on the hurling pitch. The British government stepped in. It sent troops to replace the partisian Royal Ulster Constabulary and to protect the Catholics in the area. (Lynch had stated in his speech that British troops were not the solution, and that Britain should seek a United Nations' force to protect the area. Britain, however, disregarded Lynch's request and sent in its soldiers. At first, the Catholics were quite pleased to see the British troops inviting them in for tea and offering a them warm reception—a sign of just how dire life under the RUC had become.) Lynch finished his speech by restating the constitutional claim that only reunification would bring an end to the crisis. He had grown to believe that reunification would only come from consent and not through force.

The situation in the North was deteriorating by the week. Each day seemed to bring worse news; each year a solution seemed even less plausible. To aggravate the tension in the North—and the northern Unionists' suspicions of the Republic—in 1970 two high-ranking ministers in Lynch's government were accused of importing arms for the Provisional IRA. (By that time, the IRA had split into two factions: the Official IRA and the Provisional IRA.) Lynch, showing his resolve and integrity, fired both of the men; another resigned in disgust. The party seemed in disarray, but Lynch was able to lead the party into a unified bloc before it fell apart completely. (The men were ultimately acquitted, and later Charles Haughey, one of the men, would serve as Taoiseach three separate times.)

The situation in Lynch's government paled in comparison with what was occurring in the North. Violence from both sides—from the Provos and from the Ulster Defense Association—had escalated to such a degree that Britain abolished Northern Ireland's Home Rule government. (This was the same institution that George V had announced on the day that Britian arrested de Valera in 1921.) Out and out civil war was imminent, and the chance of it spreading to the South was feared.

Whether it was possible for anyone to be in control of the situation was doubtful, but naturally it was easy to lay blame on the party then in power, Fianna Fail. But by demonstrating firmness and cool judgement, Lynch was able to keep the party in power until 1973, when it lost to a National Coalition Party composed of Labour and Fine Gael.

Four years later, in 1977, Jack Lynch and Fianna Fail returned once more— and the margin of their victory had never before been equaled. Lynch had argued that the Coalition Party had been using the "security issue" in the North to distract the people from the very real economic problems in the South that they could not resolve. So, he unveiled an economic manifesto addressing the South's market needs. (When Lynch and the Fianna Fail were in the opposition, Lynch had called on the British for a declaration to withdraw from the North. In the campaign, his opponents tried to paint this as dangerous radicalism.) Throughout the campaign in the summer of 1977, Lynch had proved an extraordinary strategist, and his work reaped better than expected rewards.

Yet, no government could have anticipated or survived the escalation of violence in the North and the deterioration of relations between the Republic and Britain. In August 1979, Lord Mountbatten was murdered in Sligo—and Lynch was criticized for being soft on Republicans. In September, de Valera's granddaughter, Síle de Valera, gave a speech attacking Lynch for abandoning the republican ideals of her grandfather. He had already considered retiring the previous year, when Fianna Fail was basking in a series of successes. The seeming split in his own party convinced him that it was time to retire. A man of unswerving loyalty, he felt betrayed by the party that had begun to question his effectiveness. In 1981, Jack Lynch retired from Irish politics.

Jack Lynch was a popular politician during a critical time in Ireland—a time of economic, social, and political change. That he remained popular was evidence of his easy-going style and his simple rapport with the common people. People considered him to be decent and honest in an age when these were not the most ready adjectives to describe a politician. Indeed, perhaps it was these very qualities—the natural decency, the loyalty, the integrity—that served him ill in the pit of governmental politics. When he died in June 1999, political partners and rivals from Britain, Northern Ireland, and the Republic, as well as your common man on the bus, in the pub or in the market, all seemed to comment and agree on the basic decency of the man called "Honest Jack," the "Nice Fellow."

CHAPTER XXXI:
CONOR CRUISE O'BRIEN

It is hard to think of anyone whose stature in Ireland is as controversial as Conor Cruise O'Brien's. What with being a writer, a professor, a journalist, and a politician, it seems he has vexed everyone at one time or another. He was labeled as being too far left in the 1940s, and too far right in the 1990s. He has annoyed radical nationalists and conservative unionists. As a young man, he worked with Sean MacBride and his anti-partition party, and today he is standing as a candidate for the "anti-agreement" Unionist party in Ulster. He was friends with de Valera, and now converses with Ian Paisley.

I only met him a few times, when he was part of the first Irish delegation to the United Nations, and I was a habitué of the watering holes throughout the city where the members unwound. They were a good bunch, the Irish delegates, full of stories and songs, and an evening with them was time well spent. For me then and there, the politics mattered little; these were men and women who were trying to leave the political world behind if only for a few hours before it would all rise up again in the massive offices of the United Nations.

But as I said earlier, Conor Cruise O'Brien's politics and opinions have certainly drawn enough heat. But that's perhaps why I like the man; it would be a dull world, indeed, if somebody didn't roil things up every so often. I don't necessarily have to agree with him—and it's not often I do—but I appreciate his mind. An intelligent man, he thinks—a rare thing in this day of ours—and explains things rationally. But as we all know, it isn't a rational world we live in, and O'Brien's insistence on applying reason to a nonsensical world is perhaps what irks people most about him.

It's now nearly fifty years since I was rubbing elbows with that Irish delegation from the United Nations, and much has happened in those times. But Conor Cruise O'Brien is still active, still writing and speaking, still inspiring admiration and loathing, still stirring things up. So more power to him. May we all be as rowdy when we reach that age.

Conor Cruise O'Brien was born in Dublin on December 3, 1917. He came from a nationalist family—his maternal grandfather was the Home Rule MP,

David Sheehy, his aunt was the famous nationalist Hanna Sheehy-Skeffington; and O'Brien claimed that his uncle was the priest who taught "patriotism" to Eamon de Valera. (Actually, this priest, who had befriended the orphaned de Valera when he was a boy in Limerick, also delivered Holy Communion to the men barricaded in the GPO during the Easter Rising.) His father, with whom O'Brien had a very close relationship, was a journalist and a friend of Yeats. He died early in O'Brien's life, but he left a particular legacy behind which O'Brien's mother followed. Frustrated with and alienated from the Catholic Church, the senior O'Brien insisted that his sons not be educated in the Catholic schools. Instead, Conor Cruise O'Brien attended the non-denominational Sandford Park school, which included Protestants, Jews, and Catholics. He then attended Trinity College, which the Catholic Church had banned on pain of mortal sin, unless one had a dispensation. (The ban was not lifted until the 1970s. It's an odd thing to consider the matters with which the Church used to involve itself not all that long ago.)

Following Trinity, O'Brien found many of the paths to academia closed to him. As a Catholic, his entrance into the Protestant world was hindered, and as a graduate of Trinity, he was suspect in the Catholic world. (In fact, O'Brien claimed that he was the first publicly avowed agnostic to hold office in ultra-Catholic Ireland.) O'Brien began a career in the civil service working for a while under Sean MacBride, the nationalist son of Maud Gonne and John MacBride. In 1944, he joined the Irish Department of External Affairs, where he remained for nearly two decades; he was also beginning to earn a name for himself as a writer and a historian.

In 1952, under the pen name Donat O'Donnell, he wrote a collection of essays on Catholic writers entitled *Maria Cross*. Two years later, he published his study of Parnell, *Parnell and his Party*. Both books were very well received and seen as the introduction of a brilliant new light in scholarship—although O'Brien's work was never burdened by scholarly arcane, but was accessible to the general public.

In 1955, O'Brien was made part of the Irish delegation to the United Nations. Among the group was the poet Maire Mac Entee—she liked to call herself the token female on the delegation—whom O'Brien married in 1962. By then, O'Brien had garnered the attention of the Secretary General, Dag Hammarskjöld—who had read and admired O'Brien's *Maria Cross*. Hammarskjöld sent O'Brien to Africa to lead the U.N. peacekeeping mission in war-torn and violent Katanga. The book *To Katanga and Back* was the result of O'Brien's mission, and it showed him to be fiercely anticolonial (and thus bitterly denounced by the conservative British press).

Following the adventures in Katanga, O'Brien spent the next several years at university. He was made vice-chancellor of the University of Ghana, and served in that position from 1962 to 1965. In the late 1960s, he was a professor of humanities at New York University. In the United States, he was very much a part of the left, protesting the war in Vietnam and embracing socialism. But by the end of the decade, he had left America in order to stand for a seat in the Dáil in Ireland. (In typical O'Brien fashion, he stood on the Labour ticket after years spent bashing the Irish Labour Party.)

Today, O'Brien brushes aside his eight years in Irish politics, stating that politicians, by the nature of their occupation, cannot be intellectually honest, for often a politician's response depends on the moment rather than on the truth. Seemingly always contradictory—but following his intellect rather than political sense—O'Brien published, in 1972, *States of Ireland*, in which he tried to debunk the allure and value of patriotism. This was at the height of the "Troubles" in Northern Ireland, when a rekindled nationalism and republicanism were much in evidence. (Throughout the previous three years, he had been a regular contributor to the intellectual journal *The New York Review of Books,* in which he had been preparing and refining his argument for *States of Ireland* as the violence in Northern Ireland flared.) As part of the Coalition Government, O'Brien made many enemies, particularly when attitudes toward Northern Ireland were concerned. He criticized Charles Haughey—who had been implicated and acquitted during the Arms Crisis—as being dangerous and still having the stain of gun-running on him; he equated the policies of Fianna Fail with those of the Provisional IRA; and he made a life-long enemy of John Hume, the founder of the civil rights movement in Ulster (and future co-winner of the Nobel Peace Prize).

After the National Coalition Party suffered a devastating defeat by Fianna Fail in 1977, O'Brien left politics—at sixty years of age, one might imagine for good. Yet, he was far from retiring. In 1979, he became editor-in-chief of the London newspaper, *The Observer.* Here too, his management style ruffled not a few feathers, and his tenure was marked by controversy. (On the other hand, his writing style was always praised and admired.) After two years, he resigned and moved back to Ireland where his days were spent writing—his book on Edmund Burke, *The Great Melody,* is considered a masterpiece—and lecturing throughout Britain and the United States. (The former self-proclaimed socialist had now become a favorite of neoconservatives in the United States.) For most men, this would have been an ideal life: he was a relatively famous figure, recognized for his writing and noted for his lectures, who could control the pace of his life. However, he chose to throw himself once more into the fray—and this time into the very dangerous arena of Ulster politics.

Despite his republican background, O'Brien had always denounced republican violence. He says this came from his ecumenical schooling as a young boy in Dublin. He derides the Good Friday Agreement and most of the players involved. But it is of little worth just to talk, so O'Brien decided to act. In the summer of 2003, Conor Cruise O'Brien—at the age of 85—chose to run as a candidate in Robert McCartney's Ulster UK Unionist party. It is an extraordinary life arc—but one that O'Brien would say has been dictated by his intellect rather than by his emotions.

There are many in Ireland today who simply cannot understand the "Cruiser." Some who had read him in their youth and followed him into social radicalism feel confused by his Unionist stance. Others less kindly say he has been a West Briton all along. And, of course, there are those who agree with him. But despite what everyone might say, he continues to assert his beliefs and act upon them. He is a proud Irishman—reflecting the love of language and the love of learning that defines the race—who has tried to intellectualize the currents of the twentieth century throughout his life, and who now, in the twenty-first century, continues to do so.

CHAPTER XXXII:

F. H. BOLAND

I wanted to do a small chapter on F. H. Boland, not because of his great importance to Irish history, or for any dramatic service he had done, or to commemorate some great act of heroism he has performed, but simply because he was a decent civil servant who made all of Ireland proud when he became president of the Assembly of the United Nations. And even that proud moment might be forgotten by many, relegating him to the footnotes of history. But I always loved him for one story; he was the man holding the gavel when that Russian fellow named Nikita Khrushchev took off his left shoe and started pounding it on the desk in front of him. And for his demeanor in those extraordinary minutes, I will never forget him. To me, it is one of the sublime moments of man at his most civilized, democratic, and appealing. Despite the Cold War, the bomb, and everything else that followed, that silly moment at the United Nations almost makes me want to forgive humanity for all its stupidity.

Frederick H. Boland was born in Dublin on January 31, 1904, and attended the Clongowes Wood School where James Joyce had gone a decade earlier. However, where Joyce had toyed with the idea of a priestly vocation at Clongowes Wood and then went on to shape the course of modern literature, Boland decided on a career in civil service, and he served his government well. He received his degree from Trinity College, Dublin, and studied law at King's Inn, where he passed the Bar. Graduate work took him to the United States, in the years following the Irish Civil War, where he studied at Harvard University and the Universities of Chicago and North Carolina, having received the Rockefeller Award for Social Science. When he returned to Ireland, he took up work in the government's foreign service, working in the Department of External Affairs. In just a few years, he was named head of the Department's League of Nations section. In 1945, he was made Ambassador to Britain, and in 1956, he was made the first permanent Irish representative to the UN. In 1960, F. H. Boland was elected President of the Fifteenth Assembly of the United Nations, a post he retained for the next three years, weathering Cold War politics, European economic upheaval, and a variety of Cuban crises. After his tenure as President of the Assembly of the United Nations, Boland retired from foreign service, but was shortly after elected as Chancellor of University College, Dublin, in 1965.

Now all of this would seem rather ordinary, the résumé of a polished career government minister who was never embroiled in scandal, who did his job and never made his personality the focus of his career. He was a sophisticated and learned man, as comfortable among diplomats as he was around academics and the man in the pub. He married the artist Frances Kelly, and had four daughters and a son. One daughter is the renowned Irish poet Eavan Boland.

However, as impressive as Boland's c.v. might be—and have no doubt it is an impressive one—perhaps his most electrifying moment came on October 12, 1960, as he presided over the assembly in the United Nations. On that day, the assembly was listening to the Russian delegation decry colonialism—in fact, the Russians wanted to pass a resolution against colonialism the world over. The Philippine representative rose to say that Russia was being duplicitous, as its satellites in Eastern Europe represented little more than the colonialism that the Russians derided. During the Filippino's speech, the Soviet Premier, Nikita Khrushchev, took off his left shoe and began banging it repeatedly on the table in an attempt to interrupt the Philippine speaker. Khrushchev continued banging, and was soon joined by Freddy Boland pounding his gavel in an attempt to achieve order. For several minutes, the austere chambers of the United Nations was the scene of a surreal percussive concert with shoe leather and a wooden gavel beating out a tattoo that fought each other for dominance. Finally, Boland's gavel shattered—reflecting the state of irritation he was in—and the moment froze into an ominous and puzzled silence. It was the British representative who broke the ice by asking how Khrushchev's pounding would be translated.

The Khrushchev/Boland incident was not a big moment in Irish history, nor a particularly important one in world history, but for anyone who was of age during those fearful, paranoid days of the Cold War, it is a moment etched forever in one's mind. Everyone knows who the Russian leader pounding his shoe was—in fact, for many, that image of Khrushchev is the most memorable, and caused him to be frequently portrayed as a blustering buffoon—but there are few who knew who was the official in charge of trying to quiet him down. And that is why I wanted to write a short piece on Freddy Boland. For in those heady days when

Russia and the United States. had their missiles pointed at each other (and at a few other places as well), it took a good old Dubliner to rattle on, beat for beat, against the wild ranting of the Soviet leader. The Republic of Ireland had come a long way since it wrested independence from Britain forty years earlier; it was now trying to impose order on one of the world's two superpowers.

F. H. Boland died on December 4, 1985.

PEOPLE OF PASSION

CHAPTER XXXiii:
BERNADETTE DEVLIN

If you drive into the Bogside area of Derry, you will see a beautiful painted mural on the side of a wall. The mural in muted blues and grays is a portrait of Bernadette Devlin, a young girl of twenty-one manning the barricades in August 1969. I can still see in my mind's eye the earliest pictures of Bernadette Devlin transmitted on the news programs around the world. And at that time what is so remarkable of those grainy photos is that she is so young, yet so forceful, so full of the hope of youth, so firm in her belief. Like so many others in Northern Ireland at the time, she had been drawn to the civil rights movement, but the overreaction of the RUC (Royal Ulster Constabulary) and later the British army turned her into a fierce republican. The cliché "a mere slip of a girl" is overused, but it seems to have been coined for Devlin herself. But her diminutive size belied the strength of her heart—and her heart was with the people of Derry. In 1969, she was elected MP to the British Parliament, and when she took her seat she was the youngest woman ever to have been elected. (In her maiden speech she made reference to the first woman ever elected to the British Parliament: the great Irish nationalist Constance Markievicz.) Part of her tenure as MP she spent in jail, tried and convicted of inciting a riot; in Parliament itself, she slapped the Home Secretary for his distorted interpretation of "Bloody Sunday" calling him a murdering hypocrite; and ten years later she and her husband were attacked in their own home by loyalist paramilitary. She was shot nine times but recovered. The most recent injustice came from the United States. Having visited the United States over thirty times—giving talks and lectures, raising funds, appearing on talk shows—she was denied entry in 2003 because she was considered a national security risk. As she herself said, she was a fifty-five year old grandmother with a bad leg, but the officials would hear none of it. Despite her visa having been previously approved, they sent her on an immediate flight back to Dublin.

Even as a child Bernadette Devlin demonstrated a remarkable feistiness. Born in 1949 into a poor, working-class family in County Tyrone, as a young girl she won a talent show not by step dancing or playing a fiddle but by reciting portions of speeches by the Irish patriots, Robert Emmet and Padraig Pearse. Her father, a carpenter, had lost his job when he was accused of Republican sympathies and died soon after, when Devlin was nine years old. While the family was never overtly Republican, such injustices to her family over time greatly helped to shape the young girl's political mind.

Devlin attended Queen's University where she found socialism as a better alternative to the republicanism of the past. She was not interested in the ancient grudges—she wanted a new world of equal opportunity for Catholics and Protestants alike based on equitable economics. This philosophy and focus on equal opportunity directed her towards civil rights activism—like many young people in Northern Ireland at the time—and the flash point for that activism came on August 24, 1968, on a small march from Coalisland to Dungannon. The march was remarkable for its pleasantness: 2,500 people out on a Sunday stroll. However, when the group reached Dungannon they were met by RUC forces and 1,500 Unionists who jeered at the marchers from behind barricades. A confrontation was avoided and the marchers changed their route. Tellingly, they sang the song "We Shall Overcome," the anthem of the African-American movement in the United States. Given the hindsight of historical perspective—this march could be considered the beginning of the Northern Irish civil rights movement or the seminal moment of the "Troubles" that would continue for the next thirty years.

Another civil rights march was planned for Derry in October—and the government banned it. Five thousand marchers showed up anyway, but before they had marched more than five minutes towards the center of Derry, the RUC appeared, beating the crowd back with nightsticks and water canon. It was an enlightening moment for Devlin, for she saw firsthand the partisanship of the constabulary force whose actual job was to protect all citizens of Ulster.

The following year brought even more civil rights demonstrations and more repercussions—the Northern Irish civil rights movement was pressing for an end to economic, social, and housing discrimination against Catholics, the same demands of black Americans. (When Devlin came to America to explain the Northern Ireland civil rights movement, her comparison of Northern Irish Catholics to American blacks alienated many of her listeners. By this time many Irish-Americans had succeeded far beyond their emigrant ancestors' wildest dreams, and in their material comfort and success, had grown conservative and closed-minded.) Devlin and other university students formed the People's Democracy, an organization of Catholics and Protestants that called for social reform.

As Unionist leaders painted the demonstrators as Republicans, violence from Protestant on-lookers escalated during the marches. As the violence continued, the Prime Minister of Northern Ireland made a speech stating that the voices for reform had been heard and that reform was imminent. This outraged hard-line Unionists who viewed reunification with the South as the inevitable follow-up to any social reform. With a loss of confidence inside his party, the Prime Minister called for a general election. Of the many upheavals that occurred during this election, perhaps the most extraordinary was the election of Bernadette Devlin, as MP from Derry.

The violence that had reigned throughout the year culminated in the summer of 1969. On August 12, an Orange Parade wound through the streets of Derry—a parade whose purpose was to reiterate to the Catholic poor the supremacy of Protestant Unionism in Ulster. When the parade reached the Catholic ghetto of Bogside, the march deteriorated into a battle. Rocks, bottles, parts of pavement were thrown; the police fired tear-gas; barricades were set up. For three days, the violence continued. And for three days, Bernadette Devlin, MP, stayed her ground, helping those who were attacked, defending their impoverished neighborhood.

For her part in the "Battle of Bogside," Bernadette Devlin was arrested. She was not the first nor would she be the last Irish MP to serve a prison sentence while sitting in Parliament. The violence continued, and Devlin was elected to a second term. But the civil rights movement would suffer its most horrible blow in the beginning of 1972 when the Derry Civil Rights Association would organize a march protesting the policy of internment that had been instituted six months before.

BLOODY SUNDAY

People have written volumes on what happened in Derry on January 30, 1972, and investigations are still going on. Approximately 15,000 people ignored a government ban and marched through the streets. This ignoring of bans was not unusual; for three years, the government had been prohibiting the right to march, and the marchers had continued to ignore it. On this day, however, the authorities had deployed the 1st Parachute Division as back-up for the soldiers who normally re-routed and guarded such demonstrations. When the fighting broke out, Bernadette Devlin was giving a speech. However, "fighting" is the wrong word here altogether. For without warning, the paratroopers moved in and began firing on the unarmed crowd. (Coroners reported that most were shot in the back as they ran away from the assault.) Devlin dived under the platform she was speaking from. Within less than an hour, thirteen people were dead; many more wounded. It had not been a fight; it had been a massacre.

When she returned to Parliament she had the right to speak on what was becoming known as "Bloody Sunday" on the fact that she had been present, but the Home Secretary—who had shamelessly transferred the blame to the marchers in an earlier speech—refused to acknowledge her. As she continued trying to say what she knew, he censured her. Finally, the petite twenty-four-year-old woman raced across the floor to attack the Home Secretary, slapping him. She had been there on that Sunday morning, and she knew the truth. She was not going to let this man silence her, or revise the facts.

BERNADETTE MCALISKEY

Bernadette Devlin was beloved by her constituents. She stated that she had been elected by "oppressed people" and that she would work for them and their concerns. But her oppressed people were also a religiously conservative people and Devlin's anti-Catholicism put off a good number of them. (She called the Catholic Church the greatest betrayer of the Irish people.) In addition to her anti-Catholicism, she further alienated them and their strict sense of morality when she announced that she was to be an unwed mother. This was all too much for the people of Derry, and in 1974, the voters turned against her and she lost her seat. (Her bid for re-election was also hurt by the SDLP party running a candidate against her which split the Catholic vote.) But by then, she had taken her husband's name and become Bernadette Devlin McAliskey.

Although not holding an elected office, Devlin continued to agitate for reform and for an end to the ever-increasing military subordination of Ulster. Life in Northern Ireland was a chaotic mess of armored cars, nighttime raids, relatives interned, and buildings blown up. This was all very far from the dreams of a fair and just workers' republic that she and the People's Democracy had conceived when she was still a young university girl. (It should be mentioned, however, that one of the People's Democracy's demands of "one-person, one vote" had been made law a few days after Devlin's first election victory.) Before long, the violence would strike very close to home.

On January 16, 1981, Bernadette Devlin McAliskey and her husband were sitting in their farmhouse in County Tyrone. A gang of paramilitaries burst through the door with a sledgehammer and sprayed the room with machine gun fire, hitting Devlin nine times as she went up to get her children. Her husband was shot twice at point blank range. At that time, Devlin had been involved in the situation of the interned prisoners in the H-Blocks at Long Kesh Prison. As Irish internees had done in the beginning of the century, those interned now were demanding political-prisoner status and prison reform and were using the hunger strike as leverage. It was an emotional campaign, and Devlin McAliskey was in the thick of it.

After the attack, Devlin McAliskey recovered and soon returned to activism. Much of that time was spent in fighting her daughter Roisin's extradition to Germany, where she had been implicated in a bombing. The case received international attention as Roisin's pregnancy and childbirth made her sixteen-month imprisonment a *cause célèbre* for human rights groups.

Today, Bernadette Devlin McAliskey continues to speak her mind. She has taken a stance against the "Good Friday Agreement" and the inclusion of Sinn Fein into Northern Ireland's government. She has also criticized the United States war with Iraq, which is what probably put her on the government's radar and caused her to be deported in 2003.

An enemy once called her a "mini-skirted Castro." An admirer called her "the Irish Joan of Arc." And like Joan of Arc she entered the battle as a young woman full of idealism and hopes. But as those successes seemed to ebb further and further away, she never gave up hope. And she certainly never gave up the activism. A tireless worker for the disenfranchised of all creeds, an activist who wanted opportunities and justice for all those for whom it had been long denied, Bernadette Devlin ranks with some of the greatest figures of our time. As a young university student, she turned to Dr. Martin Luther King Jr. for inspiration. In future years some young person, perhaps, will turn to her in the same way.

Chapter XXXiV:
Bobby Sands

There was an Irish folk-singing group called Irish Mist I remember seeing and listening to a lot back in the late 1980s. They were not particularly talented, a couple of guitars, a banjo and young girl on fiddle, but they played with passion and they played with joy. And I remember one night their doing the song "Back Home in Derry." It's a sad song about a prisoner ship in 1803 sailing to Australia—and to give them credit the good old Irish Mist played it well. But I became somewhat melancholy on hearing that song that night. Here it was a haunting song about a man missing his Irish home nearly 200 years ago, yet it was written by Bobby Sands, a sensitive fellow who gave up his home in Ireland by intentionally giving up his life in a horrible and tragic martyrdom. It has always struck me as particularly poignant, Sands writing that song, and I find myself wondering time and again about what motivated him, what pushed him back nearly to the eighteenth century, when the world around him was burning down. (And I think to myself, once again, here we have an Irish poet—in the tradition of Pearse and MacDonagh—manning the barricades of Irish freedom.)

Bobby Sands was born on March 9, 1954, in a neighborhood of Belfast that was primarily Protestant and proudly Loyalist. It was not easy for the Sands family, a Catholic family living in a hostile area in an increasingly volatile city, and when Sands was nine the family was forced to move.

The sectarian realities of ghetto life were recognized early in Bobby's life because of loyalist intimidation. Sands remembered sleeping as a pre-adolescent with a knife in his hand whenever the UDA marched threateningly close to his home. And one time, a trash can was thrown through the family's front window as they were gathered in the living room.

The situation in the North over the past forty years had created Catholic ghettos in Belfast and Derry and other smaller cities in which Nationalism and poverty were the only unifying forces and which served to further polarize the two factions: Catholic and Protestant. (It should be clear that the "Troubles" were never really fueled by "religious" beliefs. It just so happened that the disenfranchised, the poor, the unemployed, the discriminated were for the most part Catholic. The "Troubles" were originally a fight for social equality—the religious labels were merely convenient. As Bernadette Devlin argued, the situation of Catholics in Northern Ireland in the 1960s were the same as the blacks in the United States at the same time.)

Sands quit school when he was fifteen without much hope, but was fortunate to get an apprenticeship as a coachbuilder in 1970. Shortly after, he joined the National Union of Vehicle Builders and the Amalgamated Transport and General Workers Union. (The ATGWU itself has had an interesting history, as most workers in Northern Ireland continued to belong to British-based unions. A separate branch was established in the Republic of Ireland, the ITGWU. Even today there is still much politicizing of Union leadership and direction.) Sands was now a union worker and regularly employed, which was not always the case for many young Belfast teens. But after the civil rights marches began in 1968 and produced a more visible anti-sectarianism among Unionists, Sands found his position as a Catholic in this basically Protestant union to be insecure. Going to work in the morning, Sands would find workers cleaning guns and threatening to use them if he didn't get out. He would find notes in his locker and in his lunch pail with the same message—"Get out. Your kind are not wanted."

His family, which had already moved once because of harassment, was again feeling the tension. There were physical attacks on the streets; the mates he had had growing up in the mixed neighborhood followed their inherited prejudices and turned on each other. In June of 1972, the Sands family was forced to move out of their home in Rathcoole to the Catholic ghetto of Twinbrook. There were parts of Belfast where it was simply not safe for them—or any other Catholic—to live.

That an eighteen-year-old boy, who daily saw his brother and sisters harassed, his family intimidated, his work plans crushed, his home made unsafe, would ultimately join the IRA should come as no surprise. For many young men and women, Republicanism offered a glimmer of hope. It was in 1972, the year his family had been driven from Doonbeg Drive and several of his cousins had been interned, that Bobby Sands joined.

Having joined the IRA in the summer of '72, Sands was not at large for long, for in October of that year he was arrested for living in a house where four handguns had been found. He had been going out "on operations" for several months, and in that time realized the support for the IRA was growing among the oppressed. They were among the many who had lost hope and were tired of the degradation. He spent three years in Long Kesh prison—and like the internment camps and prisons that the participants of the 1916 Rising had experienced— Long Kesh functioned as a "Republican University." Sands taught himself Irish and he began to write seriously.

If the internment of political prisoners was supposed to "reform" the young men and women, it rarely worked, and more often than not they returned to civilian life more committed than before. And during those three years that Sands spent in Long Kesh, the situation in Ireland had spiraled downwards into bitter hatreds and destruction. Many men who were released became even more determined in their opposition when the saw the destruction of their homes when they returned. There was no work; there was only poverty and hopelessness. IRA membership grew exponentially. As soon as Sands was released, he reported immediately to his local unit and threw himself into activism, working with a grassroots organization known as the Tenants Association. It was a civil rights organization that was necessary to demand even the most basic of municipal services for the people in his district.

Life in Belfast during the 1970s and 1980s was tense, made so by bombings and assassinations. And quite often, anyone in the area around an incident was brought in—particularly if he or she had already been on the RUC or British Army's list. And this was many. Because for most of the young men, having gone through the prison system once, and, upon release, finding there was no work for them because of their record, there was little to do but stay in the fight.

In October 1976, there was a bombing at the Balmoral Furniture Company in Dunmurry, west of Belfast. Following the blast, there was also a gunfight, in which two men were wounded. Later that evening the RUC pulled four men over in a car in which they found a revolver. One of the men was Bobby Sands.

Taken to a prison in Castlereagh, Sands was brutally interrogated for six days.

He was then put on remand for eleven months until his trial. At the trial, the judge found no evidence that connected Sands or his companions to the bombing. He and the other three men were given fourteen years each for the possession of one revolver. (Justice, you will remember, was what they were fighting for.)

Despite their claims, the Northern Irish prison and internment system was cruel, demeaning, and brutal. For the first three weeks of his imprisonment Sands was kept in solitary confinement. Two-thirds of that time he was naked. It had always been a crucial point for Republican prisoners to be given political prisoner status and not be criminalized, and in the North at the time the prisoners ardently were agitating for both political prisoner status and reform of their conditions. The tactic being used when Bobby Sands was finally transferred from the Crumlin Road jail to the H-Block at Long Kesh was being "on the blanket"—where the prisoners, refusing to wear prison clothes, wore nothing but wrapped themselves in their blankets. Sands joined the protest upon his arrival. (It is noteworthy to understand that this was a general prison protest. Of the 1,300 prisoners "on the blanket," almost half of them were Loyalist prisoners who had had their political status removed as well.)

The physical and mental condition of the prisoners was being published in the *Republican News* and later in (the merged) *An Phobhacht/Republican News*. The reporting was being written from someone on the inside, whose articles were being smuggled out and who was writing under the pen name Marcella. The writer was Bobby Sands, using his sister's name. Bobby began teaching the other IRA prisoners Irish—which he had learned on his first prison stretch.

Another person who also alerted the world to the abject conditions of Long Kesh was the Archbishop of Armagh—Tómas Cardinal O'Fiaich. A Catholic Cardinal and the highest ranking church official in Ireland, O'Fiaich frequently made visits to both Loyalist and Catholic prisoners in Long Kesh. When he reported to the world that most humans would not let an animal live in the conditions these prisoners were in, his statements did not initiate reform. Instead he was vilified by the government and labeled a spokesman for the IRA. But he had visited many Loyalist prisoners as well and had befriended their leader, Gusty Spence, and it was for them he was speaking also. Later, when the situation in Long Kesh had worsened, he even met with Margaret Thatcher at 10 Downing Street, but the conference did not go well, was quite testy, and she accused the cardinal of supporting terrorism.

Sands was elected leader of the men on the blanket and his "negotiations" with prison authorities resulted in various spells of solitary confinement and beatings. In 1978, the blanket protest changed to the "dirty protest" where prisoners refused to wash, or use the toilets. For too long they had been abused while using showers or toilets so now they refused to use them at all. Women prisoners in a jail in Armagh who had been similarly treated joined the protest. Yet even this did not change the situation.

The prisoners were asking for five basic things: permission to wear their own clothes—they were not criminals but political prisoners; the right to have visitors; the right to receive packages; the right of free association; and the right to have books, paper, and pens. Many would suffer greatly—and some would even die— just to receive these simple basics from their captors.

The dirty protests were ineffective, and talks on the outside were breaking down, so it was decided to begin that most traditional of Irish prisoner protests: the hunger strike. Sands was the first to volunteer, but he was refused, for he was made the operations commander when the current commander, Brian Hughes, began fasting. His leadership position put him in direct negotiations with the prison authorities who gave Sands political prisoner status and allowed him to travel the three miles where the hunger strikers were in hospital. Sands negotiated with the authorities and was even allowed to meet with other leaders in other H-Blocks to formulate a strategy that would best serve both the hunger strikers and the protest. At the end—after the seven strikers had decided to end their strike—Sands realized that the authorities had been negotiating in bad faith and had never intended giving in to the strikers. At that point, Sands announced that no IRA prisoner would wear prison clothes or do prison work.

The standoff had developed into a battle of British will against Irish will and Irish bodies. Another hunger strike was called and this time Bobby Sands was part of it. In fact, he insisted on starting two weeks before the others in the hope that his death might break the deadlock, that the "five demands" would be granted, and the rest of his fasting companions could be saved.

The tactic of hunger strike works best if the outside world is aware of it. And certainly the protests of the H-Block prisoners were known. But it was a small story in most of the world except Ireland. That is until an extraordinary event occurred.

In March 1981, Frank Maguire, the Independent MP from Fermanagh-South Tyrone, unexpectedly and suddenly died. A by-election was called for, and on March 30—the thirtieth day of his fast—Bobby Sands was nominated as the candidate to replace Maguire. By this time, he was in very bad condition; he had lost nearly twenty pounds and a week earlier had been transferred to the prison hospital.

Now, a twenty-seven-year-old IRA member on a hunger strike might not necessarily make headlines in the international press, but a candidate for the British Parliament who has not eaten in over a month to protest his treatment by those very same British authorities is certain to garner attention. And Bobby Sands's situation did. Protests and demonstrations rose up immediately around the world. Bobby Sands was making five simple demands, and was willing to die for them.

Yet Britain would not budge.

When Bobby Sands won by fewer than 1,500 votes over UUP candidate H.W. West, he was in no condition to celebrate. He was in the sixtieth day of his hunger strike. His organs were failing, his vision going, yet his resolve was strong. Bobby Sands was now Robert Sands, MP. He died five days later. By that time government officials from around the world and even the pope had tried to get Margaret Thatcher to compromise and dissuade Bobby Sands from his goal. There would be nine others who would die, and still Britain would not give in. (High ranking U.S. officials, such as Senator Daniel Moynihan, Senator Edward Kennedy, and Speaker of the House of Representaives Thomas "Tip" O'Neill, all tried and failed to influence Thatcher. It says much about the long-rooted animosity involved that when a delegation of MPs from the Republic of Ireland led by Sinead de Valera tried to meet with Thatcher to try to formulate a compromise, Thatcher remarked that she was not in the habit of meeting with MPs from foreign countries.)

Bobby Sands's funeral was attended by upwards of 100,000 people and was covered by the world media. He had become a martyr; he had brought the world's attention to the plight of the H-Block prisoners; and he had proven himself steadfast and firm in the cause of his people. He also had created a public relations nightmare for Britain. (Pride in his martyrdom crossed many boundaries and inspired various causes. There is even a Bobby Sands Boulevard in Teheran, Iran.)

Ten hunger strikers in all died that year, before the families of the remaining strikers were convinced to order life-support procedures for their loved ones. It was only after the hunger strike was over that Britain gave in to each of the requests. (It also quickly worked to set up a system that would prevent hunger strikers from being nominated to Parliament.) Britain could have acquiesced to the prisoners' demands long before the first one died—a member of its own parliament, Bobby Sands. But in its need not to lose face by seeming to give in to IRA demands, it allowed the men to die. Only after the strike was over, only after the funerals were a memory, only after press coverage had died down, did it grant each and every request.

Bobby Sands was a hopeful, young boy when he first went to work as an apprentice coachbuilder. Like any boy his age, he was pleased with the wages and the freedom that a little money in his pocket gave him. But the relentless intimidation, and incessant battering turned him towards the IRA, and there he found hope. At the end, Bobby Sands's hope was never for himself—he knew that he would never live to see a better world—but for the people he was leaving behind. He truly believed that in his death, he was advancing the lot of his people, bettering the chances that their lives would know freedom and equality.

PEOPLE OF PEACE

For thirty years all that most people knew about Northern Ireland was that it was a place of violence and hatred. To them it was a place of urban blight, slashed with desperate graffiti, scattered with the shells of burned out cars, strewn with the rubble of bombed out buildings, and peopled with hard bitter men and hopeless children who were learning to hate. To the rest of the world—often believing it was simply a religious war between Catholics and Protestants—the situation seemed hopeless and senseless. Yet that picture is not altogether complete. First of all, Northern Ireland is a land of exquisite beauty. (Though, at the time, crossing the border and facing a British soldier's machine gun pointing at you while another validates your papers tended to dilute your desire for beautiful vistas.) Only a very small part of it is urban. The rest is a land of clear lakes and rich valleys, picturesque villages and magnificent natural formations. As is usually the case, the media only gets part of the picture.

But as we watched on our televisions scenes of armored cars and tanks, of barricaded streets and soldiers on patrol, of shouts and taunts, of sirens and alarms (women would bang trash can lids to warn of approaching British patrols), there was a genuine peace movement underfoot. This movement, while well aware of the need for civil and social reform, understood that at this point nothing could or would be done until the violence ended. For Northern Ireland, violence had indeed turned into a hellish cycle with the various groups on both sides attacking in reprisal for a previous attack or policy implementation and then a reprisal for that and again another reprisal. It was no place to live; it was no place to be born into.

Like many important movements, the Community of Peace People began through tragedy. In August 1976, Betty Williams witnessed the death of three children, crushed by an out-of-control car driven by an IRA operative. Williams—like many in Belfast—began marching for peace, and it was there that she joined with Mairead Corrigan, who was the aunt of the three children. Together, they formed the Peace People organization. These two women kept the organization's momentum going literally in the very face of hatred and violence and later when apathy itself seemed to seep in. These were two women from opposite sides of the conflict who saw the hopelessness within the circle of violence, who understood that continued hostilities would not bring about a resolution but would in fact further exacerbate the sectarianism, and who knew that there were plenty of others who felt exactly like them. Indeed it is a testament to the power of these two women, ordinary women in a less than ordinary world, that their efforts could resonate so clearly throughout their ravaged communities. In recognition for their work, the international community recognized them by awarding them both the Nobel Peace Prize in 1976.

Chapter XXXV:
Mairead Corrigan and Betty Williams

In August 1976, there was a clash between IRA members and the British army. This in itself was nothing new; it seemed rather commonplace in those tense days. Danny Lennon, an IRA operative, was driving a car that was being pursued by British soldiers in Land Rovers. When a soldier shot Lennon dead on the Finaghy Road North, the car veered out of control and slammed into the family of Anne Maguire who was out walking her children on that summer afternoon. In her pram was her six-week-old son Andrew, riding a bike next to her mother was her eight-and-a-half-year-old daughter, Joanne, and walking beside her was her two-year-old son, John. Another son, seven-year-old Mark, walked several yards ahead of the family and because of this he was spared. When the car slammed into them, the little girl and the baby were killed instantly; the two-year old boy was pronounced dead in hospital the following day. And Anne Maguire was comatose. When she came out of her coma, the poor woman had to be told what had happened to her family. (Tragedy has a heart-wrenching tendency to stretch itself out at times. Three years later, haunted by the horrors that were visited on her family, Anne Maguire took her own life.)

Mairead Corrigan was Anne Maguire's sister. She was a thirty-two-year-old woman who was doing her best just trying to survive the horror that was Belfast at that time. And on that day, she was returning from vacation; her holiday, however, ended with her accompanying her grief-stricken brother-in-law as he went to the hospital to identify the bodies of his dead children. Later that night, Corrigan appeared on television and appealed to all parties to cease the hostilities. The program was broadcast all over Ireland and Britain.

The death of the Maguire children was such that even the usual finger-pointing and blaming that followed such events in Northern Ireland seemed crass and vulgar. Indeed, the tragedy brought about a spontaneous call for peace. Groups of people prayed at the accident site; peace demonstrations were planned across Northern Ireland; and a petition for an end to the violence was circulated.

An office receptionist, Betty Williams, happened to be on the Finaghy Road that afternoon, and she witnessed the horrible scene. Rather than run from the violence, which would be altogether natural, she faced it and actively became part of the petitioning for peace. She called *The Irish News* and told a reporter to give out her number for any people who wished to speak to her about putting an end to the violence—and many did. Her involvement attracted the attention of

Mairead Corrigan, who called to thank her.

Now, there is also a third person involved in the Peace People that appears on the scene at this point. Ciaran McKeown was the Northern Ireland correspondent for the Dublin-based *Irish Press*. It was his task to cover the Maguire tragedy—and Northern Ireland's reaction to it. Long committed to the principles of non-violence, McKeown had written an article entitled "What Would Gandhi Do in Belfast?" and was invited to appear on a current affairs television program on the day of the children's funeral. Williams and Corrigan were invited as well, but they arrived too late to the studios. However, after the program, McKeown, Williams, and Corrigan got to meet. And from that initial meeting evolved the "Peace People." Williams and Corrigan had the passion; McKeown had the press.

The "Peace People" began organizing weekly demonstrations that drew thousands of people, people fed up with the never-ending cycle of violence. Within a month, they had assembled over 30,000 Catholic and Protestant women who marched together to voice their opposition to any form of violence. They attempted to make inroads in education—realizing that the very schools that their children attended were infested with the animosities that continued the circle of hate and prejudice. The party even reached out to the paramilitary organizations that were conducting it. But to no avail. For the violence continued, and more children were slain. And while thousands of people marched in the street, the momentum was difficult to maintain—there was really no solid organization and no strategy except to educate towards peace and to see the end of the killings. After time, "Peace People" seemed to lose its vigor.

In 1976, the two women—Corrigan and Williams—were awarded the Nobel Peace Prize. As Corrigan herself said, the prize was not for what they had done but for what they were doing. "Peace" was still very far away in Northern Ireland. Yet, the women knew that a society committed to peace was not something that a society can turn on and off—it had to be trained towards that commitment. Indeed, that was the basis of the organization's emphasis on education. And while twenty more years of violence would continue to scar Northern Ireland, the two women never ceased in their efforts to change the situation. Finally by the end of the century, it seemed that peace might be attainable after all. The seeds that Corrigan and Williams had sown had taken root somewhere in the country and in 1998 the majority of people voted to let the seeds blossom.

A CHANCE FOR RECONCILIATION

One of the collateral results of Bobby Sands's death came about through the election that was to be held to fill his seat in Parliament after he had died five days into his term. Until Sands had been nominated and won in a campaign that was merely meant as a protest of the conditions in the H-Block, the IRA had refused the political path—considering it little more than collaboration with the system that they wished to replace. Upon his death, his "agent" Owen Carron stood for election to fill the seat, and surprisingly won by a significantly larger number than Sands. The people had been greatly affected by the senseless deaths of Sands and the other nine hunger strikers and were frustrated by the stalemate that violence had brought them to. Thus, for many of those who had long held strong nationalist and republican views, the choice was no longer only the bomb and the gun. The ballot box was a viable alternative. Sands's death in a large way had opened the door for the IRA to work the political process—through their official party Sinn Fein, which was led by Gerry Adams, who argued successfully for some modification of Sinn Fein's abstention from politics policy. (The fact that the IRA, through its brutal bombing campaign of the 1980s, which had wasted most of the positive feeling that the hunger strikers had earned, postponed this political participation for a decade and placed Adams in the unenviable position of rationalizing the IRA's path.)

At the same time, John Hume, who had founded the SDLP in Northern Ireland and had been part of the original civil-rights movement in the late 1960s, helped establish the Sunningdale Agreement and was elected to the resulting "Council for Ireland." When that collapsed after a two-week national strike and pressure from hardliners on both sides, he formed the National Ireland Forum, a think tank comprised of people from Nationalist and Loyalist parties and from both Northern Ireland and the Republic of Ireland. When the NIF's proposals were brusquely rejected by Margaret Thatcher, he orchestrated a series of covert meetings among opposing parties that would result in a viable Irish Peace Initiative and ultimately to the Good Friday Accord, the first positive step towards resolution in Northern Ireland's history. The fact that Hume had gotten any of these disparate people talking to each other at all was an extraordinary thing in itself.

And in the Loyalist camp there were certain factions that were also edging away from the absolutist preaching of hardliners like Ian Paisley and embracing—however guardedly—some reconciliation with the 45 percent of Catholics who now lived in the North. Most notably was a man named Gusty Spence who had spent most of his adult life in Long Kesh prison, had educated himself there to the history of the Northern Irish situation, had become friends with Cardinal O'Fiaich, and had preached a gospel of non-violence in prison. He had made some important converts among his Loyalist prison mates, and now out of prison they were bringing their message to the party.

Much of the impetus behind this new way of thinking was brought about not only by the inspired leadership of men like Hume, Adams, and the leader of the largest Unionist party, David Trimble, but also by the situation in Northern Ireland itself. Thirty years of violence had had a devastating effect on employment, investment, and jobs. Middle-class Protestants were leaving; working class Protestants were losing jobs; and Catholics were choosing to remain—for the sad reason that British unemployment benefits were better than the Republic's. The bastions of the North's economy, linen manufacturing and ship building, had fallen on desperate times, and major investors avoided doing business in the blood-ravaged country. Thus, many Protestants gradually came to realize that their privileged status and the promise of prosperity that had come as part of their allegiance to Britain was not all they had believed it to be, and that change was imminent and necessary.

It was a slow and painful ascent up a very rickety ladder that could—and still might—collapse at any time. To be sure, violence continued throughout the 1980s and 1990s—although the death toll had fallen considerably—and the choice of targets seemed bolder and more desperate. (Gerry Adams was shot; the hotel that Margaret Thatcher was staying in was bombed; the lawyer Finucane was murdered; and a particularly horrible bombing and reprisal took place on the Shankill Road and in a Greystill pub as late as 1993 in which seventeen people were killed.) And certainly not everyone was pleased with the direction in which things were going. Hardliners on both sides derided any process of conciliation; politicians of every ilk questioned the process; and old animosities and bitter memories continued to thrive. But there was momentum—spurred on not a little by the U.S. President Bill Clinton and his mediator, George Mitchell—which in 1998 culminated in what became known as the "Belfast Agreement of the Good Friday Accord," an agreement that instituted a power-sharing assembly among all parties, an institution that has faltered and lurched since its inception in 1998.

CHAPTER XXXVI:
John Hume

John Hume was born in 1937 into the Derry ghetto of Bogside. His mother was not well read and his father was well known for a particular handsome style of handwriting. As insignificant as this seems, it had important consequences for Hume. During World War II, Hume's father was hired by the War Office to write out ration tickets, a job that lasted only for the duration of the war. Afterwards, he worked temporarily for the shipyards, and then—being Catholic in this Protestant-run country—he never could find work again. He survived by writing letters and filling in job applications for neighbors. John Hume remembers sitting at the table doing his homework, while neighbors sat across from his father dictating letters. As the letters more often than not were concerned with the hardships of poverty, unemployment, sickness, and injustice, John Hume heard first hand the miseries of the poor. (His own world was hardly opulent; there were seven children and two adults, two bedrooms and a toilet in the backyard.) And while his father assisted the neighbors in getting things written, his mother also did her share for the neighborhood. Often when she would take the bus into town, Mrs. Hume brought groceries and goods back to the older neighbors who could not make the trip themselves. From both his father and mother, Hume learned a sense of shared community and service.

Hume's secondary education was among the best, paid for by a scholarship intended for eleven-year-old boys who proved in an examination that they were on the track for university. Since the scholarship was administered from London, it was available to both Protestant and Catholic boys—something that would never have been the case if the Northern Ireland government had administered it. (Apparently, the Unionists were able to pick and choose how closely they were united with the Crown!) Hume came in the top 25 percent and was given a scholarship to the exclusive St. Columb's Catholic School in Derry. He would be the only one of his six brothers and sisters who would attend secondary school. The scholarship was the only way he could attend. (I think it is interesting that two years later, the Irish poet Seamus Heaney also attended St. Columb's on a scholarship. He too would be awarded a Nobel Prize in the 1990s, and when you think of it, for a small parochial school in the tiny city of Derry to produce two Nobel Prize winners is an extraordinary percentage.)

After St. Columb's, Hume studied in the Catholic seminary in Maynooth where for a while he considered a vocation to the priesthood. He studied French and history, and cites as a profound influence on him a history professor, Reverend Thomas Fee. (Fee would Gaelicize his name to Tomás O'Fiaich and would become the leading prelate of Ireland, the Archbishop of Armagh. It was O'Fiaich who visited the hunger strikers at Long Kesh and argued so heatedly with Margaret Thatcher.) Hume dropped out of the seminary in 1957, received his degree from the National University, and when he returned to Derry, taught French in a local school. But his studies and his background had made him fiercely committed to community action.

His first point of business was in setting up a credit union—the Derry Credit Union, which was the first credit union in Ireland. From the credit union, Hume made the logical jump to the problem of housing and set up the first housing association in Ireland as well. The association was successful in placing numerous families in houses and attempted to do some building as well as repair. But when the association applied to the government for permission to build 700 homes for needy families, it was refused. This was a Unionist government, after all, and the needs of its Catholic minority were of little concern to them. Worse, not only did the Derry government refuse the Housing Association permission, but it banned the building of houses.

As the Irish-American politician Tip O'Neill once said, "all politics is local," and if Hume didn't know it before, he knew now that in Northern Ireland everything is politics. His community activism was a direct path to politics, and before long the Credit Union evolved into the Credit Union Party, which in turn became the Social Democratic and Labour Party, the SDLP.

Such continued instances of sectarianism and blatant discrimination—witnessed from his childhood on—committed Hume to the cause of civil rights. And as he turned to Martin Luther King Jr. in the United States, he also became convinced of the power of nonviolence. He was a tireless worker in the civil rights movement, often in the front lines of the civil rights marches but always with the mandate that the marchers eschew violence. Always calm, despite being hit with water canon, tear gas, and the paint bombs that marked him as one of the organizers, he was forever working the press, getting out the message of what exactly the demonstrators were protesting, what they were asking for.

In 1969, Hume won the seat from Derry in the Northern Ireland Parliament, standing on a platform of social and economic reform. His was a completely new order of opposition, bereft of the "only unity with the twenty-six counties" rhetoric that had distinguished the previous Nationalist campaigns. Hume believed that the Nationalist party had let down the people terribly, more concerned with the shadow of the border than the overwhelming shadow of poverty and unemployment. (It is one of those historical congruencies that when asked to stand for the British Parliament, Hume declined. The seat was then won by the twenty-one-year-old Bernadette Devlin.)

Dedicated to the principles of nonviolence, in 1970, Hume, along with civil rights activists and socialists, particularly Gerry Fitt, founded the Social Democratic and Labour Party. The SDLP was an attempt to bring together a non-militant opposition to the Unionist parties that had always controlled Derry. At the time, Catholics were in the majority in Derry, but through intricate gerrymandering were largely underrepresented in the Parliament. Gerry Fitt was elected the leader of the Party and Hume was appointed secretary.

After the massacre of "Bloody Sunday" and the ensuing violence that resulted, in 1973 John Hume took part in an unprecedented series of negotiations. Representing the SDLP, Hume met with representatives of the Ulster Unionist Party, as well as with delegates from Great Britain and the Republic of Ireland.

The situation had grown so severe that all parties had to put aside their differences and come to a resolution. (At this time, Sinn Fein, as the political party of the IRA, was not included in government negotiations.) The results of the talks became known as the Sunningdale Agreement and it was an encouraging start. The agreement stated that a power-sharing body of eleven members would govern the North—and Hume was elected as one of several Catholics on that body. There would also be a "Council of Ireland" made up of delegates from Northern Ireland and the Republic of Ireland, which would consider issues that affected the entire island. It had been a very long time since Ireland had been considered an entire entity by anyone. It was hopeful plan, but the hard-liners resisted. Both Loyalist and IRA paramilitary groups engaged in the violence and Loyalist unions called a two-week strike that paralyzed the country. Finally, the pressure was such that the agreement was scrapped.

As the violence escalated further and further, Hume found it harder to find support for his principles of nonviolence. After the death of the hunger strikers, Sinn Fein began attracting increasing numbers of people to its party, so Hume countered by developing the National Ireland Forum, which included people from the North and from the Republic. The purpose again was to find some solution for the island. He knew that Ulster would never be won by violence. Perhaps Hume was optimistic at first; it seemed incredibly hopeful to have the disparate parties working towards a single goal. But momentum fell apart after a much-anticipated meeting between Margaret Thatcher and the Irish prime minister, Garrett Fitzgerald. The meeting was friendly and centered on the need to do something in Northern Ireland with many of the NIF's proposals on the table. Thatcher blindsided Fitzgerald at a press conference, negating the possibility of any of the plans the two had spoken about. Fitzgerald was thoroughly humiliated; he had accompanied Thatcher to the press conference in confidence that a breakthrough might be reached, and the "Iron Maiden" had turned on him in public.

With each road towards normalcy blocked, John Hume decided that Sinn Fein should be brought into the political process. Sinn Fein had, since Bobby Sands's death, increasing success at the voting booth, but as a matter of principle refused to sit in the Northern Ireland Parliament and the Republic of Ireland's Dáil, saying it refused to recognize the legitimacy of the two partitioned governments. While this policy may have adhered to its principles, it did nothing in affecting change. Finally, in 1983, the IRA gave notice that it would like to talk to Hume, to somehow yoke constitutional politics with their own militancy. The talks broke down even before they started, however, and once again John Hume's hopes for a solution were dashed.

In 1988, after five more years of violence, the IRA again reached out to Hume. John Hume and Gerry Adams, president of Sinn Fein, met from January to September in 1988, and continued to meet afterwards. Indeed, secret talks were held between Hume, Sinn Fein, Britain, and the White House. (Newly elected president Bill Clinton, who has perhaps done more for Ireland than any other president, had appointed Jean Kennedy Smith, the sister of Senator Edward Kennedy and of the late John F. and Robert F. Kennedy, as ambassador to the Republic of Ireland. And although she was ambassador to the Republic, as a friend of John Hume she spent much time in the North—much to Britain's dismay. Her input and her judgment were immeasurable in the movement towards an end to the conflict.) And, with several parties talking, things began to move quickly. The Downing Street Declaration issued in 1993 stated that Britain had no interest—economic, social, or political—in Northern Ireland and that the people of Northern Ireland themselves should decide their fate. The declaration was astounding—naturally reviled by hardliners, but for the most part warmly welcomed by the rest of the world. The Downing Street Declaration was followed by cease-fires on both sides—Gusty Spence's announcement was even laced with apologies to all the families of innocent victims. And while there were sporadic failures of the cease-fires, they quieted the bombs for the first time in twenty-five years.

John Hume was beginning to see what he had hoped to see all his life: the gun taken out of the nationalist agenda and a window of opportunity opened for serious reform.

In 1995, President Clinton sent a former senator, George Mitchell, to mediate talks among all the concerned parties. Mitchell's job, chairing a committee of volatile and headstrong men whose lives were shaped by a history of hatred and prejudice, was arduous at best, but he was a firm and fair diplomat and a masterful mediator. On Good Friday, 1998, a proposal was offered to the Irish people. It included a new legislature made up of any parties who had forsworn violence; it arranged for the dismantling of legislated discrimination against Catholics; and most importantly, it stated that Northern Ireland would remain part of Great Britain until the majority of its people wished otherwise. It seemed that after thirty years of bloodshed and centuries of mistrust and misdealing that the situation in Ireland would finally be settled. It all depended on the vote.

The Irish public, both in the Republic and in the North, voted on the Good Friday Agreement on May 22, 1998. More than 70 percent of the people voted yes with more than 50 percent of Northern Irish Protestants supporting the agreement. For his part in bringing it together, John Hume shared the Nobel Peace Prize with his Protestant counterpart, David Trimble. But approving the accord was one thing; implementing it would be something else.

In September 2001, John Hume retired as head of the SDLP. His health had been failing and he was busy with both the British and European Parliaments. He had taken over the leadership from Gerry Fitt in 1979, and for twenty years was a tireless exponent of its principles: economic and social justice without violence. In his role as leader, he had been tenacious, politic, intelligent, and steadfast. He had worked ceaselessly for both his people and the larger issues of nationhood, and for a while it seemed that he succeeded. Today, the permanence of his successes and the success of the Good Friday Accord are challenged daily, and what its outcome will be no one can guess. But unless "the center cannot hold," as the great Yeats once wrote, John Hume can be proud that his country is a better place because of him.

CHAPTER XXXVII:
DAVID TRIMBLE

The "Troubles" in Northern Ireland have produced all sorts of incongruities. For instance, as recently as 1995, David Trimble marched in the traditional Drumcree parade with the intractable Unionist Ian Paisley—literally hand-in-hand with the very symbol of Unionist intransigence. In 1998, however, he was the first Ulster Unionist to sit down and bargain with Sinn Fein. To be sure, it was only through such incongruities as these that the "Troubles" in Northern Ireland could ever have hope of being resolved.

David Trimble was born in 1944 and came of age as the civil rights movement in Ulster was beginning to foment. He received his education in Bangor at Queen's University in Belfast, and as the first civil rights marches were forming in Derry and Belfast in 1968, he passed the Bar and became a barrister. He also worked as a lecturer at Queen's University. As a Protestant Unionist, his was the class to which the civil rights protestors were appealing for rights. His was also the class that profited most by continuance of the status quo, by the continuance of sanctioned discrimination. Northern Ireland had been created for the Ulster Protestants, and over the course of a century they had legislated and systemized their own advantages on the backs of the disenfranchised Ulster Catholics. And as the civil rights movement attempted to bring Protestants into the struggle—before the escalation of violence—the Unionist parties, who saw all agitation for social reform as merely a guise for Republicanism and reunification with the South, also began strengthening their positions. In the early 1970s, Trimble joined the hard-line Vanguard Progressive Unionist Party. (Its leader, William Craig, once infamously stated that it was the duty of every loyalist "to liquidate the enemy." There was no doubt that the enemy to whom Craig referred were those who were marching for fair housing, equal opportunity, and an end to discrimination. In effect, they were marching against the Orange Order, and that made them the enemy in Ulster.) Trimble, who served as the party's deputy leader, was elected to the Northern Ireland Convention.

Trimble remained with the Vanguard Party throughout most of the 1970s, as the violence in Northern Ireland spiraled out of control and devolved into a war between various paramilitary factions. In 1978, however, the Vanguard Party, which had always been on the fringe, collapsed, and Trimble joined the Ulster Unionist Party. He quickly moved up the ranks and soon became party secretary.

In the 1980s, the Unionists felt themselves under attack, not only from the Republicans who they claimed were being supported by the Republic of Ireland, but by Great Britain itself, who they accused of catering to the nationalists' demands. This argument would continue throughout all negotiations in the next two decades and would be the cause for many of the arguments and resignations after the Good Friday Accord was voted in.

In 1990, Trimble was elected in a bi-election to the British Parliament. It was a difficult time to maintain hard-line Unionist views. That year, Peter Brooke, the Secretary of State for Northern Ireland, made a historical announcement: Britain had no "selfish strategic or economic interest" in Northern Ireland. Brooke went on to say that Britain was not even set against a united Ireland per se. It was against the violent attempt to achieve it. The Unionists were outraged and felt abandoned. At the same time, talks were being held secretly between Sinn Fein and the British government and between the Republic and Britain. The old world of the Orange Order seemed to be coming to a close.

In 1995, Trimble famously marched with Ian Paisley in the Drumcree Parade. It was as much a sign of unity and resolve as it was the yearly traditional Orange foot on the neck of the Catholic minority. Yet, it was also an important moment for Trimble to be seen. His presence with Paisley was arguably decisive in his being elected that year as leader of the UUP.

Three years into his leadership—years in which he must have understood where matters were headed—David Trimble took the courageous step of participating in conciliatory talks with the republicans. It was a crucial moment for Trimble and the UUP; he lost half of his support in Parliament—but he carried the majority of his party with him. Trimble opposed the appointment of the American George Mitchell as chairman, for he believed that the Americans in general were biased towards the republicans, but he was instrumental in developing the power-sharing institution that would become the cornerstone of the Good Friday Accord.

Developing the accord was one thing; getting his unionist party to accept it was something else altogether. Trimble proved himself a brave and formidable leader, and insisted to his people on the necessity of the Good Friday Accord for the good of Ulster and Unionism. It was essential if the agreement was to mean anything, that the Ulster Protestants showed a sizeable sign of support. (Since the agreement was being voted on by both countries on the island, Catholics could have overwhelmingly voted for the agreement and negated any Protestant opposition, which probably would have led to more of the same acrimonies and stalemate.) Trimble, however, was successful in getting over fifty percent of the North's Protestants to approve the agreement. In voting its approval, Northern Ireland was embarking on an unprecedented new journey.

In the months that followed, a multi-party governing body was formed and Mr. Trimble was named the first minister and the SDLP's Seamus Mallon was named his deputy. (That in itself was as extraordinary as it was historic.) Indeed, these were historic times, and like all historic times, they were not without their difficulties. When in July 1999 the new National Executive was about to meet, the UUP refused to sit with Sinn Fein until the IRA began decommissioning their guns. George Mitchell, who had returned to America, was brought back as the entire process seemed on the verge of disintegrating. Trimble—again against the wishes of many of his party—agreed to convening the executive first and having the IRA decommission later. The Ulster Unionists were split and the decision was put to a vote. Trimble's measure convincingly won by a vote of 480 to 349, yet the numbers indicated a dangerous split within the party.

When in late February 2000, the IRA had not yet handed over any of its weapons, Trimble suspended the executive and his party walked away. The UUP, he stated, would not govern with Sinn Fein as long as the IRA were armed. When the IRA began allowing weapons inspectors into its arsenal in May, Trimble returned to government.

Yet the IRA's wavering on the issue of decommissioning was proving to be Trimble's Achilles' heel, and in July 2001, he resigned as leader of the Unionist Party. He had lost the support of his party that believed he was too soft on the rebels; many even believed that he had sold out to the Republicans.

With John Hume, Trimble was awarded the Nobel Peace Prize in 1998. The Nobel committee cited his political courage in taking the first steps to opening discussion and building trust. It also emphasized that the positive institutions that had arisen from the Good Friday Accord must not be allowed to lay fallow, but should be nurtured and made to flourish.

Unfortunately, there are few others in the Unionist faction that have the political courage of David Trimble. And as his party loses confidence in both him and the Good Friday Accord, and the hardliners gain support and credibility, the future of those historic "first steps"—and the hopes of Northern Ireland—remains in danger.

Chapter XXXVIII:
Gerry Adams

A man is born into the household that begets him, and Gerry Adams was born in 1948 into a very Republican family in Ballymurphy, Belfast. His upbringing was thoroughly Irish and thoroughly Catholic. The eldest of ten children, he went to Catholic schools, learned the Irish language, played Gaelic football and hurling, and believed in the inevitability of a united Ireland. His grandfather on his father's side was a member of the Irish Republican Brotherhood in the early 1900s, and his mother's father had been an election agent for Eamon de Valera in 1918. Adams's own father had spent five years in prison in the 1940s when at the age of sixteen he was charged with the attempted murder of an RUC policeman.

As a teenager, Adams joined both *Na Fianna Eireann* and Sinn Fein; however, this was a different Sinn Fein from that of his father and uncles. The younger generation who were filling its ranks were formed in the crucible of the civil rights movement, and Gerry Adams was a visible figure in Belfast during those heady days as republicans joined the constitutional nationalists in agitating for better housing and fairer job opportunities.

In 1983, Gerry Adams was made leader of Sinn Fein. It was a difficult position at the time, for as the "political wing" of the IRA, his was the public face attached to the murderous campaign the IRA had instituted in the 1980s. As the chief spokesman of Sinn Fein, he concurred with the policy of armed conflict, of forcibly ousting the British government from Northern Ireland, but the IRA bombing campaign was brutal and appalling and did much to damage the credibility of the IRA. It was this situation through which Gerry Adams had to walk.

Despite the criminalization of the IRA, however, Gerry Adams was the major contact for all parties in dealing with the group, and he soon earned the respect of those trying to halt the hostilities. (Even before he had assumed leadership of Sinn Fein, he had commanded respect from the government authorities. In 1972, having been picked up during the days of internment—when anyone with suspicious connections could be arrested and detained without charges—Adams was secretly flown to London for talks with British authorities.)

The question always arises whether Adams himself was ever part of the IRA, and consistently, he has denied it. But those who know state that it would be impossible for him to have reached the pre-eminence that he has in his party— and maintain the loyal obedience of the IRA rank-and-file—if he had not. It is something we probably will learn for certain one day, but that day is not now.

Sinn Fein's political aspirations at the time were bogged down by their principled refusal to sit on any office they had won through election. They considered neither the Northern Ireland Parliament nor the British Parliament legitimate governing powers, and because they didn't recognize the partition of 1921, they didn't recognize the Republic's Dáil Éireann either. With the momentum gained through the deaths of the hunger strikers, Sinn Fein began to win over more voters and make incursions into the SDLP's power base. At the same time, they criticized the SDLP for being too middle-class and for being toadies to the Northern Irish system. Adams argued against Sinn Fein policy, stating that IRA victory could not come solely through violence. He asserted that the IRA could not have a military victory—the ballot box must prevail for them. These were radical words within a radical party.

In 1983, Adams scored a double victory. He was named president of Sinn Fein, and he was elected MP for West Belfast in the British Parliament. His becoming president of Sinn Fein was a result of the Northern Ireland contingent ousting the south's Ruari Ó Bradaigh on the issue of abstentionism. Adams had argued for revoking the abstention policy, and when he became president, he revoked the proscription on sitting in the Republic's Dáil. Sinn Fein continued to refuse to sit in the British Parliament and Adams accordingly did not sit in Westminster after his 1983 election.

Yet while Gerry Adams might announce that Sinn Fein was ready to enter the political arena, the IRA and the various Loyalist paramilitaries had no intention of stopping their armed struggles while he went about it. And as if to emphasize that point, in 1984, as Adams stood outside a courthouse in Belfast, three men fired twenty shots at him. He was hit four times. (Adams and his family have long been targeted by Loyalist paramilitaries and government authorities. He has had a brother-in-law killed by the British army and a brother shot. His wife and son were in their home when it was bombed; both escaped unharmed. And family members have been imprisoned.)

But regardless of whatever thoughts the militants had about Adams, mainstream politicians were concerned about Sinn Fein's dedication to electoral victory, and in many ways the Anglo-Irish Agreement of 1985 was a referendum on John Hume and his moderate SDLP party. Both London and Dublin felt that by encouraging the mainstream SDLP, they could negate any influence that Adams's Sinn Fein might wield.

But Hume was no political naïf, and he realized the influence that Adams wielded. In 1988, the two began having secret talks. Like much else in Ireland at the time, the talks ended uneasily. But the goals of the individual parties were too aligned to keep them apart for long, and soon afterward, Hume and Adams began meeting again. Hume, as well as London and Britain, knew that Adams was the pivotal key if any sort of peace initiative was to begin.

On December 15, 1993, the Downing Street Declaration was announced. It said for all intents and purposes that Britain had no self-interest in the affairs of Northern Ireland. The situation was changing rapidly, but in order for the declaration to proceed, Gerry Adams had to be brought along—and first he had to convince the IRA of the declaration's worth. It is important to state here that throughout these times of unofficial negotiations, the American President Bill Clinton was also playing a pivotal role. Besides sending the very competent Jean Kennedy Smith as ambassador to Ireland, Clinton trusted her opinions and acted on them. Her opinion was that Gerry Adams should be granted a visa to visit the United States. At the end of January 1994, a month after the Downing Street Declaration was issued, Adams was on a plane to America.

When Clinton was asked later to approve the visa of Joe Cahill, an old republican and suspected arms smuggler whom the United States had deported twice, Clinton stalled, saying he wanted something in return, some movement toward peace. The Irish Taoiseach, Albert Reynolds, promised him there would be something. After a flurry of calls across the Atlantic, Cahill was put on a plane. The following day, Gerry Adams announced "a complete cessation of military operations" for the IRA.

The IRA cease-fire in 1994 did as much as anything else to put an Irish peace initiative on track, and that track led ultimately to the Good Friday Accord. A brilliant politician, Adams was also able to deliver his party when it came time to set up the executive that resulted from the agreement. To the question of abstention and sitting at the new executive, Adams brought a sizeable 90 percent of his party in affirmation. It was a testament of his management skills, his persuasive abilities, and his political savvy.

But Adams's patience is still being tested. His status as a pariah to many Unionists has always threatened collapse for the power-sharing assembly that Good Friday brought—and any good will that surrounded it. He continues to be an exponent of the peace process despite internal dissent within the party and within the IRA. But he remains steadfast to his principles, and committed to the reality of peace in Northern Ireland.

In the past six years, the Good Friday Accord has often seemed in imminent danger of dying. Old acrimonies still exist; mistrust is everywhere; and the issue of disarmament is omnipresent. (Though some say that the disarmament question is just a plank on which to sabotage the entire process.) But saving the peace process that was formulated and voted upon in May 1998 is not the job of any one man alone. If the Good Friday initiative is to be resuscitated, if the initial hope and optimism that described the heady days of 1998 are to continue, the momentum toward peace needs to be revived by the good work of many good men, men like John Hume, David Trimble, and Gerry Adams.

THE CELTIC TIGER
AND THE NEW IRELAND

My brother Frank brought me out to America when I was just a young fella in the 1950s, twenty years old and thinking that I knew it all. I quickly got a job working in a construction gang and then later a famous stint as a bartender. But I was just one of thousands of Irish who were arriving on the shores of America, looking for work and looking to make a life. And if we Irish weren't sailing to New York or Canada or ports west, we were making the short journey across to England, where we dug the ditches and built the motorways. In South America, in Australia, we found ourselves anywhere there was work, and often it was hard and physical—the work no one else wanted. We were the navies and nannies, the cooks and cops, the bartenders and lawn cutters.

This constant flow out of Ireland seemed to have been going on forever. You couldn't pass a construction gang in Manhattan without hearing a Mayo accent or ride the subway in from Brooklyn without overhearing some Cork girls on their way to minding someone's kids. Even at the beach, the convenience stores and T-shirt shops were filled with Irish kids making a buck for the summer.

And then suddenly in the 1990s, the pipeline seemed to have stopped. Construction crews couldn't keep the Irish boys on; the rosters of available au pairs and nannies showed fewer and fewer Irish girls; American companies that depended on seasonal Irish help actually began recruiting in Ireland. It seemed that the workers were returning home quicker than usual, if they were coming out at all.

Ireland had become a booming economy, and for the first time in nearly two centuries there were plentiful jobs at home. The computer business, particularly, turned Ireland into Europe's "Silicon Valley." Investment, development, and new construction were booming. A nascent movie industry was thriving, and in entertainment it seemed that everything Irish was being desired and consumed throughout the world. (I have one friend who travels frequently, and one of her hobbies is collecting shirts from Irish pubs all over the world—in Rome, in Amsterdam, in Paris, in Madrid, in Japan.)

The name given this new era of flourishing economics was the "Celtic Tiger," after the ferocious Tiger economies of East Asian countries like Korea and Malaysia. And while the "Celtic Tiger" has had its critics—as in all vigorous economies, there were those who were left behind and those who were made redundant and those who were swept into the corners where they could not be seen—it succeeded in one very large way: the "Celtic Tiger" kept its youth at home, not only moving the nation toward the twenty-first century, but leading most of Europe along the way. (Its economy—reaching double-digit growth—outpaced both Britain's and Germany's, while unemployment sank to the lowest level in half a century.) For many of the young people, the animosities and ancient grudges that had informed their history seemed a distant and foreign thing; the vise that the Catholic Church had held on the nation had been loosened; and the Irish now thought of themselves as European. They were the "post-nationalist" Irish, proud, sophisticated, and savvy. It was indeed a "New Ireland."

During such frenetic and exciting times as these, there were many figures from all over the cultural landscape that helped shaped this new Ireland. There were business people and movie directors, impresarios and computer wizards, seasoned aristocrats and rock stars, ad men and community leaders. Ireland's path towards modernity had been usurped by business and commerce, and the job of the politicians seemed now to merely act as conduits for the whole exciting and energetic thing to work.

Typical of the new energy, of the new Ireland that the world embraced, were three very different people. Mary Robinson served as President of Ireland, and then Head of the United Nations Human Rights Commission. Bertie Ahern became Taoiseach and played a major role in implementing and sustaining the political agreements in the North; and the rock star Bono, aside from selling millions of records and touring around the world to sell-out crowds, became one of the most ardent proponents for social change, arguing for AIDS relief and debt relief in poor, developing nations. These three not only reflect the youthful vigor that is Ireland today, but also demonstrate the influential role that Ireland plays on the world stage.

CHAPTER XXXIX:
MARY ROBINSON AND BERTIE AHERN

If anything, the ascent of Mary Robinson and Bertie Ahern reflects how different Ireland is now from what it was throughout most of its history. Robinson, as the first female President in the Republic, cracked the patriarchal dominance that had defined Irish politics since the demise of the chieftains and the end of Brehon law. And Ahern, who separated from his wife and traveled openly with a female companion, reflects a world very different from the one that railroaded Charles Stewart Parnell out of Ireland. These are different times to be sure, and both Robinson and Ahern have risen to prominence because of their talents and skills: their gender and personal life are no longer the crucible in which their acceptability need be tested. I would be naïve if I said there haven't been backlashes and criticisms of both. But they have risen above petty politics and have gone on to reach great and important attainments.

Mary Robinson

Mary Robinson was not only the first female President of Ireland. She was the first non-Fianna Fail President as well, and of course the first Labour President. Her election in 1990 indicated a changing mood in the country and seemed to anticipate the modern Ireland that would emerge during that decade.

Mary Bourke was born in Ballina, County Mayo, in 1944. She was a descendant of the aristocratic Bourkes, who had arrived in Ireland in the thirteenth century with the Norman invasion, and who fast "became more Irish than the Irish themselves." Indeed, in Mary Bourke, it seemed that all of Irish history has been culminated, and with her the nation could finally shake off its past and move forward. In fact, all of Ireland's various factions seemed to be combined in her. Her relatives included Land League agitators and Elizabethan knights, members of the Irish Republican Brotherhood and colonial judges. One was a Catholic nun, and others were members of the Anglican Church of Ireland. In some dramatic way, it seemed that with all these separate factions brought together in one personage who was in a position to lead, the nation was ready to face the new millennium. (Completeing this personal unification of Irish strands, in the 1970s, the Catholic Mary Bourke married Nicholas Robinson, a Protestant in the Church of Ireland.)

Yet when Mary Bourke was young, Ireland was still mired in the prejudices of its past. As a Catholic, she was forbidden to attend Trinity College without the express permission of her bishop, so she went out and got it from him. She read law at Trinity and received law degrees from both King's Inns and Harvard University. In 1969, she became Trinity College's Reid Professor of Constitutional and Criminal Law, and she continued that professorship for six years before becoming a lecturer at Trinity in European Community Law. And if the switch from professor to lecturer seemed a step backward, it was merely because Robinson's political career was becoming more and more involved and more and more controversial.

Elected to the Senate (Sénead Éireann) in 1969, Robinson became a fierce advocate for women, arguing against laws making married women quit civil service and denying women the right to sit on juries. She also argued against the ban on contraception. (Remember, Robinson did not come into a "New Ireland": she helped create it.) Contraception had always been illegal in Ireland, although by the 1970s, it was being brought back from overseas or just from across the border. Her stance on the right to use contraception caused contentious and nasty repercussions in the Senate and in her private life. When she proposed the bill easing the restrictions on contraceptives, no one in the Senate had the courage to second it, and the bill had to be dropped from discussion. Her mail was stuffed with used condoms—illegally obtained of course—and the opposition accused her of supporting contraception for financial reasons, wrongly accusing her family of having an interest in the business. (The old world might be fading, but it was not going out without a fight.) It is a credit to Robinson's political acumen and vision, that each of these issues—the right to contraception, a woman's right to remain in civil service after marriage, and the right for women to sit on juries—all came to fruition during Robinson's time in office.

Robinson remained in the senate for fifteen years, advocating the rights of women, of homosexuals, of the disenfranchised, and of all people on the fringe. (During her presidency she signed two bills that reflected the issues she had fought for throughout her career: one eased the legislation against contraception; the other decriminalized homosexuality in Ireland.) She had originally sat in the upper house as an independent member, but in the 1970s, she switched her alignment to the Irish Labour Party. In the 1980s, Fianna Fail was ousted from power, and the Labour Party joined in a National Coalition party, but Robinson resigned from the coalition in protest of the Anglo-Irish Agreement in 1985. While the hardliners in the North protested the agreement between Britain and Ireland about the

North and threatened to sabotage it, Robinson resigned precisely because the Northern Unionists had not been involved in the negotiations in the first place. No one ever could question her integrity.

In a way, Robinson was brought out of her retirement when the Labour Party asked her to run as its candidate for president. It was a long shot by far, but Robinson proved herself a strategic campaigner, a personable politician, and an intelligent speaker on the issues. To the surprise of all the odds makers, in 1990, Mary Robinson was elected as the first female president of Ireland.

Now the office of president has usually been a secondary office, practically a sinecure formulated by Eamon de Valera for Douglas Hyde, but in recent times, it has taken on a more and more influential role. For this Robinson was perfectly fit. Her legal mind and brilliant intelligence allowed her to anticipate and cut through the obstacles of any issue, and her personable character allowed her to forge new alliances and to assuage old foes. She was particularly adept at hosting members of Britain's Royal Family, easing along the détente that had been developing between the two ancient enemies. Indeed, unlike the majority of Irish presidents before her, Mary Robinson was far too bright to take a back seat to the events of the day. On her trips to the north—to the chagrin of many in the government—she met with Gerry Adams as well as with John Hume and David Trimble. In fact, many of the people with whom Robinson met worried the more sedate politicians in her government: she invited a gay and lesbian coalition to visit the presidential home; she visited with the Dalai Lama (much to China's anger); and she visited the pope. She kept touch with Irish emigrants on her many travels, and in a way, built an international network of both the common man and the powerful.

In 1997, Mary Robinson resigned from the presidency, three months before her term ended. She had served for seven years, and in that time had proven one of the most popular presidents in the country's history. But she had other work still to do.

That year, she was appointed the United Nations High Commissioner for Human Rights. Here too, she has proven controversial, opting to do her job as she sees it regardless of the political agenda of many of the nations involved. In her new role, she was immediately charged with overseeing the merging of what had been two separate United Nations offices: the High Commission and the Center for Human Rights. Aside from the logistics of any such merger, Robinson became the leading advocate for inserting human rights concerns into every aspect of the U.N.'s mission.

Respected at home and abroad, Mary Robinson embodies the very spirit of the new Ireland: Intelligent and sophisticated, charming and personable, strong and principled. When she was president—over the boom times of Ireland in the 1990s—Mary Robinson had put a light in the window of the presidential residence, harking back to an old Irish folk tradition of keeping a candle burning for the many emigrants who had left their home and crossed the sea. In Mary Robinson's time, the emigrants are now returning home to the lighted window. And Ireland has never been the same.

Bertie Ahern

Sometime in the 1990s, Ireland shifted from being the Shan van Voght, "the poor old woman," to being a vigorous and unstoppable youth. It was only natural then that the time would also see the rise of Bertie Ahern. (Now Mr. Ahern has only been Taoiseach since 1997 so the verdict is not known, but he was the youngest man at forty-five ever to hold the office. And from the looks of things right now, he may be Taoiseach for some years to come).

Bertie Ahern was born in Dublin in 1951 into a Republican household that still had strong memories of the early struggles for independence: Ahern's father had fought in the War for independence and in the Irish Civil War. The neighborhood in which he was raised was solidly working class, and Ahern trained at the Rathmines College of Commerce to become an accountant. With his degree in hand, he worked in the offices at the Mater Hospital, Dublin.

But well before his college days, Ahern had become interested in politics and Fianna Fail. When he was a young boy, the party had him climb up light poles to hang election posters. And just as a young Jack Lynch had first spied Eamon de Valera in a campaign and forever after remained loyal to him, in this first campaign, Ahern met Charles Haughey, to whom he would remain loyal throughout his career. Now, to say that Haughey's political career was a bit of a roller coaster would be an understatement at best. He was fired by Jack Lynch on suspicion of gun-running in the 1980s—the accusations were never proven, and he was acquitted; he was elected as Taoiseach three separate times; and he was involved in a nasty financial scandal toward the end of his career. But for the fourteen-year-old Ahern, meeting the yet unscathed politician was a turning point.

Now, the year 1977 was a momentous one for Fianna Fail. They had been in the opposition when the year began, but in a general by-election, gained the largest majority in the modern era. Fianna Fail members were being nominated as constituency TDs at a feverish pace, and one result of this political activity was that Bertie Ahern was sent to the Dáil. Two years later, when a struggle developed as to who would succeed Jack Lynch, Ahern backed the winner, Charles Haughey. In gratitude, he received his first ministered appointment.

As a politician, Ahern is not a particularly inspiring man, but he is likeable, and this sat well with the electorate. In the general elections of the early 1980s, he polled highly, but the times were not kind to Fianna Fail. While Fianna Fail remained in the opposition for much of the 1980s—they did not regain power until 1987—Ahern went and got himself elected Lord Mayor of Dublin in 1986.

With the party back in power in 1987, Ahern was made minister of labour, and it was here that he thrived. There are some who argue that Ahern's tenure as minister of labour was one of the driving forces behind the economic boom that would explode a few years later. (You must remember that Ahern was trained as an accountant; as a politician, he always had one eye on the bottom line, but it was a clever eye, to be sure.)

For the next decade, Irish government would swing between Fianna Fail and various party coalitions. In 1990, there was a bid for the presidency—the first one in almost twenty years—and Ahern acted as director of elections for the hands-on favorite, Brian Lenihan. But for a variety of reasons beyond Ahern's control, Lenihan was defeated, and Mary Robinson of the Labour Party was elected. (Ahern would later work closely with Robinson and came to admire her greatly.) More damaging, however, scandal and corruption continued to disrupt the course of government, and ministers seemed to be resigning or being sacked at a pretty good rate. Ahern's man Haughey had fallen and picked himself up several times in the past, but finally, in 1992, he resigned from politics. Within two years, Ahern had seen both his men—Lenihan and Haughey—taste defeat.

In the next five years, two more men would hold the office of Taoiseach: Albert Reynolds and John Bruton. (This was indicative of the general upheaval in government. When Jack Lynch was made Taoiseach in 1966, he was only the fourth man to hold the position in thirty-four years.) When Reynolds resigned in 1994, Ahern was elected leader of Fianna Fail, and it was assumed that in a coalition between Fianna Fail and the Irish Labour Party, he would then be made Taoiseach. But Labour backed out of the arrangement at the last minute. Fianna Fail was now in the opposition, and John Bruton was made Taoiseach. Yet, Bertie Ahern had proven to be a shrewd party player, both a clever political animal and a cunning wooer of the public, and his talents served him well.

In 1997, with Fianna Fail's return to government, Bertie Ahern was made Taoiseach—the youngest prime minister Ireland ever had. In a very real way, Ahern's ascent at such a young age was symbolic of Ireland's overall youth and vigor. It was a new Ireland with an economy coveted the world over. It was also an important and historic time in the country, for the Northern Irish peace process was at a crucial stage. Here Ahern showed himself to be a politic and judicious leader in the way he stepped into the middle of the process and kept up the momentum. No matter what he does in the rest of his tenure as Taoiseach, his signing of the Good Friday Agreement on Easter Sunday 1998 is perhaps one of the most momentous events in all of modern Irish history, and one with which he will always be associated. (To be fair, the Taoiseach Albert Reynolds was most instrumental in bringing the process to fruition, but by the time the agreement had garnered the world's attention, he had retired from public life.)

Ireland today under Bertie Ahern is a country of optimism. The political agreements among the United Kingdom and Ireland and Northern Ireland are fragile at best. The economy has shown signs of stalling, and the fallout of the boom years is causing uneasiness. But the people like Bertie Ahern; they re-elected his government in 2002—the first time a government had been re-elected in twenty-three years. Ahern, still very much a young man, sees himself remaining as Taoiseach for another three years. His government is behind him, and there is no one on the horizon to unseat him. Described by his mentor, Charles Haughey, as a cunning and skillful politician, he may be around for much longer than that.

Chapter XL:

Bono

I can count the number of rock concerts I've attended on the fingers of one hand and I would still have enough fingers left to turn a doorknob. But sometime in the early summer of 2001, two sisters, Moira and Bridget Bohannon, and a sports writer from Dublin named Justin Kavanagh, took me to a see the Irish rock band U2 in concert. Kavanagh had lived in Dublin when it was still part village, part city rather than the megalopolis it is today, back when everyone seemed to know everyone else's business, and he treated us to dozens of stories about the members of the band as they were taking their first steps towards fame. (He also regaled us with a string of god-awful jokes that involved groan-inducing puns fashioned around the names of particular U2 songs. I didn't know but three or four song titles, but that didn't matter; the only response to any sort of pun—good or bad— is a proper groan.)

I remember now that U2—and their energetic front man Bono—seemed to have been everywhere that year; at a tribute concert for the victims of 9/11, at the Super Bowl halftime show, getting out the vote before a Northern Ireland election, in an Ethiopian village, on the cover of news magazines, and on all sorts of awards shows. It was by any standard a successful year. But unlike most entertainers, Bono also seemed to maintain a very high political visibility. Pictures of him on stage competed with pictures of him with Nelson Mandela, Bill Clinton, the pope; stories about Bono's work at relieving world debt or tackling the AIDS epidemic seemed more common than album or concert reviews. In fact, this is why I allowed myself to be talked into going to a concert; I was intrigued by this band that was so different from most.

The show was astounding. From our seats, which were two rows from the back, one could feel Bono's energy and passion and his flair for the dramatic. The hall literally shook—whether from the volume of the music or the intensity of the fans—and Bono was the conductor, ably manipulating the tenor of the program. He and his band mates were magnificent: talented, lyrical, and thoughtful. And this is what they do night after night throughout the world.

Seven months after my first U2 concert, I watched the band again at the half-time of the uniquely American extravaganza, the Super Bowl. I know many who can never forget that show, which the band insisted on doing live rather than lip-synching as most half-time acts do. As the band performed "Beautiful Day," their song of guarded hope and optimism, the names of all those who had died on 9/11 actually scrolled up the screen. It was a gesture of extraordinary communion; it was a gesture of U2's sense of the dramatic; it was a gesture of just how far in front these Irish rock-and-rollers actually were.

There are several stories as to the origin of Bono's name, the most common being that it is from the words *Bono Vox*. Now, it would be very nice and neat if this name—Latin for "good voice"—had clairvoyantly been conferred on the future rock singer. But the more mundane truth is that he and his friends used to hang around a store on O'Connell Street that used to sell "BonoVox" hearing aids. And boys being boys, the name looked good, and so they christened your man. Hardly a romantic, fate-filled story, but there you have it; he was named after a brand of hearing aids.

Actually, Bono was born Paul David Hewson in 1960, in the poor North Dublin neighborhood of Ballymun. His was a family of mixed religions; his father was Catholic and his mother was Church of Ireland, and in this way, perhaps, Bono avoided the common religious prejudices that many of his contemporaries had inherited. (A more universal sense of religion—or spirituality—plays a very large role in the lyrics he writes for his music.)

Growing up in North Dublin in the 1970s, there were several directions a young lad could go: there was little work to be had for anyone; the republican movement had become increasingly dangerous; there was always football and the GAA; and there was music; specifically, there was punk music. The raucous anarchy of punk, imported originally from London and typified by the Sex Pistols, struck a chord within many of these inner city boys, and soon everyone wanted to have his own punk band.

In 1972, Bono, having been asked to leave the national school in Glasnevin, was enrolled in the Mount Temple School. This was Dublin's first comprehensive, coeducational and nondenominational school. It was also at this time, when Bono was fourteen, that his mother died. Her death was extremely hard on Bono, as would be expected, but he reacted in two contrary ways: he became rebellious and he became religious. But the Mount Temple School provided the perfect haven for him at the time. There he met those people who would stay with him for the rest of his life: Alison Stewart, who would become his wife, and his classmates who would become U2.

In 1976, Bono answered an ad posted on a message board by Larry Mullen, who was looking for people wanting to form a band. And with two other fellows from school, Dave Evans and Adam Clayton, Bono went to see what it was about. (The four members of the band are the four original members.) While Bono claimed he could play guitar—he could barely—the band liked his flair for management and his comfort in assuming a particular stage persona. And so they made him their lead singer and front man. (The story is that in the early days, the band considered having Bono just manage the band.)

In those days, Dublin seemed rife with young bands. Down below Stephen's Green, an area called the Dandelion Market became popular where new bands could play and gain some attention, and the band that would ultimately become

U2 used to play there every chance they could.

Then in March 1978, the boys broke through, albeit on a very local level. U2 came in first in the "Limerick Civic Week Pop '78 Competition." Sponsored by the *Evening Press* and Harp Lager, Bono and his bandmates won 500 pounds and a trophy, but just as importantly, they got some good press and gained some confidence.

All the while, as the band was developing, Bono was writing lyrics. He had long written poetry, and had impressed the band from the beginning, so they considered him the songwriter. At first the songs were heavily laced with religion; then, they veered into the typical boy-girl adolescent love genre of pop music; but then suddenly they gained a certain weight, became more intense in personal feeling, revealing the beginnings of Bono's global humanism and spiritual depth. Undoubtedly the war in Northern Ireland inspired his writing; Britain's war in the Falklands/Malvinas affected him also; and like so many Irishmen over the past two decades, he was profoundly inspired by Martin Luther King Jr. In the course of their career, U2 have composed and played several songs dedicated to the slain civil rights leader—and they continue to play them in concert no matter how large their repertoire grows.

Now to many in the mainstream, the punk movement was violent and scary and seemed as if it sought to overturn all that they held dear—but that is what rock-and-roll had always been about, and the punk ethos arose when the music seemed to have gotten just a little too twee. Yet the music was not all *Sturm und Drang*. In Ireland, there seemed to be a pointed sort of social consciousness, as well. One Dublin musician, Bob Geldof, leader of the Boomtown Rats, had become interested in the famine that had ravaged Ethiopia for several years. For the Christmas season, he assembled some of the greatest rock stars—Bono included—and recorded a single from which all proceeds were to go to famine relief.

This was a noble and very successful venture, but in the long run, the money earned was a small bandage on a hemorrhaging country. In 1985, Geldof began to think grander. He assembled the largest concert of all time—simultaneously in London's Wembley Stadium and Philadelphia's JFK stadium—convinced the superstars of the day to donate their talents, and mounted a magnificent show from which all proceeds would go to famine relief. Geldof's work impressed many, in and out of the entertainment business, and for his efforts, he would be knighted by Queen Elizabeth II and nominated for a Nobel Peace Prize. Afterwards, his brain child would spawn dozens of similar benefits, such as FarmAid, BandAid, and WorkAid, each attempting to assist various critical issues. Geldof's heart was in the right place, and he did great things for famine relief, but he hadn't the necessary political savvy to affect change. That type of politicking would have to wait for the other Dublin frontman—Bono. (I have heard it said that the difference between Geldof and Bono is that Geldof suffers fools badly and is not particularly good at the political compromise, going for the immediate payoff rather than mapping out for the long term. Bono, on the other hand, is much better at playing the game, and his negotiating style is not as aggressive and off-putting as Geldof's.)

Anyway, by the time *Live Aid* was mounted—the name given to the Philadelphia and London concerts—U2 was slowly emerging as one of the most important bands of the 1980s—and as such, it was important to have them in the lineup. It was also the beginning of a career of benefits and tributes that the band would be involved in—sought by organizers because the world not only enjoyed their music, but took them seriously as well. Passionate and thoughtful, dramatic and mysterious, the band brought intelligence back to rock-and-roll after what seemed like decades where stupidity in popular music was the norm. And audiences of all ages seemed to like where Bono and U2 were taking them.

Like all bands, like all artists, U2 have tried hard not to become static and have gone through various changes, toying with new sounds, new strategies, and new personae. Yet underneath it all, there is always the driving honesty of their music. Of course, various albums have met with various successes, new tours are judged more or less successful than the last. But without a doubt, aside from rock's elder statesmen—Dylan, the Rolling Stones, and the surviving Beatles—there are few others who have soldiered on like U2, who have carried such influence in the capricious world of music.

And it was with this influence that Bono began to work. As the twentieth century slouched toward the new millennium, Bono took up the cause of debt relief for underdeveloped countries in Africa. Articulate and intelligent, he began assembling an eclectic group of supporters, government officials, UN ministers, and even the pope in asking the world's developed nations to give the poorer countries a step up by canceling their debt as human history entered the twenty-first century. Bono's argument—and one supported by many economists and sociologists—is that the underdeveloped countries can never expand, can never dig their way out of poverty, as long as the debts they accrue eat away at the majority of their economy, as long as money is used to pay debts rather than educate, feed, house, and care for people. Development was a no-win proposition if all the resources gained were used simply to pay off interest. Bono argued that with the new century, perhaps, the more fortunate nations could forgive all debt, allowing everyone to start afresh. The movement was called Jubilee 2000, and Bono exacted sizeable pledges from many of the nations in the G7.

When he wasn't promoting debt relief for African countries, he was arguing for relief of a much greater scourge, AIDS. He tackled famine in Africa as well— reminding people of his own history, of his own country that had had a famine which nearly halved its population. Throughout the first years of the new century, pictures of Bono—with his ever-present sunglasses—in Africa working with dying children, visiting stricken villages, and talking with government officials were more common than pictures of the star on stage. For Bono had discovered that the stage was just a stepping-stone to a much larger platform where his influence could really have an effect.

When he is not jetting around the world in support of his causes or touring with the band, Bono still lives on the east coast of Ireland, married with four children. It is for these children that he strives to make a better world. (His wife too is committed to activism, and after their wedding, the two flew off to work in a camp in Ethiopia. It was not the honeymoon that one associates with most celebrity newlyweds. But it was typical of Bono and Alison.)

While the band's success—and the success of all the Irish bands that followed on their coattails—has had a significant impact on the booming Irish economy, it is too soon to measure the success of his activism. Yet no other rock star has promoted social issues as intelligently and successfully as Bono. And in a world where pop culture usually carries more weight than economic and philosophic discourse, Bono's involvement in the global arena is immeasurable, and the world has praised him for it. He has won numerous humanitarian awards from organizations as varied as the American Ireland Fund and MTV Europe. He has pressed a petition with twenty-one million signatures into the hands of the U.N. Secretary General, Kofi Annan, as well as guided the former American Secretary of the Treasury, Paul O'Neill, on a working tour of Africa. Several organizations have given him their "Man of the Year" awards for his humanitarian work, and he has met and conferred with everyone from Tony Blair and George W. Bush to Bill Clinton and the pope. And, more importantly, he has made the developed countries listen, to such a degree that the *Times* in London asked the rhetorical question, "Can Bono save the World?"

Given all this, Bono remains nevertheless a down-to-earth Dubliner. He eschews the trappings of rich celebrities: bodyguards, limousines, and private jets. Instead he prefers to be grounded, to be very much a part of the world that he wants very much to save.

And so, how is it that we end our long history of Ireland with a rock-and-roll singer? But Bono is in fact a perfect ending. He is lyrical and has the Irish way with language. He is full of practical and engaged spirituality. He is political and willing to fight for the issues he believes in. He is musical and energetic and full of life. And more than anything else he represents, on an international platform, the New Ireland: vigorous, cosmopolitan, ballsy, committed, and proud.

EPILOGUE

As I sit putting the finishing touches on these last pages, I can already hear the voices complaining. "Hey Malachy," one says. "How in God's name could you not mention so and so?" Or "What the hell were you thinking when you included that tosser in the bunch?" Or "Why does he get ten pages, and my man only three?" And such is the inevitable reaction to a book like this. It has covered 2,500 years of Irish history through the lives of some fifty people—somebody was bound to get omitted. It has focused primarily on the Republic of Ireland, treating Ulster primarily in its relationship to the twenty-six counties to the south, and perhaps weighed in the heaviest in the late nineteenth century and early twentieth century when independence seemed within reach and Irish nationalism had burst forth heroically.

It's an extraordinary history—and one that continues to evolve. The recent economic strength, the struggle toward final peace in the North, the international acclaim of its culture, and the continued improvement of people's lives are signs of a vibrant society edging toward its Golden Age. The problem with Golden Ages, however, is that one never knows when they are occurring; there is always room for improvement.

As globalization tends to democratize us all—the boy in Mayo listens to the same music as the boy in Hong Kong; the teen in Belfast wears the same jeans as the girl in Rio de Janeiro—some bit of our individuality gets lost. Throughout their history, the Irish have always resisted assimilation into the cultures of those who invaded their island—the Vikings, the Normans, the English—and they have always put an Irish spin on the worlds of those who came to conquer. May the same continue throughout the next millennium. And may the qualities that define the Irish: their love of life and their love of freedom, their respect for scholarship and their facility with language, their wit, their courage, and their passion, spread across all cultures—for these are the very things that make our humanity bearable.

List of Works

I never intended this brief history to be an academic work, and it hasn't been written as such. I think of it more as a collection of stories that one might share across a kitchen table about people we once knew. So the list below is not a bibliography in the strictest sense. It is merely a list of books—some popular and some scholarly—for those of you who might be interested in finding out a little bit more about a particular person or event. Some of these books were very helpful in putting this book together; others I fondly remember reading long before this project was conceived.

Adams, Gerry. *A Farther Shore: Ireland's Long Road to Peace.* New York: Random House, 2003.

Arnold, Bruce. *Jack Lynch: Hero in Crisis.* Dublin: Merlin, 2001.

Bartlett, Thomas, and Keith Jeffery, eds. *A Military History of Ireland.* Cambridge: Cambridge University Press, 1996.

Bordowitz, Hank (compiled and edited by). *The U2 Reader: A Quarter Century of Commentary, Criticism, and Reviews.* New York: Hal Leonard, 2003.

Brady, Ciaran, ed. *Worsted in the Game: Losers in Irish History.* Dublin: Lilliput Press, 1989.

Brady, Ciaran, and Raymond Gillespie, eds. *Natives and Newcomers: The Making of Irish Colonial Society 1534–1641.* Dublin: Irish Academic Press, 1986.

Byrne, Francis J. *Irish Kings and High-Kings.* Four Courts History Classics. Dublin: Four Courts Press, 2001.

Cahill, Thomas. *How the Irish Saved Civilization: The Untold Story of Ireland's Heroic Role from the Fall of Rome to the Rise of Medieval Europe.* New York: Nan A. Talese/Doubleday, 1995.

Chambers, Anne. *Eleanor: Countess of Desmond.* Dublin: Wolfhound Press, 2000.

_____. *Granuaile: The Life and Times of Grace O'Malley, c. 1530–1603.* Dublin: Wolfhound Press, 1998.

Cheyney, Edward P. *A Short History of England. Revised and Enlarged Edition.* Boston: Ginn and Company, 1960.

Coe, Richard N. *Samuel Beckett.* New York: Grove Press, 1964.

Connolly, S. J., ed. *The Oxford Companion to Irish History.* Oxford: Oxford University Press, 1998.

Coogan, Tim Pat. *Michael Collins: The Man Who Made Ireland.* Boulder, Colorado: Roberts Rinehart, 1996.

Cronin, Mike. *A History of Ireland.* New York: Palgrave, 2001.

Curtis, Edmund. *A History of Ireland.* Sixth Edition. London: Butler and Tanner, Ltd., 1950.

Daly, Dominic. *The Young Douglas Hyde: The Dawn of the Irish Revolution and Renaissance, 1874–1893.* Totowa, New Jersey: Rowman and Littlefield, 1974.

Dangerfield, George. *The Damnable Question: A Study in Anglo-Irish Relations.* Boston: Little, Brown and Co., 1976.

Davis, Richard. *Arthur Griffith.* Dundalk: Dundalgan Press, 1976.

DeRosa, Peter. *Rebels: The Irish Rising of 1916.* New York: Fawcett Columbine, 1988.

Devlin, Bernadette. *The Price of My Soul.* New York: Knopf, 1969.

Douglas, Roy, et al. *Ireland since 1690: A Concise History.* Chicago: Contemporary Books, 1999.

Dwyer, T. Ryle. *Nice Fellow: A Biography of Jack Lynch.* Cork: Mercier, 2001.

Edwards, Ruth Dudley. *James Connolly.* Dublin: Gill & Macmillan, 1998.

Elliott, Marianne. *Wolfe Tone: Prophet of Irish Independence.* New Haven: Yale University Press, 1989.

Elliott, Sydney, and W.D. Flackes. *Conflict in Northern Ireland: An Encyclopedia.* Santa Barbara, California: ABC-CLIO, 1999.

Ellmann, Richard. *James Joyce.* New York: Oxford University Press, 1959.

Flood, Andrew. "The 1798 Rebellion in Ireland." 9 November 2003. < http://flag.blackened.net /revolt/andrew/1798.html>.

Forristal, Desmond. *Colum Cille: The Fox and the Dove.* Dublin: Veritas, 1997.

Foster, R. F. *Modern Ireland: 1600–1972.* New York: Penguin, 1989.

_____. *W. B. Yeats: A Life. I: The Apprentice Mage, 1865–1914*. New York: Oxford University Press, 1997.

_____. *W. B. Yeats: A Life. II: The Arch-Poet, 1915–1939*. Oxford: Oxford University Press, 2003.

Fraser, Antonia. *Cromwell: The Lord Protector*. New York: Dell, 1973.

Fry, Plantagenet, and Fiona Somerset Fry. *The History of Scotland*. London: Routledge and Kegan Paul, 1982.

Golway, Terry. *For the Cause of Liberty: A Thousand Years of Ireland's Heroes*. New York: Simon & Schuster, 2000.

Greaves, C. Desmond. *The Life and Times of James Connolly*. New York: International Publishers, 1971.

Gross, John. *James Joyce*. Edited by Frank Kermode. New York: Viking, 1970.

Hahn, Emily. *Fractured Emerald: Ireland*. New York: Weathervane Books, 1971.

Haney, John. *Charles Stewart Parnell*. New York: Chelsea House, 1989.

Heaney, Seamus. "All Ireland's Bard," Review of *W. B Yeats: A Life. Volume 1: The Apprentice Mage,* by R. F. Foster. *The Atlantic Monthly*, November 1997, pp. 155–160.

Herm, Gerhard. *The Celts: The People Who Came Out of the Darkness*. New York: St. Martin's Press, 1976.

Kinsella, Thomas. *The Tain*. Oxford: Oxford University Press, 1970.

Knowlson, James. *Damned to Fame: The Life of Samuel Beckett*. New York: Simon & Schuster, 1996.

Lavin, Patrick. *The Celtic World: An Illustrated History 750 B.C. to the Present*. New York: Hippocrene, 1999.

Lydon, James. *The Making of Ireland: From Ancient Times to Present*. New York: Routledge, 1998.

MacAnnaidh, Séamus. *Irish History: From Prehistoric Times to the Present Day.* Bath: Parragon, 1999.

MacDonald, Iain, ed. *Saint Bride.* Edinburgh: Floris Books, 1992.

MacManus, Seamas. *The Story of the Irish Race: A Popular History of Ireland.* Revised Edition. New York: Devon-Adair, 1944.

McCorristine, Laurence. *The Revolt of Silken Thomas: A Challenge to Henry VIII.* Dublin: Wolfhound Press, 1987.

McCullough, David Willis, ed. *Wars of the Irish Kings: A Thousand Years of Struggle from the Age of Myth Through the Reign of Queen Elizabeth.* New York: Three Rivers Press, 2002.

McGarry, Mary (compiled and introduced by). *Great Folk Tales of Ireland.* New York: Bell Publishing, 1972.

McGurk, John. *The Elizabethan Conquest of Ireland: The 1590s Conquest.* Manchester: Manchester University Press, 1997.

Mitchell, George J. *Making Peace.* New York, Knopf, 1999.

Ní Chatháin, Próinséas, and Michael Richter, eds. *Ireland and Europe in the Early Middle Ages: Texts and Transmission.* Dublin: Four Courts Press, 2002.

O'Brien, Conor Cruise. *States of Ireland.* London: Hutchinson, 1972.

O'Brien, Máire, and Conor Cruise O'Brien. *A Concise History of Ireland.* New York: Beekman House, 1972.

O'Connor, Frank. *The Big Fellow: Michael Collins and the Irish Revolution.* New York: Picador, 1979.

Ó Cróinín, Dáibhi. *Early Medieval Ireland: 400–1200.* (Longman History of Ireland). New York: Longman, 1995.

O'Ferrall, Fergus. *Daniel O'Connell.* Dublin: Gill & Macmillan, 1998.

Ó hEiíthir, Breandán. *A Pocket History of Ireland.* Dublin: O'Brien Press, 2000.

Sayers, Peig. *An Old Woman's Reflections.* Translated from the Irish by Seamus Ennis. Oxford: Oxford University Press, 1962.

_____. *Peig: The Autobiography of Peig Sayers of the Great Blasket Island.* Translated from the Irish by Bryan MacMahon. NP: Talbot Press, 1974.

Tanner, Marcus. *Ireland's Holy War: The Struggle for a Nation's Soul, 1500–2000.* New Haven and London: Yale University Press, 2001.

Tilley, Alan. *A Pocket History of Celtic Ireland.* Dublin: O'Brien Press, 2000.

Tone, William Theobald Wolfe, ed. *The Life of Wolfe Tone.* http://free.freespeech.org/republicansf/1798/tone_ndx.htm

Walsh, Michael Kerney. *An Exile of Ireland: Hugh O' Neill, Prince of Ulster.* Dublin: Four Courts Press, 1996.

Ward, Margaret. *Maud Gonne: A Life.* London: Pandora, 1990.

Wheatcroft, Geoffrey. "No Regrets, No Surrender." *Guardian Unlimited,* 12 July 2003; 31 December 2003. <http://books.guardian.co.uk/review/story/0,12084,995447,00.html>

Woodham-Smith, Cecil. *The Great Hunger: Ireland 1845–1849.* London: Penguin, 1991.

Yeats, W[illiam] B[utler]. *The Collected Poems of W. B. Yeats.* Definitive Edition with the Author's Final Revisions. New York: Macmillan, 1956.